THE ADVENTURES OF

LOLA BADIOLA

THE ADVENTURES OF LOLA BADIOLA

A BUSINESS ENGLISH NOVEL

SAM GRATTON

A thrilling way to advance your English

Published by:
Gratton Communications S.L.
Madrid

First edition 2023

Copyright © Sam Gratton

ISBN: 978-84-09-51563-9

*To Natalia, Carolina and Violeta
from Mamá and Daddy.*

"It's a dog-eat-dog world."
Concha

Chapter 1 - The Resignation

Lola got on the subway train, switched on her iPod and turned up the volume. It was half an hour before the start of the morning rush hour[1]. She closed her eyes and listened to a meditation playlist, trying to empty her mind of negative thoughts.

She was travelling to work earlier than normal. She wanted to arrive at the office before anyone else. She needed time to compose herself before she made the announcement.

She had hardly slept the night before. Her subconscious was still second-guessing the decision that her conscious mind had already made. How would everyone react? What would they think? Was this all just a terrible mistake? At two o'clock in the morning she had called her best friend. She needed some reassurance, someone to tell her that she was doing the right thing.

"Is this really what you want?" asked Concha in a sleepy monotone.

"Yes."

"Then you have to be ruthless[2]."

Lola's best friend worked as a recruitment consultant specialising in the placement of senior executives in the financial sector. She

---

[1] Rush hour *(adjective noun)* - The busy part of the day either in the morning when people are travelling to work, or in the evening, when people are travelling home.

[2] Ruthless *(adjective)* - Showing no pity or remorse for your actions.

knew, better than anyone, how dangerous it could be to resign from a company to join a competitor, to bite the hand that feeds[3].

"But I want to leave on good terms," said Lola.

"Good luck with that," replied Concha. "The company has nurtured you, trained you, and invested in you. You've become one of their top producers, a HiPo[4]. They won't let you go without a fight."

Lola had hoped that the telephone call would calm her down, help her get back to sleep, but it had the opposite effect.

"Resigning is not as easy as it seems." Concha continued. "So, let me give you some advice. Don't tell them where you are going. Don't get emotional. And above all else, do not change your mind. Remember Lola, it's a dog-eat-dog world out there[5]."

Lola got off the train, switched off her iPod and walked towards the glass and steel skyscraper of her downtown office in Madrid. It was a Norman Foster designed tower that stood head and shoulders[6] above the other buildings in the vicinity, a statement of a modern, multinational corporation that sought to dominate its ecosystem.

José, the only male receptionist at the headquarters, welcomed Lola with a big smile, a look of surprise evident on his face which she could only assume was due to her early arrival. As always, they exchanged a few pleasant words before Lola swiped her card on the electronic turnstiles and walked quickly towards the elevators.

While waiting, she saw the elegant figure of Mario Ruiz de Velasco enter the building, his entourage following quickly behind

---

[3] To bite the hand that feeds *(idiom)* - To mistreat someone who you depend on.

[4] HiPos - High Potential Employees *(adjective noun)* - An employee that is considered to have potential as a future leader of the company and therefore is on the fast track to promotion.

[5] A dog-eat-dog world *(idiom)* - An environment which is aggressive and competitive, either I survive at your expense, or you survive at my expense.

[6] Head and shoulders above the rest *(idiom)* - Something or someone that is significantly bigger or better than its peers or competition.

him. This was the CEO who had lifted the company out of a financial black hole[7], the CEO who was responsible for ten years of exponential growth[8]. As always, he was wearing a clean-cut tailor-made suit, that would cost the average person their monthly salary, with a singular pop of colour in the form of a green silk tie, consciously chosen to match the colour of his eyes.

Lola got into the elevator and rode it up to the fourteenth floor. She walked directly to her office in the cybersecurity services department, sat down at her desk and waited. At a quarter to nine her direct boss, Luis Bruña walked through the entrance with a cup of coffee in his hand and a newspaper tucked under his arm.

Luis was an empathetic manager. He'd always been good to her. He had fought for her promotions, trusted her with the biggest accounts and supported her Diversity & Inclusion initiatives. In the years that they had worked together, a certain closeness had formed between the two of them. She knew, therefore, that the next conversation was going to be a difficult one.

"Luis, I need to speak to you," she said as he passed by her desk.

"Just a minute Lola. There's been a ton of activity through the wires. I need to catch up."

He didn't stop. He clearly had urgent matters to deal with. Lola got up from her desk and followed him down the corridor.

"This can't wait," she said with an authoritative tone.

Luis stopped and looked at her. Lola didn't normally speak to him like this. He knew that something was obviously wrong. "Ok, follow me."

They walked to his corner office, and he politely asked his secretary to hold all the calls. He put down his coffee and newspaper, and then sat down.

---

[7] Financial black hole *(adjective noun)* - Irregular accounting activities where a company's losses are hidden by management from investors.

[8] Exponential growth *(adjective noun)* - An ever-accelerating increase in something. (In this case the revenues of TechSpania).

"What's going on?"
Lola got straight to the point[9].
"I'm resigning."

---

[9] To get straight to the point *(idiom)* - To be direct and clear in your communication.

Chapter 2 - The 51st Floor

Luis took a moment to process the news. He was shocked and upset, like a faithful long-term lover who has just been discarded for an exciting alternative.

Lola was a rainmaker[10]. Her team had beaten their budget[11] for the last four years consecutively, often going beyond the company's stretch targets[12]. Without her, the whole division's financial plans would be almost impossible to fulfil.

"Why?"

"I need a change Luis, a new challenge."

"Where are you going?"

"It's a small tech start-up. You won't have heard of it."

Luis motioned for Lola to sit down in his office. Then, as Concha had predicted, he did everything in his power to convince her to stay. He started with the logical arguments – "90% of start-ups fail in the first two years". When she wasn't convinced, he moved on to the emotional arguments – "we've been through so much together, we're like a family". As a last resort, he ended with the moral arguments – "how can you do this to me after all I've done for you?"

---

[10] Rainmaker *(noun)* - A key employee who generates revenue for a company ensuring prosperity for the whole organization.

[11] To beat your budget *(idiom)* - To exceed the financial objectives set by management at the beginning of a time-period.

[12] Stretch targets *(adjective noun)* - Business goals that are considered impossible to reach given the current circumstances, incentivising employees to find innovative solutions to a company's problems.

Lola was patient and resolute[13]. She had learned that one of the key attributes of a successful salesperson was the anticipation of objections to a proposal. She had created a mind map[14] of all the possible scenarios for this discussion. If he says X, I will respond with Y. She had filled a dozen sides of A4 paper with notes and spent most of the week practicing her lines.

"Wait here," said Luis, as he realised, he was getting nowhere. "I need to go and have my daily call with senior management, but I'll be right back."

He went into the adjoining meeting room and dialled into a conference call. Lola could see everything, but she couldn't hear anything due to the soundproofing. It gave her a moment to reflect on the course she was taking. As was often the case, the expectation of a difficult conversation was more unpleasant than the conversation itself. In verbalising her thoughts and desires, Lola fully accepted that she was doing the right thing. There was no turning back now. She was burning her boats.[15]

After about twenty minutes, Luis returned to his office. His attitude had changed. He was distant, as if emotionally detached from the situation. He no longer looked Lola in the eyes.

"Ok, follow me. We're going up to the 51st floor."

In her seven years at the company Lola had never been to the 51st floor. It was where the company had its board meetings and entertained VIPs. It was strictly for senior managers only. Even Luis looked a little nervous as the elevator doors opened and the two of

---

[13] Resolute *(adjective)* - Determined, persistent or tenacious.

[14] Mind map *(adjective noun)* - A graphical representation of concepts that connects different ideas in an intuitive manner.

[15] To burn your boats *(idiom)* - To be 100% committed to your objectives, to pass the point of no return. Hernán Cortés, the Spanish conquistador, famously destroyed his boats on arrival at the New World in 1519. There was no turning back, he and his men had to conquer the territory or die trying.

them walked out into a palatial reception. It felt like a five-star hotel[16] with double height ceilings, baroque artwork, and panoramic views of Madrid.

Luis led Lola along a corridor, passed the company's boardroom until they reached an old oak door. He knocked on the door and then turned to Lola.

"Good luck. You'll need it." Then he walked away.

The oak door opened, and a smart middle-aged[17] lady invited her in. "This way please."

Lola walked into an opulent study filled with antique furniture, old books, and Persian rugs. On the walls were oil paintings of hunting scenes framed in elaborate gilt. In the corner there was a sideboard replete with crystal glasses and vintage whisky.

"Would you like a drink?"

"No thank you."

The lady smiled politely and then walked out of the study.

Lola was left on her own. The silence was absolute. It was a room that absorbed all the ambient noise, like a music recording studio or a padded cell in a lunatic asylum.

She wandered over to the bookshelves, keen to distract herself, and ran her fingers across the shiny leather-bound volumes. They appeared to be unopened, there for decoration rather than education.

One of the oil paintings caught her attention. It was strikingly similar to a landscape by Diego Velázquez that she had seen in the Museo del Prado. She examined the picture closely. The composition, lighting and brushwork all suggested the hand of a great master. Was it possible she was looking at an original piece by one of Spain's greatest artists?

---

[16] Five-star (hotel) *(compound number adjective)* - Remember to write it with a hyphen, and in the singular form.

[17] Middle-aged *(compound adjective)* - Generally regarded as being between the ages of 45 and 65.

"Good morning, Lola."

The voice from behind her was deep and resonant, shocking her out of her reverie.

She spun around to see Mario Ruiz de Velasco at the entrance of the study. He was strikingly handsome, his silver hair slicked back, his green eyes glinting in the late morning light.

Lola was momentarily lost for words[18].

"Please, take a seat."

---

[18] Lost for words *(idiom)* - To be unable to speak due to surprise or shock.

Chapter 3 - The CEO

Mario Ruiz de Velasco was everything Lola expected him to be, charming, aristocratic and intimidating. She had seen him being interviewed on television, making company presentations and, from time to time, walking around the headquarters[19]. But she had never been up close and personal like this before.

After a couple of minutes of small talk[20], the two of them sat down either side of his antique oak desk.

"So, what's on your mind?" he asked.

"Well, after careful consideration, and with the greatest respect to you and everyone at TechSpania, I have decided to resign."

Ruiz de Velasco lit a cigarette and stared at Lola without replying. She felt obliged to say more.

"It's been an amazing seven years, but I really feel that it's time for me to move on."

Ruiz de Velasco remained silent.

"I'd like to thank you and everyone at -"

"Where are you going?"

Lola was startled by the sudden interruption.

"It's a small start-up. You wouldn't have heard of it."

---

[19] Headquarters *(noun)* - An unusual noun because it ends in an "s", whether it is expressed in the singular form or the plural.

[20] Small talk *(adjective noun)* – Informal, everyday conversation about the weather, traffic, sports, or current affairs. It is used by people who don't know each other too well, to break the ice, at the beginning of an interview, meeting, or social event.

"Try me."

The CEO waited patiently for her answer. Lola felt compelled to fill the silence.

"It's a company called JBlock."

Ruiz de Velasco nodded his head. "It's run by a young American entrepreneur. They plan to use the Ethereum blockchain [21] to reinforce security systems. It's a nice idea."

"That's right," replied Lola, trying to hide her surprise at his knowledge of the company.

"And what are they offering you that we aren't?"

It was a difficult question. Lola's decision to move was driven by instinct rather than rationale.

"I want to be part of something new. I want to build something from zero. JBlock are offering me the chance to make a difference."

"You don't think that you can make a difference here?"

Ruiz de Velasco took a long drag on his cigarette and then let it balance on the edge of a large marble ashtray. His questioning had led Lola down a dead-end road[22]. She couldn't respond.

"Listen Lola, TechSpania controls the cybersecurity sector in Spain, South America and much of Europe. Our strategic objective is to defend our monopoly position[23]. So, when a company like JBlock enters our market we observe them, we study them, then we either buy them or we bury them."

The CEO took one last drag on his cigarette and then crushed it into the ashtray.

---

[21] Ethereum blockchain *(noun)* - Decentralised global software platform powered by blockchain technology, known for its native cryptocurrency, ether, or ETH.

[22] Dead-end road *(adjective noun)* - Literally it is a street with an entrance but no way out at the other end. Metaphorically, it is an action or direction that does not lead to any progress or resolution.

[23] Monopoly position *(adjective noun)* - A company that is the only supplier of a good or service in a specific market. It faces no competition and is therefore likely to offer poor or overpriced products or services.

"You have no future at JBlock because JBlock has no future. If you want to make a difference the only place you can do that is here, with us, at TechSpania."

The CEO paused to let his words sink in. Then he softened his tone.

"You're an exceptional manager Lola. You've done amazing things over the last seven years. With my help, you can make it to the very top of this organisation. But I need to know that you're committed to our cause."

This was the moment of truth. Should she stay or should she go? Only half an hour earlier she was 100% convinced that she was leaving. Now, sitting in front of the CEO of TechSpania, one of the most revered men in the world of business technology, she was not so sure.

In the back of her mind, she remembered the three pieces of advice[24] that Concha had given her. Don't tell them where you are going, don't get emotional, and above all else do not change your mind. She had already ignored the first two pieces of advice and was on the brink of ignoring the third. She needed to buy herself some time.

"Could I get back to you tomorrow with my final decision?"

Ruiz de Velasco sat back in his chair with a look of disappointment on his face. That was not the right response. His eyes narrowed, and his head tilted slightly to one side. The atmosphere in the room darkened. Lola felt the hairs on her arms stand on end.

"Your father was a great man," he said quietly.

Lola was thrown off balance by the sudden change in direction.

"You knew my father?"

"We were close."

"Really?"

---

[24] Pieces of advice *(noun)* - "Advice" is an uncountable noun. To express it in a countable form use "pieces of advice" and never "advices".

Lola didn't remember seeing Ruiz de Velasco at her father's funeral.

"He called me when you interviewed here seven years ago. He asked me to look after you."

Lola started to feel uncomfortable. She resented the implication that her father had pulled strings for her.[25]

"Since then, I have been following your progress closely, making things happen for you."

Lola became defensive. "I think that I've made things happen for myself at this company."

Ruiz de Velasco smiled. It was the smile of shark about to bite into its prey. "Do you think a girl like you could have succeeded in a company like this without a sponsor[26] like me?"

The attractive mask slipped from his face to reveal the shadow beneath.

"I'm the invisible hand that's been guiding your career. And I can take you to the very top of the mountain. Or I can throw you off it."

A shot of adrenalin pumped through Lola's nervous system. This was the Mario Ruiz de Velasco that she had heard whispers about, the vain and vindictive tyrant who took pleasure in crushing his competitors. She knew that it was over. A line had been crossed.

"Thank you very much for your time, Mr. Ruiz de Velasco."

Lola stood up slowly, looking straight into those piercing green eyes.

"I'd shake your hand, if it weren't invisible."

And then she left TechSpania for good.

---

[25] To pull some strings *(idiom)* - To secretly influence the people around you for the benefit of your friends and family, like a puppet master controlling its puppets.

[26] Sponsor *(noun)* - In a large company it is common for a more senior manager to guide, mentor and promote a more junior manager, in other words act as their internal sponsor.

Chapter 4 - JJ Thomson

JJ Thomson's alarm went off[27] at 6am but he was already awake. He was visualising the forthcoming day, running through[28] all the issues that he had to deal with at his tech start-up. The new Commercial Director was starting at 9.30am that morning and he wanted everything to be ready for her.

He went to his kitchen and prepared a pint of detox juice using the vegetables in his pantry. Then he lay down on an exercise mat on the wooden floor of his attic apartment. He went through his daily stretching and breathing exercises followed by an ice-cold shower.

JJ opened the sliding door of his living room and stepped out onto his terrace. He looked out across the roof tops of Barrio Salamanca in the centre of Madrid, taking a deep breath of frigid air. The weather app on his phone indicated five degrees centigrade, forty-one degrees Fahrenheit. According to the meteorologists the local forecast was a chilly start to the day, followed by sunshine, as usual for this part of Spain at this time of year.

Amongst the cars parked in the street below, was a black Toyota Prius. Inside a man looked up at JJ's apartment as the lights turned on, making a note of the time.

---

[27] To go off *(phrasal verb)* - Describes the moment when a warning device starts to ring or make a loud noise.

[28] To run through *(phrasal verb)* - To quickly review or consider a set of items or actions.

JJ Thomson was born in a small, conservative community near Seattle, Washington in 1984. He was a gifted child[29] and his parents expected him to become a university professor or a doctor. But he had other plans. He was a rebel, a misfit, a round peg in a square hole[30]. As soon as he was old enough, he left home to travel the world, working in manual jobs to finance his nomadic lifestyle.

He was forced to return to Seattle when his mother was diagnosed with motor neuron disease. The family didn't have enough money for private healthcare, so he spent the next eighteen months caring for her until she passed away[31]. This experience convinced him that the status quo needed to be challenged[32]. He vowed to be one of the crazy ones who changed the world for the better.

While caring for his mother, he learned how to code in several different computer languages and created his first applications. Over the next five years he became a serial entrepreneur[33] starting more than a dozen technology companies. Three of them were outstanding successes. He sold each of them to a different tech giant giving him the financial freedom to live and work wherever he wanted. He chose Madrid, the city he had fallen in love with during his travels. This was where he planned to build his biggest and most ambitious project.

He left his apartment on Calle Hermosilla at 7:30 am and picked up an electric scooter on the corner of Velázquez. From there he headed south to Gran Vía where he had rented an entire floor of the

---

[29] Gifted child *(adjective noun)* - A child with exceptional abilities. A prodigy.

[30] A round peg in a square hole *(idiom)* - Describes someone who doesn't fit in with their environment. A person unsuitable for their situation.

[31] To pass away *(phrasal verb)* - An indirect way of saying "to die".

[32] To challenge the status quo *(idiom)* - To reject the traditional way of doing things and look for new and innovative solutions.

[33] Serial entrepreneur *(adjective noun)* - A person who creates multiple new businesses, one after another.

Adriática building. It was more space than he needed for his current operations, but if the business were to grow as rapidly as he expected it would be worth the additional cost.

His first meeting of the day was with the new Commercial Director of the company. He was really looking forward to seeing her again. He had finally found someone who truly shared his core values[34], someone who could help him realise his vision. Her name was Lola Badiola.

JJ had met Lola at an annual cybersecurity conference in Las Vegas. At the time, she was working for a technology giant that was rapidly expanding its cybersecurity business. He watched her give a presentation on multi-cloud security and was immediately impressed by her ability to take complex issues and simplify them into messages that could be understood by the average Joe[35].

He introduced himself to her and, within five minutes, he knew that she was the person he needed to catalyse the growth of his company. It was love at first sight[36], in a business sense.

Lola politely declined his initial offers. It was understandable. She had a secure job in a big company and was on the fast track to senior management. But JJ was smart and persistent. He knew that he had something special and exciting to offer her, something that would appeal to her sense of morality and adventure. Over the next six months, they had many conversations until, one day, he sent over an official contract, and, to his delight, Lola accepted.

In his mind the management team was now complete, the final piece of the puzzle had been put in place. As he rode his scooter up Gran Vía, zigzagging in and out of the morning traffic, he was full of optimism about his latest venture.

---

[34] Core values *(adjective noun)* - The underlying beliefs of a company that form the foundations of its culture, guide its decision-making process, and differentiate it from the competition.

[35] The average Joe *(idiom)* - An ordinary, typical person.

[36] Love at first sight *(idiom)* - An instant attraction between two people.

He arrived at the Adriática building at just before 8.30am and parked the scooter at one of the collection stations nearby. He checked his smartphone for any new WhatsApp messages and then jogged inside the office block. As he disappeared up the stairs, a black Toyota Prius drove slowly passed the entrance.

Chapter 5 - The Apple

It was 8.45am and JJ Thomson was sitting at his desk trying to write a mission statement[37] that truly expressed the purpose of his company. He wanted to demonstrate its core values to all the stakeholders[38]. But he found it impossible to summarise everything in one inspirational sentence. He had written more than twenty-five versions of the same idea but none of them worked to his satisfaction. He threw down his pencil in frustration and looked at the team he had assembled over the last six months.

Up until that moment his primary concern had been human resources. The success of the company depended on the success of the people. But, like many start-ups, there was little cash to pay the employees. So, to attract talent and get their long-term commitment, he had offered everyone shared ownership[39].

He wanted his team to feel like they were part of something special, like they were changing the world for the better. This sense of purpose was reflected in the environment in which they worked. JJ had invested a lot of money in the interior design of his offices.

---

[37] Mission statement *(noun)* - A short description of the fundamental purpose of the company.

[38] Stakeholder *(noun)* - Anybody with an interest, or a stake, in a specific company. In other words, someone who benefits from the company's success and suffers from its failure. This includes shareholders, bondholders, employees, suppliers, government, local community and others.

[39] Employee share ownership *(noun)* - The financial interest that employees have in the company which motivates them to help it succeed.

The objective was to bring the outside world inside the building. The rooms were filled with natural woods, plants, and flowers, and subtle but exotic aromas. There was a central meeting area with an artificial waterfall and a vast[40] ceiling light that mirrored the changing colours of the sky. All the items of furniture combined form and function and were made of sustainable materials. He wanted to lift the spirits of everyone who walked into the office, be it an employee, a client, or a pizza delivery boy.

Nobody expected the company to generate profits[41] or even revenues[42] overnight, but JJ was eager to win their first big contract as soon as possible. They had been operating in a marketing vacuum[43] for some time. Consequently, he was thrilled to have Lola on board and expected her to hit the ground running[44].

"JJ, do you have a second?"

His train of thought[45] was interrupted by the voice of Cayetano Tolosa.

"Sure."

Cayetano was the salesman who would be reporting to Lola. Despite his lack of direct experience in the cybersecurity sector, he was very well connected, *plugged in* as they say in Spain, and could open doors to some of the biggest accounts in Europe.

---

[40] Vast *(adjective)* - Very big, huge, enormous.

[41] Profits *(noun)* - The money that is left after all a company's expenses are subtracted from its sales.

[42] Revenues *(noun)* - The total sales or invoicing of a company, the total money that the company earns from all its activities.

[43] Operating in a (marketing) vacuum *(idiom)* - To work without any influence, information, or assistance from the outside world.

[44] To hit the ground running *(idiom)* - To start something, such as a job, without any period of learning or introduction, to be able to work at full capacity from the very first moment.

[45] Train of thought *(idiom)* - A series of connected ideas that somebody is considering.

JJ was well-aware of the subtle but significant differences in business culture between his native and adopted countries. It was not just an empty cliché[46] to say that trust in Latin cultures was built through personal relationships. In his years of doing business in Spain he had learned to adapt, to spend more time talking about the families of his business associates, to enjoy coffee breaks and long lunches, not as a way of avoiding work, but as a way of building confidence and credibility. He understood that if he wanted to succeed in Spain, he would need salespeople who were not only highly competent but also well connected.

Cayetano walked into JJ's office, half-eaten apple in hand, and sat down on one of the Smart Ocean office chairs. He was an archetypical salesman, supremely self-confident and smooth as butter on a hot summer's day. He was clean shaven, hair gelled back, sleeves rolled up to reveal his tanned and toned forearms. He could have been a male model, if only he'd been thirty centimeters taller.

"When is the new commercial director arriving?" he asked.

"Any time now."

"Great."

Cayetano leaned back in the chair, crossed his legs, and took a small bite of his apple.

"I have a question about her."

"Yeah?"

"Why did she get fired[47] from her last company?"

JJ was startled by the question. As far as he was concerned Lola had resigned from TechSpania following the acceptance of the offer from JBlock.

"She wasn't fired," he replied. "She quit."

---

[46] Cliché *(noun)* - A phrase or expression that is overused, and a sign of lazy thinking.

[47] To be fired *(verb)* - To lose your job, normally because of your own negligence or incompetence, as opposed to "to be made redundant" or "to be let go" which mean to lose your job because of corporate or economic issues out of your control.

"Oh." Cayetano chewed quietly on his apple. "I heard a different story."

One of the administrative assistants interrupted the conversation to inform them that Lola had just arrived at the office. JJ closed his laptop, stood up and looked down at Cayetano.

"Well, you heard the wrong story," he said. Then he walked quickly to the entrance to greet the new arrival.

Cayetano spun around in the revolving chair, then he threw the remains of his apple into JJ's rubbish bin.

QUIZ TIME

Chapters 1 to 5

COMPREHENSION QUIZ

Answer the questions with complete sentences. Say them out loud.

1. What advice does Concha give to Lola the night before her resignation?
2. How does Luis Bruña react to the resignation? And how does he try to change her mind?
3. What is on the 51st floor of the TechSpania headquarters? And why do you think both Lola and Luis become nervous on the way there?
4. Describe Mario Ruiz de Velasco in as much detail as you can. What is his physical appearance? What is his character? What are his achievements?
5. What is Ruiz de Velasco's opinion of JBlock? Why does he believe that it is a bad career move for Lola?
6. What is the exact moment when Lola finally decides to leave TechSpania for good?
7. Describe JJ Thomson in as much detail as you can. Where is he from? What is his professional and personal background? Why is he in Madrid?
8. According to JJ what are the key ingredients for a successful start-up company?
9. What is JJ's opinion of Lola and why is he so keen for her to join JBlock?
10. What is your first impression of Cayetano Tolosa?

BUSINESS ENGLISH QUIZ

Complete the sentences with the words used in the story.

1. The financial sector can be a D_____ E_____ D_____ W_____ where everyone is competing aggressively for the same clients.
2. He talks so much and yet says so little, I wish he would just G_____ to the P_____!
3. The Human Resources department is responsible for identifying H_____ and supporting them throughout their career at the company.
4. I don't know how he does it! He always closes the biggest deals with the biggest clients. He's a R_____.
5. If you want to succeed as an entrepreneur you have to be completely committed to the future, you must be willing to B_____ your B_____.
6. The management are expecting a 20% increase in revenues this year and a 25% increase in profits. We must all work together as a team to B_____ our B_____.
7. We always start the job interview with some S_____ T_____ to make the candidate feel more relaxed.
8. My father-in-law never P_____ any S_____ for his friends and family, he believed in a meritocracy.
9. Big companies use their M_____ P_____ to exploit their customers. That is why they are regulated by the Competition Commission.
10. The H_____ of our company is on 5th Avenue in Manhattan, New York.

11. We are an innovative company producing disruptive technology and we are looking for leaders who will C_____ the S_____ Q_____.

12. Whenever you have a difficult decision to make at this company always remember our C_____ V_____ of integrity, innovation, and quality.

13. We need to update our M_____ S_____ so that all our stakeholders are aligned with our corporate objectives.

14. P_____ equals revenue minus cost.

15. We need to recruit a sales manager who can H_____ the G_____ R_____ and generate new business from day one.

ANSWERS TO COMPREHENSION QUIZ

1. Concha advises Lola not to tell TechSpania where she's going, not to get emotional, and above all not to change her mind.

2. Luis is shocked and upset, like a faithful long-term lover who has just been discarded for a new alternative.

3. The office of the CEO and the boardroom are on the 51st floor along with other meeting rooms for clients. Lola and Luis are nervous because they are not accustomed to visiting this floor.

4. Mario Ruiz de Velasco is tall, handsome and elegant, with silver hair and piercing green eyes. He is charming and intelligent, but he has a reputation for being ruthless. He has enjoyed great success at TechSpania, generating exponential growth in revenues during his time as CEO.

5. Ruiz De Velasco is aware of JBlock but does not see the company as a competitive threat. In fact, he thinks the company has no future in the Cybersecurity market and therefore is a bad career move for Lola.

6. Lola finally makes up her mind to leave TechSpania when she is threatened by Mario Ruiz Velasco and recognises his true character.

7. JJ Thompson is a young, successful American entrepreneur who has founded and then sold several start-ups. He is in Madrid because he loves the city and wants to start his next company there.

8. According to JJ Thompson, the key ingredient for a successful start-up is the people.

9. JJ was particularly impressed by how Lola was able to take complex ideas and simplify them so that they could be understood by an ordinary person. As soon as he spoke to her in person, he knew that she was right for the job. It was love at

first sight. He was very keen for her to start because up until that point the company had no marketing or sales strategy.

10. First impressions are very important in business. We will find out more about Cayetano Tolosa in the coming chapters.

ANSWERS TO BUSINESS ENGLISH QUIZ

1. The financial sector can be a DOG-EAT-DOG WORLD where everyone is competing aggressively for the same clients.

2. He talks so much and yet says so little, I wish he would just GET TO THE POINT.

3. The Human Resources department is responsible for identifying HIPOS and supporting them throughout their career at the company.

4. I don't know how he does it! He always closes the biggest deals with the biggest clients. He's a RAINMAKER.

5. If you want to succeed as an entrepreneur you have to be completely committed to the future, you must be willing to BURN YOUR BOATS.

6. The management are expecting a 20% increase in revenues this year and a 25% increase in profits. We must all work together as a team to BEAT OUR BUDGET.

7. We always start the job interview with some SMALL TALK to make the candidate feel more relaxed.

8. My father-in-law never PULLED ANY STRINGS for his friends and family, he believed in a meritocracy.

9. Big companies use their MONOPOLY POWER to exploit their customers, that is why they are regulated by the Competition Commission.

10. The HEADQUARTERS of our company is on 5th Avenue in Manhattan, New York.

11. We are an innovative company producing disruptive technology and we are looking for managers who will CHALLENGE THE STATUS QUO.

12. Whenever you have a difficult decision to make at this company always remember our CORE VALUES of integrity, innovation, and quality.

13. We need to update our MISSION STATEMENT so that all our stakeholders are aligned with our corporate objectives.

14. PROFIT equals revenue minus cost.

15. We need to recruit a sales manager who can HIT THE GROUND RUNNING and generate new business from day one.

SAM GRATTON

"Have you observed any new anomalies?"
Kang

Chapter 6 - The Programmers

Leading the programming team at JBlock was Diego de la Fuente, a Spanish national who had grown up[1] in California and gotten a degree[2] in electrical engineering from Stanford University. He had worked with JJ on previous initiatives as a consultant. Now he was a partner and major shareholder in JBlock.

He was a brilliant team leader, able to get the best out of the freaks[3] and geeks[4] around him. They included a Norwegian, a Dutch, a Brit, and two Spaniards. All the coders were men between twenty-five and thirty-five years old, all of them had ethical hacking backgrounds and lived and breathed computer code.

Diego was a big, energetic man. His whole body was covered in a thick layer of hair apart from the shiny surface of his head. On the outside, he looked like a ferocious grizzly bear. On the inside, he was more like a cuddly teddy bear.

---

[1] To grow up *(phrasal verb)* - To mature from a child to an adult.

[2] Degree *(noun)* - An award from a university. It could be a Bachelor's, Master's, or PhD. Be careful not to confuse with the word "career", which describes your professional progress.

[3] Freak *(noun)* - Someone or something abnormal or extraordinary. Could have both negative and positive connotations.

[4] Geek *(noun)* - Someone who has an obsessive expertise in a specific area.

By nature, he was a nervous character and that morning he could almost be considered hyperactive. He had a lot on his plate[5]. First, he had to come up with [6] a cybersecurity solution for a pharmaceutical company. Second, he needed to give some input into the creation of JBlock's mission statement. And finally, he wanted to make a good first impression[7] on the new commercial director.

Diego knew that the key to the success of any tech start-up was the close collaboration between the product and marketing departments. At that moment, the programmers had little faith in the commercial side of the business, least of all with Cayetano Tolosa. The arrival of Lola Badiola was therefore a key moment in the development of the company.

"Ok people, unplug yourselves. We need to start the morning meeting."

From 8:30 to 9:00 am, every morning, Diego gathered his team to find out how they were progressing and if they had any problems.

"First up. Where are we with the P.O.C[8]. for the pharmaceutical company?" he asked Turner, the British programmer.

"Almost done. Just need to iron out[9] a couple of bugs."

"Good. Next. JJ wants our input on the company mission statement and slogan. Any feedback for the suggestions I sent you?"

---

[5] To have a lot on your plate *(idiom)* - To be busy, to have a lot of responsibility, and therefore, unlikely to be able to accept any other tasks.

[6] To come up with *(phrasal verb)* - To originate, create, or design.

[7] To make a good first impression *(idiom)* - Research has shown that people decide whether they can trust you or not in the first few seconds of meeting you, therefore, it's important to make a good first impression.

[8] P.O.C. - Proof of concept *(noun)* - A very common approach when offering innovative solutions. It is the opportunity for a client to do a trial of the application or software before making a commitment to a full investment.

[9] To iron out *(phrasal verb)* - To remove any final issues or problems, in the way an iron will remove the creases in your clothes.

The silence was deafening[10].

"Have a think about it. As you know, our new Commercial Director arrives today. The marketing push starts now."

The programmers looked sceptical and mumbled their disapproval.

"Ok, what's on your mind?"

Van Dyck, the Dutch coder was the first to speak. "You mean we're gonna have another Pretty Boy wasting our time." There was never any filter between what the Dutchman thought and what he said, both a strength and weakness.

"Pretty Boy is a salesman. His job is to open doors for us. And he does that very well," Diego had the patience of a saint[11] but at times he needed to assert his authority. "And from now on, we're going to stop calling him Pretty Boy. His name is Cayetano, he's our colleague and we'll treat him with respect."

"Do we really need a sales team, at all?" asked Turner.

"Is that a serious question?" replied Diego.

"The way I see it, our code sells itself."

"Yeah." agreed Velázquez, one of the Spaniards. "Salespeople just get in the way."

"The only thing they do well is book lunch," said Munch, the Norwegian.

"And ask dumb questions."

"I've explained blockchain to Pretty Boy a dozen times, but he still doesn't get it[12]."

"We do all the work, and they make all the commission," said Van Dyck.

Diego allowed the five programmers to express themselves. He understood that coding could be a lonely and deeply frustrating

---

[10] Deafening silence *(idiom)* - An oxymoron or contradictory expression, used to emphasise the fact that there is silence when there should be noise.

[11] The patience of a saint *(idiom)* - A common metaphor in English.

[12] To get it *(idiom)* - To understand intuitively.

process. These moments of communal complaining were a necessary evil[13]. After thirty seconds he interrupted their banter.

"Listen guys, I've heard through the grapevine[14] that the new Commercial Director is a rock star[15]. She was a top producer at TechSpania, she knows the industry inside out[16] and she's adored by her clients."

"The new Commercial Director is a woman?" asked Turner sceptically.

"Yes, she's a woman." sighed Diego. "And her track record and CV are impeccable. It's a miracle JJ convinced her to join us."

The programmers were unmoved by the credentials. They looked around at each other. Munch asked the question on everyone's mind.

"Is she hot?"

It took a lot for Diego to lose his temper, but this was one of the few occasions where the teddy bear showed his teeth. "You know that's exactly the type of comment that makes it so difficult for me to recruit women into this team."

"Women can't code," replied the Van Dyck.

"Women can code, they just don't want to," argued Velázquez.

"Men like things. Women like people," added Turner wisely.

Once again, the five coders started arguing amongst themselves. Once again Diego allowed them to express themselves. The discussion reached a crescendo until suddenly it stopped, and

---

[13] A necessary evil *(idiom)* - An activity that is unpleasant but can't be avoided if you wish to achieve your objectives.

[14] To hear (something) through the grapevine *(idiom)* - A common expression and a famous song by Marvin Gaye, that refers to important information that reaches you from an unspecified and unofficial source.

[15] Rockstar *(noun)* - An informal description of a high performing employee, often a salesperson or dealmaker.

[16] To know something inside out *(idiom)* - To be intimately familiar with all the aspects of an issue.

everyone went quiet. Something had caught the programmers' attention.

Diego turned around to see JJ Thomson walking through the office. With him was a smartly dressed woman in her early thirties. She gripped the handle of her leather briefcase with strong but perfectly manicured hands. As she passed by, she looked across at the coding team, exuding confidence, and authority, and smiled. Then she followed JJ into one of the meeting rooms.

Diego turned back to his team.

"Ok boys, close your mouths and say hello to Lola Badiola, our new Commercial Director."

SAM GRATTON

Chapter 7 - The Speech

Lola pressed the buzzer of the intercom and entered the Adriática building. She walked up the spiral staircase to the third floor. She needed to release the adrenalin that was flowing gently through her bloodstream. Waiting for her at the entrance to the office was JJ Thomson.

"Lola! It's great to see you again."

He moved forward to kiss her on the cheek. He had become accustomed to this southern European style of greeting having spent so much time in Madrid. Meanwhile, Lola was walking towards him with her hand stretched out ready to greet him in a more formal manner. They ended up[17] simultaneously shaking hands and kissing in a slightly awkward manner.

"Did you have any trouble getting here?"

"No, no problem. You have a great location here."

"Yes, we wanted to be central."

"You couldn't be more central than Gran Vía."

"We love it. Follow me."

JJ led Lola into the main area of the office and passed a group of employees who were having a team meeting. They all stopped and looked at her as she walked by. She smiled at them as it dawned on[18]

---

[17] To end up *(phrasal verb)* - To reach the end of a journey and often find yourself in a place you didn't expect.

[18] To dawn on *(phrasal verb)* - To slowly realise an inevitable truth, in the way the sun rises across the horizon on a clear morning.

her that she would be the only woman working at JBlock. JJ led her into his office, and they engaged in a few minutes of small talk.

"How was your trip to Las Vegas?" asked Lola.

"It was a disaster!" JJ replied shaking his head and laughing. "I bought a hot dog for three bucks[19] from a street vendor and ate it while I read through my speech. By the time I reached the conference centre I was feeling really sick. I'm not sure how I completed my presentation, but as soon as I concluded, I ran to the nearest bathroom and threw up[20]!"

Lola grimaced.

"Then I washed my face, walked back into the conference room and answered some questions from the audience!"

"Now that's dedication!" said Lola.

"Yeah."

They both laughed, a little nervously, and then JJ turned the conversation to more serious matters. He leaned forward at his desk.

"Listen Lola, I want you to take control of the marketing plan, I want you to create a brand image[21] that truly reflects our core values. I want our customers to believe in us, to trust our promises, to say great things about us when we are not in the room. I'll give you whatever you need to make it happen."

Lola was excited by the entrepreneurial challenges of her new role, and she finally felt a deep sense of purpose. There was a war being fought in the digital world. A war between truth and lies, between the fake and the real, between information and manipulation. She was ready to go into battle with JJ Thomson and his army of geeks.

---

[19] Bucks *(noun)* - An informal term for US dollars.

[20] To throw up *(phrasal verb)* - To vomit.

[21] Brand image *(noun)* - The perception of a company in the mind of a customer, the feeling they have when they think of the company and its products.

"Ok, let me introduce you to the rest of the team!" said JJ. "I'm going to gather everyone in the conference room. Would you like to make a little speech?"

"Sure," said Lola, then immediately regretted it.

She wanted to make a good first impression, but she never expected to give a speech on her very first morning. Public speaking was not something that came easy to her. In fact, making a speech was one of the biggest challenges she faced in her role as Commercial Director, particularly when it was in English. She would spend many long days and sleepless nights preparing for her conference presentations.

JJ led Lola into a small auditorium with twenty seats, a stage, and an enormous video screen, then he invited the other employees to join them. One by one, they entered the room and sat down in silence staring at the new arrival. Lola felt the sickening sensation of panic rising from her stomach, as if she were just a shy girl who had been chosen to read a poem in front of the class.

JJ jumped up onto the stage, made a few announcements and then said: "It's a great pleasure to introduce you all to the new Commercial Director. Lola Badiola!"

Everyone clapped half-heartedly[22].

"Good morning!"

Lola looked into the eyes of her all-male colleagues.

And her mind went completely blank[23].

There were no words. No ideas. No thoughts.

There was nothing.

Just a blank.

---

[22] Half-hearted *(adjective)* - To do something without full commitment or enthusiasm.

[23] Mind (to go) blank *(idiom)* - To forget completely something you planned to say, normally when under pressure in a meeting or when making a speech.

Her heart raced, her legs trembled, and the walls of the room started to close in on[24] her. She looked across at JJ who was patiently waiting for her to start her speech.

In the middle of the audience, she noticed an immaculately dressed man, his hair was gelled back, and his sleeves were rolled up. He was staring at her with a smile on his face. Was he encouraging her? Or was he enjoying her suffering? Either way, it jolted her out of the inertia. She focused her attention on her breath, cleared her head of all the negative energy and moved forwards.

"Thank you very much for such a warm welcome. I am so happy to be part of this team. I'm really looking forward to working with you to make the digital world a safer place."

It wasn't a great speech, short and bland, but it was good enough to save Lola from a public meltdown[25], and for that she was thankful.

---

[24] To close in on *(phrasal verb)* - To get nearer to something that you are pursuing.
[25] Meltdown *(noun)* - A rapid and disastrous collapse of an economy, company, or person, originating from the term used to describe an accidental melting of the core of a nuclear reactor.

Chapter 8 - The Attack

Luis Bruña opened the front door of his house and tiptoed[26] in, quietly shutting the door behind him. It was past midnight and he'd spent the last eighteen hours dealing with a crisis at TechSpania.

Lying at the bottom of the stairs was his six-year-old son Chema. The little boy was deep asleep. Luis picked him up and took him to his bedroom. He laid the little boy gently in the bed and put the sheet on top of him, watching him breathe slowly and peacefully. He kissed him on the forehead and left the room.

Then he went to check on his wife. She was still awake, lying in bed reading a novel.

"Hey, Sweetie."

"Hi."

She didn't look up from her book and it was clear from the tone of her voice she was in a bad mood[27].

"I'll come to bed in a few minutes."

---

[26] To tiptoe *(verb)* - To walk very carefully and quietly so as not disturb anyone or anything.

[27] To be in a bad mood *(idiom)* - To have a temporary negative disposition, the opposite of being in a good mood.

Luis went back downstairs for a whisky. He didn't have the energy for a late-night fight about work-life balance[28]. It had been a day of non-stop stress.

At 6 am that morning, one of his clients, SMZ, a Swiss life insurance company, had been shut down by a ransomware[29] attack. The hackers had exploited a vulnerability in the Spanish branch of the company. They had locked the customer database and given the company 12 hours to transfer 100 Bitcoin, worth more than four million euros, to an untraceable digital wallet. If the money didn't arrive on time, they promised to unleash a virus that would disrupt their systems for days and weeks to come.

Luis and his team of engineers had spent the whole day brainstorming[30] ideas, writing code and communicating with their colleagues in Switzerland. With two hours to go until the deadline[31], the CTO arrived in Madrid on a private jet from Zurich. He would have been the image of business sophistication, if his face weren't red with anger and stress. The company's reputation was at risk. People's jobs were on the line[32], including his own.

"Where are we?" he asked brusquely.

"Let me take you through our plan of defence," replied Luis with as much confidence as he could summon. At that moment, he truly missed Lola. She had managed the SMZ account. She knew the client inside out. She'd even learned some basic German to enhance the relationship. She would have been able to reassure the client and

---

[28] Work-life balance *(noun)* - A healthy equilibrium between the time and effort you put into your professional life and your personal life.

[29] Ransomware *(noun)* - A computer virus that prevents the functioning of a company's software or threatens to damage it unless money is paid to the hackers.

[30] To brainstorm *(verb)* - An idea generating activity done by a group, often guided by a moderator, to access the collective subconscious and generate creative solutions.

[31] Deadline *(noun)* - The final moment to deliver a product or service.

[32] To be on the line *(idiom)* - To be at risk.

deal with[33] the crisis. But she had resigned from the company a month earlier and Luis still hadn't found a suitable replacement.

With an hour to go until the deadline, the CTO started to take the necessary steps to transfer the bitcoin to the digital wallet. There was only one thing left that Luis could do - organise an emergency meeting with the North Americans.

Just like in Europe, the US cybersecurity market was a virtual monopoly[34]. Despite being competitors at a global level TechSpania and its US equivalent had agreed to come together[35] in moments of crisis to share their expertise. A high-profile breach of security, like the one that SMZ was experiencing, eroded the trust of the entire sector. It was therefore in everyone's interest that this problem was resolved quietly and competently.

During the emergency meeting, it became apparent that the ransomware code was almost identical to the one used to break into a life insurance company based in New Jersey, earlier in the year. With the collaboration of IT experts in the US, Luis, and his team, were able to design a program to override the malware[36] and neutralize its effect.

With less than 15 minutes remaining, SMZ's systems were unlocked, and an upgraded firewall was put in place. The bitcoin transfer was cancelled, and the company's reputation was saved.

But nobody celebrated.

Luis knew that this was probably the end of the relationship with the SMZ company and the loss of more than a million dollars of

---

[33] To deal with *(phrasal verb)* - One of the most common phrasal verbs in business English. To take responsibility for an issue or person and solve whatever problems arise.

[34] Monopoly *(noun)* - A company that is the sole provider of a good or service in a market, and therefore exercises considerable power and influence.

[35] To come together *(phrasal verb)* - To assemble in a harmonious way, or to start working successfully with each other.

[36] Malware *(noun)* - Software that is designed by a hacker to gain unauthorised access to a computer system, in order to disrupt, damage or exploit it.

revenue per year. He would have to explain the situation to Ruiz de Velasco at the next morning meeting. A prospect he dreaded[37].

As he sat on his sofa in the darkness, he took another sip of his whisky and wondered how his department was going to hit its budget, let alone its stretch targets, without the Swiss life insurance account. He also wondered how on earth he was going to be able to replace Lola Badiola.

He heard the footsteps of his wife coming down the stairs. She was wearing a dressing gown and slippers. She sat down next to him on the sofa, reached for his glass of whisky and took a small sip.

"You wanna talk about it?" she asked softly.

---

[37] To dread (something) *(verb)* - To have a very bad feeling about something that is about to happen.

Chapter 9 - The North Koreans

Park Jae-bong was a genius. He attended the University of Technology in Pyongyang, North Korea, where he obtained a master's degree in physics, graduating top of his class. He was immediately recruited by the country's state-sponsored hacking organisation. Within a year he had created and released WannaCry[38], one of the world's costliest ransomware attacks.

Over the following three years, he generated hundreds of millions of dollars for his government through brilliant and devastating computer related frauds. His victims were multinational companies like JP Morgan, Vodafone, and Yahoo.

Within the international hacking community, he was considered a demi-god. Nobody knew who he was or what he looked like, but his style of coding was unmistakable. Within his own country however, he was just another anonymous civil servant[39]. He wore the same smart casual clothes, travelled on the same public buses, and received the same benefits as everyone else in his division.

He operated in a small cubicle in an enormous room with 13,000 other hackers. Each of them spent sixteen hours a day in a

---

[38] WannaCry *(noun)* - The name of a malware application that attacked computer systems running Microsoft Windows in 2017, encrypting data and demanding a ransom to be paid in Bitcoin.

[39] Civil servant *(adjective noun)* - A person who works for a country's government but who is not a part of its military.

continuous cycle of trial and error[40] until they bumped into[41] a system weakness. Park was the most imaginative and persistent of them all.

He worked closely with his best friend and confidant, Kim Dae-won. Their personalities complemented each other perfectly. Park was in many ways a typical introverted[42] computer geek, someone who found it much easier to communicate with machines than with people. Kim, on the other hand, had a childlike enthusiasm for the real world around him.

That morning the two of them were monitoring the progress of their most recent infiltration. The target was the Spanish branch of a Swiss insurance company called SMZ. It was a classic ransomware attack. They had shut down a critical link in a company's computer systems and demanded payment in the form of cryptocurrencies.

"Midday report!"

Park and Kim's concentration was interrupted by Kang, their direct superior in Division 6523 of the hacking department. Kang was a functionary[43]. He walked around, all day, collecting reports that he didn't understand.

Park and Kim hated Kang. They hated being supervised by him. And above all, they hated the pointless routine of producing daily reports that nobody read.

"Here it is, sir," said Park as he handed over the document.

Kang then asked a few standard questions.

---

[40] Trial and error *(idiom)* - An iterative process of reaching the solution by making a series of attempts, until the correct answer reveals itself.

[41] To bump into *(phrasal verb)* - To meet someone by chance.

[42] Introverted *(adjective)* - An adjective used to describe someone who feels comfortable in their own company, focusing on their own thoughts rather than interacting with the external world.

[43] Functionary *(noun)* - Someone who performs a simple task or duty, normally a government official. The word often has a negative connotation implying that the person has little imagination or autonomy.

"Have you observed[44] any new anomalies?"

"No, sir."

"Have you crashed any systems?"

"No, sir."

"Have you concluded any infiltrations?"

"No sir."

"What is the status of the SMZ attack?"

"They have three hours to respond."

Kang made a note in his report then he walked away without any acknowledgement. Kim and Park waited until he was out of sight and then they turned back to their computers. They had some time to kill[45] before the bitcoin payment arrived.

Without anybody else in Division 6523 knowing, they bypassed the internal security systems and accessed the uncensored internet. It was a dangerous activity. If either of the programmers were caught, they would be at best demoted, at worst imprisoned. But this didn't deter them. After all, they were the smartest guys in the room[46].

For the next couple of hours, the two Koreans surfed the web, consuming the content that most interested them. Park checked the BBC, New York Times and Russia Today for international news. Kim signed into his Disney Plus account and continued watching episodes of Star Wars Rebels. To the two of them, the western world was both alien and fascinating.

---

[44] Observed vs. crashed vs. concluded *(verbs)* - These are examples of the regular past participle. In each case the final syllable "ed" is pronounced differently, D vs T vs ID. This is one the most common pronunciation errors in spoken English. For a complete review, listen to episode 9 of the Adventures of Lola Badiola podcast.

[45] To have time to kill *(idiom)* - To have nothing to do for a particular period.

[46] The smartest guys in the room *(idiom)* - A common business expression that refers to the group of people in a meeting, negotiation or department who know more than everyone else and are therefore able to get what they want.

With 15 minutes to go before the deadline of their attack they received an unexpected notification on their screens.

"Shit!" whispered Park Jae-bong.

"Shit!" whispered Kim Dae-won.

Their attack had been disarmed, their code erased, and an upgraded firewall put in place.

"I can't believe it!" said Park.

"We were so close!" said Kim.

They sat in silence in their little cubicles feeling defeated and deflated. Almost a month's work had come to nothing.

"We'll get them next time."

"Yes, we will."

Park hated being beaten by another coder. To lose like this was a humiliation. He started typing instructions into his computer.

"Let's start again,"

"Are you kidding? They've reprogrammed their whole system."

"They're still vulnerable.

"Come on comrade, it's time to go home."

"I'm staying."

Kim sighed and shook his head. He logged off, shut down and headed for the exit. He knew it was pointless to argue with his best friend when he was in this sort of mood.

Park turned back to his computer and stared into the abyss of cyberspace. He closed his eyes and tried to visualise the people he was targeting. Who were they? What were they like? What did they look like? He tried to put himself into their shoes[47].

Whoever had defeated Park Jae-bong was going to feel the full force of his revenge. He wasn't just going to re-hack SMZ, he was going to attack the company that protected them.

He was going to bring down[48] TechSpania.

---

[47] To put yourself in someone else's shoes *(idiom)* - To try to see the situation from the other person's perspective, to be understanding and empathetic.

[48] To bring down *(phrasal verb)* - To cause someone to lose power.

Chapter 10 - The Coffee

Lola stood alone in the women's bathroom looking at herself in the mirror. It had been almost three years since her last panic attack[49]. Her therapy and yoga sessions had helped control these self-destructive tendencies. Ever since she was a teenager, she had fought an ongoing battle with the little demons inside her head. She knew the triggers – alcohol, caffeine, lack of sleep, stress – and she avoided them as much as she could.

She took some cold water in her hands and splashed it over her cheeks. She was determined to keep her condition a secret from her new colleagues. Mental strength was considered essential in her line of business. She didn't want to be stigmatised[50].

Waiting for her outside the bathroom was Cayetano Tolosa.

"Hey. Nice speech."

"Thanks."

"Do you have time for a coffee?"

Lola's father had once warned her to be suspicious of the first person who wanted to be your friend when you started a new job,

---

[49] Panic attack *(noun)* - Sudden irrational feelings of fear and anxiety that cause physical symptoms like a palpitations, fast breathing, and sweating.

[50] Stigmatise *(verb)* - To treat something with disapproval or shame.

moved to a new neighborhood, or joined a new team. He believed that they always had a hidden agenda[51].

"Sure!"

She knew she would be working very closely with Cayetano. It was therefore a good idea to find out his strengths and weaknesses as soon as possible. He had never worked in the cybersecurity sector, and she had never worked in a start-up environment. So, they had something in common, they were both fish out of water[52].

"I know the best place for pinchos[53] around here." He said.

"Great."

Lola followed Cayetano out of the office and down on to Gran Vía. It was a relatively quiet morning, only a few tourists for the pickpockets[54] to target. Lola held her handbag close to her body as they headed onto one of the quieter side streets.

Cayetano was a little taller than her, but this was only because of the six-centimeter heels of his Balenciaga boots. He clearly spent a lot of money on his appearance. He wore skin-tight Armani jeans, a shiny white shirt by Karl Lagerfeld and a Burberry winter jacket. He was either living beyond his means[55], or he was independently wealthy.

"Coffee with milk." said Cayetano to the old man behind the bar at the café.

"Fresh orange juice, please."

---

[51] Hidden agenda *(adjective noun)* - When someone appears to be helping you when, in truth, they have other secret reasons for acting the way they do, normally self-interest.

[52] Like a fish out of water *(idiom)* - A familiar metaphor which describes someone that is in an unfamiliar, and often uncomfortable, situation.

[53] Pinchos *(noun)* - A delicious homemade snack that is offered in Spanish bars as an aperitif.

[54] Pickpockets *(noun)* - Thieves that operate in the streets of big cities specialising in stealing wallets from the pockets of tourists without them realising.

[55] Living beyond your means *(idiom)* - To spend more money than you earn.

"Smoke?"

"No."

"Do you mind if we sit outside so I can have a cigarette."

"Sure."

They took their drinks and sat at a small round table next to the entrance of the café. Cayetano lit his cigarette and looked coolly into the distance.

"So, what brought you to JBlock?" Lola asked.

Cayetano took a sip of his coffee, a drag of his cigarette and then smiled.

"The money."

It was an ironic comment[56]. The salary and benefits at JBlock were lower than more established companies. It was true that all the employees had an equity stake[57] in the company, but at that point it was valueless. Cayetano continued:

"My cousin[58] introduced me to JJ. I knew I had to work at JBlock. The guy's a visionary."

"Did you have a job interview?"

"Of course." replied Cayetano. "I prepared like a maniac, read everything, anticipated the questions. Then I practiced my answers in English out loud."

"What kind of questions did he ask you?"

"Oh, the usual things. Tell me about yourself. What are your weaknesses? Where do you see yourself in five-year's time? Along with a few brainteasers[59] like - what's four fifths of 1005?"

---

[56] Ironic comment *(adjective noun)* - To say the opposite of what you mean, in a way that is understood by your listener in order to emphasise the point that you are making in a humorous way.

[57] Equity stake *(noun)* - The ownership of shares in a company.

[58] Cousin *(noun)* - One of the most mispronounced words in spoken English, should be pronounced "kuh-zin".

[59] Brainteasers *(noun)* - An amusing problem or puzzle that requires mental effort and ingenuity to solve.

Cayetano crushed his cigarette into the ashtray and looked Lola straight in the eye. "You think I'm only here because of my connections, don't you?"

"No, not at all."

"All the programmers think so. They don't respect me. They make fun of me[60]. Call me names."

The expression on Cayetano face changed. The peacock strutting down Gran Vía was suddenly just a sad and vulnerable duckling. Lola couldn't help sympathising with him. She knew what it was like to be an outsider. She leaned forward. "Hey. If JJ offered you the job, then you deserve the job. As you said, the guy's a visionary."

"Thanks, Lola."

Cayetano reached forward and gently held her arm. It was an unexpected gesture and Lola wasn't sure how to respond.

"That's a beautiful watch," he said.

They both looked down at the large watch on Lola's thin wrist.

"It was my father's. It's a Patek -"

"- Philippe in white gold." Cayetano completed her sentence. "Your father was a very stylish man."

He released her arm.

"It's a pity that it doesn't have the original strap."

Once again, Lola was unsure how to respond. She had inherited the watch and replaced the crocodile skin strap with a synthetic alternative that looked almost identical. Nobody had ever noticed before.

"Shall we head back to the office?" he said. "I need to follow up a few sales leads."

Without waiting for an answer, he walked over to the bar and paid for the drinks. Lola couldn't help noticing the contours of his muscular body as it stretched the fabric of his tight-fitting designer clothes.

---

[60] To make fun of *(phrasal verb)* - To ridicule or mock someone. To laugh at them often in an insulting way.

SAM GRATTON

QUIZ TIME

Chapters 6 to 10

COMPREHENSION QUIZ

Answer the questions with complete sentences. Say them out loud.

1. Describe Diego de la Fuente, the Chief Technology Officer at JBlock. What is his management style?
2. What do the programmers at JBlock think about Cayetano Tolosa and salespeople in general?
3. What was the multicultural misunderstanding between JJ and Lola when they greeted each other outside the elevators?
4. What are Lola's responsibilities at JBlock going to be, and how does she feel about the challenges ahead?
5. What does Lola think about public speaking in English? What happened to her body and mind when she started to panic? How did she control herself?
6. How long has it been since Lola's last panic attack? When did she start suffering from panic attacks? Why does she want to keep her condition a secret?
7. Why does Luis Bruña, manager at TechSpania, miss Lola Badiola so much?
8. Who is Park Jae-bong, and what is he like? What is Park's reputation globally versus his reputation in his own country?
9. How do Park and his best friend Kim Dae-won react when their cyber-attack fails? What do each of them do next?
10. How is the relationship between Lola and Cayetano developing?

BUSINESS ENGLISH QUIZ

Complete the sentences with the words used in the story.

1. We are offering them a one-month trial of our software as a P_____ of C_____ and after that we expect them to sign a multiyear contract.
2. We need to reduce our company's headcount by 15%, it's a N_____ E_____, in order for us to return to profitability.
3. The Italian sales guy is a R_____, he just signed up Italy's largest pharmaceutical company to a five-year servicing plan.
4. It is slowly D_____ O_____ our management team that if we don't embrace artificial intelligence, we will soon become obsolete.
5. Can you believe that a cup of coffee in Starbucks in New York now costs more than five B_____?
6. Your B_____ I_____ is how your customers describe the way they feel about your product to other people.
7. I always use notes when I'm making an important speech just in case my M_____ G_____ B_____.
8. The negative economic data has caused a M_____ in the Asian stock markets and we need to reduce our exposure as quickly as possible.
9. My manager has been in a B_____ M_____ ever since he was rejected for a promotion.
10. It's important to maintain a healthy W_____-L_____ B_____, in order to be happy and successful in both your personal and your professional life.

11. Let's get the whole sales team together so that we can B_____ creative ways of marketing and selling the latest version of the software.

12. The D_____ for delivery of the final machine is 5pm on Friday, if we miss it, we will be penalised.

13. The Competition Commission is investigating our company for the abuse of M_____ power in the steel markets.

14. Before you launch this system upgrade, you need to think about the customer. You need to P_____ Y_____ in their S_____.

15. All our employees have an E_____ S_____ in our business. It is a way to incentivise them to work hard, be creative and commit to us over the long term.

ANSWERS TO COMPREHENSION QUIZ

1. Diego de la Fuente is a big, bald hairy man, with an excellent academic and professional track record, who understands and empathises with his team of programmers, and therefore, knows how to get the best out of them.

2. The programmers at JBlock have a very low opinion of Cayetano Tolosa. They think that he knows very little about the product and the market and he's just a pretty face. In fact, they have a low opinion of salespeople in general and believe that their code is so good that it simply sells itself.

3. Both Lola and JJ are trying to adapt to the culture of the other and therefore when they meet outside the elevators Lola extends her hand for a handshake while JJ moves forward for a kiss.

4. Lola is the new commercial director of JBlock responsible for marketing strategy and sales results. She is very motivated by this challenge because she believes that JBlock's software can make the world a safer place.

5. Lola is afraid of public speaking, particularly, in English, but recognises that this is a necessary part of her job as a commercial director, and therefore, does a lot of preparation before any speech. On her first day of work at JBlock, she had no advanced warning and therefore she started to panic, her body shook, and her mind went blank. In order to control herself, she breathed deeply, centred herself and took a step forward.

6. It's been almost three years since the last panic attack. She has been experiencing these episodes since she was a teenager. She wants to keep the condition secret, as she believes that mental health issues are stigmatised at work.

7. Luis Bruña, Lola's previous manager, is missing her because she was an excellent account manager, and he is now having to deal

with her ex-clients, including a Swiss life insurance company that has just been hacked.

8. Park Jae-bong is one of the world's greatest cyber security experts employed by the North Korean government to hack into multinational companies for financial gain. He is considered a demigod in the international hacking community but, in his own country, he is just a simple government employee.

9. Park and Kim are shocked and disappointed by the failure of their attack after so much work and effort. Kim suggests they go home, but Park decides to stay in the office and try again.

10. Let's see how the relationship between Lola and Cayetano develops in the coming chapters.

ANSWERS TO BUSINESS ENGLISH QUIZ

1. We are offering them a one-month trial of our software as a PROOF OF CONCEPT and after that we expect them to sign a multiyear contract.

2. We need to reduce our company's headcount by 15%, it's a NECESSARY EVIL, in order for us to return to profitability.

3. The Italian sales guy is a ROCKSTAR, he just signed up Italy's largest pharmaceutical company to a five-year servicing plan.

4. It is slowly DAWNING ON our management team that if we don't embrace artificial intelligence, we will soon become obsolete.

5. Can you believe that a cup of coffee in Starbucks in New York now costs more than five BUCKS?

6. Your BRAND IMAGE is how your customers describe the way they feel about your service and product to other people.

7. I always use notes when I'm making an important speech just in case my MIND GOES BLANK.

8. The negative economic data has caused a MELTDOWN in the Asian stock markets, and we need to reduce our exposure as quickly as possible.

9. My manager has been in a BAD MOOD ever since he was rejected for a promotion.

10. It's important to maintain a healthy WORK-LIFE BALANCE, in order to be happy and successful in both your personal and your professional life.

11. Let's get the whole sales team together so that we can BRAINSTORM creative ways of marketing and selling the latest version of the software.

12. The DEADLINE for delivery of the final machine is 5 pm on Friday. If we miss it, we will be penalised.

13. The Competition Commission is investigating our company for the abuse of MONOPOLY power in the steel markets.

14. Before you launch this system upgrade, you need to think about the customer, you need to PUT YOURSELF IN THEIR SHOES.

15. All our employees have an EQUITY STAKE in our business. It is a way to incentivise them to work hard, be creative and commit to us over the long term.

"It's David vs. Goliath."
JJ Thomson

Chapter 11 - The Interview

JJ got onto his electric scooter and rode through the rush hour traffic of central Madrid. It was already 8.30 and he had a busy morning ahead of him. He had to pick up his residency permit from the town hall. Then, he had to drop off various documents relating to his business at the tax office. After that, he had an appointment for an interview with an American journalist at CyberStory Magazine at a restaurant near Plaza Colón.

He was running late, but every time he tried to speed up, a car, truck or bus would get in his way, and he would have to slow down. He looked forward to a world where all large vehicles were banned from the city centers.

It was 11:15 am by the time he reached Platea on Calle de Goya, an art deco cinema that had been converted into a series of interconnected restaurants. The journalist was already at the bar waiting for him.

"Hi! Bradley Manson."

"JJ Thomson"

"Orange Juice?"

"Sounds good."

"You know, I've spent more than 18 months living in Spain and I still can't say Zumo de Naranja."

JJ smiled. "I can't roll my double "r"s. That's why I never travel by ferrocarril."

They both chuckled.

After only a little more small talk[1], the journalist got straight to asking JJ some standard questions about his past business life.

"Your first big success was ePort, wasn't it?"

JJ had worked with the San Francisco Port Authority to design software that would dramatically improve the logistics[2] within the port. There were great inefficiencies in the way that oil tankers, cargo ships, and yachts navigated inland. There were even greater inefficiencies in the way that the freight[3] was dropped off by the ships and picked up by the awaiting trucks and trains.

JJ had designed an algorithm that minimised the amount of time and movement of each boat using the port. The cost savings were worth tens of millions of dollars a year. When other Port Authorities around the world heard about the success in San Francisco, JJ's phone didn't stop ringing.

"And then you sold ePort to a private equity firm[4], didn't you?"

"That's right. I love creating businesses. Other people love building them."

"What's the secret to your success?"

---

[1] Small talk *(adjective noun)* - Informal, preliminary conversation used when talking to someone you don't know very well at meetings or social events. Includes discussion of the weather, the traffic and your location.

[2] Logistics *(noun)* - The organisation and implementation of a complex operation.

[3] Freight *(noun)* - The goods or cargo carried by ship, train, truck, or airplane, pronounced like the number eight.

[4] Private equity firm *(adjective noun)* - An investment firm that uses its own money to buy companies, transform them and then sell them for a profit, normally over a five-to-seven-year period.

"Every tech entrepreneur[5] needs the right mix of hard skills[6] and soft skills[7]. Clearly, you need to have the technical ability, you need to be able to write code and implement best practice in your business. But you also need to understand people. You need to be able to communicate, influence, lead, negotiate and work in a team. And you need to do all of this with integrity."

"Your current venture is called JBlock, isn't it?"

"JBlock is a start-up cybersecurity company using blockchain technology to revolutionise the fight against corporate crime."

JJ explained in detail the plans to compete against the big companies that protected the status quo in the IT sector. He explained how the software that his company was developing, would surpass any products that were currently in the cybersecurity market. Just like ePort, it would drastically reduce the operational costs of doing business. And in doing so, it would put some powerful IT companies out of business.

"It's David vs. Goliath[8]," said JJ. "And we all know how that story ended."

The journalist clearly liked the sentence and wrote it word for word into his note pad.

"How do you think the incumbents will react?" he asked.

"That's their business." replied JJ. "My job, as CEO of JBlock, is to focus on mine."

---

[5] Entrepreneur *(noun)* - A person who risks their own money to start a business.

[6] Hard skills *(adjective noun)* - Technical skills that are relevant to each position, they are easy to test and demonstrate. The hard skills of a computer programmer would be expertise in Python, C++, and other languages.

[7] Soft skills *(adjective noun)* - Personal characteristics that become more relevant as you move up the career ladder, such as communication, time management, collaboration, problem solving and leadership.

[8] David vs. Goliath - In the famous Bible story, the boy David beats the giant Goliath in a fight. David succeeds despite his youth and small size by using an innovative and unexpected strategy.

At the end of the interview, JJ, and the American journalist from CyberStory Magazine exchanged numbers and agreed to go out for a beer together before the end of the month.

JJ picked up an electric scooter just outside of Platea and headed back to the office. It was 12:45pm and streets were now relatively free of traffic.

Following close behind him was a black Toyota Prius.

"Rogue hacker or hostile government?"

"I cannot confirm or deny either of those possibilities."

A journalist from ABC raised her hand and without waiting for permission to speak, she asked the question that was on everyone's mind.

"What does it say about the safety of our data if the company protecting our data is vulnerable to attack?"

There was a murmur around the press conference. This was the elephant in the room[11]. And it needed to be addressed.

"We are living in unprecedented times," said Mario Ruiz de Velasco calmly and confidently, having prepared for the questions with a rehearsed response that was loaded with rhetorical devices[12]. "A time when the integrity of data is coming under threat from forces both foreign and domestic. A time when any company, big or small, start-up or multinational, is vulnerable to the insidious actions of criminals. It is therefore paramount that, during these times, we stick together, support each other, and present a united front. Let there be no doubt in anybody's mind, TechSpania will fight back, TechSpania will prevail, TechSpania will continue to counteract the causes of chaos. It is, therefore, an opportune moment for me to inform you of our current product pipeline."

"Son of bitch! He's turning this press conference into a publicity stunt," said JJ.

"What's happening to the share price?" shouted Diego.

---

[11] The elephant in the room *(idiom)* - An idiom that describes an important and controversial issue that everybody is aware of, but nobody wants to talk about.

[12] Rhetorical devices *(adjective noun)* - Techniques that make speeches more memorable and persuasive. In this case, the use of anaphora, the repetition of a specific word in the phrase: "TechSpania will fight back, TechSpania will prevail, TechSpania will continue to counteract the causes of chaos." And the use of alliteration, the repetition of a specific letter at the start of consecutive words - "continue to counteract the causes of chaos".

"Still down 20%," replied one of the programmers monitoring his screen.

For the next ten minutes, Mario Ruiz de Velasco spoke about the upgrades the company was making to its endpoint protection, network encryption and web application firewalls. It looked like he was going to bore the press conference into submission until a journalist from El Confidencial, interrupted him with a question that caught everyone's attention.

"Was it an inside job[13]?"

"What do you mean?"

"Most malicious attacks are made by a company's current or ex-employees. Do you think that was the case here?"

"We are pursuing all lines of investigation."

"Is it true that the account manager responsible for the Swiss insurance company recently left?"

"Yes...we had to fire her."

The journalist made a note in his book and then asked.

"Is she implicated in this incident?"

Mario Ruiz de Velasco leant back in his chair and took some advice from his lawyer. Then he said. "That is something for the cybercrime department of the police force to decide."

"What's her name?"

Ruiz de Velasco turned to Luis Bruña and waited.

Luis hesitated for a movement, then leaned forward so that his lips were touching the microphone.

"Lola Badiola. Her name is Lola Badiola."

Ruiz de Velasco gave the journalists time to write down the new information and then he looked directly into the television camera.

"I hope that I can be the invisible hand that guides the police towards these criminals, whomsoever they may be."

---

[13] Inside job *(adjective noun)* - Illegal activity perpetrated by the employees of the organisation being targeted.

One by one, the JBlock team turned to look at Lola. She was frozen to the spot. Staring incredulously at the television screen.

And the sickening sensation of panic started to rise from her stomach.

SAM GRATTON

Chapter 13 - The Blind Date

Lola stood alone on the balcony of her apartment, looking out across Plaza del Dos de Mayo in the Malasaña district of Madrid. She couldn't get the image of Mario Ruiz de Velasco out of her head - his green eyes staring into the camera, accusing her of being involved in the attack.

Everybody at JBlock had turned to look at her - the administrative staff, the programmers, Diego de la Fuente, Cayetano Tolosa and JJ Thomson. She knew what they were thinking. She knew that they were questioning her integrity. But that moment, her feelings of anger and indignation gave her strength.

"Okay, listen up everyone," she said in a loud voice. "This security breach is bad news for Ruiz de Velasco and his shareholders. But it's good news for us.

The truth is they were running outdated and inferior programs and it was only a matter of time before they were breached[14]. We need to take this opportunity to show our potential customers that we offer a superior solution.

Diego, Cayetano, I'd like you to join me in my office so that we can revise our marketing plan, in light of these developments. I have more than a dozen hot prospects lined up and I'd like to visit them this week with our new proposal.

---

[14] To breach *(verb)* - To break a law or agreement.

And in case any of you are wondering, I wasn't fired from that company. I left them to join a group of people who I believe will make the business world a better and safer place. If anybody doubts that, please speak out now."

Nobody said anything.

Lola let the silence hang in the air as she scanned their faces. Then she said:

"Right! Diego, Cayetano, let's go."

The two men dutifully followed her into her office while everyone looked on.

As she stood on the balcony of her apartment, Lola replayed the day's events, over and over again, in her head. Her little speech had been effective. She was confident that she had won back the trust of most, if not all, of her new colleagues. But she was worried about Ruiz de Velasco and what he would do next.

"Hey Lola!"

She was distracted by the sound of a familiar voice from the street below. She looked over the balcony and saw Concha, her best friend, beckoning her down.

"Are you ready?"

"Ready for what?"

"Come on! It's double date night!"

"Oh God!"

Lola had completely forgotten that Concha and her husband had organised a blind date[15] for her and one of their single male friends. She wasn't in the mood[16]. She wanted to relax in front of the TV. Eat fajitas and watch Netflix.

---

[15] Blind date *(adjective noun)* - A romantic meeting between two people who don't know each other, normally organised by mutual friends.

[16] To be in the mood *(idiom)* - To feel like doing something.

Concha sensed her reticence. "Don't let me down, Lola. We've been planning this for weeks. You've got to meet this guy. He's made for you!"

Lola shook her head and ran her fingers through her hair. She was mentally exhausted, but for the first time that day she had been distracted from work. Maybe an evening with friends was what she needed. Maybe a night of uncomplicated sex would do her some good.

"Ok, Concha, I'll be down in ten minutes."

She hung up the phone and headed to the bathroom.

***

Lola took another sip of red wine as she listened to her blind date telling a funny anecdote about his travels. He worked as an engineer for the Red Bull Formula 1 racing team and spent nine months of the year travelling from one major city to another. He was intelligent, charming and he loved the music of Leonard Cohen. As Concha had said earlier that evening, he was perfect for Lola.

But Lola's mind was distracted. It fluctuated between the conversation at the dinner table about the skyscrapers in Melbourne and the Ferris wheel in Osaka, and the conversations in her head about JBlock, Ruiz de Velasco and the cyberattack.

By the time they ordered dessert[17] Lola was feeling a little too drunk for a Wednesday evening. She excused herself from the table and headed to the ladies' toilets. Concha followed her.

"So, what do you think?"

"About what?" Lola replied, as she touched up her make up in front of the bathroom mirror.

---

[17] Dessert *(noun)* - A sweet dish at the end of a meal. It is pronounced with the emphasis on the second syllable. Not be confused with "desert" an area of terrain with no rainfall, pronounced with the emphasis on the first syllable.

"About your blind date!"

"Oh, he's lovely."

Lola paused and then turned to Concha and said, "What's his name again?"

"Come on!" Concha shook her head in genuine frustration. She had made a lot of effort to get these two together and she wanted it to work. "What's up with you this evening?"

Lola stopped retouching her make up, put down her mascara brush and then burst into tears. Big, loud, uncontrollable sobs.

Concha opened her arms and Lola fell into them like a tall, gangly teenager in need of some mother love. For a moment, they didn't say anything, they just rocked from side to side in the middle of the bathroom. A couple of other women came and went, smiling sympathetically as they passed.

"He wants to ruin me, Concha!"

"What?"

"He wants to end my career!"

"Who?"

"Ruiz de Velasco! That bastard!"

"How?"

"He's lying about me! Saying I was fired! Implying I'm a criminal!"

"Bastard!"

"I've made the worst decision of my life!"

"Ok, ok, calm down. Let it all out."

Lola took a few deep breaths and gradually regained her composure. She caught sight of her face in the bathroom mirror.

"Oh God, look at me now. What a disaster! I feel so sorry for my blind date."

She washed her hands and face and took a fresh paper towel from the dispenser. Then she turned to Concha with a smile and said:

"What was his name again?"

The two women burst into laughter. And when they had calmed down Lola dried her face, retouched her mascara, and straightened her hair.

"Thanks for listening, Concha. I needed that."

"Are you sure you're ok?"

"Yep. Let's go!"

They had one last hug and then Lola picked up her handbag, took a final look at herself in the mirror and opened the bathroom door. The two women walked confidently back to their table. Lola sat down, leaned forward and in a quiet voice said to her blind date:

"Listen, I haven't really been myself tonight."

"Oh?"

"It's a long story."

"Ok"

"Would you mind if we started this blind date from the beginning again?" She smiled at him playfully.

"Sure." he replied.

She stretched out her hand and said: "Hi, my name's Lola Badiola. What's your name?"

SAM GRATTON

Chapter 14 - Waking Up

Even before Lola opened her eyes, she knew that she was waking up in someone else's bed. It smelled different – the scent of an unfamiliar washing powder. She tried to remember what had happened the previous night and became aware of a slight ache in her head.

She could hear the movement of pots and pans in a distant kitchen. Somebody in the apartment was already awake.

Slowly she opened one eye. She was lying alone in a double bed. She asked herself the obvious questions. Where was she? How did she get there? And most critically, whose bed was she in?

A shot of adrenalin passed through her body, and she sat upright. She was wearing her bra, panties, and socks underneath an oversized T-Shirt with the Harvard University logo. The events of last night came rushing back to her - the red wine, the tears, the hugs, and Mr. Red Bull.

She heard a deep voice nearby and then the door of the bedroom started to open very slowly. She stared at it, like a dear in the headlights[18]. A man's face appeared from the other side of the door.

"Good morning," he said.

Lola rubbed her eyes.

---

[18] Like a deer in the headlights *(idiom)* - A person who sees something so surprising or confusing that they don't know how to react.

The man was tall and muscular, much bigger than the one she had met the previous night. He smiled at her and then turned and shouted in the direction of the kitchen.

"Hey Concha, Sleeping Beauty's awake."

"Perfect timing!" Concha shouted back.

Lola sank back into the bed in relief. The man was Eugenio, Concha's loving husband.

"Come on!" he said. "You've got a fruit smoothie with your name on it waiting in the kitchen."

Lola got out of bed and headed through to the kitchen, apologising sincerely to Eugenio, who had clearly spent the night sleeping on the sofa.

"I didn't know where I was," said Lola with an embarrassed smile. "When did you redecorate the flat?"

"Just after I got back from Angola," replied Eugenio.

Eugenio Hernández had been married to Concha for just over a year. He was a freelance[19] documentary filmmaker currently working for the World Wildlife Fund (WWF). That morning, he was particularly excited as he was flying out to Davos to interview politicians, environmentalists, and businesspeople at the World Economic Forum (WEF).

Lola admired Eugenio and asked him a lot of questions about his job. He was always jetting off to exotic locations to make films about endangered animals in stunning landscapes. He was incredibly knowledgeable about world affairs and spoke at least five different languages. He was also a wizard in the kitchen, the fruit smoothie he'd prepared for Lola being a testament to his abilities.

Concha and Eugenio were an odd-looking couple. She was petite and pretty. He was almost two-metres tall and had a face that had taken a few knocks from his days as a competitive rugby player. Despite their physical differences, they were perfectly matched in

---

[19] Freelancer *(noun)* - A self-employed person who does multiple short-term jobs for different businesses.

every other way. It was no secret that they were making a big effort to have a child, whenever Eugenio was in town.

"So," said Eugenio with a wicked smile, "What did you think of your blind date?"

Lola took a sip of her smoothie. Mr. Red Bull was a nice guy. He was interesting, funny, and a good listener. At the end of the evening, he had walked her back to Concha's apartment and kissed her goodnight.

Lola searched her memory for any embarrassing moments, any silly comments, or actions that she regretted. But, for once, there were none. After her tears in the bathroom, the evening had gone very smoothly. And she felt good about herself.

"He's alright," she said nonchalantly.

"Just alright?"

"Come on guys, I've got a lot on my plate[20] right now."

"Wouldn't you like to settle down with an Eugenio in your life?"

Concha wrapped her arms around her husband and pinched his chubby cheeks. Eugenio kissed his wife and pulled away.

"Listen girls, I need to pack my bags for the trip."

"Yeah, and I need to get ready for work." said Lola "Concha, can I borrow a suit?"

"Sure, let's get this show on the road[21]."

Lola had a quick shower and then squeezed herself into one of Concha's suits. It was a couple of sizes too small for her, the bottom of her thighs showing beneath the skirt and her bust pushed upwards and outwards by the jacket. It wasn't particularly comfortable, but it would do for the coming day.

Lola took a short bus ride from the apartment to the office on Gran Vía, which meant that she arrived on time for work. She smiled

---

[20] To have a lot on your plate *(idiom)* – To have a lot of work to do, and therefore to be unable to accept any more tasks.

[21] To get the show on the road *(idiom)* - To begin a significant activity or process after some time in preparation.

at the doorman as she entered the Adriática building and took the stairs up to the third floor. She was humming a little tune, feeling good about herself, as she walked into the office.

The first thing she saw was Cayetano waiting at her desk. He was with two other men - one tall, young, and Northern European, the other short, old, and Spanish. She had no meeting booked in her agenda so she wondered who the two men might be.

"Morning, Lola. Nice suit," said Cayetano as he moved to the side.

One of the strangers stepped forward to introduce himself.

"Good morning, Ms. Badiola. My name is James Buck, and this is my partner Guzmán Zunzunegui. We work for the cybercrime division of Interpol, and we would like to ask you a few questions about a recent corporate hacking incident."

Chapter 15 - Interpol

Lola sat at the table of the conference room in the offices of JBlock opposite the two agents. It was still early in the morning and most of the other employees, including JJ Thomson, had yet to arrive at the office. She felt isolated and vulnerable, as if she were swimming with sharks[22]. The young English agent, James Buck, reached for his notepad.

"You worked at TechSpania for seven years. Is that correct?"

"Yes." replied Lola

"Most recently, you were the senior account manager in the cybersecurity division reporting to Luis Bruña. Is that correct?"

"Yes."

"Are you still in contact with him?"

"No, we are not in regular contact anymore."

Buck wrote something into his notepad.

"One of your accounts at TechSpania was the Swiss insurance company SMZ. Are you aware that they recently suffered a catastrophic breach of security?"

"Yes. I am." replied Lola

Buck raised an eyebrow and wrote something into his notebook. Lola continued: "Because it's been reported in the newspapers."

Buck looked up from his notebook.

"Why were you fired from TechSpania?"

---

[22] Swimming with sharks *(idiom)* - To be in an environment with dangerous people, not knowing when or where they might attack.

"I wasn't fired[23]."

"Really?"

"Yes, really. I resigned from the company. You should speak to Luis Bruña. He'll confirm that."

The two agents looked at each other and then Guzmán Zunzunegui, the older of the two, leaned forward and in an apologetic voice said:

"We've already spoken to Luis Bruña. We've spoken to a lot of people, and they all say that you were fired."

Lola felt like she had been punched in the stomach. Luis Bruña had always been good to her. Their relationship had been one of mutual trust. They had become close friends. But now he was betraying her, lying about her, helping Ruiz de Velasco to destroy her.

The two agents from Interpol sat motionlessly, waiting for her to respond, watching her clam up[24]. But before Lola could answer, the door of the conference room burst open and JJ and Diego marched in.

"What's going on here?" said JJ forcefully.

James Buck, stood up, pulled out some identification from his pocket and explained that they were agents from Interpol interested in discussing some private matters with Lola Badiola.

JJ didn't even look at the identification. "If you want to speak to any of my team, in my office, you need to make an appointment."

"It's an urgent matter of international importance," the agent replied.

---

[23] To be fired *(verb)* - When a person loses their job because of something they have done, in other words it is their fault. Different from being "let go" or "made redundant" which is when a person loses their job due to wider economic or company circumstance. In other words, it's not necessarily their fault. You are "fired" for stealing; you are "made redundant" due to the recession.

[24] To clam up *(phrasal verb)* - To be unable to speak or express yourself due to fear or anxiety. Imagine your mouth shutting like the shell of a clam.

"I don't care what the fuck it is! If you want to speak to any of my team, in my office you need to make an appointment."

JJ and Diego stood shoulder to shoulder staring down at the two agents.

Lola had never realised how big and physically intimidating Diego could be. He was as wide as he was tall, with huge hairy hands and a solid torso that looked like it was about to rip through the Lacoste polo shirt he was wearing.

For a moment, the confrontation looked like it was about to get ugly, but Zunzunegui rose to his feet and attempted to diffuse the situation. He turned to Lola and said:

"Thank you for your time. We will be in contact. In the meantime, here is my card, in case you want to talk to us."

Then the two agents walked out of the conference room followed closely by Diego who escorted them out the building. The morning sun was shining brightly through the office window and directly into Lola's eyes. She squinted as the silhouette of JJ appeared in front of her.

"What really happened at TechSpania?" he asked.

Lola felt the emotion building up inside her. She was desperate not to break down[25] in front of her boss. She decided to be open and honest about what had happened.

"It ended badly," she replied.

"Were you fired?"

"No. I walked out[26]."

"When you say it ended badly, what do you mean?"

"I tried to do the right thing. I tried to leave on good terms. But Mario Ruiz de Velasco made it personal."

Lola's voice started to crack; she felt the tears building up inside her. "You believe me, don't you?"

---

[25] To break down *(phrasal verb)* – A verb with several meanings in a business context, in this case it means to lose control of your emotions and to start crying.

[26] To walk out *(phrasal verb)* - To end a relationship because you are upset.

"Of course, we believe you, Lola," said Diego, who had returned to the meeting room after dispatching the two agents. The ferocity from earlier had completely vanished and now he looked once again like a big, cuddly teddy bear.

Lola started to tremble as the intensity of the morning boiled over[27].

"I'm so sorry!" she said. "I feel terrible that I've dragged you guys into this."

JJ sat down opposite Lola and took hold of her hand.

"Listen carefully, Lola. This is not about you. It's about all of us. You see, our software represents an existential threat[28] to the all the incumbent[29] IT firms in the world, including TechSpania. We will do to them what the smartphone did to Nokia, Motorola, and Blackberry. Make them obsolete."

Lola had never heard JJ speak like this before. She knew that they had plans to disrupt the market but not on such a dramatic scale. He continued:

"Ruiz de Velasco will do whatever he can to stop that from happening. And he's joined forces with some very powerful friends. Come and have a look."

JJ beckoned Lola to join him at the window of the office. They looked down onto the street below where the two agents from Interpol were standing waiting. A black Toyota Prius stopped and picked them up.

---

[27] To boil over *(phrasal verb)* - Describes the moment when emotions become so intense that they can no longer be controlled.

[28] Existential threat *(adjective noun)* - A danger that is so great that it could mean the end of a person, a company, or in the case of climate change, the whole of humanity.

[29] Incumbent *(noun)* - In a business context, it is used to describe the company or companies that currently control or dominate a market.

"They've been following me everywhere since I arrived in Madrid. They're looking for a weak link[30] in our company. And now they think they've found it."

---

[30] Weak link *(adjective noun)* - The least strong part of a chain, the point of vulnerability for an organisation or a structure.

SAM GRATTON

QUIZ TIME

Chapters 11 to 15

COMPREHENSION QUIZ

Answer the questions with complete sentences. Say them out loud.

1. Describe JJ's Thomson's first big business success related to the shipping industry.
2. According to JJ Thomson, what is the key for being a successful technology entrepreneur?
3. What rhetorical devices does Ruiz de Velasco use in his speech at the press conference?
4. How does Lola feel at the end of the press conference?
5. How does she attempt to regain the confidence of her colleagues at JBlock?
6. Who does she meet on her blind date and what is her first impression of this person?
7. Describe Eugenio Hernández. What is his profession?
8. Who is waiting for Lola at her desk the morning after her blind date? What do they want?
9. How does Lola react during the interrogation by Interpol?
10. What happens to the interrogation when JJ and Diego arrive?

BUSINESS ENGLISH QUIZ

Complete the sentences with the words used in the story.

1. The interview started with some S_____ T_____ and then quickly moved on to questions about my leadership capabilities.

2. Our family-owned company is now for sale and there's interest from a number of buyers, including a P_____ E_____ firm, who plans to restructure our debt and introduce a new management team.

3. He is a S_____ E_____ who has started half a dozen successful companies and is now looking for his next big idea.

4. In the interview, they were more interested in my S_____ S_____ than my H_____ S_____, focusing on my leadership experience and my ability to sell and negotiate.

5. Our small software firm is competing against Microsoft for this business. It is like D_____ V_____ G_____.

6. Since his divorce our CEO has been a S_____ of his F_____ S_____ and we are worried about where the company is going.

7. Is anybody going to address the E_____ in the R_____ in this meeting? In order to survive the recession, some of us are going to lose our jobs.

8. His speeches are so interesting to listen to because they are filled with R_____ D_____ to capture the attention of the audience.

9. Since I lost my job, I have been working as a F_____ tax consultant and I'm making twice as much money doing half as much work.

10. I'm sorry I wasn't able to speak to you earlier. I have had a lot O_____ M_____ P_____ this week.

11. We've been planning the launch of this new product for the last six months. At last we are ready, so let's get this S_____ on the R_____.

12. Since I moved to the real estate office in New York, I have felt like I'm S_____ with S_____. I can't trust any of my colleagues.

13. When I told him we would have to make him redundant because of the economic crisis, he B_____ D_____ in front of me.

14. Blockbuster did not realise that streaming services, like Netflix, represented an E_____ T_____ to their business.

15. There are no W_____ L_____ in our commercial division. Every single one of our salespeople is a superstar.

ANSWERS TO COMPREHENSION QUIZ

1. JJ Thomson's first big success was the creation of ePort. A company which offered software solutions to Port authorities, allowing them to manage the movement of ships and cargo within their ports more efficiently.

2. According to JJ Thompson, the key to being a successful entrepreneur is having the right mix of hard and soft skills. Hard skills include technical ability and knowledge of computer languages. Soft skills include clear communication, time management and leadership.

3. Ruiz de Velasco uses two rhetorical devices in his speech. The first is known as "anaphora". The conscious repetition of the same word at the beginning of consecutive sentences: "TechSpania will… TechSpania will… TechSpania will…". The second device is called "alliteration". The repetition of the same letter at the beginning of consecutive words: "…counteract the causes of chaos."

4. Lola feels a mixture of emotions at the end of the press conference. It's clear that Mario Ruiz de Velasco is accusing her of criminal activity. At first, she is shocked and upset by what he says, and she starts to feel the onset of a panic attack. But she composes herself and becomes determined to fight back, believing that this situation is an opportunity for JBlock.

5. She regains the confidence of her colleagues with a brief but effective speech. She publicly challenges anybody within the company who doesn't believe her. Then she quickly moves forward to the next plan of action.

6. She meets Mr. Red Bull on her blind date. She considers him to be interesting, thoughtful, and patient. She recognises that they have a lot in common and, like Concha and Eugenio, feels that this relationship has potential.

7. Eugenio is a huge, powerful man, who is extremely tender and loving with Concha. A gentle giant. He's also a fabulous cook, having spent much of his childhood in the kitchen with his grandmother. He works as a filmmaker with an expertise in nature and environmental documentaries. He spends a lot of time travelling to exotic locations and is planning to visit the World Economic Forum in the coming week.

8. Waiting for Lola at her desk the morning after her blind date is Cayetano, along with two men from Interpol, a young Englishman, and an older Spaniard.

9. Lola feels isolated and vulnerable during her interrogation by Interpol. She is deeply upset by the news that her old manager and friend, Luis Bruña, has betrayed her.

10. As soon as JJ and Diego arrive, the interrogation stops, they take control of the situation, they evict the agents and give their whole-hearted support to Lola.

ANSWERS TO BUSINESS ENGLISH QUIZ

1. The interview started with some SMALL TALK and then quickly moved on to questions about my leadership capabilities.

2. Our family-owned company is now for sale and there's interest from a number of buyers including a PRIVATE EQUITY firm, who plans to restructure our debt and introduce a new management team.

3. He is a SERIAL ENTREPRENEUR who has started half a dozen successful companies and is now looking for his next big idea.

4. In the interview, they were more interested in my SOFT SKILLS than my HARD SKILLS, focusing on my leadership experience and my ability to sell and negotiate.

5. Our small software firm is competing against Microsoft for this business. It is like DAVID VERSUS GOLIATH.

6. Since his divorce, our CEO has been a SHADOW of his FORMER SELF and we are worried about where the company is going.

7. Is anybody going to address the ELEPHANT IN THE ROOM in this meeting? In order to survive the recession, some of us are going to lose our jobs.

8. His speeches are so interesting to listen to because they are filled with RHETORICAL DEVICES to capture the attention of the audience.

9. Since I lost my job, I have been working as a FREELANCE tax consultant and I'm making twice as much money doing half as much work.

10. I'm sorry I wasn't able to speak to you earlier. I have had a lot ON MY PLATE this week.

11. We've been planning the launch of this new product for the last six months, at last we are ready, so let's get this SHOW ON THE ROAD.

12. Since I moved to the real estate office in New York, I have felt like I'm SWIMMING WITH SHARKS. I can't trust any of my colleagues.

13. When I told him we would have to make him redundant because of the economic crisis, he BROKE DOWN in front of me.

14. The company Blockbuster did not realise that streaming services, like Netflix, represented an EXISTENTIAL THREAT to its business.

15. There are no WEAK LINKS in our commercial division. Every single one of our salespeople is a superstar.

"What you see is what you get."
Lola

Chapter 16 - The Mickey Mouse Watch

Park and Kim knew more about the security systems in Division 6523 of Ministry of Information than anyone else. This meant that when the office was quiet, they could override their own firewalls and surf the world wide web without any impediments. Park liked to follow international news and sports channels, while Kim preferred hacking streaming services to watch cartoons.

The previous week, they had successfully breached the defences of TechSpania and caused the share price of the company to fall by more than 20%. In doing so, the two hackers had discovered vulnerabilities in several large public[1] companies in Spain. Their next target would be Europe's largest commercial bank, Banco Cantábrico.

As part of their preparation for an attack, they always researched the target company in great depth. They learned about the culture of the company, how it was organized, where the vulnerabilities were hidden.

At that moment, they were sitting together watching the Annual General Meeting[2] of Banco Cantábrico. It was one of the biggest

---

[1] Public company *(adjective noun)* - One that is listed on the stock exchange and, therefore, its shares can be bought openly by members of the public. It is not a company owned by the government.

[2] Annual General Meeting *(adjective noun)* - A public company is obliged to organize an annual general meeting (AGM) to which all the shareholders are invited and anyone of them can ask the management a question.

lenders in Europe - from the smallest personal loans[3] to the largest and most complex corporate debt[4] instruments. It was also the most successful mortgage[5] provider in the region and therefore had a treasure trove[6] of priceless data.

Park listened carefully as Nuria Nueno, the head of Banco Cantábrico, presented the results of the company and talked about their plans for future growth. It was the first time he had listened to a woman chairing a company's Annual General Meeting. He admired the way she answered questions in a professional but conversational manner.

"Hey Park, I've got something to show you."

"Not now Kim, I'm concentrating."

"Look!" said Kim.

Kim rolled up the sleeve of his shirt to reveal a watch. It was old and scratched but functioning perfectly. It had the unmistakable image of Mickey Mouse in the middle. The cartoon character's gloved hands were pointing at the numbers on the dial.

"Where did you get that from?" Park whispered.

"I got it from a street vendor in Shanghai."

Kim had just returned from an official trip to the People's Republic of China. He had been visiting the equivalent department in the Chinese government. They often exchanged information and coordinated attacks on Western targets.

"What the fuck!" whispered Park. "If you get caught with that.... you'll get fired, or worse."

---

[3] Loan *(noun)* -Pronounced as one syllable and rhymes with "phone".

[4] Debt *(noun)* - Pronounced with a silent "b", it rhymes with "bet".

[5] Mortgage *(noun)* - Pronounced - "mor-gihj".

[6] Treasure trove *(idiom)* - Many valuable objects hidden somewhere.

Kim knew the risk he was running[7]. He knew that Mickey Mouse was considered one of the greatest symbols of American decadence. He knew the supreme leader would disapprove. But he couldn't resist.

Kim rolled his sleeve back down to cover the watch and winked at Park. "When you wish upon a star, your dreams come true[8]," he said in his best American accent.

At that moment Kang, the divisional supervisor, appeared from around the corner. As always, he was pushing a trolley full of reports that he didn't understand. He stopped at the desks of Park and Kim and looked down at them condescendingly.

"Daily report."

"Here it is, sir," Park said as he handed over the document.

The supervisor then asked him the usual questions.

"Have you observed any anomalies?"

"No, sir."

"Have you crashed any systems?"

"No, sir."

"Have you concluded any infiltrations?"

"No sir."

"The quarterly meeting will start at 7pm this evening. Don't be late."

Kang put the report into a folder and moved on to the next cubicle. As soon as his back was turned, Kim turned to Park and gave him another wink and two thumbs up. Park couldn't help smiling. He felt like a parent who simultaneously admires and disapproves of their facetious[9] little child.

---

[7] To run risks *(idiom)* - To do something worthwhile but that may result in loss or damage.

[8] When you wish upon a star, your dreams come true *(idiom)* - The signature musical theme for Walt Disney. Originally from the animated film Pinocchio.

[9] Facetious *(adjective)* - Joking in an inappropriate manner when the situation is serious.

SAM GRATTON

Chapter 17 - The Girl with the Almond Eyes

Park and Kim caught the bus outside the Ministry of Security Affairs. It was a 45-minute[10] journey to their apartment block in the Chunghwa district of the city. They passed through The Arch of Triumph and across the Tae Dong River and then headed down the Pyongyang highway towards the south of the city.

There was never much traffic, but they were often delayed by people on bicycles, horse-drawn carts, and government checkpoints. The most common problem they encountered on their journey home was the bus breaking down. It was a diesel vehicle built in China in the 1980s and it had a completely unreliable transmission system. Every time the driver changed gear it sounded like the bottom of the bus was about to collapse.

Park looked out of the window at the grey functional apartment blocks that lined the highway. Everything was uniform, all the buildings looked exactly the same. He couldn't help but imagine what it would be like to travel on a bus outside of London, passing cottages with their thatched rooves, mansions with their iron gates and bungalows[11], where all the old western people moved into when

---

[10] 45-minute *(compound number adjective)* - Remember to include the hyphen and keep the noun in the singular form.

[11] Bungalow *(noun)* - A detached house built all on one level, popular with older couples who do not wish to walk upstairs to the bedroom.

they retired. There was no property ladder[12] in North Korea, the government simply allocated you an apartment and that was where you lived and eventually died.

His thoughts turned to the upcoming attack on Banco Cantábrico. He had breached their security systems on several occasions in the past, but never progressed very far. They always managed to kick him out before he could do any damage. The bank had multiple layers of defence and reaching the sensitive information at its core was like peeling an infinite onion.

He thought again about Nuria Nueno and her presentation at the AGM. He marvelled at the fact that a woman could have so much power and influence. The Workers' Party in North Korea actively promoted gender equality[13] for the good of the economy, but everyone knew that a woman's place was at home. He remembered the old Korean saying: "It is bad for the house when the hen sings, and the cockerel is silent."

As always, sitting next to Park on the bus was Kim who was focused on the task of creating an airplane out of a blank sheet of paper. He had many talents and one of them was origami. The paper airplane that he was constructing not only looked exactly like a B52 bomber. It flew like one too.

Kim stood up in his seat at the back of the bus and aimed the airplane at a young woman at the front. He gently propelled the model forward through the air and it sailed across the heads of all the other passengers landing perfectly in the lap of the intended recipient. The young woman picked up the paper airplane and read the message that Kim had written on its wings.

---

[12] Property ladder *(noun)* - Steps in home ownership. It starts with the purchase of a small, cheap home and, through a series of transactions during your life, ends with a large, expensive home.

[13] Gender equality *(noun)* - Equal opportunities for men and women within society. This differs from the concept of gender equity, which implies equal outcomes.

She looked behind her, searching for the person who had sent her the message. Kim waved to her to catch her attention. And then he pointed at Park.

Park was, as always, lost in his thoughts about work. He was, after all, the world's greatest hacker. Feared by companies around the world. Revered by the underground hacking community. Wanted by the FBI, the CIA, the NSA[14].

His daydream was interrupted by the presence of a woman in the aisle of the bus standing next to him. She was staring at him with quiet determination. She had porcelain skin and almond eyes. For a few seconds the two of them just looked at each other in silence. Park was mesmerized by this mysterious apparition.

The woman leaned forward and gave Park the paper airplane. She nodded, then turned around and walked back to her seat.

Park looked down at the model and read the message that was written on the wings:

"Meet me at Chunghwa Park this evening at 8pm."

The bus noisily changed gear and headed over the Tae Dong River towards the south of the city.

It took a moment for Park to figure out what was going on. Then his heart skipped a beat[15] and his face turned as red as the Chinese flag.

Next to him Kim was doing his best to keep a straight face[16].

---

[14] FBI/CIA/NSA *(Abbreviations)* - Federal Bureau of Investigation, Central Intelligence Agency, National Security Agency.

[15] Heart skips a beat *(idiom)* - Literally it is a palpitation, but metaphorically it indicates surprise, excitement, or nervousness.

[16] To keep a straight face *(idiom)* - To appear unemotional when something funny or surprising happens.

Chapter 18 - The Apartment

Park arrived back at his apartment at 7:30. He took off his shoes and went to the toilet. He lived in a modern apartment on the 22nd floor of a tower block in zone 7 of the Chunghwa district. As a D grade government employee, he had certain privileges, over the general public.

He had a separate kitchen with a small fridge freezer, and an oven with two electric hobs. He didn't own any luxuries like a microwave, a dishwasher, or a washing machine, but he did have a television which was the envy of all of his neighbours.

Unlike most North Korean people, Park knew that he was poor. He knew that the standard of living[17] in the North was significantly lower than in the South. He knew that the infrastructure of his country remained backward and most of his countrymen still worked in hard, time-consuming jobs in the agricultural sector.

Park also knew that the economies of many other East Asian nations had progressed dramatically over the last 30 years, as a result of globalisation. They had successfully worked together through institutions such as the United Nations and the World Trade Organization, to promote international cooperation. The Supreme Leader was convinced that these institutions would eventually

---

[17] Standard of living *(noun)* - The level of wealth, comfort and material goods of a country or region.

collapse in the aftermath of a Marxist revolution[18]. Park wasn't so sure.

South Korea was now much richer than North Korea. It had higher levels of technology and productivity. The people seemed happier, they seemed to have more fun. Park wondered what his life would be like if he had been born 150 kilometers south. The distance between the communist[19] haven of Pyongyang and the capitalist[20] centre of Seoul.

Park looked at the analogue clock on his wall. It was 7.45pm. Chunghwa Park was a 15-minute walk from his apartment. Who was the girl with the almond eyes? Why had she invited him to meet her? Was she a member of the secret police? It was quite normal for the government to spy of its own employees. There was even a department that spied on the spies of the employees. Or was it possible that this invitation was genuine, that this mesmerizing woman actually wanted to go on a date with him? Of the two possibilities, Park was more worried about the latter. He was almost thirty years old and still a virgin[21].

He walked into the bathroom, combed his hair, and then opened the bottle of Dragon aftershave. His prized possession. A gift from Kim after one of his business trips to China. He carefully placed a

---

[18] Marxist Revolution *(noun)* - A social revolution where the working classes overthrow the ruling elite and transform the economy into a communist system.

[19] Communism *(noun)* - A social system where production is owned and controlled by the government on behalf of the people. There is no market for products or competition between companies. There are no class distinctions.

[20] Capitalism *(noun)* - An economic system in which private companies compete in the open market to provide consumers with the desired goods, with the goal of making profits for their owners.

[21] Virgin *(noun)* - A person who has yet to have sex. Metaphorically, it can be used to describe someone who has no experience in a certain activity.

drop of the liquid on his index finger[22] then spread it across the left side of his neck. He repeated the action for the right side of his neck. He didn't want to waste a drop. The liquid was more valuable to him than plutonium was to the Supreme Leader. He stepped back from the mirror and imagined himself with his arm around the Girl with the Almond Eyes. Whether she was a spy or a potential girlfriend or both, he was determined to find out.

He left his apartment and headed on to the street. It was a dark winter's night but fortunately the streetlights were working that evening. He walked along the clean and orderly streets the Chunghwa district until he reached the main road. Then, he hailed a bicycle cab and jumped into the back of the carriage.

Pyongyang was a city for the elite. It was considered a paradise by the peasants, who scraped a living from the unproductive lands in the countryside. Park felt thankful to the Supreme Leader that he had been invited to live there.

The road to Chunghwa Park was full of traffic. There was a mix of diesel buses, horse drawn carts and Chinese motorcars. The government vehicles had back number plates, the foreign residents had red number plates and the very rare privately owned cars, perhaps gifts to sportsmen or actors, had yellow number plates. However, most of the citizens of Pyongyang walked or caught the bus.

It was one of the privileges of being a D grade government employee that Park could flash his identification and hail a bicycle cab. As he sat in the back of the carriage, he wondered who the mysterious girl was, what her father did and why her family lived in Pyongyang.

At exactly 7.59pm, Park arrived at his destination. He got out of the cab and stood beneath a huge poster of the Supreme Leader. He

---

[22] Index finger *(noun)* - At the end of your hand you have a thumb, then an index finger, middle finger, ring finger and finally the little finger or pinky.

looked around the surrounding area for his date, trying to appear relaxed but feeling deeply insecure.

Walking towards him were two people. A middle-aged lady, in her mid-fifties, short and slightly bent, with grey hair and pale skin. Next to her was a tall and slim young woman with a beautiful round face and almond shaped eyes.

His date and her chaperone[23] had arrived.

---

[23] Chaperone *(noun)* - Traditionally an older person, especially a woman, who monitors a younger woman who is not married when she is in public.

Chapter 19 - The Break

Lola sat at her desk wondering how she had ended up in this situation. The simple act of leaving one company and joining another had turned her life upside down. She considered all the elements that were currently conspiring against her:

Mario Ruiz de Velasco, the powerful CEO of TechSpania, wanted to ruin her. Luis Bruña, the man she had trusted all her working life, had betrayed her. And Interpol suspected her of involvement in a series of cyber-attacks. It was overwhelming[24].

Lola made herself comfortable in her chair and started to meditate. She breathed in deeply through her nose and then out through her mouth. She closed her eyes and pictured a door opening into her grandmother's garden - the calmest, quietest, and most relaxing place she could imagine. The fear she was feeling was purely subjective and therefore could be eliminated. She was in control or her own reality.

Her phone started to vibrate in her pocket. She opened her eyes and looked at the caller ID. It was Concha.

"Hey."

"Hi."

"I'm just in the middle of something. Can I buzz[25] you back?"

"This Sunday. Paella. Our place. Eugenio's cooking."

---

[24] Overwhelming *(adjective)* - Describes a situation that affects you deeply and leaves you unsure how to react.

[25] To buzz *(verb)* - Informal term for contacting someone via the telephone.

"Ok, count me in."

"Great! Chat later."

"Yeah. Sure."

Lola put down her phone and drummed her fingers on the surface on her desk. There was only one way to deal with[26] all the problems in her professional life. And that was to move forwards. Make things happen. Prove everyone wrong.

She opened her email account and started working. She had about 20 unread messages. Most of them were from suppliers marketing their products. She transferred these irrelevant items into the trash folder. There was an internal message from Diego reminding everyone to remain compliant with the roll out[27] of the new GDPR regulations. And there was a link to an article from CyberStory Magazine about North Korean hackers ramping up[28] attacks on European targets.

Amongst all the emails, there was one message that caught her eye. It was from one of her ex-clients with whom she had a great working relationship in the past. He had just been hired as IT procurement manager at Banco Cantábrico, Europe's largest commercial bank. He was inviting her to his office for a general catch up[29]. This was the break[30] Lola needed.

---

[26] To deal with *(phrasal verb)* - To resolve an issue or a problem. Probably the most common phrasal verb in business English.

[27] To roll out *(phrasal verb)* - To launch or introduce a product in a series of stages. You might roll out a software upgrade, a new design or a vaccine. Very popular in business speeches and presentations.

[28] To ramp up *(phrasal verb)* - To increase the production or output of your goods or services. You might ramp up the extraction of oil in response to the economic recovery.

[29] To catch up *(phrasal verb)* - To talk to someone whom you've not seen for a while. To get up to date with what they have been doing.

[30] A break *(noun)* - A noun with many different meanings. In this context, it means an opportunity for improving a situation, especially one that happens unexpectedly.

She didn't waste any time responding to his email. She knew his personal number and without a second's hesitation called it. She placed the Bluetooth headphones in her ear and stood up. She always communicated better when she was walking around the office. This was an important pitch[31] and she needed to nail it[32].

"Lola!"

"Fernando! It's been too long!"

"Yeah. A lot of water under the bridge[33]."

"How're you doing?"

"Good."

"Congrats for the new role."

"Yeah, well, it's been a baptism of fire[34]. So much activity through the wires."

"Tell me about it!"

"So, what's up with you Lola? I'm hearing rumours."

"Got a target on my back[35] since I quit TechSpania."

"So, you didn't get fired?"

Lola paused for a moment. It was clear that her ex-colleagues were trying to discredit her in the market. She needed to quash[36] the rumours.

---

[31] Pitch *(noun)* - A speech to persuade someone to buy your product, service, or idea. You might have heard of an "elevator pitch", which is an attempt to persuade somebody to buy something in the time it takes for the elevator to rise from the ground floor to the top floor of a building.

[32] To nail it *(verb)* - A common shortening of the idiom "to hit the nail on the head" which means to do something perfectly.

[33] Water under the bridge *(idiom)* - Describes problems or conflicts in the past that are no longer of any consequence.

[34] Baptism of fire *(idiom)* - Describes a new situation that is extremely difficult or unpleasant.

[35] To have a target on your back *(idiom)* - A target is an object you try to hit with a weapon. If you have "a target on your back", it means that someone is planning to attack you.

[36] To quash *(verb)* - To stop something from happening or continuing.

"Fernando, you, and I go way back. We've suffered together. We've celebrated together."

"Yeah."

"You know me. What you see is what you get."

"Right."

"So, here's the thing. I quit TechSpania to join JBlock. And they don't like it. It's as simple as that."

There was a pause and then Fernando responded quietly.

"I knew it! Those bastards at TechSpania! They just wanna crush any kind of competition. Listen Lola, I'd love you to come and present your new services. How's your diary looking?"

"Well, to be honest Fernando, pretty empty at the moment."

"Ok, I'll see you at 10am on Tuesday."

"Done."

"Done."

And with that they both hung up.

Lola had booked a meeting with the biggest fish[37] in the IT procurement pond. She took off her earpiece and threw it onto the desk. It was moments like these that reminded her why she loved sales. Even though she was still behind in the game, she took a moment to celebrate scoring a goal.

---

[37] Big fish *(idiom)* - A powerful or important person within a company, industry, or specific group of people.

Chapter 20 - The Paella

Eugenio Hernández knew how to cook the perfect paella. He was a native of Denia, in Valencia, where he grew up in a big house by the Mediterranean Sea with his parents and his grandparents. From the moment he could chop a carrot, he loved to cook. While his friends were in the street playing football, he was in the kitchen with his abuela[38] boiling eggs, frying onions and baking bread.

His abuela was responsible for cooking all the food in the house and she taught him everything she knew. She showed him the best combination of seafood for a fideuá, she showed him how to pulverize the almonds to make the smoothest turrón, but most importantly, she shared with him the secrets of the perfect paella.

She explained to him that success depended on three key elements – ingredients, timing, and witchcraft. She said that it was an intuitive process - more of a feeling than a technique. She told him that the only way to develop this feeling was to spend hours and hours in the kitchen watching, learning, and assisting a master cook. And that is exactly what Eugenio did for the first 18 years of his life.

But it wasn't only the cooking that attracted Eugenio to his abuela's kitchen, it was also her stories of action and adventure. She had been a Blue Angel in the Spanish Civil War and had engaged in acts of espionage against the republican forces. Living and operating

---

[38] Abuela *(noun)* - Spanish for grandmother.

inside of Madrid, she had been an integral part of the Fifth Column, involved in countless acts of sabotage and disinformation that were the key to Franco's final victory. It was a secret that she shared with no-one other than her beloved grandson.

When Eugenio and Concha were both in town, they loved to entertain in their small apartment. They were the social epicentre of their community and, that Sunday, they had invited eight friends for lunch.

"How's it going?" asked Lola as she walked into the kitchen with a glass of Rioja in her hand.

"Fine," replied Eugenio bending down and looking at the enormous pan of simmering rice as if it were a science experiment. He had just reached the most critical stage in the preparation of the rabbit and artichoke dish.

"You know, in England they put chorizo in their paella[39]," said Lola laughing. "It's a Jamie Oliver recipe[40]."

Eugenio didn't react.

"They say he'll never be allowed back into Valencia."

Eugenio leaned forwards and inspected the rice at the edge of the paella, like a biologist might examine the specimens in a petri dish.

"How was the trip to the World Economic Forum?" asked Lola.

"Fascinating."

"Great!"

Lola took a sip of wine and watched the stock bubbling away at the centre of the paella pan.

"So, where are you going next?"

"China."

"Cool."

---

[39] Chorizo in the paella *(anecdote)* - In October 2016, the celebrity chef Jamie Oliver, tweeted his recipe for paella with chorizo causing ridicule and outrage amongst food lovers in Spain who considered this combination a sacrilege of their sacred dish.

[40] Recipe *(noun)* - It is pronounced with three syllables - "reh-sih-pi".

It was clear from his one-word answers that Eugenio didn't want any distractions at that specific moment, so Lola excused herself and walked back into the living room.

Concha was in the middle of telling a story about her recent visit to New York to the six guests who had already arrived. She had met the CFO of an investment bank who was contemplating a move to London. She had taken him out for lunch to discuss the terms and conditions of the offer. At the end of the meal, she had left some change as a tip[41]. The waiter had followed her out of the restaurant and refused to let her get into a taxi until she had paid him properly.

"Twenty percent!" shouted Concha. "He wanted twenty percent!"

The apartment intercom buzzed. The eighth and final guest had arrived. Concha was clearly distracted with the other guests. And Eugenio could not be disturbed, so Lola went to answer it.

"Hello!" she said into the mouthpiece.

"Concha?" said a man's voice.

"No, it's Lola."

"Oh! Hi Lola! Can you let me in?"

It took a moment for Lola to recognize the voice.

"Sure," she said and pressed the button that opened the entrance from the street below. She felt butterflies in her stomach[42] and her heart started to race.

It was the voice of Mr. Red Bull.

She didn't know he was coming to lunch. She thought it was going to be a simple and relaxed Sunday afternoon with friends, a chance to forget all the stress in her life. After the grilling she had

---

[41] To tip *(verb)* - To pay an extra amount of money for exceptional service. Tipping culture varies by country. For example, in the United Sates a tip 15% to 20% of the bill is expected, in Spain a few coins are enough, and in Japan it is viewed as unnecessary.

[42] Butterflies in the stomach *(idiom)* - To be feeling nervous and a little bit excited about something.

received from Interpol, her mind was fried[43]. She needed the weekend to unwind, de-stress and recover. But with the arrival of Mr. Red Bull, the atmosphere of Sunday lunch, at least for Lola, had suddenly become deliciously tense.

She opened the front door of the apartment. She could hear his footsteps running up the stairwell. She wondered if she should stay there and greet him herself, or just disappear amongst the other guests.

As the footsteps grew louder and louder her heart seemed to beat faster and faster, until the door of the apartment burst open, and Mr. Red Bull walked in.

He looked at Lola and smiled.

"Hello again!" he said and kissed her on both cheeks.

"Hi!" Lola replied.

They stood at the entrance staring at each other for a moment. And then he said:

"Wow, that Paella smells incredible!"

Lola was lost for words, like a teenager meeting her crush[44] in the school hallway. She searched deep inside her brain for something intelligent to say. And the only thing she could think of was:

"You know, in England they sometimes put chorizo in their paella.

---

[43] To fry your mind *(idiom)* - when your brain feels so overloaded with work or stress that you can't think straight.

[44] To crush *(verb)* - To compress or squeeze forcefully, in an effort to distort the shape of something. Metaphorically, "a crush" is a brief but intense attraction to someone.

QUIZ TIME

Chapters 16 to 20

COMPREHENSION QUIZ

Answer the questions with complete sentences. Say them out loud.

1. What project are Kim and Park currently working on?
2. Why is Park so concerned by Kim's Mickey Mouse watch?
3. What are the social, economic, and political differences between North and South Korea?
4. What are the key differences between communism and capitalism?
5. How does Park feel about his date with the Girl with the Almond eyes? And what does he do before he leaves his apartment?
6. What magazine does Lola like to read. And why?
7. Who does she call? And what do they talk about?
8. How did Eugenio Hernández become such a good cook?
9. What is the secret to making the perfect paella?
10. How does Lola feel when she realizes Mr. Red Bull is coming for lunch?

BUSINESS ENGLISH QUIZ

Complete the sentences with the words used in the story.

1. Microsoft, Apple, and Tesla are all P_____ C_____ because they are listed on the New York stock exchange and the general public can buy and sell their shares.
2. Throughout my life I have been climbing the P_____ L_____, starting with a very small flat in Earls Court and ending with a large, detached house in Madrid.
3. In a world of perfect G_____ E_____, do you think that 50% of plumbers would be women and 50% of nurses would be men?
4. The S_____ of L_____ in South Korea is significantly higher than in North Korea, proof that the political, economic, and social system in the south is superior.
5. Since the collapse of the Soviet Union there are very few C_____ states that are left in the world.
6. While C_____ is far from a perfect economic system, it is the most effective one that we have so far invented.
7. We are planning to R_____ O_____ the upgraded software over the next three months, starting locally, then moving regionally and finally globally.
8. They R_____ U_____ the production of chocolates ahead of the Christmas season.
9. "Hi Harry, I'm just calling to C_____ U_____ on everything that's happening in your life, at the moment. How's Meghan?"
10. You need to summarise your sales speech into a one-minute E_____ P_____ that you can use when people visit our stall at the conference.

11. That was the best presentation I've seen at this conference, perfect content, delivery, and style. You totally N_____ I_____!

12. I had to visit an angry client on my very first day of work, it was a true B_____ of F_____.

13. There is no need to apologise about the conflicts or misunderstanding we have had in the past. It's all W_____ under the B_____. Let's just move forward with the next project.

14. Our commercial director is so arrogant, he thinks that he's a B_____ F_____, when, in reality, he's just another salesman like you and me.

15. "Should we leave a T_____?" "Of course! We should. This is New York and if we don't leave one, the waiter will chase us down the street demanding his money."

THE ADVENTURES OF LOLA BADIOLA

ANSWERS TO COMPREHENSION QUIZ

1. Kim and Park are planning to hack into Banco Cantábrico, Europe's largest commercial bank. They are currently doing some background work into their target.

2. Park recognizes that Kim's Mickey Mouse watch is a symbol of western decadence and prohibited in North Korea. He is therefore deeply concerned about Kim's recklessness in owning and wearing the watch, as it could get him into a great deal of trouble.

3. South Korea is an open, mixed capitalist economy with a democratically elected government and a relatively liberal society. Its standard of living is high on a global scale. In contrast, North Korea is a closed, communist economy with an appointed dictator, in a controlled society. Its standard of living is one of the lowest on a global scale.

4. In communist societies production is owned and controlled by the government on behalf of the people. There are no markets. There is no competition between companies. There are no class distinctions, and society is relatively poor but egalitarian. In capitalist societies production is in private hands and companies compete in markets to provide consumers with what they want to generate profits for their owners. High levels of wealth and income inequality are generated by this system.

5. Park is nervous and excited about his date with the Girl with the Almond Eyes and has spent a lot of time in the bathroom beforehand preparing himself both physically and psychologically.

6. Lola likes to read CyberStory magazine to keep up to date with the news in her sector and what her clients might be doing.

7. She calls her old friend Fernando Roma who has recently been promoted to procurement manager at Banco Cantabria. They

chat about the recent events in Lola's life, before agreeing to meet to discuss business.

8. Eugenio Hernández is such a good cook because he spent his childhood in the kitchen of his Abuela, watching and helping her prepare the family meals.

9. The secret to making the perfect Paella is the correct combination of ingredients, timing, and witchcraft.

10. Lola feels excited and nervous when she discovers that Mr. Red Bull has been invited to the lunch. For her, the afternoon has become deliciously tense.

ANSWERS TO BUSINESS ENGLISH QUIZ

1. Microsoft, Apple, and Tesla are all PUBLIC COMPANIES because they are listed on the New York stock exchange and the general public can buy and sell their shares.

2. Throughout my life, I have been climbing the PROPERTY LADDER, starting with a very small flat in Earls Court and ending with a large, detached house in Madrid.

3. In a world of perfect GENDER EQUALITY, do you think that 50% of plumbers would be women and 50% of nurses would be men?

4. The STANDARD OF LIVING in South Korea is significantly higher than in North Korea, proof that the political, economic, and social system in the south is superior.

5. Since the collapse of the Soviet Union, there are very few COMMUNIST states that are left in the world.

6. While CAPITALISM is far from a perfect economic system, it is the most effective one that we have so far invented.

7. We are planning to ROLL OUT the upgraded software over the next three months, starting locally, then moving regionally and finally globally.

8. They RAMPED UP the production of chocolates ahead of the Christmas season.

9. "Hi Harry, I'm just calling to CATCH UP on everything that's happening in your life, at the moment. How's Meghan?"

10. You need to summarise your sales speech into a one-minute ELEVATOR PITCH that you can use when people visit our stall at the conference.

11. That was the best presentation I've seen at this conference, perfect content, delivery, and style. You totally NAILED IT!

12. I had to visit an angry client on my very first day of work, it was a true BAPTISM OF FIRE.

13. There is no need to apologise about the conflicts or misunderstanding we have had in the past. It's all WATER UNDER THE BRIDGE. Let's just move forward with the next project.

14. Our commercial director is so arrogant, he thinks that he's a BIG FISH, when in reality he's just another salesman like you and me.

15. "Should we leave a TIP?" "Of course! We should. This is New York and if we don't leave one, the waiter will chase us down the street demanding his money."

SAM GRATTON

"That's the life I deserve."
Kim

Chapter 21 – Banco Cantábrico

Lola walked up to the entrance of the Banco Cantábrico headquarters in La Moraleja, located 15 kms north of the centre of Madrid. It was known as the Financial Campus, a vast complex of low-rise offices within a gated community that also included a gym, a nursery, and a golf course for the employees.

Surrounding the buildings were acres[1] of gardens filled with ancient olive trees, some as old as 1500 years. Surrounding the gardens was a three-metre[2] security fence that kept unwanted visitors out, and reluctant employees within.

The Financial Campus was opened in 2004 by the legendary Spanish banker, Ernesto Nueno. At the time, it was a revolution in the way big companies looked after their employees, bringing more than 90% of the Banco Cantábrico departments together in one big productive paradise. Although some employees saw it more as a luxurious prison than a place to work.

Lola reached the security guards at the entrance of the complex, and gave them her name, telling them she was there to meet Fernando Roma, the IT procurement manager.

"Wait here." said one of the guards as he called reception to announce her arrival.

---

[1] Acre *(noun)* - 1 acre = 4047 square metres.

[2] Three-metre *(compound number adjective)* - Don't forget to use a hyphen and express it in the singular form.

Lola had never been more prepared for a sales pitch in her life. She had spent all Saturday struggling with her presentation, writing, reviewing, and practicing it, until everything was perfect. She knew all the technical features and benefits of the JBlock software, and she also knew the potential weaknesses and problems of the software that Banco Cantábrico was currently using. After all, it was supplied by TechSpania, her previous employer.

Furthermore, she had an excellent working relationship with Fernando Roma. She knew his fears and desires, both personally and professionally. They had spent many afternoons at his favourite Argentinian grill in Chueca. She had closed several deals with him over a medium rare sirloin steak[3] and a bottle of Ribera del Duero. She was confident that she could convince him to do a trial run of JBlock's software.

After five minutes waiting at the entrance, Lola asked the security guard to check that Fernando had received the notification. And for a moment her mind wandered back to the events of the previous weekend - the lunch, the paella, and the elevator ride.

She had sat next to Mr. Red Bull throughout the lunch. For three hours they had talked, laughed, and told each other secrets. From time to time[4], they joined in the debates of the others, but most of the time they were in their own little bubble – having a lunch within a lunch.

Mr. Red Bull had a flight to catch with his Formula 1 team early the next morning, so he was the first to leave the party. But he asked Lola to accompany him downstairs while he waited for the taxi.

As they rode the elevator down from the fifth floor, he gently took hold of her hand. He guided it to the emergency stop button

---

[3] Steak *(noun)* - The pronunciation rhymes with "take".

[4] From time to time *(idiom)* - Describes an activity that you do sometimes but not often.

and then he let it hover there. His eyes were bright and questioning, his pupils dilated.

The elevator slowly but inexorably descended. It passed the third floor, then the second floor and then, somewhere between the first and ground floor, Lola pressed the button, and the elevator came to a sudden stop.

They stood for a moment in the silence that followed and then, like two professional dancers reaching the end of their dance, they fell into each other's arms. Their lips touched and for the first time in months, Lola was living in the moment[5], blissfully unaware of anything other than the sweet sensation of Mr. Red Bull's kiss.

"Lola!"

The voice of Fernando Roma brought her back to the present.

"Fernando! How are you?" she said with genuine delight at seeing her old friend.

She walked forward to pass through the Banco Cantábrico security gate, but the barrier didn't open for her.

"Listen Lola, I'm really sorry but you can't come in."

Lola stopped in surprise.

"Oh," she said assuming there must be some rational reason, like a fire drill, that prevented the meeting going ahead in Fernando's office. "No problem," Lola continued enthusiastically. "We can have our meeting at one of the restaurants in La Plaza de La Moraleja. Is there an Argentinian Grill there?"

Fernando didn't smile. In fact, he had a grim expression on his face. "Lola, there isn't going to be a meeting."

"What? Have I come on the wrong day?"

"There isn't going to be a meeting today, or any other day. In fact, I shouldn't be speaking to you at all."

"Why? What's going on Fernando?"

"I'm sorry Lola. I really am. But I have to go."

---

[5] In the moment *(idiom)* - To be totally focused on the present situation.

Fernando turned around and headed back past the 1500-year-old olive trees that lined the walkways of the office complex. With him went Lola's plans of closing a deal[6] with Banco Cantábrico and proving herself to her new colleagues at JBlock.

She was left standing alone on the wrong side of the security fence, an unwanted visitor at the Financial Campus, wondering what the hell had just happened.

---

[6] To close a deal *(idiom)* - To agree and sign a contract after a period of negotiation.

Chapter 22 – The Chaperone

Chunghwa Park was sad and lifeless. Its trees were small and weak, stunted by the lack of sunlight and nutrition. The whole of Pyongyang was engulfed in a haze of pollution that coloured everything a shade of grey.

An elderly couple walked silently past Park, their clothes were old and discoloured, their faces were wrinkled and blank. They didn't acknowledge him as they went by. Making eye contact with a stranger in the city was a dangerous business. The secret police[7] were everywhere, watching and waiting for any sign of dissent. Nobody was above the law[8], not even the Supreme Leader's family and friends.

The North Korean government was unable to feed its population through the official state-run distribution system due to economic mismanagement and foreign sanctions[9]. This forced much of the population to work in the black market[10] simply to make ends

---

[7] The secret police *(noun)* - An organisation of law-enforcement that operates in a covert manner. Common in totalitarian states.

[8] To be above the law *(idiom)* - To be so powerful and untouchable that you don't need to obey the laws of the land.

[9] Sanctions *(noun)* - Actions taken by governments to prevent free-trade with the country as a form of economic punishment.

[10] Black market *(adjective noun)* - Trade in goods and services that are not declared to the government and therefore do not follow regulations or pay taxation.

meet[11]. To avoid prosecution these workers had no choice but to bribe[12] government officials. Corruption and extortion were therefore widespread within the economy.

For many years Kim Jong Un turned a blind eye[13] to this behaviour. His priority, as always, was the military sector. Then one night, without any warning, he arrested and executed a group of his closest economic advisors, including his uncle, a leading government official. The purge[14] sent shockwaves through the country and created fear and paranoia amongst the elite who lived and worked in Pyongyang.

As a result, meeting new people, making new friends, especially finding romance was a slow and tentative process. Dating was permitted but it was strictly controlled by the family. It was therefore no surprise that The Girl with Almond Eyes arrived at Chunghwa Park with a chaperone[15]. She was an older lady, possibly an aunt, with shiny grey hair tied into an impossibly tight bun. She walked up to Park and stared at him with a blank expression on her face.

"Shall we?"

"Yes."

The two of them strolled along the perimeter of the park, followed at a distance of five meters by the slender, young woman.

"Your name is?" asked the old lady.

"Park Jae-bong."

"Age?"

---

[11] To make ends meet *(idiom)* - To earn just enough money to live.

[12] To bribe *(verb)* - To make a secret payment to a public official in order to receive beneficial treatment.

[13] To turn a blind eye *(idiom)* - To consciously ignore illegal or immoral behaviour that you are meant to be controlling.

[14] Purge *(noun)* - The abrupt and violent removal of a group of people who have influence within an organisation.

[15] Chaperone *(noun)* - An older person, typically a woman, who monitors the social and romantic activities of a younger person.

"Thirty-two."

"Profession?"

"Computer technician at the Ministry of Information."

"Grade?"

"D"

The middle-aged lady stopped and turned to look at Park with the same blank expression. She repeated the question.

"Your grade at work is?"

"I am a D-grade worker, Madam."

Her expression changed, as if she were deep in thought, weighing up the pros and cons[16] of allowing Park into her family's life. Then she nodded her head, turned around and walked back towards her younger companion. She took the young lady's arm and led her towards Park.

"This is my niece," she said "She works on the switch board at the Ministry of Security Affairs. She has completed her selective conscription for the military. She is a good girl. You may speak to her for ten minutes. No holding hands." Then the chaperone walked away and sat on a bench about twenty metres from the couple.

The young lady looked down at the floor, her thin and fragile body as still as a statue. She was average height for a North Korean woman, which meant she was about as tall as Park. She had beautiful white skin and her black hair was clean and well kept. She clearly came from a good family. Her father was possibly a mid-ranking bureaucrat working in the central government. She waited patiently and calmly for her date to speak.

But Park was lost for words[17]. He had never been on a date before. He had no clue how to start a conversation with a woman. He felt insecure and inadequate. He suddenly wished that Kim had

---

[16] To weigh up the pros and cons *(idiom)* - To consider all the arguments for and against a proposal or plan of action.

[17] To be lost for words *(idiom)* - To be speechless.

never put him in this awkward situation. He felt like turning around and running back to the safety of his apartment.

For ten minutes they said nothing to each other. The couple simply stood swaying in the wind like two more trees in Chug Hwa Park. Even the chaperone found this behaviour peculiar.

"You have two more minutes," she said in a nasal and authoritative manner.

Park swallowed hard. He didn't want another two minutes. He wanted this to be over. It was a humiliation. He shifted uneasily, kicking the dirt beneath his feet.

The girl raised her hand to her mouth and gently cleared her throat. Without looking up from the floor she said in a soft voice.

"You smell nice."

Her voice was calm and melodic with a resonance that belied her delicate frame. Park had to reply. What would Kim say in this situation? How would he make the girl smile? In the background, the chaperone rose to her feet and started walking towards them. It couldn't end like this. He had to say something. Three simple words popped out[18] of his mouth, directly from his sub-conscious mind, unfiltered and to the point.

"You are beautiful."

The girl looked up at Park, her almond eyes wide open in shock. She put her hand over the mouth and stifled a laugh. The chaperone appeared from behind her.

"Ok, let's go."

Park watched them walk away, mortified. The two women exchanged some words. And then just before they disappeared into the evening darkness, the girl with almond eyes turned around and smiled at him. It was a smile of warmth and affection, a smile that suggested she wanted to see him again.

And at that moment a fire was lit in Park's heart. A fire that flowed through every artery and vein, reaching every cell of his body.

---

[18] To pop out *(phrasal verb)* - To appear suddenly and involuntarily.

It energised and empowered him. It brought colour and light to the world around him. It transformed an ordinary evening at Chunghwa Park into New Year's Eve in New York.

As he made his way home, to the 22nd floor of a tower block in zone 7 of the Chunghwa district of Pyongyang, Park looked into the eyes of every stranger he passed and grinned from ear to ear.[19]

---

[19] To grin from ear to ear *(idiom)* - To smile in the most extreme way possible.

SAM GRATTON

Chapter 23 – The Beginning of the End

Park's alarm woke him up at 6.45 am. He got out of bed, walked to the kitchen, and heated up some water to make himself a cup of barley tea. Then he very gently opened the door of his fridge. The machine had faulty electric wiring. If he pulled the door open abruptly the power would cut off and he would ruin all the food inside. He took out a bowl of boiled rice and kimchi and sat down to eat his breakfast in front of the television.

Park felt numb, but in a good way. He felt numb to the cold in his apartment, to hunger in his stomach. He felt numb to the grey day that was breaking across the sad city in which he lived, numb to the limited life in which he was trapped, numb to the frustrations of his unfulfilled potential. All of the dissatisfaction in his life was bearable because the Girl with the Almond Eyes had smiled at him. His heart pounded at the thought of seeing her again on the bus that morning. He needed to say something substantial to her, demonstrate that there was depth to his personality.

He turned on the television, background noise helped him think. There were five domestic TV channels in North Korea, all of them run by the state. The four news channels were full of the usual propaganda[20]. That morning they were reporting that one of Kim

---

[20] Propaganda *(noun)* - Ideas and information that only support one side of the argument and are spread widely to influence people's opinion.

Jung Un's generals had been charged with money laundering[21]. He was due to be executed the following day in front of the Supreme leader. In Park's mind the government sometimes resembled the Mafia, with Kim Jung Un as its godfather.

The fifth TV channel was the only one Park ever watched. It was the Sports channel and that morning it was showing a repeat of the public shaming of the women's ice hockey team following their failure to win a single game at the Pyeongchang Olympics in 2018. Park had heard rumours that many athletes were doing hard labour or were locked up[22] in prison for underachieving at international events.

After finishing breakfast, he went to his bathroom, washed, and shaved and applied some of his Chinese aftershave. He placed the bottle carefully back into the cabinet with the dragon logo facing outwards. It was a luxury that few North Koreans could afford, and Park only ever used it on very special occasions. The authorities let certain key workers get away with such acts of decadence as a reward for their achievements.

He looked at himself in the mirror. He was short and had a skinny body, far from the ideal look of the Supreme Leader whose chubbiness was admired by women around the country. He had a good head of hair; it was a little greasy but there was still no sign of baldness.

He made some martial arts moves in front of the mirror, as if he were attacking his own reflection. His adrenalin levels were through the roof, and he desperately needed to release some tension. He planned to sit next to the Girl with the Almond Eyes on the bus ride into the city centre.

At 7:30am, he met Kim at the entrance of their tower block in zone 7 and then the two of them walked together to the bus stop.

---

[21] Money laundering *(noun)* - The process of introducing money made from illegal activities into general economic circulation, in order to hide its origin.

[22] To lock up *(phrasal verb)* - To put into prison.

That morning Kim was uncharacteristically quiet. This suited Park as he was rehearsing the conversation he was about to have with his new love.

The two friends waited in silence for the bus to come. It was running late due to the ongoing problems with the transmission system. When it eventually arrived, it was followed by a cloud of thick diesel fumes. The two men covered their mouths and noses and then jumped onboard.

At that point on the route the bus was only 25% full. It had another dozen stops before it reached its destination by which time it would be full of government employees.

Sitting towards the front of the bus with an empty space beside her was the girl. Park spotted her immediately. He walked slowly up the centre aisle as the bus pulled away, practising the first line that he would say to her.

He reached her seat and looked down at her, his chest pounding, his adrenalin pumping. He was just about to sit down when Kim nudged him down the passageway towards the empty seats at the back of the bus.

The bus accelerated and the two friends stumbled forwards and ended up falling into the seats in the back row. It was by far the noisiest and least comfortable part of the bus as it was directly over the engine.

Park turned angrily towards Kim. "What are you doing?"

Kim looked at Park. "I need to talk to you."

Park couldn't hide his frustration and irritation. Whatever it was that Kim needed to say, he could easily have said it on the walk to the bus stop or while they waited for the bus.

"Listen to me carefully," said Kim just audible above the engine noise. "Our flats are bugged[23], our phones are tapped[24], and our offices are wired."

"Yes. So?" replied Park. It was common knowledge that the secret police listened to the conversations of all D grade government employees.

Kim continued: "This is the only place that I can be sure that no-one is listening."

Park's irritation turned to a mixture of curiosity and concern.

"What is it, Kim? What do you need to tell me?"

Kim looked around nervously. But there was no-one nearby. And even if there were, they wouldn't have been able to hear the conversation over the noise of 40-year-old diesel engine.

"I'm defecting." said Kim. "I'm joining the dark side of the force[25]".

---

[23] To bug *(verb)* - To place a small electronic device into a room in order to secretly listen to conversations.

[24] To tap *(verb)* - To place a small electronic device into a telephone in order to secretly listen to or record conversations.

[25] To join the dark side of the force *(idiom)* - A well-known phrase from the film Star Wars, used by Darth Vader to encourage Luke Skywalker to fight on the side of the imperial forces against the rebels.

Chapter 24 – The Secret Plan

"Did you hear me Park? I said that I was defecting," repeated Kim.

"Please tell me this is one of your twisted jokes," replied Park.

Kim shook his head slowly.

"In exactly thirty days, I will start my journey to the West. I will leave Pyongyang at midnight on the 10th of February to meet The Old Grey Man at Banshori Station. He will take me 600km north to the Yalu River, on the Chinese border, via the Dead Man's Highway.

The next day, I will cross the river on foot. At this time of year, the water is frozen, and the ice is thick enough to walk on. Most importantly, it's too cold for the guards to patrol the border at night. Waiting for me on the other side, will be an agent who works for institutions such as Interpol, Europol, and the CIA.

This agent will guide me through the security barriers on the Chinese side of the border. Together, we will travel to Paektu Mountain in the Jilin province of China. The mountain is a tourist attraction, famous for its spectacular volcanic lake.

Here, we will meet an international film crew making a documentary about the endangered wildlife around the lake. I will become part of that film crew, with a new name, a new identity, and a new passport. I will learn these personal details by heart before we travel to Changchun International Airport for the final escape.

At 10:45 a.m. on 18th February, I will be on a China Airlines flight heading to the West at a thousand kilometres per hour."

Park was speechless. He knew his best friend well enough to realise that this was no joke. All the colour drained from his face, and he stared in disbelief.

"You might ask me why I am telling you all this now. Let me explain." Kim was speaking urgently and unemotionally. He knew he had a limited amount of time to safely transmit his message. He simply stated the facts.

"If I am successful in my defection, three generations[26] of my family, including my 75-year-old grandmother, will be forced into hard labour. They will spend the rest of their miserable lives in prison eating maggots from their tortured bodies.

I can't let that happen.

Therefore, I need to defect without defecting.

So, on the 10th of February, I will commit suicide[27]. I will throw myself off the Taedong bridge, like so many of our hopeless comrades have done in the past.

In order to make my suicide convincing, I need to change my behaviour. I need to turn myself into a different person - depressed, paranoid, and unstable.

Over the next thirty days, you will witness this transformation. You will see your best friend degenerate from an outgoing and radiant optimist to an introverted and desperate pessimist.

And when the secret service eventually questions you about my suicide, you will convince them that it was real.

That is why I am telling you this now."

Park remained speechless, his head spinning. This information was toxic. It put his own life in danger. He needed to decide very quickly how to react. He could accept Kim's plan and become an

---

[26] The three-generation rule *(noun)* - A North Korean law. If you commit a crime your children and your grandchildren will also be punished.

[27] To commit suicide *(idiom)* - To kill yourself. "Suicide" is a noun and cannot be used as a verb.

accomplice to a crime against the state. He could tip off[28] the authorities and sentence Kim to a life-time in prison. Or he could try to persuade his best friend to desist from this madness. He chose the third option.

"Kim. This is lunacy. The West is dangerous, corrupt, capitalist, and full of Westerners. You have a good life in Pyongyang, a position of status in society, you may soon be promoted to a Grade C employee. In the name of Kim Jong Un, don't do it!"

The bus started to fill up with government employees on their way to work. Some of them were talking, some of them were smiling, but most of them were in their own little worlds, oblivious to the treasonous conversation that Kim and Park were having. The bus changed gear and the engine roared.

Kim leaned forward so that his mouth was almost touching Park's ear. And with a voice full of emotion and determination he said:

"Both you and I know what the outside world is really like. If we had been born in the West, we would have started our own IT company. We would have bought ourselves a car, or maybe two. We would have become somebody!"

"That's the life that I want. That's the life that I deserve. And that's the life that I am going to get, no matter what."

---

[28] To tip off - To inform the authorities of an illegal activity that you know is going to happen.

SAM GRATTON

Chapter 25 – The Journalist

Lola turned away from the entrance of the Banco Cantábrico complex in La Moraleja. She walked slowly towards the taxi stand at the corner of the street. Her hopes of closing a deal with the biggest account in the market had disappeared. Her chance of proving herself to her colleagues at JBlock had gone.

Somebody must have spoken to Fernando Roma, prohibited him from meeting with her, threatened him.

In Lola's mind, it was clear that Mario Ruiz De Velasco, the CEO of TechSpania was behind this. He was cunning[29], ruthless[30], and relentless[31]. He had an ego that was out of control. And now he was doing everything in his power to ruin her.

"Lola Badiola?"

A man walked briskly up to her with his business card in his hand.

"My name is Bradley Manson. I work for CyberStory Magazine. Do you have a moment to talk?"

Lola took his card and looked at it. She was startled by his sudden appearance.

"Let's go for a coffee and I'll explain everything."

---

[29] Cunning *(adjective)* - Skilful and clever at achieving your goals by lying or cheating.

[30] Ruthless *(adjective)* - Without pity or remorse.

[31] Relentless *(adjective)* - Persistent, implacable. Never stopping or reducing the intensity until an objective is reached.

The journalist was American. He had an East Coast accent. His manner was informal and pushy. Lola took an instinctive dislike to him.

"No," she replied, "I need to get back to the office."

She handed back the business card and looked around for a taxi.

"You should talk to me," said the journalist persistently.

Lola became agitated by his attitude.

"Really. Why? What's the article about?"

"You."

"What?"

"I've been commissioned to write a profile on you. It's due for publication on Friday, whether you talk to me or not."

Lola looked bewildered[32]. Why on earth would CyberStory be writing a profile on her? And how could they publish it without speaking to her first? The journalist continued, as if he had read her mind.

"You are a person of interest, Lola. You were involved with SMZ until they were hacked. You were involved with TechSpania until they were hacked. And I've just witnessed you attempting to enter Banco Cantábrico. A company that is currently under multiple cybersecurity attacks from foreign infiltrators. You are the common factor in all these events. Is this just a coincidence? Or is there something else going on here?"

The journalist was well-aware of the bombshell that he had just dropped in front of Lola. And he waited while the dust settled around her.

Underneath the surface, Lola was freaking out[33]. CyberStory was one of the most popular magazines in the IT sector. It was read by everyone who was anyone in the world of cybersecurity. The last

---

[32] Bewildered *(adjective)* - Extremely confused.

[33] To freak out *(phrasal verb)* - To become highly emotional through surprise, shock, or anxiety.

thing she wanted was to see her picture in this publication, particularly if the editorial agenda was against her.

She took a deep but imperceptible breath and calmed herself down. She was wise enough to know that the journalist was trying to get a reaction out of her - something emotional, controversial, and newsworthy. So, she did exactly what her father would have done. She looked the journalist directly in the eye and said: "Thank you for your interest. If you wish to pursue this matter any further, you can speak to my lawyer."

A taxi pulled up at the stand and Lola got inside.

"Can you confirm or deny that you are being investigated by Interpol?" the journalist shouted through the window.

Lola ignored him as the electric taxi pulled away from the stand.

Lola sat silently in the vehicle as it circulated the M30 motorway. The trip back to the office gave her a moment to think deeply about her predicament. She realised that her enemies would attack her from every angle. They would use her colleagues, her clients, and even the news media against her. Their objective was to skin her alive[34]. This trip had taught her one very important lesson - she needed to be better protected.

She switched on her smartphone and looked up the name 'Gonzalo Garrido'. He was an old friend from high school, and the smartest person Lola had ever met. He had graduated from Harvard Law School, magna cum laude[35]. After which he had joined Spain's most prestigious law firm, Urdangarín Mendoza. Within seven years, he had effortlessly moved up the ranks, from intern to junior associate to senior associate. Earlier that year, he had become the

---

[34] To skin someone alive *(idiom)* - To punish severely. The origins of this expression come from a mediaeval torture, where criminals had their skin removed from their body.

[35] Magna Cum Laude *(adjective noun)* - To receive a degree from university with great distinction, normally in the top 5 to 10% of the class.

youngest partner[36] in the law firm's 150-year history. He was now one of the most feared and admired lawyers in the corporate world. If someone could protect Lola from her nemesis[37], it was Gonzalo Garrido.

There was only one problem.

Gonzalo was still in love with her.

---

[36] Partner *(noun)* - A senior individual within a law firm, who is an owner of the business and therefore shares in the profits and the losses of the company.

[37] Nemesis *(noun)* - The goddess of divine retribution. Somebody who is a long-standing rival, who may eventually lead to your downfall.

QUIZ TIME

Chapters 21 to 25

COMPREHENSION QUIZ

Answer the questions with complete sentences. Say them out loud.

1. Where are the headquarters of Banco Cantábrico? What is it like?
2. What happened during the Paella lunch on Sunday?
3. What does Chunghwa Park look like?
4. What questions does the chaperone ask Park?
5. How successful is the date?
6. What is Park's routine every morning in his apartment?
7. What does he plan to do on the bus that morning? Why doesn't he do it?
8. What is Kim's secret plan?
9. What does the journalist from CyberStory say to Lola?
10. Why does Lola think she needs a lawyer? Who does she contact?

BUSINESS ENGLISH QUIZ

Complete the sentences with the words used in the story.

1. We've been negotiating this contract for the last six weeks. We need to C_____ the D_____ before the end of the quarter.

2. No politician or businessperson is A_____ the L_____. We must all face the consequences of our actions.

3. Since S_____ were imposed on Russia, we have been unable to import the raw materials that we need and export the machines that we manufacture.

4. Billions of euros of tax revenue are lost due to the illegal trade of goods on the B_____ M_____.

5. The only reason this apartment block was built on the coast is because the developer gave a $1 million B_____ to the local politician.

6. If you T_____ a B_____ E_____ to the bullying and intimidation, you are failing as a manager and as a human being.

7. Before we construct a new factory in Chile, we must W_____ U_____ the P_____ and the C_____ of making this investment.

8. Don't believe the P_____ that the government is disseminating regarding the safety of nuclear energy.

9. If you are aware that M_____ L_____ is taking place and cash from illegal activities is entering the financial system, you must immediately report it to your supervisor.

10. Every quarter, our security team checks the boardroom to make sure that it hasn't been B_____ by corporate spies.

11. One of the junior members of the accounts team T_____ O_____ the police that our company was hiding revenues in order to evade taxes.

12. I F_____ O_____ when the fire alarm suddenly sounded, but I calmed down when I realised that it was only an exercise, and nobody was in danger.

13. Have you seen the CV of this job applicant? She graduated from Harvard University with a philosophy degree, M_____ C_____ L_____.

14. If you are promoted to a P_____ of this law firm, the first thing that you have to do is invest $500,000 of your own money, to help capitalise the company.

15. Everybody has a N_____. Somebody they consider to be their greatest rival. Somebody they consider to be a threat. Who is yours?

ANSWERS TO COMPREHENSION QUIZ

1. The headquarters of Banco Cantábrico is located in La Moraleja. An affluent, gated community in the north of Madrid. It is designed as a campus with many small buildings, attractive scenery, a golf course, and social spaces.

2. During the paella lunch, Lola and Mr. Red Bull enjoy each other's company and then, as they are leaving, they have a brief kiss in the elevator.

3. Chunghwa Park is sad and lifeless; the trees don't grow properly, and it is engulfed by the pollution of the city.

4. The chaperone asks Park several questions about his work and is impressed by the fact that he is a D-grade employee.

5. Park has no experience of dating women, and therefore, does not know what to do on the date. He is self-conscious, embarrassed, and lost for words. He wants the experience to end as quickly as possible. However, The Girl with the Almond Eyes makes an effort to break the ice, and after a brief conversation, she smiles warmly at him, indicating that she wants to see him again.

6. Park wakes up, prepares himself a breakfast of kimchi stored in his unreliable fridge, and then watches the sports channel on public television.

7. Park plans to sit next to The Girl with the Almond Eyes on the bus in the morning and continue the conversation from the previous evening. He is unable to implement his plan because Kim pushes him to the back of the bus, to where the engine is noisiest, in order to explain the secret plan.

8. Kim's secret plan is divided into several parts. First, he will pretend to commit suicide. Second, he will travel to Banshori station to meet the Old Grey Man. Third he will journey along Deadman's Highway to the border of North Korea and China.

Fourth, he will cross the Yalu River into China with the help of a secret agent. Fifth, he will join a film crew who are making a documentary at Paektu mountain. Finally, he will fly from China to Madrid, where the headquarters of Interpol are located.

9. The journalist from CyberStory tells Lola that he is going to write an article about her as she is implicated in several hacking incidents. He wants to get her reaction to the accusations of improper behaviour.

10. Lola realises that her enemies are very powerful and persistent and will attack her from every angle. She also realises that she is vulnerable and unprotected, and therefore, she seeks the services of a lawyer. She contacts an ex-boyfriend, Gonzalo Garrido. He is a senior partner and one of Spain's post prestigious law firms. The only problem is, Gonzalo is still in love with her!

ANSWERS TO BUSINESS ENGLISH QUIZ

1. We've been negotiating this contract for the last six weeks. We need to CLOSE THE DEAL before the end of the quarter.

2. No politician or businessperson is ABOVE THE LAW. We must all face the consequences of our actions.

3. Since SANCTIONS were imposed on Russia, we have been unable to import the raw materials that we need, and export the machines that we manufacture.

4. Billions of euros of tax revenue are lost due to the illegal trade of goods on the BLACK MARKET.

5. The only reason this apartment block was built on the coast is because the developer gave a $1 million BRIBE to the local politician.

6. If you TURN A BLIND EYE to the bullying and intimidation you are failing as a manager and as a human being.

7. Before we construct a new factory in Chile, we must WEIGH UP THE PROS AND CONS of making this investment.

8. Don't believe the PROPAGANDA that the government is disseminating regarding the safety of nuclear energy.

9. If you are aware that MONEY LAUNDERING is taking place and cash from illegal activities is entering the financial system, you must immediately report it to your supervisor.

10. Every quarter, our security team checks the boardroom to make sure that it hasn't been BUGGED by corporate spies.

11. One of the junior members of the accounts team TIPPED OFF the police that our company was hiding revenues in order to evade taxes.

12. I FREAKED OUT when the fire alarm suddenly sounded, but I calmed down when I realised that it was only an exercise, and nobody was in danger.

13. Have you seen the CV of this job applicant? She graduated from Harvard University with a philosophy degree, MAGNA CUM LAUDE.

14. If you are promoted to a PARTNER of this law firm, the first thing that you have to do is invest $500,000 of your own money, to help capitalise the company.

15. Everybody has a NEMESIS. Somebody they consider to be their greatest rival. Somebody they consider to be a threat. Who is yours?

"Welcome to the big-league, Lola."
Gonzalo

Chapter 26 – Gonzalo Garrido

Lola attended the Lycée Français, in Arturo Soria, Madrid. She was a quiet, hard-working[1] student who liked to remain anonymous. The only place where she let her emotions run free was on the volleyball court. She was extremely competitive and captained her team to the district finals two years in a row.

It was at the Lycée that Lola met Gonzalo Garrido. She was seventeen years old. He was eighteen. She was young, pretty and innocent. He was mature, wise and on his way to Harvard.

They fell deeply in love, and although they attended university in different continents, they spoke on the telephone almost every day. They were soulmates[2], childhood sweethearts[3], and one day they were going to get married. But time passes. People change. And Lola grew up.

After almost five years with Gonzalo, she ended the relationship. It happened on a Sunday afternoon while they were walking around the galleries of the Museo del Prado. Gonzalo had started working in Madrid and he wanted her to move into his apartment. Lola suddenly felt claustrophobic. It was as if the great portraits by Titian,

---

[1] Hard-working *(adjective)* - Diligent, always putting in a lot of effort. Avoid the common mistake of using "hard-worker" as an adjective.

[2] Soulmate *(noun)* - Someone with whom you share a deep personal understanding and connection.

[3] Childhood sweethearts *(noun)* - A romantic relationship you have when you are young and innocent, most likely at high school.

Raphael and El Greco were all staring at her, judging her, and reminding her that she was just a little girl pretending to be a woman.

At the time, it was the most difficult decision of her life. There was no specific reason, there was nothing he had done wrong. She still loved him, but it wasn't what she wanted. She was only 23 years old, and she didn't want the story of her life already written.

Gonzalo was distraught[4]. He felt like he'd been widowed. He seemed to pass slowly through the five stages of grief[5]. At first, he was in denial, convinced that it was just a temporary pause in the relationship. He thought and dreamt about her all the time.

Then he became filled with wrath[6]. After all, he was an overachiever and his pride had been wounded. Then he tried to bargain with her. He would send her flowers, write her letters, in an attempt to charm her back into his life.

Eventually, he fell into a state of mild depression. He decided that the best way forward was to ghost[7] her, disconnect from her on LinkedIn, Twitter, and Facebook, and dedicate himself to his career. He worked 100-hour weeks at Urdangarín Mendoza.

Many people saw this as a sign of avarice and ambition. But, in reality, it was his way of coping with the loss of the love of his life.

Lola sat silently in the taxi looking down at the name of Gonzalo Garrido on her smartphone. For ten minutes, she reminisced about their time together. It was a bittersweet[8] sensation.

---

[4] Distraught *(adjective)* - So worried or upset that you are unable to think clearly.

[5] The five stages of grief *(idiom)* - Denial, anger, bargaining, depression, and acceptance. It is known as the Kubler-Ross model and describes the emotional journey of someone who has lost a loved one.

[6] Wrath *(noun)* - Extreme anger, often used in a religious sense, for example, the wrath of God.

[7] To ghost *(verb)* - To stop all personal and electronic communication with someone without warning or explanation.

[8] Bittersweet *(adjective)* - A mixed and contradictory feeling.

A message from the office popped up[9] on the screen asking her what time she would be back. She ignored it, pressed the call button of her phone, and waited for Gonzalo to answer.

Once, twice, three times it rang. A part of her was desperate for him to answer. Another part hoped that he wouldn't. Four, five, six times it rang. She started to doubt herself. This was a bad idea. Seven, eight… on the ninth ring, he answered.

"Lola?"

His voice hadn't changed. It was clear and deep."

"Hello, Gonzalo. Do you have a moment?"

There was a long pause. And then in a professional and courteous tone he replied.

"Yes. Of course."

Forty-five minutes later, Lola arrived at Gonzalo's offices in Vallecas, in the south of Madrid. He had some space in his diary, so he suggested that she drive directly to his office. It was not the shiny, corporate skyscraper that she had imagined. Instead, it was a humble shopfront in one of the poorer districts of Madrid.

Gonzalo had quit Urdangarín Mendoza three months earlier to start his own boutique[10] law firm with a couple of friends. He wanted to focus on start-ups, social impact businesses, and charities.

His firm had recently become the European representative of the Centre of Humane Technology. An organisation that campaigned against the negative elements of social media such as trolling[11], spamming[12] and behaviour manipulation by big tech companies.

---

[9] To pop up *(phrasal verb)* - To appear suddenly and unexpectedly.

[10] Boutique *(noun)* - A small and fashionable shop.

[11] Trolling *(noun)* - Deliberately provoking an argument with someone online in order to get attention.

[12] Spamming *(noun)* - Sending unwanted and unsolicited messages to a large group of people on an email distribution list, often with the intention of promoting a product or service.

He was waiting for her at the entrance as her taxi arrived. He was dressed informally, in a tight-fitting jumper, designer jeans, and Reebok trainers. He was in good shape, his skin was tanned, his hair was long, and the dark rings around his eyes had disappeared.

He opened the door to her taxi after it stopped. "It's really good to see you again," he said with a smile, as he kissed her on both cheeks.

It was the kind of greeting you would expect from an old friend – warm and genuine. Gonzalo exuded contentment. He was clearly in a good place in his life.

"Would you follow me!" he said as he led her into his office. He introduced her to his partners, and then took her to a meeting room at the back of the building. Everything smelt of fresh paint.

He offered her a coffee and motioned for her to sit down. Then, he took out his notebook and a fountain pen, and started asking her questions. He treated Lola like just another potential client in need of legal advice. There was no mention of the past, no chat about mutual friends, no catching up [13] on each other lives. He was interested in her predicament from a purely professional perspective.

---

[13] To catch up *(phrasal verb)* - To get up to date with an activity or with someone else's life after an absence.

Chapter 27 – The Wild West

Lola told Gonzalo all about her career move; the accusations made by Ruiz de Velasco, the interview with Interpol, the rejection by Banco Cantábrico, and finally, the conversation with the journalist from CyberStory.

"Would you mind telling [14] me, once again, exactly what happened after you resigned?"

Lola recounted the meeting with Ruiz de Velasco, and how he had threatened her when she refused to reconsider her resignation.

"What happened next?"

"I spoke briefly to Luis Bruña, my direct manager. I gave him my company laptop, my mobile phone, and my security pass. And then a guard escorted me out of the building."

"Did anybody else hear what you said to either Ruiz de Velasco or Bruña?"

"No."

"But everyone saw you being escorted out of the office by the security guard."

"Yes."

Gonzalo scribbled[15] something down on his pad.

---

[14] Would you mind *(polite imperative)* - Used in formal business situations. Remember it is followed by the gerund and not by the infinitive. "Would you mind waiting here?"

[15] To scribble *(verb)* - To write or draw something quickly and without attention.

"Was there any confidential information on your company laptop?"

"It had everything on it - business plans, company accounts, client information."

"Did you download any of that information onto your personal computer?"

Lola paused. She wasn't quite sure how to respond. Gonzalo continued.

"It's quite common for employees to download confidential data from their company just before they quit. Did you do this?"

"Yes."

"How exactly did you download it?"

"I plugged[16] a pen drive into my PC. Then I keyed in[17] my password and downloaded all the files."

Gonzalo wrote another note onto his pad.

"Did Luis Bruña ask you to sign any documents before you left the company?"

"No."

"Have you received any written messages from TechSpania since you resigned?"

"No."

"Are you sure?" he asked patiently, "Have you checked all your email accounts?"

Lola started to doubt herself. The questions were becoming more and more uncomfortable.

"I'll double-check[18]," she said.

"Ok."

Gonzalo continued.

---

[16] To plug in *(phrasal verb)* - To connect a piece of electrical equipment to the main electricity supply.

[17] To key in *(phrasal verb)* - To type a username or password into a computer.

[18] To double-check *(verb)* - To review something for a second time to make sure it is correct.

"Did you have a non-compete clause[19] in your contract with TechSpania?"

"Yes."

Lola thought for a moment and then elaborated:

"In the event that I resigned from the company or was fired, I was prohibited from speaking to any of my clients on a professional basis for 90 days."

Gonzalo put down his notepad.

"So, when you approached Banco Cantábrico earlier today you were in breach[20] of that non-compete clause."

Lola looked up at the ceiling as she realised the mistake that she had made. In her desire to make an impact at JBlock she had neglected her obligations to TechSpania. She thought that she was being proactive but in reality, she was being impatient and irresponsible.

"Yes," she eventually replied.

"Ok, here's my assessment of the situation," Gonzalo said intently, "TechSpania will say that you were fired, they will say that you stole confidential information, and they will say that you acted in breach of your contract. Then, they will claim that you were a malicious insider helping a group of hackers to breach their systems. After that, they will try to connect this crime to JJ Thomson and your colleagues at JBlock. In doing so, they will discredit a dangerous competitor and regain the trust of their investors."

Lola listened carefully to Gonzalo's conclusions. It was clear that she needed protection from Ruiz de Velasco. It was also clear that she'd come to the right place. Gonzalo was as brilliant as she had hoped and expected him to be. But there were other issues that were worrying her, issues that he hadn't addressed.

---

[19] Non-compete clause *(noun)* - A commitment to avoid competition between two parties, most commonly between an employee and an employer, written into a legal contract.

[20] To breach *(verb)* - In everyday English it means to break through a wall or a fence. In legal English it means to violate a law, obligation or agreement.

"What about Interpol?" she asked.

Lola was deeply concerned about the meeting with the two agents. They had arrived at the offices of JBlock unannounced and proceeded to interrogate her about her possible involvement in the hacking scandal. It wasn't just her career at risk, it was her freedom.

"I wouldn't worry too much about them," Gonzalo replied.

Lola looked perplexed.

"Law enforcement agencies are kind of irrelevant in the world of cybercrime," explained Gonzalo, "You see, the issues are so technical that it's almost impossible for them to understand, let alone demonstrate to a judge or a jury."

Gonzalo smiled, "The digital world is like the wild west. The hackers are the outlaws, the IT departments are the local sheriffs, and you guys are the vigilantes[21]. The law, as we know it, doesn't really exist."

Lola thought back to her meeting with the two agents. It was true that they hadn't shown any expertise in the area of cybersecurity. They didn't have any concrete evidence, and they were treated like a couple of travelling salesmen by JJ Thomson.

Gonzalo leaned forward. "If Interpol bothers you again, just call me, and I'll deal with it."

Lola was impressed by Gonzalo's knowledge and certainty. In less than an hour he had understood all the issues and was ready for action. She started to feel a little safer, as if the arm of an old friend had been wrapped around her shoulder.

"And what about the magazine article?" she asked hopefully.

"What about it?"

"Well, I'm worried about what they are going to write about me."

Gonzalo chuckled[22].

---

[21] Vigilantes *(noun)* - A group of citizens who try to prevent or punish a crime outside of the normal legal process.

[22] To chuckle *(verb)* - To laugh quietly and inwardly.

THE ADVENTURES OF LOLA BADIOLA

"Welcome to the big-league, Lola. You're a person of interest now. That's something you'll just have to get used to."

Lola looked upset.

"Listen, CyberStory is a reputable magazine. Its articles are read all over the world on the internet. They won't make any false accusations. It will just be a lightweight profile of your professional and personal background."

Lola wasn't convinced. She frowned. "I need to get back to the office." She said curtly.

"Sure."

"Thank you, Gonzalo. You don't know how kind and helpful you've been."

"Wait until you receive my bill."

They both smiled.

And then there was a long pause, as if they were waiting for the other to say something. But neither of them did.

They walked back through the offices and out onto the main street. It was one of those clear winter days that feels extremely cold in the shade and wonderfully warm in the sun. They stood in silence as they waited for Lola's taxi to arrive, the tension between them exposed by the cold light of the day. It was easier to talk about professional issues in the office than the personal ones outside of it.

Suddenly Lola turned to Gonzalo and said, "I want you to know how sorry I am that -"

He interrupted her.

"Lola," his voice was gentle. "It's okay."

They stood looking at each other for a few seconds.

"I'll call you on Friday when they publish the article," he said.

Then he kissed her goodbye and walked back into his offices. Gonzalo had clearly moved on[23].

And Lola wasn't sure if she felt relieved or disappointed.

---

[23] To move on *(phrasal verb)* - To take the next step. To make progress.

SAM GRATTON

Chapter 28 – Salvador Badiola

Lola woke up late on Saturday morning. She had switched off her alarm and disconnected her phone the night before. She had closed the blinds and curtains so that none of the morning light would enter her room. She needed to rest after a stressful week at work.

It was already noon when she finally switched on her phone. Her WhatsApp inbox was inundated with messages. She scrolled down to the earliest message from Concha.

"Saw the article. You ok? Call me when you're free."

Lola's heart skipped a beat[24]. She quickly checked the other messages, and they were all regarding the same subject – the profile of her in Cyberworld Magazine.

She ran to her desk and opened her laptop. She googled the online version of the magazine. As the front page appeared on her computer screen, she took a step backwards in shock.

Her own face was staring back at her. Below the image was the following headline:

Lola Badiola: Cybersecurity Saint or Sinner?

Lola frantically clicked on the link to the article and zoomed in to see the content. She started scanning through the paragraphs, unable to really focus on the details.

---

[24] Heart skips a beat *(idiom)* - In a literal sense it is a palpitation of the heart. In a metaphorical sense it is a sudden sensation of excitement and anticipation.

The piece started by summarising the state of the cybersecurity sector in Spain. Over the previous ten years, TechSpania had become a monopoly power [25] through a series of hostile acquisitions[26] of smaller service providers. Its ultimate ambition was to become a global player in all IT services, competing with the likes of Oracle, IBM, and Accenture.

The article then described the recent emergence of start-ups like JBlock, companies that were using blockchain technology to offer an alternative solution. They represented a new competitive threat to TechSpania. The cybersecurity sector was, therefore, entering a period of disruption[27].

At this point, the article introduced Lola Badiola. She was the human story at the centre of these developments. She had started her career at TechSpania, but she had recently moved to JBlock. She was therefore the link between the two competing worlds.

There was a photograph of Lola as a teenager standing next to her father.

The article described Lola's upbringing – her childhood, her education, and her family life. She was the only child of Salvador Badiola - entrepreneur, politician, and philanthropist. His rags-to-riches story[28] was well known in Spain, particularly in Cantabria, where he was treated like a folk hero[29].

---

[25] Monopoly power *(noun)* - A monopoly is the only provider of a good or service in the market. It is therefore in a very powerful position relative to the consumer and can raise prices, lower costs, and maximize profits.

[26] Hostile acquisitions *(adjective noun)* - Where one company takes over another, without the approval of the target company's management.

[27] Disruption *(noun)* - An innovation that radically changes a business sector, normally created by a smaller organisation, to challenge the established and traditional way of doing things.

[28] Rags-to-riches story *(idiom)* - When someone from a poor and disadvantaged background becomes rich, successful and famous.

[29] Folk hero *(noun)* - Someone who is greatly admired by ordinary people for representing and supporting them.

According to sources close to the family, the relationship between father and daughter was extremely close. Lola spent her adolescent summers working in her father's factories. She was getting hands-on experience[30] of the business - peeling anchovies, processing olives, and storing wine - so that one day, in the distant future, she could take over the food production and retail empire.

But Lola had other ideas.

After graduating from the Lycée Français in Madrid, she was accepted into the prestigious École Polytechnique in Paris to study Engineering, specialising in telecommunications. As much as she loved her father, she wanted to be in charge of her own destiny. That was why she chose to pursue a career as far away from the food and drinks industry as possible.

She graduated in the top 5% of her class and then joined the training program at TechSpania. It was a two-year rotation[31] around the different parts of the company, after which Lola began as a sales assistant in the cybersecurity division. It was exactly the role she wanted – challenging, exciting and, in her mind, heroic.

It wasn't long before she was signing up the company's biggest accounts. She became a star performer, smashing her sales targets and creating new business, not just in Spain, but throughout Europe. She was the first of her graduate intake to get a promotion, and within five years, she was managing a team of seven professionals, six of them were older than her.

Before long, she caught the eye[32] of Mario Ruiz de Velasco, the CEO of the company and, according to internal sources, he started mentoring her on a regular basis. With his help, she took on some

---

[30] Hands-on experience *(noun)* - Knowledge or skill that comes from actually doing a job or activity rather than studying it.

[31] Two-year rotation *(idiom)* - A structured program for talented graduates entering a large company, giving them experience of many different departments.

[32] To catch the eye of someone *(idiom)* - To be noticed by someone with influence.

high-profile responsibilities within the company, such as the Diversity and Inclusion initiative. She teamed up with the network division to create secure products for their 5G roll out[33]. And she worked with the R&D[34] team to gather real-time data[35] on security breaches. Many people believed that she was destined to reach the very top of the organisation.

But then, things started to go wrong.

Her father died all of a sudden of an unexpected heart attack while on a business trip to Lima. Lola was devastated. She flew to Peru to bring back his body. Then she took some time off to grieve.

When she returned to TechSpania she wasn't the same person. According to sources within the company, she no longer had the same passion or direction. She had lost the instinct to close deals. There were rumours that she was suffering from panic attacks. Her clients started to experience serious breaches of security. Was this neglect, or something more sinister?

One day, she revealed to a colleague that she planned to quit and join a competitor. The colleague then discovered that she was stealing sensitive client information and breaching confidentiality agreements. An internal investigation was launched, the evidence was conclusive, and the company had no other choice but to fire her.

An unnamed source at TechSpania was quoted as saying:

"It's probably no coincidence that shortly after Lola Badiola was fired, we suffered our most serious breach of security.".

It was a clear implication that Lola had been acting as a malicious insider, assisting external forces to hack into TechSpania's systems.

The article then returned to the general theme of the disruption in the cybersecurity market. It concluded that the battle between the

---

[33] To roll out *(phrasal verb)* - To launch and distribute a new product or innovation in stages.

[34] R&D *(noun)* - Research and Development.

[35] Real-time data *(concept)* - Information that is available as soon as it is created.

monopoly power of TechSpania and the new entrants into the market, such as JBlock, could be long and dirty.

At the very end, it stated that CyberStory had attempted to speak to Lola Badiola, but she had refused to respond to the allegations. The magazine hoped that she would take the opportunity to contact them at some point to present her side of the story. The Badiola name was synonymous with integrity. It would be a shame if that reputation were ruined.

Lola shut her laptop.

She couldn't bear the sight of the website for a second longer.

She walked into her small rectangular bathroom and opened the cold tap of the shower. She forced herself underneath the freezing water. Her body went into shock, her lungs gasped for air, her limbs shivered uncontrollably.

She closed her eyes and focused on her breathing. Little by little she regained control of every square centimeter of her body, until she was completely relaxed. And one thought came into her head.

She needed to speak to her mother.

SAM GRATTON

Chapter 29 – The Crime Against the State

Park sat at the back of the bus considering his options. He was stunned by Kim's recklessness[36] - the fake suicide, the journey Vía the dead man's highway, crossing the Chinese border in mid-winter, and finally escaping with a film crew from Changchun International airport. Was he going to help Kim with his crazy plans, or inform the authorities?

Park's anger and disbelief were mixed with a strange sensation of admiration and jealousy. Kim was clearly determined to create a better life for himself. If he succeeded, he would be living the dream in the West, working as a freelance[37] IT specialist, hanging out[38] with Western women, buying as many Mickey Mouse watches as he wanted.

The authorities in the West clearly valued his knowledge and skillset[39]. They were making a huge effort and expense to assist his defection. If they valued Kim Dae-won so highly, what might they think of Park Jae-bong, a far superior hacker, the architect of the

---

[36] Reckless *(adjective)* - Taking excessive risks.

[37] Freelancer *(noun)* - An individual who does specific pieces of work for different organisations without a long-term commitment to one company.

[38] To hang out *(phrasal verb)* - To spend time relaxing with a particular group of people.

[39] Skillset *(noun)* - A collection of abilities that a person has in order to do a particular job.

WannaCry virus, and a tormentor of multinational companies around the world?

Park banished the thought from his mind. He was a patriot. Despite the poverty and paranoia caused by the dictatorship of Kim Jong Un and his predecessors, he loved his country. It was where he was born, and it was where he would die. Moreover, he was in love with the Girl with the Almond Eyes, and he imagined a romantic future ahead of them.

The bus stopped outside the Ministry of Information, and everyone stood up and got off. The crowd made its way into the functional concrete building, each person heading to their own little cubicle within the vast complex.

Park thought again about Kim's plan. His best friend was, by nature, a people person[40], always friendly and optimistic. In fact, he had been singled out[41] by Human Resources to lead the division's Happiness Initiative. How would it be possible for Kim to convince the authorities of his suicidal intentions?

The two men sat down at their desks and turned on their computers without exchanging another word. They went through their morning routine, checking the infiltration programs that had been working overnight.

In the distance, Kang, their direct superior, was pushing a big trolley of files towards them, stopping to exchange words with each of the workers in Division 6523 of the Cybercrime Department.

Park needed to make a decision before Kang arrived at his desk. If he was going to inform the authorities, he had better do it immediately. It was one of the unbreakable rules of being a citizen of the Democratic Republic of Korea. If he delayed for just a moment, then he became part of the crime.

---

[40] People person *(adjective noun)* - Someone who enjoys socialising with other people.

[41] To single out *(phrasal verb)* - To select one person from a group for special treatment.

Kang reached Kim's desk first and asked him the same questions as always.

"Have you observed any anomalies?"

"No, sir," said Kim

"Have you crashed any systems?"

"No, sir."

"Have you concluded any infiltrations?"

"No sir."

Kang pushed his trolley a little further down the corridor and repeated the routine with Park.

"Have you observed any anomalies?"

This was a defining moment of Park's life. The universe was splitting into two parallel branches, one in which he betrayed his best friend, the other in which he betrayed his country.

"Park! I'm talking to you," said Kang impatiently. "Have you observed any anomalies?"

Park could hardly contain his contempt of the divisional manager. The man knew nothing about the complexity and beauty of computer coding. He knew nothing about the world beyond the walls of the Ministry of Information. He did nothing for the cause of the Fatherland, apart from push a trolley full of papers around the ministry. And yet, he was Park and Kim's direct superior with the power of life and death over them.

"No, sir," said Park quietly.

"Have you crashed any systems?"

"No, sir."

"Have you concluded any infiltrations?"

"No sir."

Kang hovered for a moment, staring at Park, as if the government employee were a stranger. Then he walked away slowly, pushing his trolley down the corridor to the next cubicle.

Park was now the accomplice to a crime against the state. A crime that carried the death penalty. A crime from which he would receive no direct benefit. He was risking everything for nothing. He felt empty inside.

The only way forward was to pretend that the conversation in the bus had never happened and to focus entirely on his work.

Chapter 30 – The Game

Over the following two weeks Park watched the slow but perceptible deterioration of his colleague and best friend Kim Dae-won.

Kim's personal hygiene gradually disappeared, his hair became greasy and uncombed, and he started to lose weight. He didn't speak to anyone apart from answering Kang's repetitive questions. Some nights, he slept in his chair at the Ministry. Other nights, he wandered alone around the grounds of the complex. He could no longer be counted on as a colleague or a friend. It was a thoroughly convincing performance. And if Park didn't know any better, he could easily believe that Kim had fallen into a state of deep depression.

Other people started to notice the change. One morning, Kang arrived at Kim's desk and went through the usual routine. Then he leaned forward and looked closely at Kim. An expression of disgust appeared on his face.

"What's wrong with you?" he asked. "You smell like an American."

Kim shrugged his shoulders and continued staring at his computer screen.

"I want you to have a health check tomorrow at 9am."

Park tried to distance himself from the behaviour of his friend. He let his mind wander to more pleasant thoughts. He had set up another meeting with the Girl with the Almond Eyes. He hoped the chaperone would leave them alone for a few minutes. He didn't want this trial period to drag on[42] any longer. He wanted to hold her hand, caress her hair and kiss her rosebud lips.

He started to feel aroused by the anticipation of the meeting. Impure thoughts now entered his mind. He imagined the two of them in his apartment. He was standing behind her, removing the coat from her shoulders, unbuttoning the back of her polyester dress, unclipping her bra, and lifting its straps over her shoulders. He imagined gently turning her body to face his own, looking into her eyes, moving forward to kiss her.

But something was wrong. They weren't the beautiful almond eyes he knew so well. They were the eyes of another person. They were the eyes of Kim Jong Un, president of North Korea. Park suddenly realised that he was embracing the chubby, half-naked body of the Supreme Leader.

He screamed and was instantly transported back to his desk in the Ministry of Information. A couple of his colleagues were looking at him inquisitively. It took him a moment to compose himself.

He told himself to put The Girl with Almond Eyes out of his mind. To focus 100% on his work and career. To fulfil his duty to the Fatherland. He opened the file of active targets and continued to research three inter-related companies - TechSpania, SMZ and Banco Cantábrico.

He went online and googled TechSpania to catch up with the latest news about the company. There was some stock price information, details of recent investments in South America, and some mergers and acquisitions speculation. Park was about to move on to the next company when something caught his attention.

It was the picture of a strikingly beautiful western woman on the front page of a publication called CyberStory Magazine. The headline of the article was: Lola Badiola: Cybersecurity Saint or Sinner?

---

[42] To drag on *(phrasal verb)* - To take longer than expected or than is necessary.

Park clicked on the link and read the article three times. He reviewed the story of Lola's life. How she got the job at TechSpania, how she succeeded as a manager in the Cybersecurity department, and how she was eventually fired by the company for her involvement in a series of hacking incidents.

He sat back in his chair and brooded[43]. Why was Lola Badiola getting the credit for his work? Did the world really believe that Park Jae-bong needed inside assistance to hack into TechSpania? It was an insult.

Park went onto the JBlock website and studied Lola's profile. She wasn't a hacker, she wasn't even a programmer, she was just a commercial director. It didn't make any sense.

He looked through all the pages of the company website and concluded that JBlock was just another cybersecurity start-up that would either go bankrupt[44] or be acquired by one of the bigger players. Like so many other start-ups, the founders would lose control and the employees would be laid off[45] with no notice period[46] or severance pay[47]. It seemed a very cruel system. But this was the Western way.

---

[43] To brood *(verb)* - To think long and hard about something that is upsetting you.

[44] To go bankrupt *(verb)* - When a company is unable to service its debts, or pay the money it owes, it goes through a process of bankruptcy. Its assets are taken over by a third party to be sold or managed, in order to repay the company's creditors.

[45] To lay off *(phrasal verb)* - To terminate somebody's employment due to financial difficulties at the company.

[46] Notice period *(noun)* - The period between the moment a company terminates someone's employment and their last day at work. It is usually a period of one to three months, allowing the employees to prepare for the change and hopefully find a new job.

[47] Severance pay *(noun)* - The amount of money an employee will receive as compensation if the company decides to terminate their employment. It will vary according to law of the country, the contract of the employee and the number of years of service.

He scrolled down to the very bottom of the landing page, and something caught his eye. It was the company address:

JBlock
4th Floor
Adriática Building
121 Gran Vía
Madrid
Spain
aha ck usa

He wondered what the bottom line of the address meant.

aha ck usa

It could have been a postcode, but he knew that in Spain there was a system of numbers rather than letters.

He looked closely and noticed that the middle figures were a quarter of a font size smaller than the others. It was almost imperceptible to the naked eye, but Park was trained to recognise these types of patterns.

a**ha ck us**a

There was a clear and intended message hidden within the letters. And the message was:

"hack us"

Park moved the cursor over the words and double clicked his mouse.

His computer screen went completely blank. Low-resolution graphics appeared and electronic music started playing. It looked and sounded just like an arcade videogame from the 1980s.

The following words popped up on his screen.

Welcome.

You are player 231.

Your challenge is to hack our system.

You must breach ten levels of protection.

Each level is protected by increasingly sophisticated software.

If you reach level 5, you will be invited to join us as an intern[48].

If you reach level 6, you will automatically be offered a job with no trial period.

If you reach level 7, you will automatically be offered a job with a $20.000 sign-on bonus[49].

Are you ready to play?

Park was intrigued. He had never seen anything like this before. It was a smart way of recruiting cybersecurity specialists. It was also a great way of testing proprietary software[50].

If he played the game, JBlock would track every move that he made. They would observe how he circumvented their systems. They would use him to perfect their product.

Under normal circumstances Park would discuss this discovery with Kim. But his best friend and colleague was just a shadow of his former self[51].

So, Park decided to act alone. His ego couldn't resist the challenge. He would show this start-up just how easy it was to hack their systems. He would make the world aware that Park Jae-bong didn't need any inside assistance with his work.

He hit the return button and started to play.

---

[48] Intern *(noun)* - A young person, often a university student or recent graduate, who is gaining work experience at a company for a temporary period.

[49] Sign-on bonus *(noun)* - A way of attracting talented recruits, by offering them a large sum of money to join the company before they have started working.

[50] Proprietary software *(adjective noun)* - Applications that have been designed by a company's own programmers rather than purchased from an external supplier.

[51] To be a shadow of one's former self *(idiom)* - Someone who is no longer as healthy, powerful, or influential as they once were, implying that they have been affected by difficulties in their life.

SAM GRATTON

QUIZ TIME

Chapters 26 to 30

COMPREHENSION QUIZ

Answer the questions with complete sentences. Say them out loud.

1. What was Lola Badiola like at school?
2. Describe Lola's relationship with Gonzalo Garrido at school.
3. How does Gonzalo treat her after she calls and asks for his help?
4. What advice does Gonzalo give her regarding TechSpania, Interpol and CyberStory?
5. How does the CyberStory article describe Salvador Badiola, Lola's father?
6. Do you think the article is accurate and balanced? Explain your answer.
7. What does Park think of Kim's plan to escape and how does he react?
8. How does Park react when he reads the CyberStory article?
9. Why does JBlock have a game hidden on their website?
10. What does Park do when he discovers the game?

BUSINESS ENGLISH QUIZ

Complete the sentences with the words used in the story.

1. Three partners from Clifford Chance, one of the largest law firms in the world, recently left to set up a small B_____ operation focusing solely on copyright law.

2. In most employment contracts there is a N_____-C_____ C_____ that prevents managers from contacting their clients for at least six months after they leave a company.

3. Amancio Ortega, the man behind Zara and the Inditex empire, is a classic R_____-T_____-R_____ story. From humble beginnings in rural Galicia, he has become one of the wealthiest men in Europe.

4. During my internship at BMW, I gained some H_____-O_____ E_____ working on the factory floor with the engineers manufacturing the latest models.

5. We have spent the last six years testing the new vaccine and we plan to start R_____ O_____ the first batches in Europe at the end of this quarter.

6. Pharmaceutical companies spend more money on R_____ & D_____ than companies in almost any other sector.

7. The S_____ required to be an effective computer programmer include knowledge of multiple languages, logical reasoning, and a great deal of patience.

8. The new commercial manager is a P_____ P_____. She loves socialising with her employees, clients, and suppliers. It's one of the reasons she's so successful.

9. Due to the economic crisis of the last six months, most banks have had to L_____ O_____ 10 to 15% of their staff.

10. I have read the terms of my employment contract and I am concerned about the very short N_____ P_____, in the event that I lose my job and the lack of S_____ P_____.

11. When the economy is booming and law firms are competing for the best talent, they are willing to pay significant S_____ O_____ B_____.

12. After his divorce and the loss of custody of his children, our sales manager no longer has the same passion, motivation, and determination. He has become a S_____ of his F_____ S_____.

13. We need tougher regulations to prevent people from S_____ us with marketing material and T_____ us on social media.

14. The competition commission prevents large and influential companies from abusing their M_____ P_____.

15. Our biggest competitor is now attempting a H_____ A_____ of our company and our own management will fight back in the interests of our shareholders.

ANSWERS TO COMPREHENSION QUIZ

1. Lola was a quiet, hard-working student, who did very well academically and enjoyed success in the school's volleyball team, where she was the captain.

2. Gonzalo was a year older than Lola at high school, and the two of them fell madly in love. They were together for five years before Lola decided to end the relationship.

3. Gonzalo treats Lola with kindness and concern, but above all he is professional and does not allow their past relationship to affect their current interaction.

4. Gonzalo advises Lola that she needs to be prepared for an attack by TechSpania, who will claim that she stole confidential information from their files and breached her employment contract. He tells her not to worry about Interpol as they don't have the expertise to fully understand the issues of international cyber security. And finally, he tells her to accept that she is a person of interest for magazines such as CyberStory, and trust that the article will say nothing damaging about her.

5. The CyberStory magazine describes Salvador Badiola as a successful businessman, local politician, and philanthropist. He is considered a folk hero by the people of Cantabria.

6. While the journalist claims to take a balanced view of the situation saying that he had sought Lola's input into the content of the article, in reality, the article is extremely one-sided. It uses unnamed sources from TechSpania to support its argument and implies that she is guilty of the crimes.

7. Park is shocked by Kim's plan to escape. At first, he is unsure how to react to the dilemma that he faces. If he allows Kim to go ahead with the plan, he is implicated in a crime against the state. If he tells the authorities about Kim's plan, he will betray

his best friend. He thinks the best course of action is to try to dissuade his friend from this madness.

8. Park is curious about what is written in the CyberStory magazine about Lola Badiola. However, as the architect of the intrusion, he is surprised and disappointed by the suggestion that she acted as an insider helping the hackers with their activities.

9. The game that JBlock has hidden in its website is designed to catch the attention of potential recruits. If someone is observant enough to discover the game and skilful enough to play the game, then that is the kind of person that JBlock wants to recruit. It's also a way that the company can test the efficacy of its cybersecurity systems.

10. Park understands exactly why JBlock have this game hidden in their website and decides to play it to prove to himself and to the outside world that he is an unstoppable force.

ANSWERS TO BUSINESS ENGLISH QUIZ

1. Three partners from Clifford Chance, one of the largest law firms in the world, have recently left to set up a small BOUTIQUE operation focusing solely on copyright law.

2. In most employment contracts there is a NON-COMPETE CLAUSE that prevents managers from contacting their clients for at least six months after they leave a company.

3. Amancio Ortega, the man behind Zara and the Inditex empire, is a classic RAGS-TO-RICHES story. From humble beginnings in rural Galicia, he has become one of the wealthiest men in Europe.

4. During my internship at BMW, I gained some HANDS-ON EXPERIENCE working on the factory floor with the engineers who were manufacturing the latest models.

THE ADVENTURES OF LOLA BADIOLA

5. We have spent the last six years testing the new vaccine and we plan to start ROLLING OUT the first batches in Europe at the end of this quarter.

6. Pharmaceutical companies spend more money on RESEARCH & DEVLOPMENT than companies in almost any other sector.

7. The SKILLSET required to be an effective computer programmer include knowledge of multiple languages, logical reasoning, and a great deal of patience.

8. The new commercial manager is a PEOPLE PERSON. She loves socialising with her employees, clients, and suppliers. It's one of the reasons she's so successful.

9. Due to the economic crisis of the last six months, most banks have had to LAY OFF 10 to 15% of their staff.

10. I have read the terms of my employment contract and I am concerned about the very short NOTICE PERIOD in the event that I lose my job, and the lack of SEVERANCE PAY.

11. When the economy is booming and law firms are competing for the best talent, they are willing to pay significant SIGN-ON BONUSES.

12. After his divorce and the loss of custody of his children, our sales manager no longer has the same passion, motivation, and determination. He has become a SHADOW OF HIS FORMER SELF.

13. We need tougher regulations to prevent people from SPAMMING us with marketing material and TROLLING us on social media.

14. The competition commission prevents large and influential companies from abusing their MONOPLOY POWER.

15. Our biggest competitor is now attempting a HOSTILE ACQUISITION of our company and our own management will fight back in the interests of our shareholders.

"Shall we talk about the elephant in the room?"
Perla

Chapter 31 – Lola's Mother

Lola agreed to meet her mother at the Retiro Park, in the centre of Madrid. It was a cold winter's morning, but the sun was out, and the air was still and dry.

Perla Manchón arrived wearing a long, dark cashmere coat, a Burberry scarf, and a trilby hat. She was a tall, thin woman with white hair accentuated by platinum highlights. She walked quickly and purposefully; she was the kind of woman who expected you to move out of her way.

The moment she saw Lola, her face lit up into a radiant smile. Her smooth skin stretched tight across her prominent cheekbones, her perfect white teeth dazzled, and her arms stretched out to embrace her beloved daughter.

"It's been too long!" she said, as the two women hugged.

"We spent the whole of Christmas together Mum."

"Exactly! Way too long! How have you been?"

"Good."

Perla instantly perceived that Lola was upset, and she knew the reason. She had read the CyberStory article the day it was published. She didn't say anything at that moment. She knew, from her own personal experience, that these unauthorised profiles were full of rumour and gossip, and best ignored. She simply wrapped her arm around Lola and guided her towards the central promenade of the park.

"Let's go to the lake!" she said enthusiastically.

It was a weekday so there were only a few people scattered around the grounds. To Lola it felt almost empty, a contrast to the happy, noisy weekends she had spent there with her three cousins as a child.

"Ofelia has left me," said her mother.

"Oh?"

"One of her brothers passed away[1]."

"I'm sorry to hear that."

"She flew back to Peru yesterday."

"How long will she be gone?"

"Five weeks. I don't know how I'm going to survive!"

Lola couldn't help but laugh. Her mother lived in a five hundred square meter penthouse apartment at the bottom of Calle Velázquez with panoramic views of the Retiro Park. She had a part-time driver and two housekeepers. One of them was an old Peruvian lady called Ofelia. Lola was in no doubt that her mother would not only survive the next five weeks but continue to enjoy a life of comfort and luxury.

"Do you need any help around the house, Lola?"

"I'm fine, Mum. I can manage on my own."

"Ofelia is planning to bring a sister back from Peru, if you need..."

"I'm fine."

The two women continued to walk through the Retiro park. They eventually arrived at the man-made lake, its peaceful waters shimmering in the morning sun, the massive statues of the Alfonso XII monument standing proudly at the water's edge.

Lola contemplated telling her mother about Mr. Red Bull, the man who made her smile, laugh, and forget about the stress in her professional life. Perla would be thrilled to hear that her daughter was starting a relationship. Having grandchildren was her number

---

[1] To pass away *(phrasal verb)* - To die. Sometimes shortened to "to pass".

one priority, as important as her role as Chairman of the Board of Directors[2] of Grupo Badiola.

But Lola decided to stay quiet about the new boyfriend. She knew from bitter experience that if she revealed any part of her private life to her mother it would complicate the situation. Perla would interfere and, with the best intentions, try to take control.

"How's the company?" Lola asked.

"Fine."

"What's the latest news?"

"Well, your cousins are still determined to issue[3] corporate bonds to finance the South American expansion."

"You need to keep an eye on them[4]."

"Yes, I do."

Grupo Badiola was run by Lola's three cousins. Margins[5] were good but there had been no revenue[6] or profit[7] growth in the three years since Salvador Badiola had passed away. The cousins were looking to issue public debt[8] to finance strategic investments in

---

[2] Chairman of the Board of Directors *(title)* – A person responsible for leading the Board, whose fundamental role is to ensure that company managers work in the best interests of the company shareholders. The board advises on strategic issues, corporate governance, and financial matters.

[3] To issue corporate bonds *(finance concept)* - One of the ways a company raises money is through the issuance of corporate bonds. These are certificates that promise to repay the lender the full amount of the loan at a specific moment in the future plus regular interest payments. These certificates or corporate bonds can be bought and sold by investors in the secondary bond markets.

[4] To keep an eye on someone *(idiom)* - To look after someone. To take care of them or to observe them closely during a critical time.

[5] Margin *(noun)* - The ratio of profit to sales. It is a simple indication of the profitability of a certain activity.

[6] Revenue - The total amount that the company invoices representing its sales. Also known as turnover.

[7] Profits *(noun)* - Revenues minus costs equals profits.

[8] Public debt *(adjective noun)* - The amount of money that the company owes to its creditors through the issuance of corporate bonds in the open markets.

Argentina and Brazil. Perla thought it was a reckless move and, as Chairman of the Board, had convinced the directors to block the move.

The succession[9] of the family company had been a source of tension between Lola and her parents ever since she had decided to pursue her own career path. Her mother still hoped that one day Lola would return to Grupo Badiola. She knew there was no-one better to run the company in Salvador's style than his own daughter.

"What about you Lola? How's the new job? Shall we talk about the elephant in the room[10]?"

The two women stood in silence for a moment.

"You mean the CyberStory article?"

"Listen, darling, you've just got to ignore these journalists. It's sensationalist nonsense."

"That's easier said than done[11]."

"Remember, today news is tomorrow's trash."

That was a typical sentence from Perla Manchón, the eternal optimist. Lola's mother had the ability to brighten up a room with her smile, to motivate her team with a stirring speech, to fill the people around her with hope. But her optimism also had its drawbacks.

Whenever Lola had a problem or concern as a child, she would always receive the same sort of advice.

"Everything will be ok in the end."

or

"Time heals all wounds[12]."

---

[9] Succession *(noun)* - The process of deciding who takes over running a business when the CEO retires.

[10] Elephant in the room *(idiom)* - An extremely important issue about which everybody knows but nobody is willing to talk about.

[11] Easier said than done *(idiom)* - A decision or an action that is easier to talk about that it is to implement.

[12] Time heals all wounds *(idiom)* - The idea that, as time passes, the pain that we feel from loss or injury gradually declines and eventually disappears.

or

"Always look on the bright side of life."

Positive words and fine sentiments, but not very helpful for an only child suffering from insecurities, loneliness, and more than her fair share of bullying at school.

Lola took hold of her mother's arm and guided her to the nearest park bench. She motioned for the two of them to sit down.

"Listen, Mum, it's not the CyberStory article that worries me. It's the person behind it."

She looked directly into her mother's eyes and said:

"I need you to tell me everything you know about Mario Ruiz de Velasco."

SAM GRATTON

Chapter 32 – Pluto

Lola arrived at the JBlock office after her morning meeting in the Retiro. Her mother had said very little about Ruiz de Velasco, other than the news, rumours, and gossip that everyone in the Spanish business community already knew. She did, however, confirm that Ruiz de Velasco had attended her father's funeral, but had kept a very low profile.

She then moved the conversation quickly onto other subjects.

As Lola walked up the steps to the third floor of the Adriática building, she couldn't help feeling that there were important questions left unanswered. Her mother rarely lied, but she could often be economical with the truth[13].

She paused for a moment before entering the front door. She wanted to prepare herself for the reaction of her colleagues to the CyberStory article. She knew that JJ and Diego were on her side. But she was worried about the reaction of everyone else. What would Cayetano and the team of programmers think? Would they still respect and trust her?

She opened the door, walked into the open plan office[14] and immediately realised something wasn't right. There was nobody

---

[13] Economical with the truth *(idiom)* - To deliberately withhold critical information when answering a question or explaining something. A way of avoiding the truth without lying.

[14] Open plan office *(adjective noun)* - Design of office space where there are no walls or barriers between employees.

working in the management, marketing, or administration sections of the room.

She looked around and saw everyone squeezed around a single computer. All nine members of the JBlock team were standing behind Diego. All of them were silently watching his huge hairy fingers punch frantically into a computer keyboard. He was clearly under pressure.

Lola observed the surreal scene without moving, until at last the typing stopped.

"Level 9." said Diego quietly.

There was a brief pause and then everyone erupted into conversation. JJ started shouting instructions, the team of programmers exchanged strong opinions, and the administrative staff picked up their telephones. Lola felt like she was standing on stage in the middle of a dramatic scene in which everyone knew their lines apart from her.

She ran over to Cayetano "What's going on?"

"I'm not really sure," said Cayetano. "Something to do with Pluto."

This was a technical issue, and Cayetano was clearly the wrong person to ask. Lola grabbed the arm of one of the programmers as he was running back to his computer terminal.

"Van Dyck, what's up?"

"Level 9, Pluto got to level 9!"

Diego was now on his feet directing his team of ethical hackers, he looked like a man on the verge of a nervous breakdown[15].

"Velázquez, run a complete analysis of every instruction he completed. Turner, I want you to track and trace every line of code

---

[15] To be on the verge of a nervous breakdown *(idiom)* - To be so stressed or worried that you have almost reached a point where you can no longer function either physically or mentally.

he left on our system. Munch, run diagnostic checks on all of our software. I don't want any more surprises.

Everybody else listen up!

There is a hacker out there who reached level 9 of our game. His name is Pluto. If he comes back tomorrow and reaches level 10, we're all dead. Do you understand? This is an existential threat[16] not only to our business, but to the security of global information. Speak to anyone you know in the cyber world. Ask for favours. Use the dark web. Get creative! Do whatever you need to do.

Just find me this Pluto!"

***

There was a collective feeling of fear and excitement in the team meeting that evening. Lola imagined that this must be what it felt like in The Situation Room[17] of the White House after a terrorist attack. On the one hand, the team was facing an imminent crisis, on the other hand they were trained to deal with this eventuality. It was, in fact, the reason they existed.

JJ stood up and waited for everyone to stop speaking.

"Ok, let me summarise the current situation. Last night, between the hours of 2 am and 6 am Central European Time, a hacker entered our system to play our recruitment game. As you know the game is designed to attract talent to our company. In fact, all of the programmers who currently work here reached Level 7 of the game.

Last night, the intruder reached level 9. This is unprecedented. He was able to break through, not only our conventional firewalls,

---

[16] Existential threat *(adjective noun)* - A danger so great that it threatens your existence.

[17] The Situation Room *(noun)* - A safe room located in the White House, where the President of the United States can meet with his or her military leaders to discuss their response to a domestic or international crisis.

but also some of our proprietary software. In doing so, he highlighted weaknesses in our coding that we are now addressing.

This hacker was not interested in a job at JBlock. He was not interested in stealing any data from us. In fact, we are not entirely sure why he played our game. We can only suppose it is because he enjoyed the challenge. But we need to find out who he is and what his motivation is.

He left us two clues. The first is the way that he hacks. He has a distinct style. On the surface, it appears random and pointless, however, deeper down there is a penetrating logic.

The second clue is his name, Pluto. This could be a reference to the dwarf planet in our solar system, it could be related to the ancient God of the underworld, or it could be something to do with Mickey Mouse's canine friend.

Finding Pluto is our number one priority. So, from now on we are in crisis mode. That means we work around the clock[18] until this problem is solved. I don't mind if you come into the office, you work remotely or become a digital nomad, as long as you are searching for Pluto. Does anyone have any questions?"

There were murmurs around the room, but nobody put up their hand to speak. The programmers knew exactly what they had to do. They understood the power and the skill of the adversary they were confronting.

JJ was about to terminate the meeting, when Cayetano raised his hand, like the cool schoolboy sitting at the back of the classroom.

"Yes, I have a question."

"Go ahead."

"Do you think that this is an inside job[19]?"

---

[18] To work around the clock *(idiom)* - To work continuously all day and all night.

[19] Inside job *(idiom)* - A crime that is committed against a company or institution by its own employees or members.

The murmuring stopped and the room fell silent. Cayetano was asking if JJ suspected somebody in the room was responsible for the attack. It was a deeply uncomfortable moment. He continued.

"Most attacks are orchestrated by current or ex-employees, right? That's what it said in the CyberStory article."

He leaned forward in his chair and looked across at Lola. Then, he smiled innocently and said:

"What do you think Lola? Is this an inside job?"

Lola felt the eyes of everyone in the meeting room turn towards her. She understood the implication of Cayetano's words.

JJ stood up and walked around the room until he was standing behind Cayetano. He placed his hands on the salesman's shoulders.

"Let me explain something to you Cayetano. I recruited everyone sitting in this room for three reasons. Firstly, I believe that they are the best people for the job. Secondly, I believe that they share my vision and my values. And finally, I believe that they are trustworthy. If you think that I have misjudged anyone, please tell me now."

Cayetano sat silently in his chair. He seemed to shrink back into the ergonomically designed and environmentally friendly seat. JJ patted him on the shoulder. And then returned to the top of the conference table.

"Now, more than ever, we need to speak openly and directly. Now, more than ever, we need to trust each other. Now, more than ever, we need to come together[20] as a team."

He clapped his hands, like a football manager who has just finished his half-time speech.

"Ok, let's do this!"

And everyone followed him out of the room.

---

[20] To come together *(phrasal verb)* - To start working successfully as a team.

SAM GRATTON

Chapter 33 – The Empty Space

Park woke up at 7am on a dark winter's morning. He had a freezing cold shower, then shaved the few hairs that grew from his chin. He opened his bottle of Dragon aftershave and breathed in the smell, then he practiced some martial arts moves in front of the mirror. He was seeing the Girl with the Almond Eyes that evening. One day, very soon, he would lose his virginity.

He walked into the living room and turned on the television. As always, he watched the sports channel. There was a documentary about the conflict between men and women in the US football federation. The women were campaigning against the gender pay gap[21] that existed in their sport and the unconscious bias[22] against them in all areas of American society. The presenter of the TV program argued that this conflict was evidence of an imminent Marxist revolution[23] in the US. She proudly exclaimed that no such

---

[21] Gender pay gap *(noun)* - The difference in the average hourly earnings of male and female employees, expressed as a percentage of the earnings of the male employee. In the European Union the gender pay gap is currently between 12 and 13%.

[22] Unconscious bias *(adjective noun)* - A prejudice we feel against a certain group based on gender, race, age etc. of which we are unaware.

[23] Marxist Revolution *(adjective noun)* - Based on the writings of Karl Marx, it is the idea that the working class in an industrial society will violently revolt against the elite and replace the capitalist mode of production with a communist alternative.

gender discrimination occurred in the People's Democratic Republic of Korea.

Park carefully opened the door of his dodgy[24] electric fridge, making sure that he didn't trip the electric circuit. It had been broken since he moved into the apartment two and half years earlier. He took out some leftover Kimchi from the previous night and prepared his breakfast.

Half an hour later he was on his way to work. It was a bitterly cold morning in early February and there was a sprinkling of snow on the ground, so he decided to wear his Russian manufactured army coat and boots. They were a gift from the Supreme Leader to all the hackers of section 6523 of the Ministry of Information following the successful ransomware attack of the English Post Office the previous year. The coat was made of compressed sheep's wool wrapped in canvas and was incredibly heavy. But it did the job and kept out the cold. By the time Park reached the bus stop, he was sweating.

He sat at the back of the bus. It was a forty-five-minute journey to work, which gave him time to review his assignments. His targets were three inter-related companies, Banco Cantábrico, TechSpania, and SMZ. He also had a personal project in the form of a cybersecurity start-up called JBlock. He intended to return to their system later that week and finish the job.

There were few people on the bus at that time of day. He normally chatted with Kim on his way to work, but his best friend had degenerated even further in his attempt to convince the world that he was suicidal. Kim had become completely anti-social and spent most nights sleeping at the Ministry underneath his desk. It was February 8th, two days to go until his escape from the Fatherland.

---

[24] Dodgy *(adjective)* - Something that is unreliable, low quality, or likely to cause problems.

Park got off the bus and entered his workplace. He passed under the huge clock at the entrance of the Ministry of Information. It was five minutes to nine, so there was still a little time before his workday officially began. He walked up the stairwell with several other hackers until he reached his department.

The moment that he entered the open plan floor of section 6523 of the Ministry of Information, he knew that something was wrong. As he got closer to his workstation the feeling of fear inside him grew stronger. His heart started to pound, his head started to throb, and his vision started to blur. It was dreamlike, as if the world around him had become slow and distorted.

He sat down at his desk and mechanically turned on his computer. Then he took out a pen and pretended to make some notes. He was almost too afraid to look up, but he had to make sure that what he'd seen was real. Very slowly and carefully he raised his head and looked across the hallway.

His worse fears were confirmed.

Kim was not there. Kim's computer was not there. Kim's desk was not there.

There was nothing left but an empty space.

SAM GRATTON

Chapter 34 – The Health Check

Park spent most of the morning speculating about the disappearance of Kim. It was Tuesday, the 8th of February, two days before the intended escape. One possible scenario was that the conditions were perfect, and they had expedited[25] the plan. Another scenario was that Kim hadn't revealed the whole truth to Park in order to protect him. He hoped and prayed that one of these scenarios was real, but deep down he was very worried.

Park's priority was now his own safety. He needed to act normally and distract his mind from the events surrounding Kim. He forced himself to concentrate on his current projects.

He had made good progress in his attempt to re-enter the systems of TechSpania. He had found a vulnerability in the software that controlled the supply of electricity to the headquarters.

Every large company and government institution in the world had a backup supply of electricity in the event of a systemic failure of the electrical grid. They needed to be prepared for what was called a Black Sky Event[26] - a terrorist attack, a meteor shower, or nuclear war that rendered the electrical gird inoperable.

---

[25] To expedite *(verb)* - To speed up the process in order to reach a conclusion.

[26] Black Sky Event *(idiom)* - A catastrophic event such as a natural disaster, cyber-attack, physical attack, or act of war that causes the electrical grid to cease functioning for a significant period, leaving a country or region without electricity.

It was unthinkable for a bank, airline, or data centre to be without power under any circumstances. Therefore, companies, such as TechSpania had two lines of defence. The first was known as an Uninterrupted Power Supply or UPS. This was a system of powerful batteries that guaranteed the uninterrupted flow of electricity to essential parts of the company for a temporary period. The second was the Automatic Transfer Switch or ATS that controlled a series of backup generators, normally diesel fuelled, that provided electricity for an indefinite period, or until the grid was once again functioning.

Park had hacked into the software that controlled the UPS and ATS at the headquarters of TechSpania. He was able to fool these machines into believing that there had been a Black Sky Event. He could therefore turn on both the batteries and the diesel generators while the grid was still supplying power to the headquarters. This would overload the internal electrical system and cause all the machines connected to the grid to blow their fuses. This would leave the company naked, vulnerable to further cyberattacks. It was a little like disarming the force field of the Death Star before the rebels struck.

Park had yet to carry out his plan, but he was optimistic about the prospects for success. He was deep in thought when Kang appeared in the distance, pushing his aluminium trolley full of papers towards him. Park needed to behave as if he knew nothing about Kim's plans, as if he had never been an intimate friend of Kim.

The supervisor arrived at Park's desk and went through the usual routine.

"Have you observed any anomalies?"

"No, sir."

"Have you crashed any systems?"

"No, sir."

"Have you concluded any infiltrations?"

"No sir."

Kang moved on to the next cubicle without any acknowledgement.

Park knew that he had to bring up the issue of Kim's disappearance. It would appear unusual or even suspicious if he didn't question the whereabouts of his colleague and friend. He cleared his throat.

"When will Kim be back?"

Kang stopped and slowly turned around. "What?"

"When will Kim be back? I need his assistance today."

Kang reversed the trolley to Park's desk. He took a chair from another workstation and placed it right next to Park's. Then he sat down and stared into Park's eyes.

"Kim won't be back today."

"Oh."

"Kim won't be back for the rest of his life."

Kang continued to stare at Park as if he were searching for the thoughts behind the façade[27].

Park's amygdala, the most ancient part of his brain, started sending signals to his adrenal glands to release cortisol into the bloodstream. This triggered an automatic fight-or-flight response[28] throughout his body. He had to use all his powers of self-control to appear unemotional even though his heart was pounding, and his head was throbbing.

"I will need a new assistant then," he said in a monotone voice.

"Yes, I suppose you will." replied Kang.

The functionary stood up and straightened his jacket and tie. He took hold of his trolley and slowly pushed it down the hallway. Then he turned back to Park and said:

---

[27] Façade *(noun)* - In a literal sense, it is the front of a building that faces the street. In a metaphorical sense, it is an attractive outward appearance that hides an unpleasant reality beneath.

[28] Fight-or-flight response *(idiom)* - An instinctive physiological response to danger in which the body releases cortisol and adrenaline, in preparation to either fight the danger or run away from it.

"By the way, you have a health check tomorrow at 9am. Go straight to the medical centre before you start work."

And with that, he walked away.

Chapter 35 – Aftershave

Park was in a state of high anxiety throughout the rest of the day. He was unable to do any work. His mind kept going back to the conversation with Kang. Where exactly was his best friend, Kim? What were they doing to him? Was he still alive?

Park was equally concerned about himself. He was sure that he was going to be interrogated about every element of his relationship with Kim. He would probably receive a lie detector test or be drugged with a truth serum.

Every North Korean knew that if you did not immediately report a crime, you became an accomplice to that crime and suffered the same consequences as the criminal. How was Park going to be able to convince the secret police that he knew nothing of Kim's plans without getting tongue tied[29]?

At exactly 6pm Park shut down his computer and made his way home. He sat at the back of the bus looking through the window at the urban wasteland surrounding him. He felt like a beautiful big fish that had jumped out of a dirty little pond and now found itself gasping for air. The sense of helplessness was overwhelming. He was the world's greatest computer programmer, a genius, and yet his talents would never be fully realised or appreciated. His life was a miserable failure.

---

[29] To be tongue-tied *(adjective)* - To be unable to find the right words to express yourself due to surprise or stress, as if your tongue were tied in a knot.

He looked at all the other functionaries[30] on the bus in front of him. They were the same pathetic faces that he saw every day going backward and forwards in a pointless process of production. They filled in forms and went over reports until one day they were sent back to their villages to grow old and die. He didn't know whether to cry, scream, or hijack the bus and drive it to the Chinese border.

But before Park could do anything silly, something caught his attention and brought him out of his self-indulgent daydreams. There were two men sitting half-way down the bus that he had never seen before. He was sure that he knew everyone on this daily commute[31], but these men were new.

The strangers were wearing the typical clothes worn by government employees, but their shoes were different - leather, shiny, high quality, built for outdoor activities, built for the military. Both men had very sharp haircuts and the backs of their necks were muscular and slightly tanned.

It didn't take long for Park to figure out[32] that they were from the secret police. But not the regular secret police. They were too well-fed for that. They must have been from the Special Operations Force (SOF)[33], North Korea's finest and bravest soldiers.

What were they doing on the bus? What were they doing on this specific bus at this specific moment? It was very unlikely that this was just a coincidence. They must have been following him. Park's sense of paranoia started to grow.

---

[30] Functionary *(noun)* - A person who works in an administrative role for an organisation or institution usually with little autonomy, creativity, or responsibility.

[31] Daily commute *(adjective noun)* - The trip to work in the morning and the trip home in the evening, that coincides with millions of other workers.

[32] To figure out *(phrasal verb)* - To solve a problem after some thought and deliberation.

[33] Special Operations Force (SOF) *(adjective noun)* - The elite military units that are specially trained and equipped to perform military or political operations in North Korea.

The bus arrived at Park's stop, he stood up and walked quickly down the aisle to the exit. He didn't look back. He jumped off the vehicle and made his way directly to his apartment. It was getting dark but there were still plenty of people around. As always, everyone who was out on the street minded their own business[34], nobody looked anyone else in the eye.

As he got closer to his apartment he started to speed up, and by the time he reached the entrance to the building he was running. He didn't dare look backwards, but he sensed the presence of the two secret servicemen breathing down his neck[35].

He took his keys out of his pocket and clumsily unlocked the front door of the building. He closed it behind him and, for the first time, looked to see if anyone had been following him. There was no-one, just the neighbours going about their daily business.

He realised he was out of breath and sweating. The Russian army coat felt like it weighed a ton. He took it off and carried it up the stairs and into his apartment. As soon as he was inside his living room, he breathed a sigh of relief. He was home, in his castle, protected by his four flimsy walls.

He opened the fridge door to get himself a drink of cold water, but the fridge wasn't working. The dodgy electric circuit had been tripped[36] and the contents inside of the machine were at room temperature. Park shook his head and swore. He was sure that he had opened and closed it carefully earlier that morning.

He poured himself a class of tepid water and sat down on the sofa to watch television. He needed to distract himself from the current events in his life. The 7pm news was just finishing and the

---

[34] To mind your own business - To not show interest or ask questions about the activity and behaviour of others.

[35] To breathe down someone's neck *(idiom)* - To get so close to someone that they can feel your breath on their neck. In a professional sense, it implies you are monitoring their activity closely and obviously.

[36] To trip an electrical circuit *(idiom)* - To automatically shut off the electrical flow in a circuit in order to prevent damage and overheating

next program on the schedule[37] was a documentary about rice production in the North Hamgyong province between 1994 and 2009.

Park checked the remote control and realised that the television was on the news channel. This didn't make any sense. He was sure that he had left it on the Sports channel that morning.

There could only be one explanation for why his fridge wasn't working and the television channel had been changed. Someone had been in his apartment.

Park started to feel like he was sinking into his sofa, like a great weight had been placed on his shoulders and was pushing down from above.

Were the intruders still there?

---

[37] Schedule *(noun)* - In British English, the first syllable is pronounced "SH". In US English, the first syllable is pronounced "SK".

QUIZ TIME

Chapters 31 to 35

COMPREHENSION QUIZ

Answer the questions with complete sentences. Say them out loud.

1. Describe Perla Manchón and the relationship she has with her daughter.
2. Describe the way in which Grupo Badiola is managed.
3. What is happening at JBlock when Lola returns from her walk in the park?
4. What does Cayetano say at the team meeting later that day, and how does JJ respond?
5. What is Park's routine each morning when he wakes up?
6. How does he feel when he discovers that Kim has disappeared two days earlier than planned?
7. What vulnerabilities has Park discovered at TechSpania and how does he intend to exploit them?
8. Why is Park worried about his supervisor Kang?
9. How does Park feel as he looks out of the window of the bus on the way home?
10. Who are the two strangers on the bus and how does Park react when he sees them?

BUSINESS ENGLISH QUIZ

Complete the sentences with the words used in the story.

1. We have recruited a new C_____ of the B_____ of D_____, to ensure that the board does its job effectively and protects the interests of the shareholders of the business.

2. Our company intends to I_____ C_____ B_____ at the beginning of next quarter. We are seeking to raise €500 million from the bond markets. We will pay an interest rate of 6% and repay the debt in 10 years' time.

3. I suspect that the commercial director is in the process of looking for a new job at another company. Could you K_____ an E_____ on him and report back to me?

4. Our revenue is stable, but our P_____ M_____ has increased because we have successfully reduced our cost of doing business.

5. We need to address the E_____ in the R_____. Our current CEO is mentally unstable and needs to be replaced as soon as possible.

6. He didn't lie on his CV, but he was E_____ with the T_____, because he omitted the fact that he had been accused of bullying at his previous company.

7. With the demanding financial targets, half of the sales team are on the V_____ of a N_____ B_____. I think we need to organise a weekend team-building event to help people relax, and boost morale.

8. Artificial intelligence represents an E_____ T_____ to many traditional service businesses such as translation, proofreading and legal administration.

9. With the end of the quarter approaching, we all need to W_____ A_____ the C_____, in order to hit our production targets.

10. The majority of cyber-attacks are I_____ J_____, where either current or former employees assist the hackers with their intrusion.

11. The G_____ P_____ G_____ in the European Union is between 12 and 13%. It has fallen dramatically over the last few years, but more effort needs to be made to eradicate it entirely.

12. We all have U_____ B_____ against people who are unlike us or with whom we are unfamiliar, we must make ourselves aware of these prejudices and act fairly and appropriately.

13. The D_____ C_____ is killing me! I spend two hours stuck the traffic on the M-30 every day.

14. My colleagues keep asking me about my private life, they want to know if I am single or if I have a partner, and I wish they would just M_____ T_____ O_____ B_____.

15. The new commercial director is a micromanager, he's always B_____ D_____ O_____ N_____ and making it difficult for us to work freely and independently.

ANSWERS TO COMPREHENSION QUIZ

1. Perla Manchón is an intelligent, glamorous, and confident woman who is currently the Chairman of the Board of Directors at Grupo Badiola. She has a complex relationship with her daughter over whom she wishes she had more control.

2. Group Badiola is currently managed by Lola's three cousins. It is a profitable company but has not experienced any growth over the last three years. The cousins are eager to expand the business into Latin America, and would like to borrow money from the financial markets. As Chairman of the Board of Directors, Perla Manchón has blocked this move.

3. There is drama and tension in the office of JBlock when Lola returns. Everybody is crowded around a computer as Diego analyses the intrusion into their systems by a mysterious hacker called Pluto.

4. At the team meeting later that day, Cayetano asks if the intrusion was the work of somebody inside of JBlock, he implies that Lola may have been involved. JJ responds very forcefully by stating his complete confidence in the integrity of everybody in the team.

5. When Park wakes up every morning, he makes himself breakfast, turns on the TV and watches the sports channel.

6. Park has discovered a weakness in TechSpania's connection to the electrical grid. He knows how to overload the electrical circuits of the company, to temporarily shut down their power supply, making them vulnerable to further cyberattacks.

7. Park is extremely concerned about Kim's unexpected disappearance. He tries to convince himself that there is a rational explanation for what has happened, but deep down he believes that the authorities have become aware of Kim's plan and arrested him.

8. Park is worried that Kang suspects him of helping Kim with his plan to escape.

9. Park feels frustrated and depressed that he is trapped in a country in which his true talents are neither appreciated nor fully realised.

10. Park is concerned about the two strangers who have appeared on the bus. Given the way they look and the way that they are dressed, he assumes that they are two members of the Special Operations Forces (SOF) who are now following him.

ANSWERS TO BUSINESS ENGLISH QUIZ

1. We have recruited a new CHAIRMAN OF THE BOARD OF DIRECTORS, to ensure that the board does its job effectively and protects the interests of the shareholders of the business.

2. Our company intends to ISSUE CORPORATE BONDS at the beginning of next quarter. We are seeking to raise €500 million from the bond markets. We will pay an interest rate of 6% and repay the debt in 10 years' time.

3. I suspect that the commercial director is in the process of looking for a new job at another company. Could you KEEP AN EYE ON HIM and report back to me?

4. Our revenue is stable, but our PROFIT MARGIN has increased because we have successfully reduced our cost of doing business.

5. We need to address the ELEPHANT IN THE ROOM. Our current CEO is mentally unstable and needs to be replaced as soon as possible.

6. He didn't lie on his CV, but he was ECONOMICAL WITH THE TRUTH, because he omitted the fact that he had been accused of bullying at his previous company.

7. With the demanding financial targets, half of the sales team are on the VERGE OF A NERVOUS BREAKDOWN. I think we need

to organise a weekend teambuilding event to help people relax, and boost morale.

8. Artificial intelligence represents an EXISTENTIAL THREAT to many traditional service businesses such as translation, proofreading, and legal administration.

9. With the end of the quarter approaching, we all need to WORK AROUND THE CLOCK, in order to hit our production targets.

10. The majority of cyber-attacks are INSIDE JOBS, where either current or former employees assist the hackers with their intrusion.

11. The GENDER PAY GAP in the European Union is between 12 and 13%. It has fallen dramatically over the last few years, but more effort needs to be made to eradicate it entirely.

12. We all have UNCONSCIOUS BIAS against people who are unlike us or with whom we are unfamiliar, we must make ourselves aware of these prejudices and act fairly and appropriately.

13. The DAILY COMMUTE is killing me! I spend two hours stuck the traffic on the M-30 every day.

14. My colleagues keep asking me about my private life. They want to know if I am single or if I have a partner, and I wish they would just MIND THEIR OWN BUSINESS.

15. The new commercial director is a micromanager. He's always BREATHING DOWN OUR NECKS and making it difficult for us to work freely and independently.

SAM GRATTON

"Lies. Lies. Lies"
Park

Chapter 36 – Knife

Park jumped up onto his feet and grabbed a knife from his kitchen countertop. It still had some Kimchi sauce on it, but it was sharp and would do the trick[1]. He slowly and silently walked up to his bedroom door and listened carefully. There was no sound from within.

He closed his eyes and counted to three. One. Two. Three. Then he burst into[2] the room screaming at the top of his voice and slashing the air with his kitchen knife.

There was nobody there. His bedroom and bathroom were empty. He checked all the cupboards and curtains and found nothing and nobody else in the apartment. The intruders had long since left the premises.

He sat down on his bed and let the adrenalin dissipate through his body. Gradually, his normal breathing returned, and he came back to his senses. He needed to think clearly. He needed to plan his next move. He was a brilliant problem solver and tactician. That's what made him such an effective hacker. Now, more than ever, he needed to rely on his resourcefulness[3].

---

[1] To do the trick *(idiom)* - To get the intended result.

[2] To burst into *(phrasal verb)* - To suddenly start doing something. You can burst into song, burst into a room, or a building might burst into flames.

[3] Resourcefulness *(noun)* - The ability to find clever ways to overcome difficulties given what is available to you.

There were three layers of law enforcement in North Korea. The first and most obvious was the police force. Over 150,000 security personnel employed to maintain public order and investigate criminal activity. They wore uniforms and carried badges, they walked the streets and directed traffic. They were the public face of the Ministry of Security Affairs.

The second layer of law enforcement was the bowibu, or the secret police. Nobody knew exactly how many officers were employed in this division, but it was several times the number of uniformed policemen. They were responsible for capturing dissidents and preventing anti-government activities. They ran the internment and re-education camps for political prisoners.

The third and final layer of law enforcement, the most feared and revered, were the Special Operations Forces or SOF. They were an independent organization charged with the protection of Kim Jung Un himself. They had the authority to carry out[4] pre-emptive strikes against any threat, real or imaginary, against the Supreme Leader. If a factory full of striking workers burned down[5] with the staff inside, if an airplane full of government officials flew into a mountain, if a notable family was massacred at a wedding, the SOF was probably behind it.

Park knew how the three layers of law enforcement operated. He had seen each of them in action. The people who worked for the regular and secret police were, like so many government workers, functionaries doing their jobs to put bread on the table[6]. He believed that he was smart enough to stay one step ahead of them.

The agents of the SOF were a different category altogether. They had the intelligence, the equipment and above all the psychological

---

[4] To carry out *(phrasal verb)* - To fulfil an objective, to complete a job or activity.

[5] To burn down *(phrasal verb)* - To completely destroy something with fire.

[6] To put bread on the table *(idiom)* - The process of earning money to survive.

commitment to track down[7] and eliminate anyone they felt was a threat. They were, as Kim had once described them, an army of Terminators[8].

As Park senses gradually returned to him, he became aware of a strong smell in his bedroom. A smell that was familiar. It was sweet, floral, and somewhat acrid. He got up, walked over to his bathroom, and opened the door. The smell became even stronger. It was the distinct essence of Dragon aftershave.

He looked closely at the bottle of pungent perfume on the shelf in his bathroom and noticed two things that were wrong. Firstly, the bottle was positioned with the logo facing inwards. Secondly, the level of fluid had dropped from earlier that morning. Whoever had been in Park's apartment had helped themselves to a large quantity of his most treasured possession.

Park's emotions had been on a rollercoaster[9] that day. From hope, to paranoia, to fear and now, finally, he was moved to anger. Was there nothing sacred in this society? The Fatherland had taken his talent, his best friend, and now, his aftershave, the one thing that made him feel unique and human. He could not contain his bitterness and resentment. He attacked the air around him with the knife in his hand, stabbing an imaginary Kang, slashing the two-secret policeman, cutting the jugular vein of the Supreme Leader, and watching him collapse on the bedroom floor in a pool of blood.

This physical expression of his inner emotions made him feel much better. It allowed him to release the adrenalin that had built up in his system. And, for a moment, it made him feel powerful.

In the background, he heard the 8pm news starting on the television. It brought him back to the present moment. And he

---

[7] To track down *(phrasal verb)* - To find someone or something after a long and difficult search.

[8] The Terminator *(noun)* - A 1984 film by James Cameron, starring Arnold Schwarzenegger, as an almost indestructible cyborg from the future.

[9] On a rollercoaster *(idiom)* - A journey with moments of excitement and terror.

suddenly remembered that he needed to be somewhere at 8pm. He remembered that he needed to be sitting on a bench in Chunghwa Park with the Girl with Almond Eyes. He was already late for his date.

He ripped off his clothes and jumped in the shower. Then he got dressed, fixed his hair, and grabbed his Russian coat. In one pocket he placed the bottle of aftershave, he didn't want to risk losing any more of his most valued commodity. In the other pocket he placed the kitchen knife just in case he had to defend himself.

Despite all the uncertainty in his life, despite all the questions surrounding his future at the Ministry of Information, there was one thing of which, he was sure.

Park Jae-bong was not going to die a virgin.

Chapter 37 – The Final Date

It was a fifteen-minute walk to the meeting point with the Girl with the Almond Eyes, but Park was running late[10], so he hailed a taxi. A small but powerful man on a bicycle stopped and Park jumped into the carriage at the back. He told the rider where to go and flashed his identity badge from the Ministry of Information. He warned the rider that he had official government business, so speed was essential.

The bicycle and carriage dodged through the mixed traffic on the roads of Pyongyang. There were horses and carts, big diesel buses and black limousines competing for the smoothest parts of the road. The rider peddled as fast as he could, weaving in and out of the other vehicles and doing his best to avoid the potholes that scarred the road.

During this brief but bumpy journey, Park had a moment to think back to what had happened during the day. He went through all the events that had taken place and all the conversations that he'd had. Slowly but surely, it dawned on[11] him that he was being tricked.

Why had Kang acted in such a sinister manner? Why were the two secret policemen sitting right in his line of sight on the bus? Why had the intruders in his apartment used up some of his aftershave?

---

[10] To run late *(idiom)* - To be behind schedule in your activities.

[11] To dawn on *(phrasal verb)* - To slowly realise the truth about something, like the sun slowly rises above the horizon to give light at the beginning of the day.

It was all too obvious.

If Kang really suspected him, he would have been more subtle about it. If the secret police really wanted to follow him, they could have done it without being noticed. If an intruder really wanted to break into his apartment, he could have done it without leaving a trace.

This was an intimidation tactic, a psychological trap. They wanted to make him feel like he was under suspicion, put him under pressure, force him to make a mistake that would then reveal the truth. He was being tested.

On that short ride, Park realised that all was not lost. He just needed to be careful, strip away the fear and paranoia, and focus on his work. After all, if the authorities really believed he was an accomplice to Kim's crime they would already have arrested him.

The bicycle carriage arrived at its destination and Park jumped out feeling a whole lot better about the world. He thanked the driver for his incomparable speed. Then he headed swiftly towards the bench for his romantic rendezvous[12].

The Girl with the Almond Eyes was sitting alone, dutifully waiting for him. Her chaperone was pacing backwards and forwards in the distance. They both looked pleased to see him when he finally appeared. He sat down on the bench and apologised for being late. He explained that he had been delayed by his work, which was not very far from the truth.

It was their seventh meeting together and they had developed both mutual trust and respect. Their personalities complemented each other. He was serious and introverted, a D level employee at the Ministry of Information, with a tendency to take himself too seriously. She was young and curious, with a good sense of humour and plenty of self-confidence. That evening she was particularly excited to see him again.

---

[12] Rendezvous *(noun)* - A pre-arranged meeting.

"I have some good news for you!" she said, as she looked around to make sure the chaperone wasn't listening. "You have won my family's approval."

"Really?" replied Park.

"They are very impressed with your CV[13] - the double bachelor's degree[14] in maths and physics, the master's degree[15] in computer science, and now the position at the Ministry of Information. Your career progress has been impressive."

Park smiled. He was proud of his resumé but didn't want to appear that way. "My qualifications are not who I am as a person." He said with false modesty.

The girl looked at him flirtatiously.

"Do you know what this means?"

"What?"

"It means that the next time we meet each other, we will be completely alone."

The significance of this news started to sink slowly into Park's brilliant but naïve brain. "Without the chaperone?"

The Girl with the Almond Eyes nodded her head and looked at Park with strange intensity. "You can show me your fridge. You can show me your television. You can show me your bed."

She gently kissed Park's cheek, then she pulled away and looked down at the floor.

Every cell in Park's body came alive. It was as if his whole nervous system was wide awake for the first time in his life. He searched for inspiration, he wanted to arouse her in the way that she

---

[13] Curriculum Vitae (CV) *(noun)* - A written summary of someone's work history, education, skills, and achievements.

[14] Bachelor's degree - A three or four-year course offered at an accredited university.

[15] Master's degree - A one or two-year post-graduate degree offered at an accredited university.

had just aroused him, but no ideas came to him. Eventually three simple words popped out[16] of his mouth.

"I love you."

The girl looked up at him in shock. She put her hand over her mouth and started giggling. She couldn't control herself. She bent over double with laughter. Park joined in. His laugh was nervous. Her laugh was hysterical.

Eventually they calmed down and recovered their composure.

"I love you too," she replied.

There was nothing quite as intoxicating as young love. It could move mountains, make rivers runs backwards and bring the whole world to a stop. But it could also be dangerous, it could lead to foolishness, obsession and in the case of Romeo and Juliet, tragedy.

In this state of euphoria, Park temporarily lost control of his mental faculties. He forgot where he was, who he worked for and how to behave in the People's Democratic Republic of Korea. He made exactly the mistake that the authorities were waiting for.

And the next words that came out of Park's mouth were the last he would ever say as a citizen of the Fatherland.

---

[16] To pop out *(phrasal verb)* - To suddenly appear.

Chapter 38 – In The Moonlight

"Let's escape together." said Park.

The Girl with the Almond eyes smiled back at him. "Not tonight. My auntie is watching. Next time."

Park leaned forward[17] and took hold of her hand. It was small and delicate. The skin was as soft as the petal of a Lilly.

"I don't mean escape from your Auntie; I mean escape from everyone."

"I don't understand." she replied.

"There's another world out there. A world of light and colour. It's beautiful."

"What are you talking about?" she said with genuine confusion.

"I'm talking about a place where we can buy a house, own a car, maybe two, a place where our children will never go hungry."

"Where is this place?"

"The West."

The Girl with the Almond Eyes snatched back[18] her hand. She turned away from Park. The milky white skin of her face wrinkled into an expression of disgust.

---

[17] To lean forward *(phrasal verb)* - To bend your body towards something of interest.

[18] To snatch back *(phrasal verb)* - To aggressively take something from someone.

"Listen to me." said Park lowering his voice to a passionate whisper. "This country is a lie. The Supreme Leader is a fake. We're all being cheated."

The Girl with the Almond eyes didn't react.

"They say that we are fighting a glorious battle against the evil of American capitalism. They say that only through self-reliance and a strong independent state, can true communism be achieved.

Lies. Lies. Lies.

We live a country run by a family of gangsters. We have the highest rates of corruption[19] and lowest level of democracy[20] in the world. The government and bureaucracy is wrapping itself up in red tape[21], while more than 12 million of our fellow citizens suffer from a lack of basic human needs."

Park shifted closer to The Girl with the Almond Eyes and put his hand gently on her shoulder.

---

[19] Corruption *(noun)* - Transparency International is a non-governmental organization (NGO) that has been analysing corruption in business and government across the world since 1995. It defines corruption as the abuse of a public position for personal gain. It ranges from small bribes (secret payments to public official in return for favourable treatment) to large scale election interference. Every year Transparency International publishes a global ranking of corruption. Denmark, Finland, and New Zealand are the least corrupt countries in the world with a score of 88. Somalia, Syria, and South Sudan are at the most corrupt with a score of 11. North Korea has a score of 16.

[20] Democracy *(noun)* - The Economist Intelligence Unit produces an index which ranks countries according to their level of democracy. The rank depends on five main criteria - electoral process, civil liberties, functioning of government, political participation, and political culture. Norway, New Zealand, and Iceland are the most democratic states in the world. Afghanistan, Myanmar, and North Korea are the least democratic, and are considered authoritarian states.

[21] Red tape *(idiom)* - The level of bureaucracy in a political institution. The origin of the expression dates back to the 16th century when Carlos V was running the Spanish Empire, used red tape to bind the most important official documents.

"I can take you away from all this. I can find a way out. We can escape together."

There was a scattering of people around the park, some were on their way home from work, others were doing exercise. In the distance, there was the sound of the big diesel buses ferrying the final passengers to their destinations. Park waited patiently for his new love to react.

Slowly she turned to face him. She looked like a little girl who'd lost her parents at the fairground. She whispered something that Park couldn't hear. Then she whispered it again slightly louder. And then again. Each time increasing the volume. It was a mantra expressed in a monotone.

By the fifth repetition, Park understood what she was saying, and his blood ran cold[22]. He suddenly realised that he had made a terrible misjudgement. He'd taken his eye off the ball[23] and put his own life in mortal danger.

The words that the Girl with the Almond Eyes was repeating were: "Traitor. Traitor. Traitor…" By the tenth repetition, she was shouting. By the fifteenth, she was screaming. People in the park started to notice.

The girl's chaperone appeared from behind a tree and ran towards her in a state of panic. She grabbed hold of her niece and shook her until she stopped screaming. They had a brief conversation and then the older woman looked at Park in disbelief.

Without a second's hesitation the chaperone ran to the nearest person in the park, got their attention and pointed at Park. Then she ran to the next nearest person and did the same. Each one of the people the chaperone spoke to, did exactly the same thing as her. In this way the news of Park's treachery spread like a virus.

---

[22] Blood runs cold *(idiom)* - To be filled with great fear or horror.

[23] To take your eye off the ball *(idiom)* - To stop concentrating on something important.

Every North Korean knew that, if you were aware of a crime, you had to report it immediately, otherwise, you would suffer the same fate as the criminal. By a simple law of probability, the news would eventually reach the member of the secret police who was closest to the crime. No form of communication in a totalitarian state[24] was faster and more efficient than word of mouth[25].

Park was frozen to the spot. It seemed like the whole of Pyongyang was pointing at him. In the distance, he saw two suited men running in his direction. Park needed to deal with the immediate danger.

He looked at the Girl with the Almond Eyes, standing like a withered sapling[26] in front of him. Was this the last time he would ever see her? If so, he had nothing to lose. He stepped forward, pulled her towards him and kissed her passionately on the lips. He felt her body relax in his arms and start to tremble. And for a very moment the world stopped, and a beam of moonlight shone from the heavens on the two young lovers.

Shouts in the distance brought Park back to the harsh reality of his current predicament. He placed The Girl with Almond Eyes gently back onto the bench.

"Goodbye Song Sook-Ja," he said tenderly.

Then he ran as fast as he could in the direction of the taxi stand. He spotted the rider that had brought him to the park earlier that evening and jumped into the back of the carriage.

"Take me to Jungi Forest!" He shouted. "I have more government business to take care of. So, make it fast!"

---

[24] Totalitarian state *(adjective noun)* - A government with total power over its subjects, controlling their activities, movement, speech, and every other aspect of their lives.

[25] Word of mouth *(idiom)* - The passing of information from person to person using oral communication.

[26] Withered sapling *(adjective noun)* - A sapling is a small, immature tree that is between 90 cm to 3 metres. If something is withered, it is dry and decaying.

THE ADVENTURES OF LOLA BADIOLA

"Yes sir," the rider replied. He headed off down the main road at full speed dodging in and out of the evening traffic with breathtaking skill. Park looked back and could see a group of people gathering around the taxi stand, trying to work out where he had disappeared to. He ducked down[27] in the carriage so that no-one could see him.

As he lay on his side, he knew that there was only one course of action he could take, there was only one way to survive this situation. He had no choice but to assume the identity of his best friend Kim Dae-won, and carry out[28] his original plan of escape.

---

[27] To duck down *(phrasal verb)* - To move your head or the top part of your body quickly down, especially to avoid being hit.

[28] To carry out *(phrasal verb)* - To perform a task as intended.

SAM GRATTON

Chapter 39 – Good News and Bad News for Lola

Lola sat in the back of a Cabify taxi, on the way to meet Gonzalo Garrido at his law offices in Vallecas. They had agreed to meet at 5pm, but the M-30 ring road around Madrid was hardly moving. Lola hated arriving late to meetings. She sent a text message to Gonzalo explaining why she wouldn't be there on time, saying that she hoped to arrive by 5.30pm. Then she sat back in the taxi and ruminated on the events of the last couple of days.

The CyberStory article was now yesterday's news. No-one at the company was talking about it. Nobody was questioning Lola's loyalty or integrity. They were all too busy dealing with the recent intrusion into their systems.

JJ and Diego were at the office twenty-four seven[29], supported by the team of programmers who were working on a rotational basis. The programmers were split into three teams. The first team was responsible for finding the mysterious hacker, Pluto. The second was in charge of upgrading the company's software. And the third continued to work on designing new products. There was a sense of urgency in the office as the JBlock employees came together to fight this new and unknown threat.

The only person who was not part of the team effort was Cayetano. He sat quietly in the marketing department, observing all that was happening around him. Since Lola had first met Cayetano

---

[29] Twenty-four seven *(idiom)* - Short for twenty-four hours a day, seven days a week, used to emphasise that an action is continuous.

she had been equally attracted to him as repelled by him. But after their last team meeting, she had seen him for what he truly was, a snake in the grass[30].

As her Cabify taxi continued to crawl around the M-30 ring road, Lola thought about the upcoming meeting with her lawyer and friend Gonzalo Garrido. Up to this point, Gonzalo had been a Godsend[31]. He seemed to know how to handle the Cyberworld article, the situation with TechSpania and the investigation by Interpol. However, in his recent message he sounded less assured. He asked her to come to his office as soon as was practically possible. He said that there was both good news and bad news.

At last, the traffic cleared, and as Lola had predicted, she eventually arrived in Vallecas at 5.30pm. She sat down in the reception of the law firm and started flicking through a legal magazine that was on the table next to her. There was nothing particularly interesting in it, but she wanted to keep her mind occupied and distracted.

After a couple of minutes Gonzalo arrived, kissed her on the cheek and guided her to his office at the back of the building. They exchanged some small talk before Lola moved the meeting onto more serious matters.

"You said that there was good news and bad news."

Gonzalo sat forward in his chair and rested his elbows on the desk in front of him.

"Yes, let's start with the good news. Interpol won't be pursuing any action against you. You won't be charged, and you won't have

---

[30] Snake in the grass *(idiom)* - Someone who is a hidden danger.

[31] Godsend *(noun)* - Something that you didn't expect to receive but is extremely useful for whatever cause you are fighting, as if it were a gift from the gods.

to defend yourself in criminal court. As we thought, they don't have enough evidence and anyway, they have bigger fish to fry[32]."

Lola felt elated. This was the first positive piece of news that she had received since she started at JBlock. The sensation only lasted a few seconds because she could see from the expression on Gonzalo's face that all was not well.

"So, what's the bad news?"

"The bad news is that TechSpania have decided to pursue a civil case[33] against you."

"What does that mean?"

"That means that you will have to defend yourself in civil court against the charges of corporate espionage. TechSpania are claiming that you stole confidential information and passed it on to competitors and cybercriminals. They are arguing that this has had a tangible negative impact on the company's value."

Lola shook her head in dismay.

"They are suing[34] you for 150 million euros in damages[35]."

Lola's dismay turned to disbelief.

"What? That's crazy."

"It might sound crazy," explained Gonzalo, "but it's legally justifiable. The share price of TechSpania hasn't recovered since the recent attack. Hundreds of millions of euros have been wiped off the value of the company."

---

[32] Bigger fish to fry *(idiom)* - Somebody with power and influence might be called a "big fish". If you have bigger fish to fry, it means that you have more important things or people to consider and pursue.

[33] Civil case *(adjective noun)* - A disagreement between two parties, such as a breach of contract, that will be decided by a judge in civil court.

[34] To sue *(verb)* - To take someone to civil court and demand compensation for actions that have negatively and unjustly impacted you.

[35] Damages *(noun)* - Money paid for injury or loss. The amount is determined by a judge in a civil court.

Gonzalo stood up and walked to the glass door of his office. He looked into the hallway to make sure nobody was listening. Then he turned back to Lola and said:

"I need to ask you a personal question."

Lola was lost in thought and didn't respond. Gonzalo continued:

"What assets[36] do you have Lola? I need to know what's at risk here."

Lola was quiet. She thought about her father and all the legal battles that he had faced in his career. She needed to be more like him. She needed to put her emotions to one side and remain objective.

"My father owned 51% of Grupo Badiola," said Lola "When he died, he left half of that to my mother and half to me."

"So, you own 25.5% of Grupo Badiola."

"Yes. But I'm a silent partner[37]. I pass all my voting rights[38] over to my mother. She has ultimate control of the company."

"And how much is Grupo Badiola worth?"

"It's a private enterprise so it's difficult to say."

Gonzalo took out a note pad and a piece of paper.

"What were the operating profits[39] for the last three years?"

---

[36] Assets *(noun)* - What you own that has some value, be it tangible or intangible. It is a resource that will provide a future benefit. A company's assets will be listed on the balance sheet of their annual report. For example, factories, machines, and land.

[37] Silent partner *(adjective noun)* - Somebody who has partial ownership of an asset or business but wishes to have no active involvement in the managing of that asset or business.

[38] Voting rights *(adjective noun)* - Anyone who is an ordinary shareholder of a company has voting rights, giving them the power to elect directors at annual or special meetings and make their views known to company management. The more shares someone owns, the more voting rights they have and the greater influence they carry in the decision making of the company.

[39] Operating profits *(adjective noun)* - The amount of money that the company receives in product sales, minus all the costs related to the creation of those product sales.

THE ADVENTURES OF LOLA BADIOLA

"They've been quite flat, ranging between 50 and 55 million euros a year."

Gonzalo typed something into his computer.

"Ok, food and drinks companies listed on the Spanish stock exchange trade on a multiple[40] of 11 times operating profits. Let's assume that this is the case for Grupo Badiola. That means, at the low end of the range, the company is worth 11 x 50 million euros which equals 550 million euros."

Gonzalo took out a calculator.

"Your stake is therefore 25.5% of 550 million euros."

He plugged in the numbers.

"That equates to 140.25 million euros."

Gonzalo put down the calculator and looked up at Lola.

"It's no coincidence that Ruiz de Velasco is suing you for 150 million euros. He knows what your holding in Grupo Badiola is worth. And he wants it all."

Lola sat in silence absorbing the implications of the lawsuit.

Grupo Badiola had been founded by her father forty years ago. He had worked like hell, taken risks and made many sacrifices along the way. In doing so, he had turned a small distributor of anchovies into a global food and drinks empire.

When he died, he had passed control of the business to his wife and daughter for safe-keeping. It was their responsibility to continue to nurture the company for the benefit of future generations.

Lola knew exactly how much her 25.5% stake[41] in Grupo Badiola was worth, but she never considered that it truly belonged to her.

---

[40] Financial multiples *(adjective noun)* - A valuation tool based on ratios from a company's financial data, to illustrate the health of the company and compare it to others in the same sector.

[41] Stake *(noun)* - An interest in something. If you have a stake in a company, then you will benefit if the company succeeds and you will lose if the company fails. Shareholders, employees, suppliers, local communities are all examples of company stakeholders.

She was simply a guardian of what her father had created and what her children would inherit.

And now all that was under threat. If Lola had to sell her stake to finance the legal damages, the family would lose control of the business. Her mother would be unable to direct the actions of the other shareholders. And the legacy would be lost forever.

Chapter 40 – Pretty Boy

Cayetano sat at his desk eating an apple. It was late evening, and JBlock was quiet. A small group of programmers were tapping away on their keyboards, completely oblivious to his existence.

He unbuttoned the top of his shirt and took out the small golden cross that was hanging at the end of his necklace. He was Catholic by birth but had long since given up practicing Christianity. He held the cold, smooth metal between his thumb and forefinger as he contemplated his next move.

At the other end of the room, JJ and Diego were deep in discussion. The door to JJ's office was slightly open and Cayetano could hear the murmurs of the conversation within, but he was unable to understand anything that was being said.

He took a final bite of his apple and then walked over to the rubbish bin that was nearest to JJ's office. He stood there, hidden from their sight, but close enough to hear the discussion.

"No trace[42] of Pluto," said Diego. "Nobody has heard of him. The guy's a ghost."

"So, who do we think he is?"

"There are only two options. An anonymous hacker working for a hostile government. Or an inside job."

There was a long pause.

---

[42] No trace *(idiom)* - A trace is a sign that someone or something has been present. If there is no trace of something it means, there is no evidence of its existence.

"Ok." replied JJ quietly.

He walked over to the window of his office and looked down at Gran Vía below. It was full of people coming and going. There were tourists discovering the centre of Madrid, groups of teenagers shouting and screaming, and young couples on the way to enjoy a romantic meal for Valentine's Day.

JJ turned back to Diego.

"I'm running out[43] of money."

His voice betrayed a tone of vulnerability that Diego had never heard before. He continued.

"We've fallen a long way behind the business plan."

He opened a printout that his accountant had prepared for him and flicked though[44] some of the pages.

"On the revenue side, we'd projected income streams[45] from January, with a steady monthly increase throughout the year. In reality, we don't have a single client signed up. We don't have anyone on the horizon."

He turned to another page of the report.

"On the cost side, we're running about fifty percent above budget since I started paying everyone overtime to search for Pluto."

He threw the report onto the table in front of him.

"The cash burn[46] is killing me, Diego."

Diego stroked his big bushy beard and thought for a moment. Then he said:

---

[43] To run out *(phrasal verb)* - To have no more of a resource.

[44] To flick through *(phrasal verb)* - "To flick" is to move or hit something with a short sudden movement. To "flick through" is to quickly scan or read a magazine or book by turning the pages with short sudden movements.

[45] Income streams *(noun)* - The movement of money from various sources flowing into a company.

[46] Cash burn *(noun)* - The rate at which a start-up company is spending its initial investment capital on the running of the business before it starts generating revenue and making profits.

"We could reduce costs. For a start we don't need to be in this big, fancy office."

JJ shook his head.

"I signed a long-term lease with the landlord."

Diego suggested another option.

"We could stop working overtime. We could even take a pay cut."

Once again, JJ shook his head.

"Even if we reduce costs to a bare minimum, it doesn't make the business viable. For that we need a source of revenue, we need to make some sales, we need to find some God-damn clients."

JJ ran his fingers through his hair, took a deep breath and then sat down on his chair. He leaned back with his hands behind his head.

Cayetano leaned closer to the open door to ensure that he could hear every word that was being said. He needed to know exactly what was happening to the business, what they thought about Lola, and what they planned to do next.

The two managers were speaking quietly and Cayetano had to strain his ears to hear the words. He hadn't noticed that the keyboard typing around him had stopped. He hadn't noticed that all the programmers were now silently staring at him.

"What are you doing, Pretty Boy?" asked Van Dyck.

Cayetano looked up in surprise.

"Are you lost?" asked Velázquez.

Like any consummate salesman, Cayetano was able to think on his feet[47]. "My apple core." He said, regaining his composure. He showed them the remains of his fruit and then threw it into the nearest rubbish bin. Then he flashed them all a diamond white smile and walked back to his desk.

---

[47] To think on your feet *(idiom)* - To be able to respond quickly to changing circumstances. For example, when a public speaker is able to answer spontaneous questions from an audience.

Little by little, the noise of typing once again filled the office as the programmers got back to work.

Cayetano sat down, took out his iPhone and scrolled down his contact list.

Then he sent the following message:

"It's time!"

QUIZ TIME

Chapters 36 to 40

COMPREHENSION QUIZ

Answer the questions with complete sentences. Say them out loud.

1. What are the three layers of law enforcement in North Korea and how do they differ?
2. Why was Park so upset that his aftershave had been used?
3. What conclusion did Park come to about his predicament, on the ride to Chung Hwa Park?
4. What news does the Girl with the Almond Eyes have for Park? How does he react to this news?
5. How does the Girl react when he asks her to go to the West with him? Why does she react like this?
6. What happens when the Chaperone hears about Park's proposal?
7. What good news does Lola receive from Gonzalo? And what bad news does she receive from him?
8. How does Gonzalo calculate the value of Lola's stake in Grupo Badiola?
9. How does Lola feel about her substantial financial position in Grupo Badiola?
10. What are JJ and Diego quietly discussing at the offices of JBlock?

THE ADVENTURES OF LOLA BADIOLA

BUSINESS ENGLISH QUIZ

Complete the sentences with the words used in the story.

1. Despite the poverty of rural Spain in the mid-20th century, my mother and father were always able to P_____ B_____ on the T_____ and support their family.

2. This is a very impressive C_____ V_____. The candidate got a first-class B_____ D_____ in economics, before taking a one-year M_____ D_____ in econometrics. I think she would be perfect for the role of junior analyst.

3. If you want to build a factory just outside of Shanghai, you have to be aware of all the R_____ T_____ required to obtain permission from the local authorities.

4. We don't advertise in magazines or on television. The growth of our business comes from recommendations and W_____-O_____-M_____.

5. Since I launched my company 18 months ago, I have been working T_____-F_____ S_____ to make a success of this business and, at last, we have started to make profits.

6. Why are you focusing on this small domestic account? There are much B_____ F_____ to F_____ in the international market.

7. Our competitor is pursuing a C_____ C_____ against us, they claim that we copied their idea, and they are S_____ us for $50 million worth of D_____.

8. In any law firm, the most important A_____ is the people - their knowledge, connections, and expertise.

247

9. I would like to remain a S_____ P_____ in this new business venture. I will provide the money required but I will let you manage the day-to-day operations.

10. The O_____ P_____ of our start-up company have been growing at 20% per year, and we are now able to pay our shareholders dividends for the first time.

11. The most common F_____ M_____ for assessing the profitability of a company relative to its competitors is the operating profit margin. We divide the operating profit of the company by its revenues and multiply the result by a hundred.

12. Everybody has a S_____ in the company - shareholders, employees, suppliers, and the local community. If we allow it to go bankrupt, we will all suffer the consequences.

13. Our company has three I_____ S_____. The first is our online business English platform, the second is our public speaking workshops and the third is our keynote speaking activities.

14. We need to reduce the C_____ B_____ of our company as we are quickly running out of initial capital, and we still don't have enough revenue to cover our ongoing costs.

15. When you make a speech at a conference, it is often the Q&A that is the most stressful because you have to T_____ on your F_____.

THE ADVENTURES OF LOLA BADIOLA

ANSWERS TO COMPREHENSION QUIZ

1. The first layer of law-enforcement in North Korea is the official police, who are responsible for investigating everyday crimes. The second layer is the secret police, who are responsible for ensuring all citizens comply with the rules of the state. The third layer is the Special Operations Forces (SOF), who are in charge of the protection of the supreme leader.

2. Park is so upset about the fact that his aftershave has been used because it is not only a treasured possession and very valuable by North Korean standards, but also a symbol of who he is as an independent human being.

3. Park realises that if the authorities thought he was guilty of aiding his friend Kim to escape from North Korea, they would have already arrested him. As he is still free, he believes that he is under suspicion and being watched but not considered guilty of any crimes.

4. The Girl with the Almond Eyes tells Park that this is the last time that they will be accompanied by a chaperone on their dates, which means that they can become more intimate. Park is thrilled by this news and momentarily forgets the danger that's around him.

5. When Park asks the girl to go to the West with him, her immediate reaction is disbelief, which then turns into disgust. Like most North Koreans, she believes the propaganda about the West and now considers Park to be a traitor to the Fatherland.

6. As soon as the chaperone hears about Parks plan, she informs the people around her, as it is her duty to immediately report any crime that threatens the state.

7. The good news that Lola receives from Gonzalo is that Interpol will not be pursuing criminal charges against her, as they don't

have enough evidence and they are focused on bigger cases. The bad news, that Lola receives from Gonzalo, is that TechSpania will be pursuing a civil case against her for the negative impact her actions have had on the company's share price.

8. Gonzalo makes a simple calculation about the value of Lola's stake in Grupo Badiola. He multiplies the operating profit of the company by the financial multiple that is used to value other companies in the same sector, to reach a value of €550 million euros. He then multiplies this number by 25.5%, the percentage of the company that Lola owns, to reach a value of €140.25 million.

9. Lola doesn't think that her stake in Grupo Badiola truly belongs to her. She feels that she is simply the temporary guardian of this asset for future generations of her family.

10. JJ and Diego are quietly discussing the future of JBlock. JJ is voicing his concerns about the potential for the company to get its first client and compete with TechSpania in the Cybersecurity market.

ANSWERS TO BUSINESS ENGLISH QUIZ

1. Despite the poverty of rural Spain in the mid-20th century, my mother and father were always able to PUT BREAD ON THE TABLE and support our family.

2. This is a very impressive CURRICULM VITAE. The candidate got a first-class BACHELOR'S DEGREE in economics before taking a one-year MASTER'S DEGREE in econometrics. I think she would be perfect for the role of junior analyst.

3. If you want to build a factory just outside of Shanghai, you have to be aware of all the RED TAPE required to obtain permission from the local authorities.

4. We don't advertise in magazines or on television. The growth of our business comes from recommendations and WORD OF MOUTH.

5. Since I launched my company 18 months ago, I have been working TWENTY-FOUR SEVEN to make a success of this business and, at last, we have started to make profits.

6. Why are you focusing on this small domestic account? There are much BIGGER FISH TO FRY in the international market.

7. Our competitor is pursuing a CIVIL CASE against us. They claim that we copied their idea, and they are SUING us for $50 million worth of DAMAGES.

8. In any law firm, the most important ASSET is the people - their knowledge, connections, and expertise.

9. I would like to remain a SILENT PARTNER in this new business venture. I will provide the money required but I will let you manage the day-to-day operations.

10. The OPERATING PROFITS of our start-up company have been growing at 20% per year, and we are now able to pay our shareholders dividends for the first time.

11. The most common FINANCIAL MULTIPLE for assessing the profitability of a company relative to its competitors is the operating profit margin. We divide the operating profit of the company by its revenues and multiply the result by a hundred.

12. Everybody has a STAKE in the company - shareholders, employees, suppliers, and the local community. If we allow it to go bankrupt, we will all suffer the consequences.

13. Our company has three INCOME STREAMS. The first is our online business English platform, the second is our public speaking workshops and the third is our keynote speaking activities.

14. We need to reduce the CASH BURN of our company as we are quickly running out of initial capital, and we still don't have enough revenue to cover our ongoing costs.

15. When you make a speech at a conference it is often the Q&A that is the most stressful because you have to THINK ON YOUR FEET.

SAM GRATTON

"Welcome to Dead Man's Highway."
The Old Grey Man

Chapter 41 – Richard Gere

Lola arrived back at her apartment in Malasaña at 9pm. She had gone for a quick drink with Gonzalo following their meeting. They both needed to wind down[1] after the discussion about finances.

Lola decided to keep the news of the civil lawsuit from her mother for the time being. The involvement of Perla Manchón would only add melodrama to the story. Lola needed to think clearly and independently.

As she inserted the key into the front door, she heard a familiar voice behind her.

"Hey!"

"Concha! What are you doing here?"

"It's St. Valentine's Day. And I'm your date."

"What?"

"What do you fancy? Chinese? Indian? There's a new Lebanese around the corner."

Concha was in one of her irrepressible moods and Lola decided to go with the flow[2]. Neither of them had partners in town, so it seemed like a good plan. Concha was not only a great teller of

---

[1] To wind down *(phrasal verb)* - To relax. To release all the pressure and stress after a period of work of activity.

[2] To go with the flow *(idiom)* - To be relaxed and willing to accept the situation and circumstances in which you find yourself and the decisions made by others.

anecdotes and jokes, but she was also a patient listener. This would be an opportunity for Lola to externalise all her thoughts and ideas. It would help her clarify a way forward.

"Lebanese."

"Perfect."

Maroush, the new restaurant on the corner of Carranza and Monteleón, was packed with thirtysomethings[3] who lived locally. The noise, colour and smells of the place were intoxicating. The two friends ordered a selection of breads, sauces, and meats from the menu.

"Do you prefer red or white wine?" asked Lola.

"I'm not drinking tonight."

"No?"

"Actually, I'm not drinking for the next seven months."

Lola looked up from the wine menu. "No way!" she screamed.

"Yes way! I visited the doctor this morning."

"I can't believe it!"

Lola jumped out of her chair and gave Concha the hug of her life.

"I'm so happy for you both!"

She felt tears of happiness streaming down from her eyes.

"Does Eugenio know?"

"Yeah, I managed to contact him somewhere in the wilderness."

It was the most wonderful news that Lola could have imagined. Her two friends had been trying for ages to get pregnant. She was convinced that they were both going to be amazing parents.

For the next hour, the two women planned the birth, education, and marriage of the unborn baby. If he was a boy, he would be tall, like his father, attain a basketball scholarship to Yale University, marry young and have half a dozen children. If she was a girl, she would be petite but powerful, start her own online business and win the Nobel peace prize. As the dishes of Lebanese delights came and

---

[3] Thirtysomethings *(noun)* - People who are in their 30s.

went, they discussed all the activities that the pregnant couple would need to complete in preparation for the new arrival, until eventually, they ran out of ideas and Concha changed the subject.

"Hey! I saw your Mum yesterday."

"Oh."

"Does she have a new man in her life?"

"I don't think so. Why?"

"I was stuck in some traffic on Serrano, and I saw her walking into a restaurant with a Richard Gere lookalike[4]."

"Richard Gere?"

"Yeah, you know, tall, confident, silver hair. Old but extremely sexy."

Lola burst into laughter. "My Mum has a few companions, but I don't think any of them are serious."

Perla Manchón was a businesswoman and a socialite. When she wasn't overseeing the activities of Grupo Badiola as the Chairman of the Board, she was attending charity events, modern art exhibitions and fashion shows. If there was a party featured in Hola magazine, Perla would have an invitation for it, often accompanied by an eligible CEO, aristocrat or intellectual.

Lola wasn't concerned about her mother at that moment. She had more pressing matters on her mind that she needed to talk about. She was no longer speaking to a therapist, so Concha was the next best thing.

"Listen Concha, I'm in a bit of trouble at the moment."

"Really? Tell me about it."

For the next two hours, Lola and her best friend discussed everything that was happening in Lola's professional life - the article in CyberStory magazine, the interview with Interpol, the lawsuit

---

[4] Lookalike *(noun)* - Someone or something that is similar in appearance to someone or something else. An interesting synonym is the word "doppelgänger", borrowed from the German language that literally translates into "double-walker".

from TechSpania, the rejection by Banco Cantábrico and the office politics[5] of Cayetano Tolosa.

Concha listened carefully, offering sympathy and advice, firing Lola up[6] when she sounded depressed, spurring her on[7] when she sounded unsure. It helped Lola release the pressure that had been building up for the previous two weeks. It helped her to put things into perspective. But it didn't solve any of the fundamental problems. How was she going to succeed at JBlock? How was she going to respond to the civil lawsuit from TechSpania? How was she going to protect the future of Grupo Badiola?

The two women were so engrossed in their conversation that they were unaware that the restaurant had emptied, and they were the last two customers. The waiter asked them if they would like some chupitos on the house[8], but they hadn't had a single drop of alcohol all evening, so they politely declined and asked for the bill.

"Why don't you sleep over at my place tonight?"

"I'd love to, but I've got a busy day tomorrow."

"Ok, well, come over this weekend."

"Sure."

The two women walked arm in arm through the pedestrian streets of Malasaña. There were still plenty of people wandering from one bar to another, impervious to the cold, dry air of the February night. There was no better country than Spain to get pregnant and start a family. Lola was reminded of the important things in life and for a moment her troubles seemed very far away.

---

[5] Office politics *(noun)* - Activities performed by individuals at work to improve their status and advance their personal agenda, sometimes at the expense of others.

[6] To fire up *(phrasal verb)* - To motivate and inspire somebody so they feel passionate or emotional about something.

[7] To spur on *(phrasal verb)* - To encourage somebody to move forwards or to accelerate.

[8] On the house *(idiom)* - When a bar or restaurant offers you a free drink to demonstrate how much they value your custom.

"So, you really think my Mum is dating Richard Gere?"
"A Spanish version."
"Even better," said Lola with a smile.

SAM GRATTON

Chapter 42 – The Tomb of the Glorious Farmer

Park remained hidden in the bicycle carriage until the rider had taken him beyond the streetlights of the city. It was a clear night, and the moon illuminated the way into the empty countryside. It wasn't long before the urban sounds diminished, and all Park could hear was the squeaking of an unoiled bicycle chain and the panting of his diligent[9] rider.

It was a bitterly[10] cold night. The temperature was just above freezing but the humidity made it feel a lot harsher. Park pulled the enormous collar of his Russian army coat around his head so that only his eyes and forehead protruded from the material. He sat silently in the carriage, looking out into the shadowy trees that lined the route into Jungi Forest.

"Keep going until we reach the Tomb of the Glorious Farmer."

The rider of the carriage acknowledged his instructions with a grunt.

As each kilometre passed, the road became more potholed. The rider had to weave from one side to the other in order to avoid the deepest cracks. Eventually the surface disappeared entirely to leave a rutted pathway that only a horse could navigate.

"This is as far as I can go."

---

[9] Diligent *(adjective)* - Hard-working. Performing a task with a lot of care and attention.

[10] Bitterly *(adverb)* - In a resentful and angry way.

"How far is it from here?[11]"

"About 2 kilometers."

"Ok, wait here."

"Yes sir."

Park jumped out of the carriage, stretched his legs, and then continued his journey on foot, into the darkness and the wilderness of the unwelcoming forest.

The Tomb of the Glorious Farmer was built in 1999, following the great famine[12] of the previous five years. Nobody knew how many peasants had died during the period of mass starvation, but the estimates were between 240,000 and 3.5 million. The government had labelled it "The March of Suffering" blaming the shortage of food on foreign enemies - the Japanese, the Capitalists, or the Imperialists. The Tomb commemorated this noble struggle against the forces of evil.

Park knew the truth. He had read about it from a wide variety of international sources. It was a homemade disaster. The result of economic mismanagement, political isolation, and endemic corruption.

In the winter of 1996, hundreds of thousands of starving peasants had made their way from their drought ridden and infertile lands to the outskirts of Pyongyang. This was not a revolution, it

---

[11] How far is it from here? *(Interrogative)* - An interrogative structure concerning distances. Try to use this structure rather than "How many kilometres are there?" which is often used by non-native speakers.

[12] The great famine *(history)* - North Korea experienced a catastrophic famine in the mid-1990s that killed hundreds of thousands if not millions of citizens. During that time, the country pursued an economic policy of self-reliance. North Koreans were expected to feed themselves without any form of international trade. In 1995 and 1996 there were extreme weather patterns that led to flooding across the generally infertile farming lands. Whatever food was produced went to the elites and to the military. This left the peasants who made up the majority of the North Korean population suffering from mass starvation.

was not an attempt to overthrow the government, it was a desperate cry for help.

The pathetic mass of humanity had been blocked by the military. They were prevented from entering the gates of city and left to perish at the perimeter of Pyongyang. The piles of dead bodies were collected in trucks and dumped in mass graves in Jungi Forest.

As Park made his way along the path that led to the Tomb, he shuddered at the thought of the bones that were buried beneath his feet and the lost souls that floated between the trees.

Amongst the dead were his mother, his father, and his little sister Dal-Rae.

Where were they now?

What part of this god-forsaken graveyard did they occupy?

It was starting to get light by the time Park arrived at the monument. It was a pyramid consisting of 1996 blocks of stone about 20 metres high. At each apex was the statue of Chollima, a mythical winged horse, too rapid to be ridden by any mortal. An ironic symbol of North Korea's economic future.

In the years since the tomb had been built, the country had moved on, reforms had been made and further famines narrowly avoided. Two Supreme leaders had come and gone, and the current dictator wanted to distance his regime from the apocalyptic events of the 1990s. Consequently, the monument was no longer celebrated or even mentioned. It was left to decay and fall into ruin. It was only prevented from disappearing into the forest by the relatives who, like Park, came to pay their respects to the loved ones that they had lost.

Park sat at the foot of one of the statues and meditated. He journeyed deep into his childhood memories:

I am in a field planting seeds with my father. I'm in the house washing plates with my mother. I'm catching cockroaches with my sister.

We march with many others to the city.

Now I'm in a windowless orphanage[13]. A man from the government visits. He tests our physical and mental abilities.

I am moved to a boarding school[14]. There is the soap, hot water, and clean bedsheets.

I receive classes in maths, physics, and computer science. I excel. I am the best in the class, the best in the school, the best that they have ever taught.

The other children bully me[15]. They call me "The Peasant". They attack me while I'm sleeping.

I win a place at a prestigious University. I obtain a master's degree in physics. I am recruited by the cybercrime division of the North Korean government.

Park curled up at the foot of the monument, wrapped up in his Russian Army coat, and fell into a restless sleep, the memories of his life flashing before him in an abstract and mixed-up manner. He had journeyed to the Tomb of the Glorious Farmer to bid a final farewell to his family. He was closing one chapter before the next was opened.

As the sun rose on a bright winter's morning, two agents from the Special Operations Force, North Korea's finest and bravest soldiers, quietly observed Park's sleeping body.

---

[13] Orphanage *(noun)* - A home for children whose parents are dead or unable to care for them.

[14] Boarding school *(adjective noun)* - A school where students both study and live.

[15] To bully *(verb)* - The act of hurting or frightening someone, often over a period of time, and often making them do things that they do not want to do.

Chapter 43 – Checkpoint

The rider was exactly where Park had left him, where the tarmac of the road into Jungi Forest disintegrated. He was asleep in the carriage wrapped up[16] in a thick blanket that he kept under the passenger's seat. He was awoken by the sound of Park's return. He got out of the carriage and put away[17] the blanket. Then he pulled out a small container of food and offered Park some kimchi and dumplings.

Despite Park's hunger, he politely declined. It was the North Korean way to always refuse the first offer of kindness. The rider insisted and this time Park accepted. The two men sat silently munching[18] the spicy vegetables and doughy carbohydrates, and then the rider turned to Park and said:

"My family is buried here too."

Park stopped chewing[19] and looked carefully at his companion.

"What's your name?

"Hyun."

---

[16] To wrap up *(phrasal verb)* - To cover or enclose something in material. It has a second and unrelated meaning in business English which is to bring a meeting or event to a quick conclusion.

[17] To put away *(phrasal verb)* - To put something in the place where you usually keep it when you are not using it.

[18] To munch *(verb)* - To eat something steadily and often noisily.

[19] To chew *(verb)* - The process of crushing food between the teeth within the mouth to make it easier to swallow.

"Do you know where Banshori station is?"

Hyun nodded his head, "My wife is originally from Banshori. Some of her family still live there."

"Can you take me there?"

Hyun thought about it for a while, as if he were imagining the route from Jungi Forest to the station.

"It's a four-hour[20] journey if the weather is good and there aren't any checkpoints."

"We can take it in turns."

Hyun looked at Park quizzically.

"I can ride half of the way there."

Hyun shook his head and laughed.

"I insist."

Hyun stopped laughing. He could see that Park was entirely serious. So, he accepted the generous proposal.

Without any further discussion, they left Jungi Forest, heading North-East away from Pyongyang and in the direction of Park's rendezvous point with the Old Grey Man at Banshori station. They agreed that Hyun would ride the first half of the journey and Park the second.

Park knew that he was now very vulnerable. He couldn't be sure about how much information Kim had told the authorities about the escape plan. It was possible they knew nothing of the meeting at Banshori station, Dead Man's Highway, and the border crossing. It was possible that Kim had given them a completely different story, in order to protect all the accomplices to his crime. But it was more likely that they had tortured some of the details out of him. If that were the case, there would be policemen waiting for Park at various points along the way. He had to be extremely vigilant.

The carriage started ascending a long and winding country road and it was clear that Hyun was tiring. Park leaned forward and

---

[20] Four-hour journey *(compound number adjective)* - Remember to include the dash and express it in the singular form.

tapped him on the shoulder, it was time for them to swap over[21]. Park lowered the seat, as he was shorter than Hyun, then he pushed down on the pedals and got the carriage moving again. It was significantly harder than he had imagined. The chain needed oiling, the wheels were slightly bent and the whole machine seemed to weigh a ton. By the time he reached the crest of the hill, he was panting like a dog on a hot summer's day. He gave the pedals one last big push to take it over the top of the hill and allow the momentum to take it back down the other side.

As the bicycle carriage accelerated downhill, Park stopped pedalling, sat up in the seat and looked around. From this high point in the landscape, he could see the road winding back down the other side of the hill. At the bottom of the valley, he saw something that shocked him.

There was a police checkpoint positioned at a crossroads, with a line of vehicles moving slowly through it. Park immediately squeezed the brakes of the bicycle as hard as he could. It was an instinctive reaction to avoid the danger ahead. But the carriage didn't slow down[22]. In fact, it continued to accelerate under its own inertia as the gradient of the hill became more pronounced.

Park squeezed and released the brakes three more times, but still the carriage would not slow down. He started to panic. He turned back to Hyun and shouted.

"The brakes don't work. I can't stop it!"

"Don't worry," replied Hyun, perplexed by Park's state of anxiety. "We'll slow down as soon as we reach the bottom of the hill, and it flattens out[23]."

---

[21] To swap over *(phrasal verb)* - To exchange places, roles, or activities.

[22] To slow down / to speed up *(phrasal verb)* - To slow down simply means to decelerate and to speed up to accelerate.

[23] To flatten out *(phrasal verb)* - To stop rising or falling and stay at the same level. It is used quite frequently, in investment reports or economic analysis, when talking about the trend of a particular price. For example, you might say

Park ignored the advice and continued to frantically squeeze the brakes until they reached the bottom of the hill and, exactly as Hyun had predicted, the carriage slowed down to a stop just behind a big diesel bus that was waiting at the crossroads to be inspected.

Park watched as the police walked onboard the bus, moving slowly up and down the central aisle, looking into the eyes of all the passengers. Then the officers jumped off the bus and waved the driver on. They motioned for Park to move forwards.

He did as they instructed until he was surrounded by policemen. He could feel the sweat of his palms on the handlebars of his bicycle. He sat still and looked straight forwards, avoiding eye contact with anyone else.

The policemen weren't interested in him. Instead, they leaned forward and looked very closely at Hyun, who was sitting comfortably in the passenger seat.

"Where are you going?"

"Banshori," said Hyun.

"Why are you going there?"

"My mother-in-law is sick."

"What is her address?"

"The house on the corner of Ponghwa and Kyonghung."

Satisfied that he was not the man they were looking for, the policemen waved them on without another word. Park pushed down hard on the bicycle pedals, but the carriage wouldn't move. He had no power left in his skinny little legs after the exertion of the hill ascent and the panic of the descent.

The policemen shouted at him to move on. Once again Park pushed down with all his might but the front wheel was trapped behind a stone and the carriage wouldn't move.

---

the house prices have started to flatten out after their steady decline during the economic recession.

THE ADVENTURES OF LOLA BADIOLA

The policemen walked to the back of the carriage, bent down[24] and forced their bodies against the vehicle to get it moving. Once the wheels were rolling, Park could maintain the forward motion and slowly ride away from the checkpoint. Although he was tempted, he didn't thank the officers for helping him escape the law.

There was no doubt in Park's mind that if he had been sitting in the carriage through the checkpoint, he would now be on his way back to Pyongyang in handcuffs. There was also no doubt that Hyun had covered for[25] him.

Two hours later they reached the outskirts of Banshori, and Park rolled the carriage to a stop on a quiet side road. He got off the bicycle seat and looked around. Apart from the birds that cut across the sky above them, they were completely alone.

"I'll walk from here."

"Ok."

Hyun got out of the carriage and stretched his legs. Then he opened up the box below the passenger seat and took out another container of food. He handed it to Park.

"You'll need this for your journey."

For a moment the two men stood in silence, looking at each other. It was a connection that could only occur between two souls who have suffered the same fate. They were one mind in two bodies, and they understood each other completely.

"Thank you," said Park.

Then he reached into one of the enormous pockets of his jacket and took out the bottle of Dragon Aftershave that he had been carrying since he left his apartment.

"Here," he said, passing it to Hyun.

---

[24] To bend down *(phrasal verb)* - To move the top part of your body downwards and forwards.

[25] To cover for *(phrasal verb)* - To provide an excuse for someone, or an explanation for something that has gone wrong. If you cover for someone, it means that they are in trouble, and you do something to protect them from any negative consequences.

The two men exchanged gifts.

Park turned around and started walking slowly towards the centre of Banshori. The light was fading at the end of an exhausting day, but he knew that this was just the beginning of his escape to the West.

Chapter 44 – Deadman's Highway

It was dark by the time that Park reached the railway tracks that would lead him to Banshori Station. He walked cautiously along the embankment, hiding himself in the vegetation. As soon as he could see the lights of the station, he stopped and climbed a tree to get a better view. It was deserted, or at least it seemed that way. He jumped down and continued on his knees, until he was 50 metres from the building. He made himself comfortable[26] and sat down amongst the plants with an unimpeded view of the entrance. He didn't know what to expect.

It was a clear night, and the moon was out. The same moon under which he kissed the Girl with the Almond eyes. He wondered what she was doing now. If she really hated him as much as her reaction to the escape plan suggested. She didn't resist him when he kissed her. In fact, she melted in his arms. Surely this was a sign of love rather than hate.

Something moved in the distance. A small shadowy figure approached the entrance to the station. Park sat up to get a better look. It was a young boy running up and down the platform, playing with a rubber tyre. It must have been a local boy entertaining himself before bedtime.

---

[26] Comfortable *(adjective)* – It's pronounced with only three syllables - /kamf-ta-bl/. There are several important words that have fewer syllables than most non-native speakers expect. They include words like vegetable, chocolate, interesting and restaurant. For an in-depth review of this pronunciation point please listen to Episode 44 of the Adventures of Lola Badiola podcast.

Park sat back and took the container of food out of his pocket. He carefully opened the lid and extracted a piece of kimchi. He placed it in his mouth and chewed slowly. In the quiet of the empty railway grounds, it sounded like a metal crushing machine had just been switched on.

To his right, about 15 metres away, he saw a blue plume of smoke rise up above the vegetation in which he was hiding. He stopped chewing and raised his head to get a better look. A tiny round orange glow appeared for a second and then disappeared. To his left, about 20 metres away the same thing happened, a blue plume of smoke and an intermittent orange glow. It happened in three other places close to where Park was hiding. And then the unmistakable smell of tobacco diffused into his nostrils. A nauseating feeling overwhelmed [27] Park as he realised that he was completely surrounded by the secret police, who, like him, were watching the entrance to the station.

Before he could vomit out his Kimchi, he felt a tug[28] on his shirt. He looked around to see a young boy amongst the vegetation next to him.

"Kim Dae-won." The boy whispered.

Park was too confused to respond.

"Kim Dae-won." The boy whispered again.

"Yes." Park responded, his wits returning to him.

"Follow me."

In the distance, they could hear the rumble of an approaching train. The little boy disappeared back into the vegetation. Park crawled as quickly and as quietly as he could, staying as close as possible to the boy's feet in front of him. Eventually the vegetation

---

[27] To feel / be overwhelmed *(adjective)* - To receive too much. To be unable to cope with the quantity of something such as work, noise, love etc…

[28] To tug *(verb)* - To pull something hard or suddenly. There is a well-known game that is played at local festivals and school events called the "Tug-of-War" where two opposing teams hold either end of a rope and try to pull the other across a line in the ground.

cleared, and they arrived at a quiet road that led to the outskirts of a small village. The noise of the train trailed off into the distance.

The little boy jumped over a fence and into a farmyard. There was a small, detached house next to a big industrial building. The door of the house opened, and Park followed the little boy inside. He blinked in the bright artificial light of the hallway. A man in his sixties, with long grey hair and beard was peering at him.

"Kim Dae-won?"

"Yes." Park replied.

"Why are there so many secret police?"

"I don't know."

"Did you tell anyone about the plan?"

"No."

The old man stroked his beard and then ushered Park into his kitchen, a worried look on his face. There was hot soup and rice on the stove. After almost 48 hours on the road with only cold kimchi and dumplings as sustenance, Park could not have imagined a more welcome treat. The old man served the three of them and the atmosphere in the room became more relaxed.

"Ok, listen carefully," said the old man. You have to prepare yourself psychologically for what comes next. Some of the defectors we have helped in the past have not coped well with this part of the journey."

Park put down his soup spoon, wiped his mouth and nodded his head. The old man continued:

"China imports[29] cadavers from North Korea. They are religious and respect their dead, we are atheist and do not. The Chinese use the bodies for research and training purposes in medical universities around the country. This business relationship is a win-win

---

[29] To import *(verb)* - To bring in products or goods from another country for sale or use.

scenario[30]. They cover a supply shortage, and we generate foreign income.

The bodies of anyone who dies in North Korea between the ages of twenty and forty are sent to my team for processing in the building next door. Every night, we transport the cadavers up to the border in refrigerated trucks. Our police know what's inside the vehicles and they let us through their checkpoints. No questions asked. We transfer the cadavers to the Chinese authorities who take them across the border."

Park thought that he knew everything about the economic activity of the Fatherland from his extensive reading of reports on the internet. But this international trade agreement came as a complete shock. The old man continued.

"In fifteen minutes, the next truck will leave with the three of us on it. I will be driving, my grandson will be in the passenger seat, and you will be hiding in the back with the merchandise. We will make a stop at the Yalu River and let you out. There will be a foreign agent waiting for you on the other side of the river. He will give a signal when it is safe to cross the border into China.

Understood?"

Park felt the hot soup rise up from his stomach, travel back through his oesophagus and then into his mouth. He swallowed hard to keep it from escaping.

"Yes."

The old man and the young boy stood up and cleared the plates from the table. Then they put on their coats, hats and gloves and led Park out the front door. The refrigerated truck was parked beside the large building. As they walked towards it, the old man said:

"It's a six-hour drive to the drop off point. There is enough oxygen in the cabin to last about seven hours. So don't breathe too deeply. It's going to be cold, but you'll survive."

---

[30] Win-win scenario *(idiom)* - An action that is good for both parties.

He opened the back doors of the truck. The lights went on to reveal three shelves running along either side of the interior. Lying on the shelves, packed in clear plastic bags, were the bodies of the dead that were ready for export to China.

"Jump in!"

Park did what he was requested to do, as if he were on autopilot.

"Welcome to Dead Man's Highway." said the old grey man as he slammed the doors shut.

Park was left in a pitch black, freezing cold compartment, with two dozen cadavers for company.

SAM GRATTON

Chapter 45 – The Crossing

No-one can imagine what it's like to spend six hours trapped in a cold, dark container, surrounded on all sides by dead bodies. No-one can predict what an experience like that might do to a person's sanity. And so, when the old grey man and his grandson opened the doors to their refrigerated truck, they had no idea in what state of mind[31] they would find their passenger.

Park stepped out and rubbed his eyes.

"Are you ok?"

Park looked around at the environment in which he found himself, then he focused on the boy and his grandfather.

"I'm fine."

The old man nodded his head in approval. This defector had character and his chances of completing the journey were good.

"Head straight to the river and await the signal."

The old man patted Park on the back[32] and then got back into the car. "Don't forget to send us a postcard[33]." He said in a

---

[31] State of mind *(noun)* - A person's mental or emotional condition at a given point in time.

[32] To pat someone on the back *(idiom)* - To show appreciation to someone for a job well done.

[33] Postcard *(noun)* - A message sent to family and friends while on holiday. Normally a pretty picture on one side with some space to write a brief message on the other side.

deadpan[34] voice as he accelerated away to his business rendezvous with the Chinese.

Park's legs were like jelly[35]. He tripped over a couple of times as he headed to the banks of the river. Then he sat down and waited for the signal to cross, whatever that might be. In the darkness of that cold winter night, he noticed something ominous about the ice and snow that covered the water. It was moving. It had been a mild winter by North Korean standards and, therefore, the river wasn't frozen solid. This was going to be a more difficult and dangerous crossing than he had imagined.

As the minutes and then hours passed, Park started to feel sleepy. He kept his eyes firmly fixed on the other side of the riverbank, but every time he blinked, his eyelids felt heavier. There was no sign of the secret police, no puffs of cigarette smoke, no noises in the distance, so he started to relax. He watched a bat swoop up and down the river in front of him chasing insects for its dinner. It was a hypnotic sight. Slowly but surely, his mind wandered from the conscious to subconscious. The last thing he remembered, before he fell into a deep sleep, was the sound of the bat's wings as it fluttered past his forehead.

Park was awoken by the lights of a torch shining in his eyes.

"Kim Dae-won?"

Park grunted[36].

"Do you speak English?"

---

[34] Deadpan *(adjective)* - To be deliberately unemotional, particularly when telling a joke to enhance the comedic delivery.

[35] Jelly *(noun)* - A soft, sweet desert, usually brightly coloured, made from sugar, gelatine, and fruit flavours, that shakes or wobbles slightly when it is moved. Known as "jello" in US English.

[36] To grunt *(verb)* - To make a short, low sound. Animals and humans can grunt.

Park was utterly[37] disorientated. He hadn't slept for more than a couple of hours in the previous three days. His whole body was stiff from sitting in a stress position for six hours in the refrigerated truck.

A huge hand grabbed his stick-thin arm and lifted him to his feet. He found himself standing next to a giant.

"Look at me!"

Park looked up and into the eyes of the stranger. He had never seen a westerner in the flesh, nor smelt one. He was equally as fascinated as he was fearful of this foreign creature.

"I am here to take you across the border. Do you understand?"

Park nodded.

The Westerner put a harness around Park's waste and attached it to the back of his own belt with a rope so that the two of them were physically inseparable.

"Follow me. Put your feet exactly where I put mine."

The Westerner took two steps towards the river, pulling Park's flimsy body along with him. Park stumbled into the back of his new companion, as if he were a drunkard walking into the great wall of China. It became immediately obvious to both of them that this way of getting across the river wasn't going to work.

The giant knelt down and motioned for Park to jump onto his back. Park followed the instruction and, like a little boy on the back of his father, was raised to a height that felt both frightening and exhilarating.

The Westerner stood at the river's edge and plotted a path across the slow-moving ice. If either of them fell into the water at this time of year, they would perish[38] from hyperthermia within the hour.

---

[37] Utterly *(adverb)* - An intensifying adverb popular with native speakers to emphasise the adjective. Synonyms include completely and absolutely.

[38] To perish *(verb)* - To die, especially, by accident or in a violent way. In business we use this word to distinguish between perishable goods, such as fruits and vegetables, and non-perishable goods such as furniture, cars and equipment that have a much longer lifespan.

The giant was about to take his first step when he was hit hard by something from the side. Both he and Park fell to the ground, still attached by the rope and harness. Park quickly recovered his senses, and, from the floor of the embankment, he could see the boots of two soldiers standing either side of them. They were not the boots of the secret police, who had proved easy to evade over the last 56 hours. They were the boots of the Special Operations Forces. North Korea's finest and bravest soldiers. The two agents must have tracked every step that Park had taken up until this point.

One of the boots lifted in the air and moved in the direction of Park's head. The little programmer moved out of the way just in time to avoid his skull being cracked open. He felt himself being pulled to his feet by the harness, as his giant companion stood up to face the enemy.

The two soldiers attacked the Westerner from both sides. They didn't use guns or knives. They wanted to overwhelm him. He was worth much more to them alive than dead.

There was no doubt in Park's mind that the giant would have been able to withstand the onslaught, if he had been free from the harness, but, as it was, Park acted as a deadweight[39], preventing the westerner from properly defending himself.

For two minutes, Park was thrown around like a rag doll[40] as the three men fought each other, until eventually the two tough Koreans had their man pinned to the ground. One of them was lying face down on top of his chest, the other had his arm around the giant's throat in a stranglehold. Slowly, they were squeezing the oxygen out of his system until he was on the brink of fainting.

---

[39] Deadweight *(noun)* - Something that cannot move by itself but needs to be carried by someone else. It is a burden, and it makes a task more difficult without bringing any help or benefits.

[40] Ragdoll *(noun)* - A soft child's toy in the shape of a person, made from cloth.

Park watched in horror. He assumed that, as soon as they had the westerner under control, they would eliminate him from the equation. It was the agent that they wanted, not him.

A survival instinct was triggered in the primordial part of Park's brain. He reached inside the pocket of his Russian army jacket. He felt the cold, sharp steel of the kimchi knife that he had grabbed before heading out on his date with the Girl with the Almond eyes. He drew the knife from his pocket and raised it above the neck of the soldier who was holding down the agent's chest, taking careful aim at the thick, tanned, throat of his enemy.

The agent, his eyes bulging from the lack of oxygen, could see what was about to happen. He nodded his head vigorously, urging Park to follow through. The soldier who was strangling the agent shouted a warning to his prostrate companion.

With a sudden downwards thrust, Park drove the sharp jagged point of the Kimchi knife directly into the jugular vein of the soldier. The reaction was immediate – an initial spurt of blood that covered everything in a one-metre radius, followed by the pulsating flow of liquid over the bodies of the combatants. The injured man let go of the giant and writhed around[41] in agony before he quickly passed to another world.

Park then used the knife to cut through the rope and free the giant to fight the other soldier unimpeded. It wasn't long before their roles were reversed, and the Korean officer now found himself in a headlock. The giant used his immense strength to subdue his adversary until he fainted from the lack of oxygen. Then the westerner pulled out a gun, attached a silencer and shot three bullets into the head of the unconscious soldier.

He checked both men for weapons and documentation. He took a photo of their faces, their equipment, and the environment in which they lay. Then he filled the soldiers' pockets with stones and,

---

[41] To writhe around *(phrasal verb)* - To make exaggerated twisting movements with the body.

one by one, dragged them to the river, pushing their bodies under the slow-moving ice.

Finally, he turned to Park, and said:

"Good work. Let's go."

QUIZ TIME

Chapters 41 to 45

COMPREHENSION QUIZ

Answer the questions with complete sentences. Say them out loud.

1. Why does Lola decide not to tell her mother about the civil lawsuit?
2. What good news does Lola receive from Concha and how does she react?
3. What was the cause of the famine in North Korea in the mid 1990s?
4. What is the Tomb of the Glorious Farmer and why does Park visit it?
5. Why does Park feel vulnerable as they travel to Banshori Station?
6. Why do the policemen let him pass through the checkpoint?
7. What is Park thinking about while he waits in the vegetation next to Jungi Station?
8. What exactly is Dead Man's Highway?
9. How does Park feel after his journey in the truck?
10. How do Park and the agent escape from the Special Operations Forces?

BUSINESS ENGLISH QUIZ

Complete the sentences with the words used in the story.

1. After a long week at work, I like to W_____ D_____ with a glass of red wine and a Monte Cristo cigar.

2. She is very easy to work with. She is always willing to G_____ with the F_____. If we need to work weekends, she'll be there.

3. I can't stand O_____ P_____. It's one of the reasons that I work as a freelancer, so I can focus on work, rather than being distracted by gossip and rumours.

4. The pub just across the road from our office is great. The landlord is always giving us drinks O_____ T_____ H_____ because he knows we're such important customers.

5. The commercial director has been warned twice about B_____ junior members of staff. If we receive one more complaint, about aggressive behaviour or rude language, we will have to fire him.

6. Before we W_____ U_____ this meeting let me just summarise the key takeaways from our recent research project.

7. I've been photocopying the documents and you have been binding the reports for the last half an hour. Shall we S_____ O_____ to stay motivated?

8. After a period of rapid expansion, our business is maturing, and our sales growth is starting to F_____ O_____.

9. I have to take my daughter to the doctor's this morning, but I am meant to be attending the online compliance webinar.

Would you mind C_____ F_____ me while I'm away from my desk?

10. I feel completely O_____ by all the work that we have to do in the final days of the quarter. We need to organise our time better, to avoid this stressful situation.

11. We are trying to I_____ the raw materials from Sudan, but the war has made that extremely difficult, and we will have to look for new suppliers.

12. If we transfer her from your division to my division, you won't have to fire her, and I will gain an experienced employee. It's a W_____-W_____ S_____.

13. What was his S_____ of M_____ after you told him that he was being made redundant?

14. During this heat wave, the transportation of P_____ goods needs to be extremely well planned and executed.

15. The new US manager is interviewing all the employees to find out if there are any D_____ amongst us, who he can fire.

ANSWERS TO COMPREHENSION QUIZ

1. Lola decides not to tell her mother about the civil lawsuit because she thinks her mother will interfere and add drama to the current situation.
2. Lola is told by Concha that she and Eugenio are expecting their first child. Lola is thrilled by this news because she believes that the couple will make amazing parents and she knows they have been trying to have a baby for some time.
3. The famine in North Korea in the mid-90s was caused by a mixture of infertile soil, poor weather, and disastrous economic management.
4. The Tomb of the Glorious Farmer is a memorial for all the peasants who died during the Great Famine of the 1990s. This includes Park's own family and that is why he has come to the tomb, to pay his last respects and say a final farewell before he escapes to the West.
5. Park feels vulnerable as they travel towards Banshori station because he is unsure about the amount of information Kim has revealed, and fears that the authorities will be waiting for him at some point on the journey.
6. The policemen allow Park through the checkpoint because they do not look closely enough at him, as they assume that he will be sitting in the passenger seat and not driving the carriage.
7. Park thinks back to the Girl with the Almond Eyes, he considers the mistake he made in telling her of his plan, and wonders if she despises him as much as it appeared.
8. Dead Man's Highway is the route for all the cadavers that are being exported from North Korea to China. The two countries have an international trade agreement, whereby North Korea sells the bodies of healthy young people who have died in

accidents to the Chinese authorities so that they can be used in medical research.

9. Park is exhausted after his trip in the back of the truck, his legs are like jelly. However, he has a clear mind and a strong character, and therefore is ready for the next part of his journey.

10. After a fierce fight, Park uses the kimchi knife in his pocket to kill one of the North Korean soldiers, allowing the foreign agent to neutralise the threat from the other soldier. Park and the agent then make their way across the icy waters of the Yalu River.

ANSWERS TO BUSINESS ENGLISH QUIZ

1. After a long week at work, I like to WIND DOWN with a glass of red wine and a Monte Cristo cigar.

2. She is very easy to work with. She is always willing to GO WITH THE FLOW. If we need to work weekends, she'll be there.

3. I can't stand OFFICE POLITICS. It's one of the reasons that I work as a freelancer, so I can focus on work, rather than being distracted by gossip and rumours.

4. The pub just across the road from our office is great. The landlord is always giving us drinks ON THE HOUSE, because he knows we're such important customers.

5. The commercial director has been warned twice about BULLYING junior members of staff. If we receive one more complaint about aggressive behaviour or rude language, we will have to fire him.

6. Before we WRAP UP this meeting, let me just summarise the key takeaways from our recent research project.

7. I've been photocopying the documents and you have been binding the reports for the last half an hour. Shall we SWAP OVER to stay motivated?

8. After a period of rapid expansion our business is maturing, and our sales growth is starting to FLATTEN OUT.

9. I have to take my daughter to the doctor's this morning, but I am meant to be attending the online compliance webinar. Would you mind COVERING FOR me while I'm away from my desk?

10. I feel completely OVERWHELMED by all the work that we have to do in the final days of the quarter. We need to organise our time better to avoid this stressful situation.

11. We are trying to IMPORT the raw materials from Sudan, but the war has made that extremely difficult, and we will have to look for new suppliers.

12. If we transfer her from your division to my division, you won't have to fire her, and I will gain an experienced employee. It's a WIN-WIN SCENARIO.

13. What was his STATE OF MIND after you told him that he was being made redundant?

14. During this heat wave, the transportation of PERISHABLE goods needs to be extremely well planned and executed.

15. The new US manager is interviewing all the employees to find out if there are any DEADWEIGHTS amongst us who he can fired.

"Trust me, JJ."
Lola

Chapter 46 – Snake in the Grass

Lola arrived early for work. She couldn't let the lawsuit[1] distract her from her job. She had been hired to catalyse the growth of the business at JBlock and she needed to deliver as much for her own self-respect as for the company shareholders.

One of the main obstacles to achieving her goals was the productivity of her subordinate, Cayetano Tolosa. Not only had he been ineffective in his role of opening doors to big accounts, but he had also revealed himself to be a snake in the grass.

It was time to chop off his head.

One by one, the computer programmers filed into the office, plugged in, and started typing. The search for Pluto had gone cold so they were once again writing code, resolving bugs, and chewing gum. JJ and Diego were out of the office for the day. Lola had checked their diaries and it simply said: "External Meeting".

At exactly 9:00 am, Cayetano entered the office. He had a Starbucks Frappuccino in one hand and the latest copy of CyberStory magazine in the other. He walked past the programmers and stopped at the desk of the admin team. They were all Real Madrid supporters and it had been a good result for the football team the previous night. They started chatting and laughing.

Lola stood up from her desk.

"Cayetano." She threw her voice forcefully across the office.

---

[1] Lawsuit *(noun)* - A conflict between two or more private parties that is brought to a court room for a legal decision. One party will sue the other party, in other words they will file a lawsuit.

The salesman flashed her a 5,000-euro smile - he liked to talk about how much money he had spent on is teeth - then continued discussing the game with his colleagues.

Lola walked over to where he was standing.

"Where are we with the Dell account?"

"Good morning, Lola!"

"Where are we with the Dell account?"

"I've just arrived. Give a minute. I'll update you."

"It's a simple question Cayetano."

"I'm working on it."

"You're working on what?" Lola's intonation became noticeably more hostile. She was no longer asking about the specific account. She was questioning Cayetano's professionalism.

Around the office, the tic-tac sound of typing ceased as the programmers sensed that a much-anticipated fight was about to start. It was clear to everyone that the commercial team had not been functioning effectively. Cayetano was constantly making little comments to undercut Lola's authority, and she had done nothing to stop it. Perhaps things were about to change.

"I'm setting up[2] a meeting with the guy who pulls the trigger[3]." replied Cayetano, maintaining his 5000-euro smile, but lowering his voice a semitone.

"You mean Jorge Costa, the head of procurement at Dell?"

"Yeah. He's really difficult to pin down[4]. I'm calling in favours[5]. Be patient."

---

[2] To set up *(phrasal verb)* - To arrange a meeting or event.

[3] To pull the trigger *(idiom)* - The trigger is the part of the gun that causes the bullet to be fired, so when you squeeze the trigger or pull the trigger it fires the gun. It is often used metaphorically in business situations, when referring to the person who starts a process.

[4] To pin down *(phrasal verb)* - To stop somebody escaping from you so that you can get some information or a decision out of them.

[5] To call in favours *(idiom)* - To ask somebody for help in return for the help that you have offered them in the past.

THE ADVENTURES OF LOLA BADIOLA

Cayetano's voice dropped another tone as he sought to demonstrate his authority over the situation.

Lola was aware that everyone in the office was now focused on the drama unfolding before them. And she had no intention of disappointing the crowd. Her father had once told her that business meetings were like theatre. It's the people watching the action that are more important than the actors themselves.

"I just spoke to Jorge Costa." Lola stated calmly "I just booked a meeting with him."

The office absorbed the implication of the statement. Cayetano was either incompetent or deceitful.

The smile vanished from the salesman's face as he realised that this was now a public confrontation. It wasn't something he had expected, nor prepared for. He had always perceived Lola as just another cute girl pretending to be a professional. Someone who had flirted[6] their way into a position of power. He was momentarily lost for words[7].

"And where are we with the Bosch account?"

Lola was now on the attack. She knew she had the upper hand. The element of surprise had given her a distinct advantage. Once again, her question was rhetorical[8] rather than literal, designed to expose incompetence rather than reveal information.

Cayetano didn't reply. He wasn't going to fall into another trap. His eyes narrowed and his expression changed from defence to offence.

"What's wrong with you this morning, Lola?"

---

[6] To flirt *(verb)* - To act as if you are attracted to somebody but in a playful way.

[7] To be lost for words *(idiom)* - To be unable to respond. To be speechless.

[8] Rhetorical question *(adjective noun)* - A question that does not require a response. Beneath the question is an implicit message, a point that is being made.

"I checked the outgoing calls on your company smartphone. You haven't been speaking to Dell, or Bosch, or any of the other big accounts."

The computer programmers and admin staff all leaned forwards. This was the moment they had been waiting for. A climax to the repressed conflict within the commercial division. Lola continued.

"There is, however, one mobile number you've been calling over and over again."

For the first time since he joined JBlock, Cayetano's impeccable[9] façade[10] started to crack. And through these cracks Lola shined a bright white light. And everyone in the room could see the truth that was hidden within.

"I know that mobile number because I used to work with the man who owns it, Luis Bruña, senior manager at TechSpania."

There was a collective intake of breath as the audience sitting in the stalls[11] simultaneously deduced that Cayetano was a mole[12]. He was an informant, working for JBlock's biggest competitor, secretly updating them on the start-ups technological and business progress. It was not only a crime against the company, but it was also a personal betrayal of every single employee. He had made fools of them all, and the bitterness in the room was palpable.

Van Dyck, the two-metre-tall Dutch programmer stood up and folded his arms. One by one, the other programmers did the same.

---

[9] Impeccable *(adjective)* - Perfect, faultless, without any problems or bad parts. It has the Latin origin "impecabilis" which means not capable of sin.

[10] Façade *(noun)* - Literally the front of a building, especially an impressive or decorative one. It is also used to describe a false appearance that makes someone or something seem more pleasant or better than they really are.

[11] Stalls *(noun)* - The area of seats on the ground floor of a theatre nearest to the stage or screen.

[12] Mole *(noun)* - Literally, it is a small, semi-blind mammal with dark fur, that lives in passages that it digs underground. The word is also used to describe a person who works for an organisation or government, and secretly gives information to its competitor or enemy.

Some of them were shaking their heads, others had expressions of indignation, his fellow Real Madrid supporters looked down at the floor in shame.

Lola stepped forward to apply the coup de grace[13].

"You know where the door is Pretty Boy."

Cayetano was frozen to the spot, staring at her, perplexed, as if he had something important to say, but he couldn't find the right words. He looked around the room at the others. He had no allies. In fact, a number of the programmers wanted to throw him out of the second-floor window.

Men of a weaker character would have crumbled under the weight of the collective disapproval. But Cayetano Tolosa de los Monteros had noble blood running through his veins. His ancestors had thrashed their way through the jungles of South America, fought English pirates on the stormy North Atlantic, and brought treasures back from the New World. He knew that even though this battle was lost, and it was time to retreat, the war would continue[14].

As the programmers started to move forward to eject him from the premises, he calmly took a sip of the Starbuck's Frappuccino and said with an ominous smile:

"You have no idea what is just about to hit you."

Then he turned around and exited by the main door. And the curtain closed on the morning's drama.

---

[13] Coup de grace *(idiom)* - A "stroke of grace". An action that kills a person or animal in order to end their suffering.

[14] The battle may be lost but the war goes on *(idiom)* - A common expression that you hear in conflicts in business and in sports. It is a reminder that even if you face failure and disappointment in the short run, you can still succeed and win in the long-term.

SAM GRATTON

Chapter 47 – Ribera del Duero

Cayetano Tolosa was a bad apple[15]. It was good that he was gone. The confrontation had brought the rest of the team together and, finally, won Lola the respect of the programmers.

She called JJ's mobile, and it went straight through to voicemail. She asked him to call her back as soon as possible. She needed to explain what had happened, before he heard it from anyone else.

She went through her contact list and set herself the task of booking four more key meetings that morning. She needed to make up for lost time.

She was more convinced than ever that their product was a winner. While it was true that Pluto had reached level 9 of the game, he hadn't breached the most enhanced level of protection. Furthermore, the intrusion had alerted the team to weaknesses which they had subsequently addressed. In her opinion, JBlock's software was now at least three years ahead of its closest competition.

She spent the next four hours on the phone, mixing cold calls[16] with sales pitches and relationship building chats. It was what she did best. If Lola really believed in a product, she was irrepressible.

---

[15] Bad apple *(idiom)* - An expression that is used to describe somebody who has a negative influence on everybody else around them, in the way that a bad or rotting apple starts to affect all the other apples in the box.

[16] Cold calls *(adjective noun)* - Connecting with somebody for the very first time and trying to get them interested in learning more about your product. It is often regarded as the most difficult, and at times soul-destroying, part of sales.

She would wear down procurement managers with her charm, intelligence, and enthusiasm until they had no choice but to take the meeting, sample the software or sign on the dotted line.

At 2pm, she received a call from JJ. It was her opportunity to explain how and why Cayetano had left the company.

"Lola what's up?"

"Hi JJ. Listen, I had an issue with Cayetano. I had no choice but to fire him."

There was a long pause on the other end of the line.

"Ok" he replied dispassionately.

Ok? Thought Lola. Was that it? No questions? No emotion?

JJ continued in the same detached manner.

"I'd like you to come for dinner with me and Diego this evening. 9pm at Benarés. Can you make it?"

"Sure."

"Great. See you then."

And with that he hung up.

Alarm bells rung in Lola's head. That was not the voice of the boss that she knew and admired. Something was up. Her rational mind started to work through all the possibilities. She wanted to prepare herself for any surprises.

***

JJ and Diego were already sitting at the table, looking solemn, when Lola arrived at Benares at 9pm that evening. They stood up and greeted her as she arrived. Then they all sat down, and Diego slid a menu across the table.

"Shall we order?"

Lola didn't pick up the menu. She looked directly into the eyes of the two men sitting opposite her. She wasn't going to play any games.

"What's going on?"

JJ looked across at Diego, then he put down the menu and leaned forwards. In a quiet but firm voice, he said:

"We have an offer on the table."

Lola didn't react. The sale of the company was one of the possible, albeit unlikely, outcomes that she had anticipated after her brief telephone conversation with JJ.

"From whom?"

"TechSpania."

Once again Lola didn't react. It was the worst-case scenario[17], but one she had considered. She chose to remain silent and let JJ explain.

"We're in a difficult situation Lola. We're burning cash[18] like its kindling[19]. We have no sign of revenues. And there are forces, powerful forces, working against us. TechSpania have offered us a way out. With our software and their distribution, we would be unstoppable."

"Our software and *their* distribution?"

It was clear to everyone that Lola was the loser in this deal. TechSpania wanted the programmers and the technology, and nothing else. Considering the current lawsuit, there was no way Lola was going back to TechSpania.

"They are offering us 6 euros a share."

It was undeniably a generous offer. Proof that TechSpania valued the intellectual property of JBlock very highly. JJ continued:

---

[17] Worst-case scenario *(adjective noun)* - A scenario is simply one of multiple outcomes and, in this case, we are considering the most negative alternative of them all.

[18] Cash burn *(noun)* - The money that a company, normally a start-up, has raised from internal and external investors and is now spending to build the business. It is the ongoing costs of running a business that has yet to make a profit, and is, of course, unsustainable.

[19] Kindling *(noun)* - Small pieces of wood and dry organic material used to start fires.

"We all have an equity stake[20] in the JBlock, you, me, Diego, the programmers. We all benefit financially from this deal. It's too sweet to refuse."

"You're surrendering." Lola didn't hide the bitterness in her voice.

"What happened to the idea of disrupting the market? What happened to David versus Goliath? We're going to be just like all those other start-ups who begin with good intentions and end up selling their souls to the devil."

JJ sat back in his chair and scratched his head. Lola was now on a roll[21].

"This deal is going to cement TechSpania's monopoly position in the cybersecurity market for the next generation," she said, her voice trembling with indignation "It's going to allow them to kill their competition, squeeze their suppliers and screw their customers. It's a complete betrayal of everything we stand for."

Diego looked at Lola with admiration. She was a fighter. And in his heart, he completely agreed with her. He quietly ordered a bottle of red wine.

"So where is the next client gonna come from Lola?" JJ responded forcefully. "When are we gonna start seeing some cold hard cash?"

"Trust me, JJ. It's just around the corner[22]."

"Trust you? You've brought in no clients, you're being sued by TechSpania, and you've just fired half the sales team. I think I've trusted you enough already."

That hurt. And JJ knew it. He softened his tone.

"Listen Lola. If we had one big client, just one, that would be enough. That would prove to me that we have the ability to build

---

[20] Equity stake *(noun)* - Ownership of shares of the company.

[21] On a roll *(idiom)* - Having momentum, making progress.

[22] Just around the corner *(idiom)* - Something that is not visible but nevertheless is extremely close.

this business ourselves. Do we have one big client, even on the horizon?"

Lola shook her head.

Diego looked down in disappointment. He had hoped that the conversation would go a different way, that Lola would be able to convince the entrepreneur to keep going.

JJ scrutinised his two faithful colleagues, giving them as much time as they needed to respond. But his question was met with silence.

"Ok. Tomorrow, I have a meeting with the CEO of TechSpania. I'm going to accept his offer. We will then meet with the Board of Directors. And they will ratify the deal."

Lola could hardly believe what was happening. Every prediction that Mario Ruiz de Velasco had made at their fateful meeting was coming true. He said that she had no future at JBlock, because JBlock had no future. He promised that he would either buy the company or bury it. He threatened that he would either take her to the top of the mountain or throw her off it.

The waiter arrived with the wine. It was a fine bottle of Ribera del Duero. He carefully popped the cork and then filled Diego's glass with a small amount of the crimson liquid for tasting.

Lola stood up from her chair and looked down at the two men.

"Ok JJ. You know best. But let me just say. This company isn't worth 6 euros a share, or 600 or 6000. It's worth way more than that. And you're selling it for a song[23]."

And with that she walked out of the restaurant. The two men watched her go, and then sat for a long time in silence. Eventually,

---

[23] To sell something for a song *(idiom)* - To sell something extremely cheaply, a long way below its true value. The expression originates from the small amounts of money given to wandering musicians outside pubs and bars in medieval times.

Diego picked up his glass of Ribera del Duero and took a sip. It was sour, the wine had gone off[24], and he spat it back into the glass.

Outside the restaurant Lola burst into tears[25]. She had lost more than a job. She had lost a dream, a vision of a better, safer world that she could play one small part in building. For almost an hour, she wandered aimlessly around the streets of Barrio Salamanca reliving all the injustices that had been perpetrated against her, until she found herself standing outside a traditional bar on one of the quiet side streets that ran parallel to Velázquez. She walked inside, ordered a tequila, and knocked it back[26] in one go.

A small, middle-aged man with a bald head and glasses entered the bar after her. He sat down on the stool next to her and ordered a Rum and Coke. He put his right hand inside his jacket pocket and checked that his handgun was switched to safety. Then he turned to Lola and said:

"Can I buy you another drink?"

---

[24] To go off *(phrasal verb)* - In this case, it means that food or drink has started to rot and is therefore no longer edible.

[25] To burst into tears *(idiom)* - To start crying suddenly and vigorously.

[26] To knock back *(phrasal verb)* - To rapidly consume an alcoholic beverage.

Chapter 48 – Corruption

It took a moment for Lola to recognise the man who was sitting next to her. He was one of the agents from Interpol who had questioned her about her involvement in the hacking of SMZ and TechSpania.

"Guzmán Zunzunegui." said the man.

"I know who you are. What do you want?"

"I gave you my business card the last time we spoke. I had hoped that you would call me."

Lola was on her guard[27]. She couldn't understand why an agent from Interpol would approach her in a bar at midnight. He sensed her tension and tried to put her at ease.

"I'm originally from Laredo. I used to spend my summers working on the fishing boats in Santoña. I knew your father."

Lola remained distant and suspicious. She thought about calling Gonzalo. He had instructed her to contact him if Interpol ever approached her again. But she didn't feel threatened by the old man, and the shot of tequila was already filling her heart with courage. She remained silent and let the agent make the next move.

Zunzunegui took a sip of his Rum and Coke, then lowered his voice and said:

"I need your help. Do you have five minutes to hear my story?"

---

[27] To be on your guard *(idiom)* - To be alert and attentive, prepared for something unexpected to happen.

Lola raised an eyebrow. It had already been one of the most dramatic days of her working life. Now it was taking a turn for the surreal. She had no idea where the conversation was going to lead, but her innate curiosity needed to be satisfied. She asked the barman for a bottle of beer, and then, turned her body in the direction of the agent.

"Go on then."

"I'm not an expert in Cybercrime. I was transferred to the department three years ago. I'm just passing time until I retire and claim my pension."

The agent looked around the bar to check that nobody was listening. Apart from a young couple making out in the corner and the disinterested barman, they were alone. He pulled his stool nearer to Lola's, then he leaned in until he was on the verge of invading her personal space. He cleared his throat and started his story.

"Corporate corruption is my bread and butter[28]. For almost thirty years, I worked in the anti-corruption department of Interpol. I was based in different cities in South America, investigating Spanish companies who were growing their business in the region.

What is considered corrupt in Madrid, is considered normal practice in places like Caracas, Managua, and Asunción. What we call a bribe[29], they call a commission. What we call blackmail[30], they call persuasion. So, by whose rules do you play? Yours or theirs?

---

[28] Bread and butter *(idiom)* - Something you do every day in order to earn a living, and therefore something that you are very familiar with.

[29] Bribe *(noun)* - The secret payment of public officials to benefit certain individuals. For example, a local politician taking secret money from a construction company to give them a license to build on protected land.

[30] Blackmail *(noun)* - Forcing someone to pay money or give another kind of benefit, in return for not revealing damaging information about them to the public or the authorities.

Some foreign companies take a cynical approach. They say: "When in Rome do as the Romans[31]." Others take a moral stand. They simply refuse to enter markets where the standards of regulation are lower than their own. Then there is a third type of company, the one that wants the best of both worlds. They want to build factories without paying bribes.

Your father chose the third option."

The agent paused to take the tinniest sip of Rum and Coke. He knew how to make his listeners feel comfortable, how to feed them the right amount of information with the right number of pauses. After thirty years of interrogating white-collar criminals[32], he understood the psychology of the professional mind. He ran his fingers over the stubble of his chin and continued.

"Your father was clean, and he expected everyone around him to be clean. He denounced the politicians who engaged in corrupt practices. He publicly criticised foreign businesses who played by the local rules."

Lola was now fully invested in the story. She knew that her father was working hard to grow the South American business before he passed away, but she didn't know the details of the problems he encountered.

The agent continued.

"When a high-profile businessman or politician, particularly one who takes a stand against corruption, suddenly dies of a heart attack, his death needs to be investigated."

The agent leaned forward, lowered his head slightly and gently took hold of Lola's arm.

"This didn't happen in the case of your father. When I insisted on an autopsy I was ignored. When I started to make noise about a

---

[31] When in Rome do as the Romans *(idiom)* - To adapt your behaviour to the environment in which you find yourself.

[32] White collar crime *(idiom)* – A crime that is typically committed by a professional person, someone who wears a shirt with a white collar to work. The crimes include corporate fraud, money laundering and illegal hacking.

cover-up[33], I was transferred to the cybercrime department in Madrid. I'm now four months away from retirement. Before I leave the force, I want to know what really happened to your father. And I think you might be able to help me."

Lola was speechless. She didn't know how to react. Was the agent being genuine or manipulative? Was this a true story or was it a setup? If it was true, who was responsible for the death of her father? Why had the authorities covered it up? And why hadn't she asked more questions at the time?

She knew that she needed time to process the information, time to consider its veracity. She summoned all her strength of character and composed herself.

"That's an interesting story Mr. Zunzunegui. But the truth is my father died of natural causes. I, myself, brought his body back from Lima. And I wouldn't be surprised, if the pressure of being harassed by people like you, contributed to his death."

She took a twenty euro note out of her wallet and threw it on the bar. "You want my help? Buy yourself another Rum and Coke." Then she got up from her stool, walked out of the bar and headed straight over to Concha's house.

The agent didn't follow her. He paid for the drinks and headed home, leaving the twenty euro note for the barman.

He knew that Lola would be back in contact with him.

Sooner, rather than later.

---

[33] Cover-up *(noun)* - The systematic concealment of criminal activity. For example, if the management of a company is aware that some of their employees have been stealing from their clients but want to avoid any negative publicity, they might cover up the crime.

Chapter 49 – Touchdown

The wheels of the 777 touched down[34] in Madrid Barajas and the agent was finally home. It had been a two-week mission that had almost cost him his life. He promised himself that this would be his last assignment as a freelance operative. He had a wife who adored him and a child on the way. He couldn't afford to put himself in such danger again.

Sitting next to him on the plane was the man who he assumed to be Kim Dae-won. This was the package that he was hired to deliver from North Korea to the offices of Interpol in Madrid. The man who had saved him from a painful death. The man who was worth 150,000 euros after expenses. With this final pay day, the agent was sure that he could transition into a new career. He could settle down[35] and start his own business. As the airplane taxied along the runway to its allotted gate number, the agent recalled the events of the last five days.

After their confrontation with the Special Operations Forces, he and Park had crossed the Yalu River and travelled through the night to a safe house in China. With the help of local agents, they had cleaned themselves up and changed their clothes. Park was given a false identity, a fake passport, and a cover story.

---

[34] To touch down *(phrasal verb)* - To land an aircraft. When the wheels touch the runway.

[35] To settle down *(phrasal verb)* - To start living in a new place where you intend to stay for a long time.

His new name was Moon Dong-woo. He was a South Korean location scout working for a film crew making a documentary about the wildlife that inhabited the volcanic plains of Paektu Mountain. Filming was a chaotic process, with large numbers of specialists coming and going all the time. Nobody would question the arrival of another Asian man in the team.

Thus, Park Jae-bong was pretending to be Kim Dae-won, who was pretending to be Moon Dong-woo. Even Park admitted to becoming confused, so he took a vow of silence and only answered yes or no to essential questions.

Throughout the five days of filming, the agent observed the little computer programmer moving amongst the crew with an awestruck expression on his face. Everything he was experiencing - the sights, the sounds, and smells - must have been a culture shock[36].

Park was fascinated by the equipment that the team used to shoot their documentary. He wanted to touch the cameras, the sound mixers, and the video monitors. He wanted to play with the walkie talkies and the microphones. He was like a little boy in the toy department of El Corte Inglés. The agent had to follow him everywhere to make sure he didn't disrupt the filming with his silent curiosity.

Park was equally intrigued by the food served up in the temporary canteen. Like an army, a film crew marched on its stomach[37], and the producers of the documentary had spared no expense in this area. They hired a Chinese chef who had been trained at a school of haute cuisine[38] in France, so that the kitchen could produce both local and international dishes. Park was overwhelmed by the quantity and diversity of food. Each meal was presented as an all-

---

[36] Culture shock *(adjective noun)* - The feeling of surprise or anxiety when moving to a new and unfamiliar country, job, or environment.

[37] An army marches on its stomach *(idiom)* - The idea that you have to keep people well fed in order to keep them moving forwards.

[38] Haute cuisine *(adjective noun)* - Cooking of a very high standard, particularly sophisticated French food.

you-can-eat buffet. He would spend 15 minutes walking up and down the table, examining all the items before filling a small bowl with rice and soy sauce.

Of all the weird and wonderful things that Park experienced those first few days, it was the western women in film crew who really seemed to blow his mind[39]. They were tough and dynamic, and at least a head taller than he was. They spoke to the men as equals, in some cases telling them what to do and showing them how to do it. They were confident in both body and mind. On one occasion, he tripped over the root of a tree and one of them helped him back to his feet. She smiled kindly at him, and he was dazzled by the perfection of her teeth.

During the five days of filming, the agent watched his companion very closely. He was worried about the Korean's state of mind, particularly following the events on the banks of the Yalu River. The agent remembered the first time that he, himself, had killed a man in combat. It was something he was trained to do. It was something for which he was psychologically prepared, but it still took him a long time to process the event. In contrast, his companion was a civilian with no previous experience of life-or-death situations. It was possible that the Korean was suffering from post-traumatic stress[40], or on the verge of a nervous breakdown, or haunted by nightmares. However, he showed no signs of fragility, no evidence of mental weakness. Despite his meagre physique he seemed to have a resilient character.

Every evening, the agent spent some private time, preparing his companion for the journey back to the West, testing his knowledge

---

[39] To blow your mind *(idiom)* - To impress or surprise someone in an extreme way.

[40] Post-traumatic stress disorder (PTSD) - A psychological condition in which a person feels deep anxiety at the recurrent memories of an extremely shocking or stressful event.

of the cover story[41], making sure he remembered not only his own name, Moon Dong-woo, but also the names, birthdates and backstories of his mother, father, and an entire imaginary family back in South Korea. The agent needn't have worried. Park's memory was like a sponge. He had perfect recall of all the information.

After five days at Peaktu Mountain, the crew dispersed. Some of them went to the next location, twenty kilometers north, and others flew home to commence the post-production work on the raw footage. The agent and his companion joined the latter group. They travelled in convoy to Changchun airport, in the Southeast of China. This was the third time the production team had filmed in the area, so they knew which local officials to bribe in order to process the necessary paperwork efficiently.

There were no problems at Changchun Airport. They breezed through[42] passport control and onto a China Airlines flight to Hong Kong. From there they transferred to a 777-airplane run, by Cathay Pacific, for the non-stop journey back to Madrid.

They had now almost reached their destination, and as the plane slowly taxied towards the airport finger of the terminal building, the agent made sure that both he and his companion had all their documentation ready. This was the final barrier to delivering his package intact. The last obstacle to collecting his 150,000-euro bonus. He switched on his mobile phone and sent an encrypted message to his contact at Interpol, James Buck, to inform him that he would be at his office, for the drop-off and debrief[43], at 11.30am that morning as planned.

Then he turned to Park and said:

---

[41] Cover story *(noun)* - A story somebody tells to conceal the truth. Often used by police officers who work undercover, and spies who infiltrate their targets.

[42] To breeze through *(phrasal verb)* - To pass through a place or process without any difficulty or impediments, like the breeze (gentle wind).

[43] To debrief *(verb)* - To review a mission or experience in detail after its completion, in order to assess how it went, and what could be improved.

"Welcome to the West, Moon Dong-woo. Let's go!

Chapter 50 - Mistaken Identity

The agent and his companion had no problems passing through Spanish customs. Park's fake identity and false passport had been fully integrated into the international passenger database. The immigration officer let them through, without a second glance, and they headed straight to the carousels, to await their equipment and suitcases.

Park walked around the Adolfo Suarez airport in a daze[44], mesmerised by the undulating architecture of the Richard Roger's designed building. In the agent's opinion, there was no more impressive welcome to a city than this iconic masterpiece. A vibrant and colourful statement of Madrid's growing influence in Europe.

Their baggage arrived without any delay, and they made their way to the exit of the airport. It was a bright morning, clear and dry, and it put a smile of the agent's face. He always loved returning to Madrid from his travels. It felt like the dust was being wiped from his eyes.

The two men jumped into a white taxi, waiting at the exit to the airport, and the agent instructed the driver to go to an industrial estate to the west of the M40 ring road[45]. Interpol had built its

---

[44] To be in a daze *(idiom)* - To be unable to think clearly, often because of shock or surprise.

[45] Ring road *(noun)* - A road that encircles a town or city designed to assist in reducing traffic volumes in the city centre. Madrid has three ring roads, or partial ring roads, of increasing circumference - the M30, M40 and M50.

European headquarters in an anonymous functional building that looked more like a warehouse than a high security centre for police intelligence. It was here that Buck and his team would be waiting for them, eager to hear all the details of the mission and meet their prized asset.

As the taxi travelled along the motorway, the agent looked out the window at the everyday life occurring around him and started to relax. His package was sitting beside him safe and sound[46], and his payday was assured. He would have the opportunity to transition into a new and less precarious career, one that was fit for a husband and father.

The taxi dropped the two men and their baggage at the entrance of Interpol. A golf cart picked them up and carried them through two sets of security gates, before they finally reached the main entrance of the building. Two armed guards escorted them from the hallway to a large conference room on the fourth floor of the building. One of the guards placed his palm on a sensor and the door of the room slid open. Inside the room were half a dozen people standing around chatting. As soon as the agent entered, the talking stopped, and everyone looked in his direction. James Buck, a tall thin man, with a big nose and pinkish cheeks, stepped forward.

"Pleasant trip?" he asked ironically[47].

"Beautiful. I highly recommend it." replied the agent knowing that Buck had never spent a single day of his career in the field. He

---

[46] Safe and sound *(idiom)* - To be unhurt or undamaged after facing some form of danger or risk.

[47] Irony *(noun)* - Verbal irony is when you say the opposite of what you mean to emphasise your point and connect with the listener at a deeper level. When it's raining you say: "Lovely weather." When you get fired from your job you say. "Wonderful." When a presentation is boring, you say "fascinating."

was a functionary, a desk jockey[48] who used freelancers to do all the dirty work[49].

The two men shook hands and then Buck looked at Park.

"So, here he is."

The Englishman inspected the package like a zookeeper might inspect a newly acquired baby Panda - with eagerness and insecurity.

"Right! Let's do the photos, fingerprints, and irises."

He and two of his colleagues led Park into another room for a complete physical examination. It was a standard routine that took about an hour to complete. The agent helped himself to a cup of coffee and took a seat at the conference table. A short bald-headed man with glasses sat down opposite him.

"Here's the paperwork. Usual stuff." He slid a thick document across the table.

The agent took out a pen and, without reading any of the notes, started signing the bottom of each of the sheets. He had been through this process several times before. Of all the intelligence agencies that he worked for; Interpol was the most bureaucratic[50]. The debriefing process took several days, required dozens of interviews and a huge pile of paperwork. Furthermore, they operated 90-day payment terms[51]. He wouldn't receive his money for at least another three months.

---

[48] Desk jockey *(idiom)* - A modification of the term disc jockey, and here we simply mean somebody who spends all their time in an office sitting at a desk.

[49] To do the dirty work *(idiom)* - To do the unpleasant or difficult duties that are nevertheless essential to get the job done.

[50] Bureaucratic *(adjective)* - Highly structured environment with many layers of hierarchy causing inefficiencies and slow decision making.

[51] 90-day payments *(adjective noun)* - An agreement where a company pays its service providers 90 days after they have finished providing their service. It is normally applied by powerful multinationals to their smaller suppliers, and means that they can increase the amount of cash on their balance sheet at the expense of their counterparty.

The agent was almost halfway through signing the document when Buck and his two colleagues burst back into the conference room.

"Is this some kind of joke?" asked the Englishman aggressively.

The agent put down his pen and looked up. "What do you mean?"

"Who the hell is this guy?"

"Kim Dae-won," said the agent perplexed by the line of questioning.

Buck was momentarily lost for words. His face went bright red. And then he consciously calmed himself down.

"Ok, we have a serious problem here."

"What is it?" asked the agent starting to feel concerned about the turn of events.

"Where did you find this guy?"

"I found him sleeping at the pick-up point on the North Korean side of the Yalu River."

"Fuck!"

Buck looked like his head was going to spontaneously combust.

"You got the wrong guy! This is not Kim Dae-won!"

"What are you talking about?"

"Look at him! Look at his body, look at his hands, he's a fucking farmer. You were meant to bring back one of the world's most dangerous hackers and you've delivered us some random North Korean peasant!"

"But that's not possible."

Buck threw a file onto the table in front of the agent. It was a comparison of the physical information they had on record for Kim Dae-won and the physical examination that they had just done on the man the agent had delivered. Nothing matched.

"But this guy speaks English, he's well educated, he saved my life."

"He's also the wrong fucking guy!"

Buck put away his pen and picked up his documents.

"Your mission has failed. You will need to meet with the assessment committee at 9am tomorrow morning. You will receive an invitation with all the details in your email inbox."

Buck opened the door and left the room. His team followed directly behind him.

The agent was dumbfounded[52]. He looked at the little North Korean still unable to believe that he wasn't Kim Dae-won. Then he jumped to his feet and ran after Buck.

"What do you want me to do with the package?"

Buck stopped in his tracks and turned around to face the agent.

"He's your problem. I suggest you contact the Korean embassy in Calle González Amigó and start the application process for asylum seekers."

The agent was lost for words. Buck continued. "And, by the way, don't even think about sending us an invoice."

And with that Buck and his entourage disappeared down the corridor.

The agent walked slowly back to the interview room, his head spinning. Was it possible that he had picked up the wrong guy from the banks of the Yalu River? Was it possible that he had confused one Korean for another? The man he had brought back was indeed small by East Asian standards, his hands were rough, and he looked like a farmer's son. However, he was extremely intelligent and seemed to understand everything that was happening around him.

The agent returned to the conference room where Park was sitting between the two security guards. The Korean had a guilty look on his face, like a kid who had just been caught stealing candy from the sweet shop.

"I don't know who you are, little man, but I'm going to find out."

---

[52] Dumbfounded *(adjective)* - So shocked by what you have experienced that you are unable to speak.

The agent gathered all his things and then grabbed the Korean and led him out of the conference room, followed closely by the guards.

"There's one thing I do know. You're not some random North Korean peasant.

QUIZ TIME

Chapters 46 to 50

COMPREHENSION QUIZ

Answer the questions with complete sentences. Say them out loud.

1. Why does Lola confront Cayetano in public rather than in private?
2. How does Cayetano react when he is asked to leave the company?
3. Who has offered to buy JBlock, why and at what price?
4. Why is JJ considering the offer?
5. Why does Guzmán Zunzunegui want to speak to Lola in private?
6. What does Zunzunegui think happened to Lola's father in Peru?
7. What is the Interpol agent thinking as they land back in Madrid?
8. How did Park feel during his time as a member of the documentary film crew?
9. What do Park and the agent have to do when they arrive at the offices of Interpol?
10. What does James Buck do when he realises that the person the agent has brought back from North Korea, is not Kim Dae-won?

BUSINESS ENGLISH QUIZ

Complete the sentences with the words used in the story.

1. I keep receiving C_____ C_____ from people trying to sell me mobile phone contracts. It's really annoying!
2. We are considering all the alternatives, but in a W_____-C_____ S_____, the company will have to file for bankruptcy.
3. We offer an E_____ S_____ to all our employees so they feel like they are owners of the business, and therefore benefit from our success.
4. They need the cash this week, so they are selling the factory for a S_____. We'll never buy it at a better price!
5. We've been negotiating this contract for the past three months. It's time to P_____ the T_____ on the deal and move forwards.
6. The company is facing multiple L_____, after it was revealed that its new factory had been contaminating the local river with toxic materials.
7. Since he joined the team, the atmosphere in the office has become unpleasant and people have been arguing with each other. He's a B_____ A_____ and we need to do something about him, before he affects the whole department.
8. At the current rate of C_____ B_____, we will run out of money within six months. We, therefore, need to close some deals quickly.
9. The sales department is O_____ a R_____. They've signed half a dozen major contracts, so far this quarter, and have another half dozen on the horizon.

10. I believe that we lost the business to our competitor because they B_____ a local politician, who supported their proposal.

11. In my experience of international business, I have always believed that when in R_____ do as the R_____, in order to fully appreciate the culture in which you're working.

12. Prior to the financial crisis, there was a steep increase in W_____-C_____ C_____, as senior directors of public companies hid their losses in offshore companies.

13. Working with the Japanese for the first time was a C_____ S_____. It has taken me many years to understand their implicit forms of communication.

14. Before the new CEO arrived, this company was a B_____ organisation that was neither effective nor efficient.

15. We will not do business with any customer who operates with 90-D_____ P_____ T_____. We believe payment for services should be paid within a month of delivery.

ANSWERS TO THE COMPREHENSION QUIZ

1. Like her father, Lola believes that managing a team can sometimes feel like theatre. She confronts Cayetano in public, not only to ensure there are witnesses who can support her, but also to gain the respect of the people who are watching.

2. At first, Cayetano is shocked. He doesn't expect the confrontation with Lola and isn't prepared for it. However, he quickly regains his composure and, as he leaves the office, he makes a threat, not only to Lola, but also to the whole team.

3. TechSpania have offered to buy JBlock for €6 a share because they believe that, with the combination of their marketing operation and JBlock's technology, they can dominate the cybersecurity market for years to come.

4. JJ Thomson is considering the offer because his company has spent a lot of money without generating any revenues or making any sales. He, therefore, feels that the offer from TechSpania is a good one, from which he and the other shareholders can benefit.

5. Guzmán Zunzunegui wants to speak to Lola in private because he believes that her father died in mysterious circumstances, while doing business in Lima, Peru. Before he retires from Interpol, he wants to find out the truth and he believes that Lola can help him.

6. Zunzunegui believes that Lola's father did not die of a heart attack but was murdered because of his willingness to confront corruption within his business sector.

7. As he lands back in Madrid, the Interpol agent is thinking about his family and his future. He is considering a new and less dangerous career, as he has a wife who adores him and a child on the way.

8. Park's experience as a member of the documentary filmmaking team was a culture shock. He was particularly intrigued by the food, the women, and the technology.

9. When Park and the agent arrive at the offices of Interpol, they have to complete a series of administrative tasks. The agent signs some documentation. Park receives a physical examination, in order to confirm his identity.

10. James Buck is furious when he finds out that the agent has not brought Kim Dae-won back from North Korea. He believes that Park is a random peasant. He, therefore, refuses to neither accept delivery of the "package" nor pay for the agent's work.

ANSWERS TO BUSINESS ENGLISH QUIZ

1. I keep receiving COLD CALLS from people trying to sell me mobile phone contracts. It's really annoying!

2. We are considering all the alternatives, but in a WORST-CASE SCENARIO, the company will have to file for bankruptcy.

3. We offer an EQUITY STAKE to all our employees, so they feel like they are owners of the business and, therefore, benefit from our success.

4. They need the cash this week, so they are selling the factory for a SONG. We'll never buy it at a better price!

5. We've been negotiating this contract for the past three months. It's time to PULL THE TRIGGER on the deal and move forwards.

6. The company is facing multiple LAWSUITS after it was revealed that its new factory had been contaminating the local river with toxic materials.

7. Since he joined the team, the atmosphere in the office has become unpleasant and people have been arguing with each other. He's a BAD APPLE and we need to do something about him, before he affects the whole department.

8. At the current rate of CASH BURN, we will run out of money within six months. We, therefore, need to close some deals quickly.

9. The sales department is ON A ROLL. They've signed half a dozen major contracts, so far this quarter, and have another half dozen on the horizon.

10. I believe that we lost the business to our competitor because they BRIBED a local politician, who supported their proposal.

11. In my experience of international business, I have always believed that WHEN IN ROME DO AS THE ROMANS, in order to fully appreciate the culture in which you're working.

12. Prior to the financial crisis, there was a steep increase in WHITE-COLLAR CRIME, as senior directors of public companies hid their losses in offshore companies.

13. Working with the Japanese for the first time was a CULTURE SHOCK. It has taken me many years to understand their implicit forms of communication.

14. Before the new CEO arrived, this company was a BUREAUCRATIC organisation that was neither effective nor efficient.

15. We will not do business with any customer who operates with 90-DAY PAYMENT TERMS. We believe payment for services should be paid within a month of delivery.

SAM GRATTON

"My name is Park Jae-bong."
Park

Chapter 51 – Capitalism

The security guards from Interpol escorted the two men out of the main building. They were driven by golf cart to the exit, where a white taxi was waiting for them. The agent instructed the driver to take them to his apartment, in the centre of Madrid. Then he turned once more to Park.

"Ok, you're coming home with me, and we are going to sort this mess out[1]. Now listen carefully. My wife has no idea that I work as a freelance spy. That means that we have to maintain your cover story when we arrive back at my house. You are Moon Dong-woo, as it says on your passport, and you are working for my production team, as location scout, for our next documentary. You are going to stay with us because your Air BnB got cancelled at the last minute."

The agent sat back in the seat of the taxi and swore.

"You have no idea what that means, do you?"

Park shook his head.

"Ok, just answer yes or no to any questions you are asked. And I warn you, my wife can be very inquisitive."

The taxi stopped in front of an apartment block in the centre of Madrid. The two men got out of the vehicle, took their luggage from the boot, entered the building, and rode the elevator to the fourth floor.

---

[1] To sort out *(phrasal verb)* - To resolve a problem or overcome a difficulty.

The agent's head was still spinning[2] from the events earlier in the day at Interpol. Why had his mission gone so badly wrong? Who was the man he had brought back from North Korea? And why was he pretending to be Kim Dae-won? But the agent had to clear his head of these doubts and questions. He was about to see his wife for the first time in two weeks. He had to take off his spy hat and put on his husband hat[3]. His wife had informed him of the pregnancy while he was in the middle of the extraction plan. It hadn't yet sunk in, and he was desperate to celebrate this special moment with her in person.

The agent opened the front door of his flat and shouted.

"Hi Honey, I'm home."

A women screamed with delight from inside the apartment.

"Eugenio! My love!"

The woman came running through the hallway and jumped into the arms of her husband.

"Concha!"

They kissed and hugged, and then, kissed again.

"We're going to be parents!"

"Yes, we are!"

Eugenio picked his wife up in his big strong arms and the two of them pirouetted on the oak parquet floor, until Concha noticed the presence of another human being in the room. The couple came to a halt and looked at the small oriental man who was standing on the threshold of their flat.

---

[2] Head spinning *(idiom)* - Feeling dizzy or confused because you have an overload of information, you are stressed, or you've had a little bit too much to drink.

[3] Wearing different hats *(idiom)* - When you have different roles or responsibilities in a situation, you are often said to be wearing different hats. In the past, everyone wore hats, and many of those hats were for a specific job or function.

"Sweetie this is... this is... Moon Dong-woo. He's part of the crew. They cancelled his Air BnB with no notice. He's gonna stay with us for a couple of days."

"Oh. Ok. Hi Moon. Or should I call you Dong. Or Woo?"

Park looked at Eugenio then back to Concha and said:

"Yes."

Concha smiled kindly. In her job as an international recruitment consultant, she had experience dealing with professionals from many different cultures. She knew that Asian men could be both taciturn and humble in the presence of strangers. She tried to make her guest more comfortable.

"You must be hungry. Let's have a bite to eat[4]."

She led the two men into the kitchen. The table was already set. It was clear that Concha had been eating with someone earlier. She turned to Eugenio and said:

"You just missed Lola. She stayed here last night. Her life is a complete mess, poor thing. I'll tell you about it later."

Concha opened the fridge door and took out a tin of anchovies, some cold meats, cheeses, and salads. Then she cut some fresh bread and motioned for the two men to sit down at the table.

"How was your trip[5]?"

"Great. We got all the shots we needed."

"So, the WWF is going to be happy?"

"Yeah, totally thrilled."

As the couple chatted about the events of the previous two weeks, Park walked slowly towards the fridge. His fascination with Western technology continued unabated. He stood next to the mighty Smeg machine and ran his hands over its smooth surface. Then he grasped the handle and gently pulled the door. It wouldn't move. He summoned all his strength and with a sudden sharp movement wrenched the door open to reveal the contents inside.

---

[4] A bite to eat *(idiom)* - A small, light meal.

[5] Trip *(noun)* - To travel is the verb. A trip is the noun (not a travel).

It took his breath away[6].

He could not, in his wildest dreams, have imagined a fridge full of so many multi-coloured products. Beautifully sculptured jars of glass full to the top with pickles. Artistically covered tins of beans of all different shapes and sizes. Bottles of wine and soda, cartons of milk and yogurt. It was a cornucopia of nutritional delight. How was it possible for so many different products to be available to the average citizen of a country? How was it possible to organise the production and distribution of each and every item that filled this fridge, from the carrots that were stored in the bottom drawer, to the pigment of paint that was used on the label of the Coca Cola bottle? Who was instructing the landowner, the farmer, the transporter, the wholesaler, and the retailer to fill this fridge with exactly the contents that the consumer desired?

Park had an epiphany. He fell to his knees. This was capitalism.

"Are you looking for something in particular?" asked Concha from the kitchen table.

"The truth." he whispered.

Concha turned to her husband and in a quiet voice said:

"Who *is* this guy?"

---

[6] To take your breath away *(idiom)* - To surprise or shock someone, normally in a pleasant way.

Chapter 52 – Confusion

Concha knew when people were telling her the truth, when they were exaggerating and when they were outright lying. In her work as an executive head-hunter[7], she had seen thousands of CVs and interviewed hundreds of executives.

"Well, who is he?" she asked for a second time.

Eugenio had to tread very carefully, if he wanted to maintain the cover story that the little Asian man in their apartment was a location scout. But before he could reply, the buzzer sounded from the hallway. Concha stood up from the table and hurried to the videophone to see who it was.

"It's Lola," she shouted from the doorway. "She forgot her iPhone."

"It's here on the kitchen table!" Eugenio shouted back to his wife. "Tell her to come up. I wanna say hello to her." He was thankful for the distraction her presence would create.

He turned to the Korean and whispered: "Hey! I told you just to say yes or no."

Park wasn't listening. He was too fascinated by the individual items in the fridge.

There were sauces from Mexico, drinks bottled in China and fresh produce from all over Spain. No central planning committee could co-ordinate production and distribution as complex as this.

---

[7] Head-hunter *(noun)* - Synonymous with recruitment consultant but sounds much cooler. Someone who helps a company fill vacant positions, normally senior roles, by persuading their targets to leave their current jobs.

No Supreme leader could deliver anything as impressive to his people. The only possible explanation for this well-ordered abundance could be Capitalism. The idea that consumers directed the system through their buying patterns in the open market.

Park had read so much about the theory but never been convinced. He didn't believe that it was possible for an economy to function without anyone controlling it. But here it was in black and white and vivid green. A fridge full of food delivered by the magic of the market.

Like an atheist who has just witnessed the tears rolling down the cheeks of the statue of the Virgin of Guadeloupe[8] in New Mexico. Park was a convert. He could have spent the whole afternoon indulging in this revelation but the sound of Concha and her friend entering the kitchen brought him back down to earth[9].

Park got up from his knees and watched from behind the fridge door as Eugenio greeted the visitor. He instantly recognised her face. She was the woman he had seen on the cover of CyberStory magazine, the woman who had been wrongly connected to the hacking of SMZ and TechSpania. She worked for JBlock, the company who had invited him to breach their systems with an ingenious game that they kept hidden inside their website.

She was far more beautiful in the flesh[10] than she was in the photos of the magazine. She was tall and strong with luxurious long black hair and dark penetrating eyes. Having read the article about

---

[8] Virgin of Guadeloupe *(noun)* - A statue in a church in Mexico that receives thousands of visitors a week because it is said to weep tears of olive oil. The phenomenon has yet to be explained and many people believe it is a miracle.

[9] To be brought back down to earth *(idiom)* - To stop daydreaming or fantasising about something and focus on the practical realities of life.

[10] In the flesh *(idiom)* - The flesh is the part of your body that is not the bone, it is your muscle, ligaments, and skin. "In the flesh" means to meet someone in person, physically, face-to-face. If you work remotely, it is important to meet your colleagues in the flesh from time to time.

her life story three times, Park already felt a cosmic connection to her.

"Lola Badiola," he said out loud.

The three friends stopped what they were doing and looked at the little oriental man, who was peering at them over the kitchen door. Concha turned to Lola.

"Oh! You two know each other. That's nice."

Lola looked confused. "We do?"

Eugenio looked even more confused. "You do?"

Park closed the fridge door to reveal himself. He had the body of an underfed teenager, and the skin of a heroin addict, but his eyes were bright and intelligent.

"My name is Park Jae-bong," he said quietly.

"I thought it was Moon," said Concha.

"I thought it was Kim," said Eugenio.

"My name is Park Jae-bong." He repeated with more confidence, and then he turned to Lola and added "but you may know me as Pluto."

Lola, Eugenio, and Concha stood in silence trying to process the information. Each one of them had their own questions to answer. Concha was wondering what her husband was doing with this strange man. Eugenio was wondering why he had assisted Park, rather than Kim, to escape from North Korea. And Lola was wondering how it was possible that Pluto, the hacker that everyone at JBlock feared and respected, was standing in her best friend's kitchen. Lola was the first to speak:

"What are you doing here?"

"I have just defected from North Korea."

Eugenio groaned and put his head in his hands.

Concha turned slowly to her husband and said: "You and I need to have a little chat. Excuse us." Then she led her two-meter-tall rugby playing partner out of the kitchen and into the living room, slowly closing the door behind them.

Lola and Park were left alone in the kitchen. They could hear the muffled sounds of the couple arguing in the room next door.

"You are *the* Pluto?"

"Yes."

Lola was sceptical. It was no secret within the hacking community that JBlock had been looking for a brilliant and mysterious coder called Pluto. It was possible that the man in front of her was a fake. She needed to know the full story.

"Why did you play our game?" she asked.

"For fun."

"How did you discover the game?"

"Your website."

"Why were you on our website?"

"I read about you in CyberStory."

"Why were you reading the article?"

"Research."

"Research for what?"

"My targets."

"Who were your targets?"

"Banco Cantábrico, SMZ, and TechSpania."

The hairs on the back of Lola's neck stood on end[11].

"You're the hacker behind the attack on TechSpania?"

"Yes."

If this were true, the implications were mind blowing. Lola needed to be sure.

"How did you do it?"

Park explained the vulnerabilities that he had exploited in the cybersecurity software protecting TechSpania. He illustrated the steps that he had taken to overcome the firewalls, insert the virus and cover his tracks. He spoke fluently, confidently, and

---

[11] Hairs on the back of your neck stand on end *(idiom)* - When you experience an adrenalin rush from fear or excitement, your skin distorts to create goosebumps, this causes the hairs on your skin to rise up, a process known as piloerection.

convincingly. It was clear that he was proud of his work. He wanted someone to hear his story and appreciate his talents.

Lola knew the software inside out. Working as a salesperson at TechSpania she had sold it to half the IBEX 35[12] companies in Spain. She realised that everything that Pluto was saying made sense, every element of his story was consistent.

"Incredible," she said, gently stroking the ego[13] of the North Korean defector. "*You* are incredible."

Lola started pacing nervously around the kitchen. She had a hundred and one more questions, but the seed of a plan had been planted inside her head. And her heart was now pounding with possibilities.

"Is TechSpania still vulnerable?" she asked.

"*Everyone* is *always* vulnerable," he replied.

Lola looked at her watch. It was 2.15pm in the afternoon. JJ's meeting with the CEO of TechSpania had already started. It was possible she had enough time to accomplish her plan. But she needed to convince the North Korean defector to come with her. She walked forwards and gently took hold of his stick-thin arms.

"I can help you Pluto. I can help you build a life here in the West. I can help you with anything you need. Do you understand me?"

Park looked up at the woman who was holding him so gently and yet so securely. He had become accustomed to the smell of Westerners during his journey and, as he breathed in her floral

---

[12] IBEX 35 *(noun)* - All developed stock markets have a benchmark index. This is a combination of the largest and most frequently traded stocks. The performance of the index is an indicator of how the overall stock market is performing. In Spain, the index it's called the IBEX 35 and it constitutes the 35 largest Spanish companies listed on the Spanish stock exchange. The benchmark index in France is known as the CAC 40, in Germany it's called the DAX and in London it's known as the FTSE 100.

[13] To stroke someone's ego *(idiom)* - In general terms, your ego is the perception you have of yourself. Your self-worth or self-esteem. If you stroke somebody's ego, you are comforting them, supporting them, agreeing with how wonderful they think that they are.

essence, he knew that she was someone he could trust. She was exactly the kind of person that he needed in the alien world in which he had landed.

He nodded his head.

"Ok," continued Lola, "but I need you to help me first. And I need you to help me now. Will you do that?"

Once again, the little North Korean nodded his head.

Lola smiled reassuringly, then she pulled the little man towards her and embraced his bony body.

Chapter 53 – The Rush

Lola was now a force of nature, a tornado sweeping any obstacle aside. She hurried into the living room where Concha and Eugenio were having a heated argument.

"I'm gonna borrow your guest, I'll bring him back this evening."

Neither of her friends paid any attention to her. Concha was on the attack. She suspected her husband of the worst. She demanded to know everything about his double life. Eugenio was doing his best to placate her, but he looked like a man on the way to the guillotine.

Lola didn't have time to intervene in the domestic dispute. She was certain that once everything was out in the open, the couple would reconcile their differences. She grabbed Park and dragged him out of the apartment.

They didn't wait for the elevator, instead they hurried down the winding wooden stairs. Lola had to catch her companion a couple of times to prevent him from falling face first down the stairwell.

They reached the exit of the building and ran around the corner to the main road. It was lunchtime, so there was a lot of competition for the cabs heading down Fuencarral. One stopped about twenty metres away to pick up an overweight couple wearing baggy jeans and sneakers, most likely American tourists on their way to the Prado[14]. Lola grabbed Park's hand, ran towards the cab, and pushed

---

[14] El Prado - One of the world's great art galleries, located in the centre of Madrid, exhibiting famous works of the Renaissance, Baroque and Romantic periods.

the couple out of the way. "Welcome to Madrid," she said as she jumped into the back seat.

"Better for them if they walk. You know what I mean…" she said to the cab driver, a typical Madrileño, who didn't know whether to defend the fat Americans or laugh at the joke. Lola gave him the address of the TechSpania headquarters and offered him a 50-euro tip if he arrived there before 3pm. This focused his mind and he accelerated away from the scene without any further comments.

Lola took out her mobile and called Diego. She got straight to the point[15].

"Hey."

"Lola!"

"You don't want JJ to sell the company, do you?[16]"

"What?"

"It was obvious at dinner last night."

"What are you talking about?"

"I don't have time to explain right now. Just listen carefully. I need you to meet me at the Headquarters of TechSpania in thirty minutes. If you leave now, and travel on your Vespa, you'll get there in time. You need to bring a laptop, the most powerful one that we have, and a standard contract for signing. You got that?"

"What's going on Lola?"

"See you at the entrance to TechSpania headquarters in thirty minutes."

Lola hung up the phone and then immediately scrolled through her contact list until she reached the name of Gonzalo Garrido. She clicked on his number.

---

[15] To get straight to the point *(idiom)* - To talk directly and immediately about an issue without any unnecessary information.

[16] Question tags *(grammar)* - A way of confirming something that you believe. The general rule is that you reverse the pronoun and verb and then you add a negative interrogative tag to a positive affirmative sentence, or a positive interrogative tag to a negative affirmative sentence.

"Gonzalo. Whatever you are doing right now, you need to drop it."

"Lola?"

"I need you to prepare me the following legal document. A confirmation that TechSpania agrees to drop all pending and future lawsuits against me related to any cyber security breaches of their company, their clients, and affiliates."

"What are you talking about?"

"I need you to do that right now and then meet me at TechSpania headquarters in 30 minutes."

"Lola, are you crazy?"

"Never been saner in my life. I'll see you in 30 minutes."

Then she hung up the phone and turned to the skinny little man sitting next to her.

"Now, Pluto, tell me everything you know about TechSpania."

As the taxi weaved frantically in and out of traffic on the M30 ring road, Park explained the weakness he had exploited in the software that controlled the company's electrical infrastructure. He told her how he was able to access the automatic transfer switch that determined whether the power entering the headquarters came from the electrical grid or from its own internal generators. He explained that he was able to trick the system into believing that there had been an external power cut, thus triggering the internal power generators to switch on and cause an electrical overload. Most machines, from desktop computers to the company elevators, would temporarily cease to function until the building management understood the problem and rebooted the system.

Lola listened carefully asking questions about how Park had discovered the vulnerabilities, what TechSpania had done to patch[17]

---

[17] To patch *(verb)* - To fix or to cover a damaged area or a weak spot. Often used in computer programming when updating or improving an application or software

them and whether he still believed these weaknesses existed. By the time they arrived at the headquarters[18], her plan was taking shape.

She got out of the taxi and looked up at the gleaming tower of steel and glass in front of her. Somewhere at the top of the building, JJ was in a meeting room finalising the terms of a deal. Lola needed to get into that room before the deal was signed.

She heard the sound of a Vespa's straining engine in the distance and spotted Diego arriving with a leather bag wrapped around his massive torso. He parked his bike on the pavement and strode over to where they were standing, his face was flushed with tension.

"I brought the laptop and contract. Now could you please tell me what the hell is going on. I almost killed myself three times on the way over here."

"This is Pluto," said Lola, introducing the little man standing next to her.

"Hi, nice to meet you" Diego replied, offering his huge, hairy hand to the stranger, too distracted by the drama to register the man's name.

Park didn't move a muscle. He'd never met anyone like Diego before, more mythical creature than human being, half man, half bear.

Lola repeated herself, this time with a little extra emphasis.

"This is *Pluto*."

Diego looked at Park, and then back to Lola and then back to Park, and finally, the penny dropped[19].

"You're kidding me. You are fucking kidding me! How did you find him?"

---

[18] Headquarters *(noun)* - A noun that ends in "S" in both the singular and the plural.

[19] The penny drops *(idiom)* - When you finally understand or realise the truth about something you can say the penny drops. In the past, a penny coin would be inserted into some mechanical machines to make them operate. Sometimes this penny would get stuck. Only when it eventually dropped would the machine start working.

"Doesn't matter. The point is he's now on our side."

Diego instantly understood the significance of the situation. Not only would they no longer have to worry about the threat of this unknown hacker, but also, they could learn from his skills and expertise.

"So, what's the plan?"

"Give Pluto the laptop. And have the standard contract ready for me when I ask for it. We're gonna gate-crash[20] JJ's party and change the music."

"Understood."

Diego reached into his satchel, pulled out the laptop and handed it over to Park.

The North Korean programmer had never used or even touched a portable computer before, everything he did in the cybercrime department was on a Chinese desktop.

He took the machine like a classical guitar prodigy might take a brand-new Fender Stratocaster. He caressed its silky body, then opened it up and ran his fingers delicately across the robust plastic keys. An expression of awe once again beamed from his face.

"Hey, what's going on?"

A taxi had just pulled up outside the entrance of the building and a man was striding towards the three of them.

"Gonzalo!"

Lola ran up to him and, in her nervous excitement, wrapped her arms around him in an enthusiastic embrace. Then she introduced him to the other two men.

"Do you have the legal document?" she asked breathlessly.

"Yeah. Just a one-pager. It's basic but it's binding[21]."

"Great!"

---

[20] To gate-crash *(verb)* - To arrive uninvited to a party and attempt to mix with everyone else as if you were meant to be there.

[21] A binding contract *(adjective noun)* - To bind is to tie something or someone tightly together. A "binding contract" is any agreement where the two parties are compelled to behave in a certain way, they are bound to the terms of the contract.

Lola took a deep breath. She now had everything that she needed to carry out her plan. But first she had to get them all past security and into the boardroom on the 51st floor of the building.

"Ok guys, follow me."

And without any further discussion, she led her three warriors: a Harvard-educated lawyer, a bearlike technology manager, and a North Korean defector, into the headquarters of TechSpania, into the house of Mario Ruiz de Velasco, deep into enemy territory.

Chapter 54 – The Entrance

Lola led her team through the revolving doors of the headquarters of TechSpania. They entered a corporate atrium with soaring ceilings, granite columns and infinite light. Like the cathedrals of medieval Spain, it was designed to both inspire and intimidate the visiting pilgrims. As the four interlopers walked quickly to the reception desk, their heals clicking randomly on the marble floor, it was not only Park who was affected by the transcendental nature of the architecture.

It had been just over three months since Lola had been escorted out of the building following her resignation. In that time nothing seemed to have changed. The same receptionists were at the desk. The same security guards were at the door. Not even the crystal vase full of flowers on the reception desk was any different. Everywhere, employees continued their seemingly critical yet ultimately trivial discussions, oblivious to the world around them.

Lola looked at the team of receptionists. She knew them well. Some could be stubborn; others could be flexible. Amongst them, she spotted José, her favourite. The man who always had time for a quick chat about everyday life. She headed straight towards him, followed closely by the gang of three.

"José! It's been too long."

He looked up as she arrived, his face revealing surprise and then happiness.

"Ms. Badiola, how are you?"

"Fine. How are Nico, Matilda, and the dogs?"

"Couldn't be better."

"I'm here with the team from JBlock. We're joining the meeting on the 51st Floor."

José looked confused.

"It's a matter of urgency."

The receptionist checked his systems and when he was unable to find any information about their visit, he politely asked the team to take a seat while he called the reception on the 51st floor.

"It was a last-minute change[22] in the agenda," said Lola, with a hint of panic in her voice. "Perhaps you could just let us through."

José's face betrayed the slightest suggestion of suspicion. He was experienced enough to sense when someone was trying to trick him. He picked up his phone and waited for the top floor reception to answer.

Lola looked back at her companions who were standing stiffly in a huddle behind her. Over their shoulders she noticed a group of grey-haired and smartly dressed businesspeople gathering in the waiting area. They greeted each other with warm smiles and firm handshakes. One of them cracked a joke and they all laughed loudly. They behaved as if they owned the place. And indeed, they did.

For this was the board of directors[23] of TechSpania. They were there to ratify the acquisition of JBlock as soon as the final agreement had been reached. Lola felt a sudden rush of adrenalin. There was no time to lose.

She leaned across the reception desk and gently pushed the crystal vase full of flowers over the edge. It bounced on the table in front of José, splashing water all over his equipment before hitting the marble floor and splintering into a thousand jagged pieces. The

---

[22] Last-minute change *(adjective noun)* - Plans that have been changed at the latest possible moment.

[23] Board of Directors *(noun)* - A team of people who are elected to represent shareholders. The board is responsible for protecting shareholders from the self-interest of the management. They establish policies for management concerning mergers and acquisitions, hiring, and paying senior managers.

other receptionists, already stressed due to the presence of the Board of Directors, were startled by the noise and commotion. They immediately looked for someone to blame, someone who would have to deal with the mess. That person was José.

While the attention of the room was distracted by the unfortunate accident, the four interlopers made their way quickly and quietly to the turnstile barriers. Diego was the first to hop over, then he helped both Park and Lola, but when he reached out his hand to Gonzalo, the lawyer wouldn't move.

"This is unlawful entry[24]."

He started to slowly back away from the turnstiles.

"Gonzalo!" hissed Diego. "You're already committed. It's too late to turn back."

"Actually, from a legal perspective, it's not."

"For Christ's sake, it doesn't matter what the law says, we're the good guys!"

Gonzalo once again shook his head and took another step backwards.

"The end doesn't justify the means."[25]

Diego threw his arms in the air in exasperation. In the distance he could see José, the receptionist, with a couple of security guards pointing in their direction. He was tempted to jump back across the turnstile, pick up the lawyer and carry him to the meeting.

Lola stepped forward. She knew full well that no logical argument would dissuade Gonzalo from his course of action, so she chose another approach. She held out her hand and said:

---

[24] Unlawful entry *(adjective noun)* - For something to be considered 'illegal', there has to be a specific law that is broken. For something to considered "unlawful" there may be no specific law broken, but it is considered to be morally wrong or unconventional.

[25] The end doesn't justify the means *(idiom)* - A question of moral philosophy. On one side, there is the utilitarian approach where the moral quality of an action is completely determined by its outcome. On the other side, there is the deontological approach, which states that there are moral rules that do not change under any circumstances.

"Please."

And for a moment the two of them were in the Prado Museum and she was guiding him to another gallery. They were walking through the pedestrian zones of Malasaña, and she was leading him to a quiet backstreet. They were strolling through the Retiro, and she was taking him to the cherry orchard.

Gonzalo shook his head again, then under his breath he said: "Fuck it!"

In one athletic leap he jumped over the turnstile and grabbed hold of Lola's hand. The two of them dashed to the nearest elevator followed by Diego and Park. The doors had just opened, and a large group of employees were flowing out. As soon as the way was clear, they ran inside, and Lola hit the button for the 51st floor.

They could hear the voices of the security guards getting closer. Before the elevator doors could fully close, a big fat arm appeared between them. The two guards, flushed with the exertion and excitement, stepped inside, and grabbed Lola by the arms.

"You need to come with us!"

Gonzalo protested. "Take your hands off her. That's an unnecessary use of force. I'm a lawyer and…"

He couldn't finish his sentence before Diego had planted his huge hairy hands on the faces of the guards and pushed them violently backwards out of the elevator and onto the marble floor. Then he turned to Gonzalo and said, "If I need a lawyer, I know where to go. Now let's get upstairs."

And with that, the doors of the elevator finally closed, and the four comrades stood in the muffled silence of the small square space. It was a moment of tranquillity, the eye of the storm[26], time

---

[26] The eye of the storm *(idiom)* - This is literally a circular area in the middle of a hurricane, which can be up to 65km in diameter, it is characterised by light winds and clear skies which last for a short period before the turbulence returns. If you are metaphorically in the eye of the storm, you are at the centre of a disagreement or conflict that affects many people.

for each of them to gather their thoughts and prepare themselves for the next challenge.

The vibration of a mobile phone disturbed the peace. They all looked at each other wondering where the noise was coming from. Lola opened her handbag and the noise of the vibrations intensified. She took out her phone and looked at the caller ID.

Mr. Red Bull.

The three men couldn't help but see the name. There was nowhere else to look. They waited for her to answer it, pretending not to care. Lola quickly declined the call and put the phone back into her bag.

"Mr. Red Bull?" asked Gonzalo.

Before Lola couldn't respond, the doors of the elevator opened onto the 51st floor and the group were immediately met by two middle-aged secretaries who acted like a couple of schoolteachers in charge of detention.

"You are not allowed up here."

"This is most irregular."

"Security is on the way."

"We will call the police if we have to."

Lola simply ignored the verbal harassment and marched down the corridor. It had been three months since Luis Bruña had led her past the panoramic views from the 51st floor, along the hallway lined with oil paintings and to the old oak door of the office of Mario Ruiz de Velasco. Now she was back in the building in order to save her job, her career and her reputation.

She reached the boardroom, paused to take three deep breaths, then opened the door and entered.

SAM GRATTON

Chapter 55 – The Setup

The boardroom was comfortably cold, kept at a steady temperature by the silent air-conditioning system. There was a faint smell of tobacco mixed with potpourri from the pots of petals on the sideboards. All the ambient noise was absorbed by the padded walls and carpeted floor.

The central feature of the room was a long thin maple wood table. It could seat about twenty-five people. At the end of it was a group of men working on a deal. None of them noticed that Lola and her team had entered, they were completely focused on some small but significant element of the contract.

At the centre of the table was Mario Ruiz de Velasco, impeccably dressed in a tailor-made[27] suit, high collar shirt and a Windsor knotted tie[28]. His silver hair was lustrous and shiny, his skin was tanned and smooth, his body language exuded confidence and invincibility. Either side of him were his lawyers, senior partners from Urdangarín Mendoza, Spain's most prestigious law firm, guarding their master like two German Shepherds[29]. To the left of

---

[27] Tailor-made suit *(adjective noun)* - A suit where the material is cut by a tailor to fit the body perfectly, as opposed to an "off-the-peg" or "ready-to-wear" suit that you would buy in a high-street shop.

[28] Windsor-knotted tie *(adjective noun)* - A way of wearing a tie that is popular with British royal family, the Windsors. A thick triangular tie knot that is meant to project confidence.

[29] German Shepherd *(adjective noun)* - Also known as an Alsatian. A German breed of working dog of medium to large size.

this group was Luis Bruña, looking thin and sallow[30], like the life had been sucked out of him by a Death Eater[31], and to the right was Cayetano Tolosa scrolling through his mobile phone.

Sitting opposite them was JJ Thomson, wearing one of his ACDC T-shirts, skin-tight jeans, and Air Jordan basketball boots. He clearly hadn't read the dress code for the party. Next to him was a wise looking man, presumably JJs legal counsel and business mentor, the man that had assisted the entrepreneur in all of his previous contract negotiations.

Lola stood at the entrance of the boardroom observing the face-off[32] in front of her - five men on one side of the table, two on the other. It seemed distinctly unbalanced, symbolic of their relative power in the cybersecurity market. It was clear that they had yet to reach an agreement and therefore Lola and her team had arrived in time. Now, she had to put her plan into action.

"Good afternoon." she said in a loud commanding voice.

All seven men stopped what they were doing and looked in her direction. What they saw was a tall, dark-haired woman, silhouetted by the boardroom's panoramic window, staring down at them with a hungry look in her eyes. Standing behind her were three shadowy figures of varying shapes and sizes. For the men, in the midst of an intense and protracted negotiation, it must have been a strange and confusing sight.

Luis put down the document he was reading, Cayetano stopped scrolling through his smartphone, and Mario Ruiz de Velasco slowly

---

[30] Sallow *(adjective)* - When the skin of light-skinned people is yellowish and looking unhealthy due to poor nutrition, stress, or lack of sleep.

[31] Death-Eater *(noun)* - A reference to one of the creatures in the books of Harry Potter. The followers of the evil Lord Voldemort. Black cloaked faceless beings that fly around at night-time and suck the life out of their victims.

[32] Face-off *(noun)* - When you stand face to face with an opponent in an attempt to intimidate them before a contest.

took off his reading glasses. They all sat in silence trying to figure out what was going on.

"Lola? What are you doing here?"

It was JJ who asked the question that was on everyone's mind.

"We have new information about JBlock that materially affects the value of the company." She replied.

Her words were met with silence. The contract negotiation was so advanced that it seemed impossible that anything could derail[33] it. All of the terms and conditions had been agreed, all the major clauses [34] had been written and the lawyers were simply proofreading[35] the final document before it was printed and signed.

"What new information?" asked JJ slowly, still unable to believe what he was witnessing.

Before Lola could answer, a group of five security guards burst into the boardroom, followed by the two receptionists from the 51st floor and José from the ground floor. The guards had their batons drawn and were ready for a riot.

"You need to come with us!", said the biggest and ugliest of them.

"Wait!" said Lola. "You need to hear what we have to say."

The guards ignored her plea and moved in to grab the intruders. One guard for each of Lola, Gonzalo, and Park, two guards for Diego. They started to push the intruders aggressively towards the entrance of the boardroom, encouraged by the three receptionists.

While this commotion was happening, nobody noticed that the wise old man sitting next to JJ had gotten to his feet. In a deep and powerful voice, he shouted:

"Hold on! Hold on!"

---

[33] To derail *(verb)* - To knock a plan or process off course, in the way a train might be knocked off it rails.

[34] Clauses *(noun)* - A specific point in a legal document that addresses a particular matter of importance to both parties.

[35] To proofread *(verb)* - The process of making sure that there are no grammatical errors, spelling mistakes or inconsistencies in a document.

The man had such a commanding presence that everyone in the room stopped and looked at him. He continued:

"If there is new information that affects the value of the company, I, for one, would like to hear it. In fact, it is my duty as legal counsel to the vendor to hear it." Then he looked at the two stony faced lawyers sitting opposite him and said, "And it is your duty to the purchaser to do the same."

Everyone now looked towards Mario Ruiz de Velasco who commanded the room like a King amongst consorts. His poker face[36] had not indicated even the faintest sign of any emotion, either positive or negative, during the whole altercation. He looked in the direction of the security guards and simply nodded his head. One by one, they released Lola and her team and reluctantly left the boardroom, followed shortly afterwards by the receptionists.

"Please take a seat," said Ruiz de Velasco calmly, motioning for the four newcomers to sit opposite him, as if they had been genuinely invited to the meeting. "Would you like something to drink? Water? Coffee?" he looked at Lola with a charming smile.

"No thank you," said Lola as she took her seat next to JJ.

Diego and Gonzalo sat either side of them. The face-off between the two companies was now more balanced, six to five in JBlock's favour.

"First of all, let me introduce you to my team," said Lola. "This is Mr. De la Fuente, Technology Manager. This is Mr. Garrido, Legal Counsel. And this is Mr. Plu To, my Personal Assistant."

JJ leaned forwards and looked across at Park with a quizzical expression on his face. He turned to Lola who nodded her head almost imperceptibly. He turned to Diego who did the same. Then he sat back in his chair, in a state of shock.

---

[36] Poker face *(noun)* - Poker is a card game where players try to work out if their opponents have a better set of cards. They do this on the basis of statistics, body language and facial expressions. If you have a "poker face", you are able to control your facial expressions during stressful situations to hide your emotions from your opponents.

"Mr. Plu To will be taking some notes today," said Lola "Do you have a WiFi password?"

Luis Bruña slid a piece of paper across the table with the relevant information on it. Park opened up the laptop, signed into the network and started to hack TechSpania.

SAM GRATTON

QUIZ TIME

Chapters 51 to 55

COMPREHENSION QUIZ

Answer the questions with complete sentences. Say them out loud.

1. Why is Park so amazed by the contents of the fridge in Concha's house?
2. What does Lola promise Park? And why does Park trust her?
3. What does Lola instruct Diego to do before they enter the TechSpania headquarters?
4. What does Lola instruct Gonzalo to do before they enter the TechSpania headquarters?
5. What group of people are waiting in the entrance of the TechSpania headquarters? And how are they behaving?
6. Why is Gonzalo reluctant to follow Lola to the elevators?
7. Who calls Lola while they are in the elevator? And how does everyone react?
8. How does Lola feel as she walks to the boardroom?
9. How do the men in the boardroom react when Lola arrives?
10. What stage have the negotiations reached between TechSpania and JBlock?

THE ADVENTURES OF LOLA BADIOLA

BUSINESS ENGLISH QUIZ

Complete the sentences with the words used in the story.

1. As a manager, you need to wear several different H_____. Sometimes you have to be a businessperson, sometimes a coach and sometimes a therapist.

2. I was contacted by a H_____ who says that she has the perfect role for me, working at a competitor with greater responsibility and twice the salary.

3. Over the last six months, we have had many meetings via webinar, but I think it's time that we met in the F_____ to get to know each other better.

4. The B_____ of D_____ have decided to reject the proposal to acquire our biggest competitor as they believe that it is not in the long-term interests of the shareholders.

5. The Spanish benchmark stock market index, the I_____ 35, rose 2% during today's trading as a result of better than forecast GDP figures.

6. We are moving the H_____ of our consulting firm from London to Paris, in order to protect ourselves from the negative impacts of Brexit.

7. After two weeks of unusual activity in the office the P_____ D_____, and I realised I was about to be fired.

8. This is a B_____ C_____. If you sign it, you are obliged to deliver the raw materials at the agreed place on the agreed date.

9. Last night we G_____ the Christmas party of one of our competitors and managed to obtain a lot of interesting information about their plans for the future.

10. The head of sales always wears a T_____-M_____ suit because he believes that the clothes you wear not only affect the way that other people perceive you, but also the way you perceive yourself.

11. I am a very demanding manager. I expect my team to do whatever it takes to get the results. In my opinion, the E_____ J_____ the M_____.

12. The recession is now at its most damaging. We are in the E_____ of the S_____. We need to stay strong and keep moving forwards, because the good times will return.

13. Your contract has a noncompete C_____, which means that if you leave the company, you cannot approach any of our clients for the following six months.

14. The report is full of typos! Who was responsible for P_____ this document?

15. It's very difficult to negotiate with our Chinese supplier. He always has a P_____ F_____ and never shows any emotion or reaction to the things that we propose.

ANSWERS TO THE COMPREHENSION QUIZ

1. Park cannot believe the quantity, diversity, and beauty of all the different products that appear in Concha's fridge.

2. Lola promises to help Park integrate into western society. She says that she will get him anything that he needs to be happy and successful. Park trusts Lola because he feels cosmically connected to her after reading about her in the CyberStory magazine.

3. Lola instructs Diego to bring a contract with standard terms and conditions for signing. She also instructs him to bring the most powerful laptop computer that they have in the office.

4. Lola instructs Gonzalo to bring a legal document stating that TechSpania will drop all current and future lawsuits against her related to her time as an employee of the company.

5. The Board of Directors of TechSpania are waiting at the entrance of the headquarters. They are chatting to each other in a relaxed manner before going upstairs to the boardroom to ratify the deal between TechSpania and JBlock.

6. Gonzalo is reluctant to follow Lola into the elevators because he considers it to be unlawful entry and therefore morally wrong. At that moment he believes that the end does not justify the means.

7. Mr Redbull calls Lola while they are in the elevators on the way up to the first 51st floor. The other three men are curious to find out who this mysterious man is.

8. Lola feels excited and nervous as she walks into the boardroom. In order to calm herself down and prepare herself mentally and physically, she takes three deep breaths before entering.

9. There is stunned silence as Lola enters the boardroom. The men are focusing on finalising the details of the contract and are unable to understand the purpose of the intrusion.

10. Although the contract has yet to be signed or ratified by the board of directors, the terms of the agreement have been reached and the lawyers are proofreading the final draft.

ANSWERS TO BUSINESS ENGLISH QUIZ

1. As a manager you need to wear several different HATS. Sometimes you have to be a businessperson, sometimes a coach and sometimes a therapist.

2. I was contacted by a HEADHUNTER who says that she has the perfect role for me, working at a competitor with greater responsibility and twice the salary.

3. Over the last six months, we have had many meetings via webinar, but I think it's time that we met in the FLESH to get to know each other better.

4. The BOARD OF DIRECTORS have decided to reject the proposal to acquire our biggest competitor as they believe that it is not in the long-term interests of the shareholders.

5. The Spanish benchmark stock market index, the IBEX 35, rose 2% during today's trading as a result of better than forecast, GDP figures.

6. We are moving the HEADQUARTERS of our consulting firm from London to Paris, in order to protect ourselves from the negative impacts of Brexit.

7. After two weeks of unusual activity in the office the PENNY DROPPED, and I realised I was about to be fired.

8. This is a BINDING CONTRACT. If you sign it you are obliged to deliver the raw materials at the agreed place on the agreed date.

9. Last night, we GATECRASHED the Christmas party of one of our competitors and managed to obtain a lot of interesting information about their plans for the future.

10. The head of sales always wears a TAILOR-MADE suit because he believes that the clothes you wear not only affect the way that other people perceive you, but also the way you perceive yourself.

11. I am a very demanding manager; I expect my team to do whatever it takes to get the results. In my opinion the END JUSTIFIES THE MEANS.

12. The recession is now at its most damaging. We are in the EYE OF THE STORM. We need to stay strong and keep moving forwards because the good times will return.

13. Your contract has a noncompete CLAUSE, which means that if you leave the company, you cannot approach any of our clients for the following six months.

14. The report is full of typos! Who was responsible for PROOFREADING this document?

15. It's very difficult to negotiate with our Chinese supplier. He always has a POKER FACE and never shows any emotion or reaction to the things that we propose.

SAM GRATTON

"I am not my father."
Lola

Chapter 56 – The Hack

Lola sat on one side of the maple wood conference table and faced her five opponents. The two lawyers looked back at her with disdain[1], as if she were a little girl interfering with her big brother's birthday party. Luis Bruña and Cayetano Tolosa shifted in their chairs. They had reason to feel uncomfortable, considering the way they had treated Lola in the recent past. In the middle of the group was Mario Ruiz de Velasco. His green eyes fixed firmly on the only woman in the room like laser sights on a rife.

"So, what is this new information Ms. Badiola?" he asked.

Lola's throat was dry from the air conditioning and the tension. She reached forward, picked up a jug of water and poured herself a drink. It was a bad idea. Her shaking hands revealed to everyone in the room how nervous she was. She took a deep but imperceptible breath to calm herself, then stared back at Ruiz de Velasco.

In this life-or-death moment, all of her senses were heightened, and time seemed to slow down almost to a stop. She could feel the cool air entering the room from the vents above them, she could smell the remnants of the coffee in the cups of the lawyers, and she could hear somebody's leg, twitching nervously, beneath the conference table.

---

[1] Disdain *(noun)* - The feeling that someone or something is not worthy of your attention or your respect. If you treat someone with disdain, you treat them with contempt, as if they are inferior to you.

She regarded Mario Ruiz de Velasco very closely. She noticed how cleanly shaven his skin was, how perfectly symmetrical his eyebrows were. There was not a single strand of hair out of place, not a single imperfection in his presentation. He looked like a movie star. He looked like a Spanish version of Richard Gere.

"Well, what's this new information?" Ruiz de Velasco repeated.

Lola was instantly brought back to the conference room. She cleared her mind and her throat.

"You are greatly undervaluing JBlock."

Ruiz de Velasco smiled patronisingly[2]. "Our offer is extremely generous, all things considered. And your boss, Mr. Thomson agrees with us."

"6 euros a share doesn't come close to the true value."

The lawyers murmured their disapproval. Cayetano shook his head and snorted. But Ruiz de Velasco remained unemotional. He leaned forward putting his hands on the table, palms facing upwards.

"Ms. Badiola, or may I call you Lola?"

Lola recognised the negotiation tactic. If she allowed him to call her by her first name, it would be a concession, a sign of weakness. If she refused, it would appear confrontational, also a sign of weakness. So, she didn't react. Ruiz de Velasco continued regardless.

"Lola, let me explain something to you. It is very difficult to put a value on a technology company. Particularly, one like JBlock that has no profits, no revenues, and no clients. It could be worth something, it could be worth nothing, or it could be worth less than nothing.

Our offer recognises the *potential* of the company, the potential for clients, revenues, and profits. And on that basis, it's extremely generous.

---

[2] Patronisingly *(adverb)* - To treat someone in way that is apparently kind or helpful but betrays a feeling of superiority over that person. The word patronise comes from Latin patronus "protector, master," related to "pater" or father. So if you patronise a person, you talk to them like a master to his apprentice or a father might do to his child.

You see, without us, JBlock is worthless. Without us, JBlock cannot get a foothold[3] in the cybersecurity market. Only with us can this potential be realised. Only with us can revenue synergies[4] be exploited, and shareholder value created.

You may not understand this Lola, but your boss does."

Ruiz de Velasco received a text message. He read it and then he turned back to Lola.

"The Board of Directors are on their way up. We really need to finish proofreading these documents. So, I'd kindly ask you and your little friends to leave the conference room."

In response to Ruiz de Velasco's condescension, Lola decided it was time to reveal the first ace that she had up her sleeve[5].

"Thank you for the lesson in finance Mr. Ruiz de Velasco. I completely agree with your analysis of the situation apart from one fundamental difference."

"Really, and what is that?"

"JBlock does have a foothold in the cybersecurity market. It does have its first client. And this client is a whale[6]."

---

[3] Foothold *(noun)* - A place where you can safely put your feet when climbing. In business, we use it, metaphorically, to refer to a solid position from which further progress may be made.

[4] Synergies *(noun)* - An extremely important concept in business, in particular, in the world of mergers and acquisitions. Where the combined power of two companies working together is greater than the total power achieved by each company working separately.

[5] To have an ace up your sleeve *(idiom)* - In most card games, the ace is the highest card. Someone cheating in the game might hide *an ace up their sleeve,* in order to use it to win. The expression has evolved into meaning you have secret knowledge or a secret skill, that will give you an advantage at the appropriate moment.

[6] A whale *(noun)* - Salespeople often use fish metaphors. If you lose a client, you might say: "Don't worry there are plenty more fish in the sea". If you are going to pitch to an important client, you might say: "This guy is a big fish". In this case "a whale" is much larger than your usual target, it is a sales prospect so big that it could make a major difference to your company's sales.

There were confused looks from the businessmen on both sides of the table.

"JBlock has no clients, Lola, I can assure you of that."

"As a matter of fact, it does."

"Who?"

"You."

There was a moment's silence and, then, the men sitting opposite reacted in their own peculiar way. Cayetano laughed at the ridiculousness of the suggestion. The lawyers complained about their time being wasted. And Ruiz de Velasco instructed Luis Bruña to call the security guards back into the conference room.

Lola stood up from her chair, walked over to where Park was sitting and whispered something into his ear. Then she said in a loud voice.

"You are vulnerable, TechSpania, and you need our technology to protect you." The five men, sitting opposite, stopped what they were doing and looked up at her.

"What are you talking about?"

Lola clicked her fingers and the lights in the room went out. The air conditioning system stopped functioning. And the coffee machine switched off.

"What's going on?"

Lola didn't respond, she wanted the effects of her actions to sink in[7], like a magician allowing her audience to absorb a particularly astounding trick. One by one, Tolosa, Bruña and Ruiz de Velasco received calls on their mobiles from their respective deputies, telling them that all power had been lost and asking what should be done next. The door of the conference room burst open and one of the receptionists from the 51st floor rushed in, a look of panic on her face.

---

[7] To sink in *(phrasal verb)* - To gradually start to understand something or realise the effect it will have on you.

"The Board of Directors!" she blurted out. "The Board of Directors are trapped in the elevator!"

There was only one person who knew the next move. That person was Lola Badiola. She sat back down in her chair and calmly repeated her earlier statement.

"You are vulnerable, TechSpania, and you need our technology to protect you."

SAM GRATTON

Chapter 57 – The Offer

Ruiz de Velasco stood up from his chair, his face incandescent with rage.

"Whatever game you are playing, stop it right now!"

Lola didn't flinch[8]. It was her turn to show a poker face in the heat of the moment.

"Take a seat Mr. Ruiz de Velasco and let me explain something to you."

Ruiz de Velasco looked down at his two lawyers.

"Do something! You overpaid sons of bitches!"

The two lawyers had no idea what Ruiz de Velasco expected them to do, so they decided to play it safe and do nothing.

"Sit down Mr. Ruiz de Velasco," repeated Lola. "We are here to help you."

Lola took the next ace from her sleeve. She pointed at Park who was quietly tapping away on the laptop, oblivious to the commotion around him.

"My assistant has been scanning your digital infrastructure. It appears you have a weakness in the electrical systems of your headquarters. We have been able to access the automatic transfer switch and cut off all your power."

Ruiz de Velasco's eyes almost popped out of his head.

---

[8] To flinch *(verb)* - To make a sudden, small reaction to pain or the fear of pain.

"You've hacked us! This is an outrage. Desist from this activity immediately!"

The CEO's lawyers suddenly found their voices. They started quoting all the laws that Lola was breaking by her actions, including the fines that would be imposed on her and the time she could spend in prison. At this point, Gonzalo stepped in to respond to each of their claims, giving reasons why they were irrelevant for the current situation. Although, in truth, he couldn't disagree with them.

As the noise and commotion in the room rose to a crescendo, Cayetano took the opportunity to verbally insult Lola, accusing her of lying, cheating, and stealing. This brought Diego to Lola's defence. He'd been waiting for an opportunity to confront Cayetano, the traitor, and he didn't hold back. It became impossible to hear anything above the noise of the insults being thrown around the room.

Once again, it was the wise old man, acting as JJ advisor, who brought order back to the proceedings. In his deep and booming voice, he managed to recapture the attention of the room.

"Hold On! Hold On!"

The combatants stopped screaming at each other and looked at the old man.

"Ms. Badiola has something to say. The sooner that we hear it, the sooner we can fix the problem."

Lola waited for the testosterone in the room to subside, and for everyone to settle back down into their chairs. Then she started her speech.

"Yes. We have hacked you." she said in a calm and confident voice. "We've hacked you to protect you.

You may say it is an outrage. Your lawyers might accuse me of criminal activity. But isn't it better that we hack you before someone else does? Isn't it better that we discover your weaknesses before a malicious intruder does?

Last month, your share price dropped 20%, following a breach of your systems. We know who was responsible for this attack, we

THE ADVENTURES OF LOLA BADIOLA

know how they did it, and we know how to ensure it never happens again. We also know how to prevent them from exploiting other network vulnerabilities, like the one in your electrical systems.

That is why you need our technology, Mr. Ruiz de Velasco".

The CEO squirmed[9] in his chair. His left eye twitched[10]. And he drummed his fingers[11] on the surface of the maple wood conference table.

"There is something that you don't seem to understand Ms. Badiola." His voice was trembling with suppressed rage. "I am in the process of buying your technology. Mr. Thomson and I have already come to an agreement. Now stop playing games, turn the electricity back on and get out of my office."

JJ's advisor leaned forward to clarify a legal point.

"Technically, we haven't reached an agreement until everyone has signed the contract and it has been ratified by the Board of Directors." He looked across at Lola with a twinkle in his eye[12]. It was clear that he wanted her to keep going.

"As I said before this agreement dramatically undervalues JBlock," continued Lola. "With TechSpania as a client, the value of our company rises dramatically. It is a "proof of concept"[13], a signal

---

[9] To squirm *(verb)* - To twist your body.

[10] To twitch *(verb)* - To make a very sudden, unintentional movement.

[11] To drum your fingers *(idiom)* - To rapidly tap your fingertips on a surface, normally due to impatience or frustration.

[12] A twinkle in your eye *(idiom)* - To twinkle is to emit light in a flickering manner. It is what stars do on a dark cloudless night. If there is a twinkle in your eye, there is a sparkle that indicates happiness, amusement, or knowledge of a secret.

[13] Proof of concept *(noun)* - A way of ensuring that the investment of time and money in a new service or technological innovation is worth it. You create a basic version, or prototype, to test on your market. If the prototype works and generates demand, then you have "proof of concept" and you can take the next steps in product development.

to the market that our technology not only functions but is also best in class[14]."

Ruiz de Velasco snorted at the absurdity of her argument.

"TechSpania is not, nor ever will be a client of yours! And JBlock is worthless without us!"

JJ sat quietly listening to the confrontation around him.

Less than half an hour earlier he had been on the verge of selling his company for 6 euros a share to TechSpania. When Lola and Diego burst into the meeting room, he was as confused as he was intrigued. He knew that neither of them wanted him to sell the company, but he didn't realise what lengths they would go to in order to disrupt the process.

He decided to remain silent. He could see that Lola was on a roll. He wanted to find out what else she might have up her sleeve. And she didn't disappoint him.

"Well, Mr. Ruiz de Velasco," she said shaking her head slowly. "That is a pity. For both TechSpania and JBlock."

Then she stood up and walked out of the conference room.

There was a stunned silence.

Gonzalo packed up his notes and followed her. Diego grabbed hold of Park and they did the same. The conference room was left in exactly the same state as it was just half an hour earlier. Five members of the TechSpania team facing two members of the JBlock team.

Mario Ruiz de Velasco leaned over the Luis Bruña and in a voice filled with bitterness and frustration, he said.

"Bring them back here."

---

[14] Best in class *(adjective)* - The most superior product within a category. It does not necessarily mean the best product overall. For example, the best-in-class product in a low-priced category may be inferior to the best product on the market. Best in class means that it is the best relative to its peer group.

Chapter 58 – The Signature

Before Lola and her team could reach the end of the corridor, Luis Bruña caught up with them and convinced them to return to the meeting. They followed him back to the conference room to find Ruiz de Velasco in a huddle with his two lawyers. JJ and his advisor were also exchanging words.

Lola sat back down knowing that she now held the upper hand[15] in the negotiation. She waited for Ruiz de Velasco to finish his consultation and speak.

"Before we go any further," he said, "you need to turn our electricity back on."

"Have you decided to retain our services?" replied Lola.

"It's an option that we are considering."

"Diego." Lola turned to the technology manager and indicated that this was his moment. He reached into his bag and pulled out the one sheet document which he slid across to Ruiz de Velasco.

"This is a contract with our standard terms and conditions," said Diego. "As you are our first client, we are offering a 25% discount to our normal fee."

Ruiz de Velasco passed it on to one of his lawyers.

"Thank you. We will consider it and get back to you. Now turn the electricity back on."

---

[15] To hold the upper hand *(idiom)* - If you hold the upper hand, you have more power than anyone else. You have control over a situation.

"There's not much to consider. It's only one page long. Here, you can use my pen to sign it." Diego slid a biro across the shiny surface of the table.

The two men stared at each other. Ruiz de Velasco was the first to blink[16].

"Are you telling me, only if I sign this document are you going to turn our electricity back on." He was almost unable to get the words out of his mouth.

"Not at all," replied Diego. "We're saying only if you sign this document can you benefit from the protection of our technology."

"This is blackmail!" screamed the CEO through gritted teeth.

Lola leaned forward. "In some places it's called blackmail, in others it's called persuasion."

Diego continued. "It's just a one-year contract. We are not locking you into a long-term agreement. You're under no obligation to renew it."

Lola added: "But we will be issuing a press release, stating that TechSpania will be using JBlock's cybersecurity technology for the next twelve months."

Ruiz del Velasco looked around the room in a state of panic and fury, he turned to his two lawyers. "Do something you useless bastards!" Once again, the two suits started quoting the laws that JBlock was breaking, once again Gonzalo responded to the accusations, knowing full well that they were right.

The secretary from the 51st floor re-entered the office. She rushed over to the CEO to update him on all the major issues the power cut was causing around the building. Of greatest concern to her was the fact that the Board of Directors had been trapped in the lift for more than five minutes. One of them suffered from claustrophobia and another was feeling nauseous. The Chairman of

---

[16] To blink first *(idiom)* - This expression comes from a game where two children stare at each other with their eyes open until one of them blinks and loses the game.

the Board was trying to contact him on his mobile at that very moment.

Ruiz de Velasco snatched the contract from the table in front of him and scanned its contents. Then he passed it to Luis Bruña and instructed his subordinate to sign it.

Bruña put on his reading glasses and started to carefully study the document that would bear his signature.

"Just sign the damn thing!" shouted the CEO.

"I need to read it first, sir."

"Oh, for Christ's sake, give it to me."

Ruiz de Velasco grabbed the document back from Bruña, pulled out a Mont Blanc fountain pen from the inside of his tailor-made suit and scrawled his signature at the bottom of the paper. Then he slid the document back to Diego.

"Thank you," said Diego, as he put the signed document back into his leather bag.

"Just one last thing," said Lola. "I, myself, will be your account manager."

"Wonderful," replied the CEO transmitting his sarcasm[17] and impatience in equal measure.

"Therefore, it wouldn't be right if you were suing me for 150 million euros, would it?"

Gonzalo knew that his moment had arrived. He took out the legal document that Lola had asked him to prepare. He passed it to the lawyers from Urdangarín Mendoza, who started to read through it. He explained to them in elaborate legal language that all current and pending lawsuits against Lola, relating to the recent breach of TechSpania and its consequent drop in share price, needed to be immediately and permanently withdrawn. He said that everyone in the room knew that Ms. Badiola was innocent, and the lawsuit

---

[17] Sarcasm *(noun)* - Previously we have explained what "irony" is - the implicit form of communication where you say the opposite of what you mean, in order to emphasise your point. Sarcasm is a negative form of irony, where the intention is to embarrass or insult someone.

represented a malicious[18] and slanderous[19] attack on her character. He then started to explain in great detail, the individual clauses of the document that the lawyers had in front of them.

Before they had time to finish reading or responding to it, Ruiz de Velasco grabbed the document from under their noses, signed it in the appropriate places and then threw it back at Gonzalo.

"Now turn the electricity back on!"

Lola turned to Park, who was waiting for the signal, and nodded her head. He typed some code into the laptop and, all at once, the lights went on, the air conditioning restarted, and the coffee machine beeped three times.

There was a moment of silence in the boardroom before JJ's legal counsel cleared his throat and spoke in a conclusive manner.

"Well, ladies and gentlemen, it appears that there has been a material change in the circumstances, and hence the value, of JBlock. It is, therefore, appropriate to suspend our current negotiations. On behalf of JJ Thomson and the other shareholders, I would like to thank you for your offer but, at this juncture, I respectfully decline it."

Ruiz de Velasco sat motionless in his chair staring at Lola. His aura, which had blazed like a forest fire for the last fifteen minutes, cooling down to a steady green glow.

One of the character traits of a great leader is the ability to move on, to understand that these moments of victory and defeat are merely signposts on the road of success. The CEO was once again the embodiment of elegant composure.

---

[18] Malicious *(adjective)* - From the Latin word *malus*, for bad. A malicious person derives pleasure from hurting others.

[19] Slanderous *(adjective)* - Making statements or claims about someone that you know to be untrue, in order to damage them or negatively impact their reputation.

"Your father did everything by the book[20], Lola." he said with eerie calmness. "He was a straight shooter[21], known throughout Spain and South America as someone who did things right. What would he think of his one and only daughter? Would he be proud of her?"

Lola stared back at Ruiz de Velasco, not losing eye contact for a second. She slowly reached for her glass of water, her hands steady and strong, and took a small sip.

"I am not my father," she replied.

There was silence in the boardroom.

And then Ruiz de Velasco, slowly rose to his feet and buttoned up his jacket. It was the signal that the meeting was over. Everyone else stood up in unison.

"It's going to be an interesting business relationship Ms. Badiola," he said unemotionally.

He turned to his lawyers and told them to wrap up the meeting[22] and join him in his office with the Board of Directors. Then he walked quickly out of the conference room.

Lola immediately turned to JJ. He had been quiet throughout the meeting. She wondered what he was thinking. She needed his validation.

"I brought you JBlock's first client," she said "I recruited Pluto as a programmer and I'm free of all my legal distractions. Now let's fulfil our mission and make the digital world a safer place."

JJ had a one-word reply, or perhaps it was two words combined into one.

"Un-fucking-believable!"

---

[20] To do everything by the book *(idiom)* - To always follow the rules or regulations. Its origin comes from swearing over the Bible, done in court before giving testimony.

[21] A straight shooter *(idiom)* - An informal phrase that describes a person who behaves and communicates in an honest and direct way, like the straight path of a bullet shot from a gun

[22] To wrap up a meeting *(phrasal verb)* - To conclude a meeting.

All five members of the JBlock team burst into laughter at the communal release of tension. They shook hands, kissed, and hugged each other, and then made their way to exit the conference room. Waiting for them, at the door, were the two lawyers from Urdangarín Mendoza.

"You know these contracts aren't worth the paper they're written on[23]," said one of them.

Gonzalo had anticipated the argument and stepped forward.

"You might think these contracts are worthless. You might say that we coerced you into signing them. You might be tempted to break them.

Here's what will happen next.

You will find yourself in court explaining how a relatively unknown company called JBlock was able to hack into your systems, temporarily shut down your headquarters, and convince your CEO to sign a contract.

Think about how this will appear to the outside world, only two months after the press conference, in which you explained, in great detail, all the improvements you were making to your cybersecurity systems.

Just think about what that would do to your share price."

Without another word, Lola opened the door and led the team along the corridor, passed the oil paintings and the panoramic views of Madrid, to the 51st floor reception.

The elevator arrived and Lola allowed the four men to enter before she did. She patted them each on the back as they walked inside, then she pressed the button and the doors closed.

A song could be heard from the elevator as it descended past each floor of the TechSpania headquarters, a song which was being sung with enthusiasm and delight, albeit slightly out of tune.

---

[23] Not worth the paper it's written on *(idiom)* - An agreement or contract that cannot be enforced and is, therefore, worth nothing. It's worth less than the paper it is written on.

"Cámpeones! Cámpeones! Oeh! Oeh! Oeh![24]"

---

[24] Campeones! ¡Campeones! Oeh! Oeh! Oeh! - A popular football chant, sung by the winning team of a tournament and their supporters, most notably in The Champions League.

SAM GRATTON

Chapter 59 – The Aftermath

The team from JBlock stood in a circle outside the glass and steel skyscraper of the TechSpania headquarters. The centre of attention was Park Jae-bong, the little North Korean hacker whose programming skills had allowed Lola to make her audacious, some might say outrageous, sales pitch to Mario Ruiz de Velasco.

JJ and Diego were fascinated by his tiny physique, his mighty skills, and his personal story. They inundated Lola with questions that she couldn't really answer. Who was he? Where did he come from? How did she find him? She avoided answering directly until she had spoken to Eugenio. In fact, she felt responsible for returning Park to her friend, as soon as possible.

The older man who was working as JJ's legal counsel stepped forward and introduced himself to Lola. He told her that in all his years of negotiating deals in Silicon Valley, he'd never been involved in one as surprising as this. Then he turned to Gonzalo and gave him his business card. "Let's talk," he said, patting the young lawyer on the shoulder. "My firm is looking for joint ventures in Europe."

"Drinks?" suggested Diego.

"Where's the nearest bar?" replied JJ.

Lola shook her head.

"I'd love to guys, but Pluto and I have got some loose ends to tie up[25]. We'll be at the offices in Gran Vía at 9am tomorrow."

Diego and JJ protested in an exaggerated manner, but Lola wouldn't budge. She gave them both a kiss and a hug. Then she turned to Gonzalo to thank him. She realised what a difficult situation she had put him in. If the meeting hadn't gone exactly as planned, he could have lost his licence to practice law. Without him at the meeting, the lawyers from Urdangarín Menéndez would have taken control and the outcome would have been very different.

She stepped forwards and embraced him, wrapping her arms tightly around his muscular back. He smelled like a fresh pine forest on a crisp winter's morning. She held onto him longer than was professional, longer than what is normal for a friendship. And he didn't resist her.

The other men in the group made small talk.

"Why don't you come over to my office tomorrow evening," said Gonzalo. "We can run through[26] the details of the legal agreements. And then we can go out for dinner."

Lola looked up into his familiar eyes and smiled.

"I'd like that," she replied.

Then the two of them pulled away from their embrace and wished each other well. Gonzalo joined the JBlock team for a quick drink, while Lola led Park to an empty taxi stand.

Her mind replayed the events of the previous hour. She thought about what she had said, what she could have said better and how everyone reacted. She wondered what Ruiz de Velasco would do next. Would he just ride out the twelve-month agreement, would he try to break the contract, or would he find some devious way to

---

[25] Loose ends to tie up *(idiom)* - To complete the minor tasks that are outstanding. When sailors prepare their boat for departure, they make sure that any loose strings or ropes on board the boat are securely fastened.

[26] To run through *(phrasal verb)* - To quickly review a document.

exact his revenge on her? In any case, she was ready for a fight, and, in the form of Pluto, she had a nuclear weapon.

An empty taxi arrived, and Lola helped Park inside. As she joined him in the back seat, she noticed a black Toyota Prius parked directly opposite them. Inside of it was a man looking in their direction. As the cab pulled away from the taxi rank, Lola looked closely at the stationary car. Inside of it, making no attempt to conceal himself, was Guzmán Zunzunegui.

Lola thought back to their late-night conversation. She still hadn't processed the suggestions of the Interpol agent. The first thing she planned to do that weekend was speak to her mother about the business of Grupo Badiola in South America. And this time she was going to get the whole truth.

It was a fifteen-minute ride to Concha's house. Sitting outside on the steps of the entrance was Eugenio. He got slowly to his feet as they arrived.

"How did it go?" he asked.

"Well." she replied.

Lola and Eugenio stood in the street staring at each other, waiting for the other one to speak first. In the end, they both started talking at the same time.

"So, what's happening with…"

"Listen, I need to explain…."

They both stopped abruptly, and then Lola asked very quietly.

"Are you a spy?"

Eugenio burst into fake laughter. "No! No! No!" he said, but his face blushed crimson red and he looked down at the pavement to avoid Lola's eyes.

She stood very still and waited for him to recover his composure.

"Well, actually, I don't call myself a spy." he said, "I'm a geopolitical consultant. I specialise in the extraction of dissidents, political prisoners, and persons of interest from rogue nations[27]."

"Wow!" Lola's eyes opened wide with astonishment. "So, the documentary film making is just a cover[28]."

Eugenio looked around nervously. But there was nobody in the vicinity.

"It's the perfect cover." He replied with a satisfied smile. "I travel the world - Russia, China, Venezuela – acting as the executive producer. I integrate our targets into the film crew and bring them back to friendly territory."

"Does Concha know?"

Once again Eugenio's face betrayed his embarrassment.

"She does now."

"Uh oh."

"Yeah. She's kicked me out[29] of the house. It's gonna be some time before she lets me back in. Would you mind holding onto the little man for a couple of days until I sort things out with her. I can see that he trusts you."

Lola was delighted by the suggestion. The more time she spent with Park, the higher the probability of him settling into a working life at JBlock.

"Sure. No problem."

"Thanks. I'm gonna try the buzzer again."

---

[27] Rogue nations *(idiom)* - A rogue is a person who does not behave in the way expected by civil society. They might appear attractive on the surface but deep down they are dangerous. A rogue nation is a country that doesn't wish to be part of the liberal, democratic world order. The term was first used, by the American government, in 1994 to describe five states: North Korea, Cuba, Iran, Iraq, and Libya.

[28] A cover *(noun)* - A word with multiple meanings. In the context of international espionage, it is an alternative identity that hides the fact that someone works as a spy.

[29] To kick out *(phrasal verb)* - To expel somebody from a room or an event.

"Ok, good luck with that."

Eugenio hugged Lola. He bowed at Park. And they parted company.

Lola decided to take the Korean for a walk through Malasaña on the way back to her apartment. She wanted him to start getting used the sights, smells, and sounds of the neighborhood. She wanted him to experience the very best that Madrid had to offer, like the seafood at La Sirena Verde, the soups at Casa Fidel and the steaks at El Balón."

"So, Mr. Plu To where would you like to eat this evening. The world is your oyster[30]."

"Burger King." he replied without hesitation.

"Burger King?"

Park nodded his head with the enthusiasm of a 10-year-old boy organising his birthday party.

"Ok, Burger King it is then." said Lola with a shrug.

It was a short walk to the nearest branch. They waited in line for a couple of minutes then ordered two Whopper meals. They sat opposite each other at one of the uncomfortable plastic tables taking huge bites out of the hamburgers.

Park was in ecstasy, a North Korean defector, sitting in a restaurant in Madrid, eating the American dream. He finished every morsel of the food, then spent a moment with his eyes closed allowing the serotonin to course through his blood system. Eventually he came back to the real world. He looked down at the paper covering his tray and ran his fingers backwards and forward over the Burger King logo.

"Lola Badiola," he said in a quiet voice.

"Yes." replied Lola attentively.

"You said that you would help me."

---

[30] The world is your oyster *(idiom)* - An idiom, of Shakespearean origin, that indicates that there are opportunities for you in life. There is a pearl inside the oyster shell. The idiom is often used to motivate and inspire young people as they graduate from school or university.

"Yes."

"You said you would get me whatever I wanted."

"Yes."

"I want you to find Kim Dae-won."

"Who?"

"I want you to bring Kim to the West."

"What?"

"I want you to help him escape from North Korea."

QUIZ TIME

Chapters 56 to 59

COMPREHENSION QUIZ

Answer the questions with complete sentences. Say them out loud.

1. In what way is Ruiz de Velasco patronising to Lola?
2. Why does he believe that 6 euros a share is a generous offer for JBlock?
3. What is Lola's argument to prove that the offer undervalues JBlock?
4. What is Lola's justification for hacking TechSpania?
5. Is Lola blackmailing Ruiz de Velasco?
6. How does Ruiz de Velasco act at the very end of the confrontation?
7. What do the lawyers from Urdangarín Mendoza say about the contracts? And how does Gonzalo respond?
8. Why doesn't Lola go for a drink with the team to celebrate?
9. What does Eugenio tell Lola about his secret life?
10. What does Park ask Lola to do at the end of story? Will Lola be able to fulfil his wishes?

BUSINESS ENGLISH QUIZ

Complete the sentences with the words used in the story.

1. With this first big sale to a national supermarket, we have finally got a F_____ in the fruit and vegetable market.

2. We consider there to be tremendous S_____ from this merger which will allow us to produce higher quality goods at a much lower cost.

3. He always goes into a negotiation with an A_____ up his S_____, a proposal that nobody expects, helping him get the best deal possible for the company.

4. One of our junior salespeople has just caught a W_____. They have signed up the biggest purchaser of metallic paint in the market.

5. Before we invest a lot of money in this new technology, we would like you to offer a basic version for our London office to test, over the next quarter, as a P_____ of C_____.

6. We may not be the largest supplier of language classes in the market, but we do offer B_____ in C_____ business communication coaching.

7. I think we can demand another 2% discount because our supplier is very dependent on our business, and we, therefore, hold the U_____ H_____ in this negotiation.

8. In the battle between Coke and Pepsi for the domination of the Cola market, it was Coke that B_____ F_____ in the 1980s and introduced a new recipe, called "New Coke", that nobody liked.

9. The regulators are watching us very carefully after the recent financial scandals in the banking sector so I would like everyone to do everything B_____ T_____ B_____.

10. The new head of sales is a real S_____ S_____. She's honest, open, and direct, and even though you might not like what she says all the time, she does at least tell you the truth.

11. Before we W_____ U_____ this meeting and head off for lunch, I would just like to thank you all for making a really big effort to be here today.

12. Let's R_____ T_____ the speech one last time before you go up on stage.

13. This contract is not W_____ the P_____ it's W_____ O_____ because it was signed by the wrong person.

14. I'm a bit stressed, at the moment, because I have a lot of L_____ E_____ to T_____ U_____ in the office, before I leave for my summer holiday.

15. Just remember, as recent graduates of this university, you have opportunities waiting to be grasped. The W_____ is your O_____.

ANSWERS TO COMPREHENSION QUIZ

1. Ruiz de Velasco speaks to Lola as if she doesn't deserve to be in the boardroom and she doesn't understand the process that is underway. He calls her by her first name, he smiles at her like a parent to a child and he explains concepts to her that she already understands.

2. Valuing a company is a complex and subjective process, particularly if the company is a start-up with no revenues and no sales, which is the case with JBlock. Ruiz de Velasco, therefore feels that an offer of €6 per share for the company is a generous offer, considering the unproven business model and the uncertainties ahead.

3. Lola argues that the price undervalues JBlock because the company does indeed have a client and a source of revenue, and therefore, a proven technology and business model.

4. Lola's justification for hacking TechSpania is that the company has a security weakness that could be exploited by a malicious intruder. Her team is simply demonstrating these weaknesses and how they can be eliminated.

5. Absolutely.

6. At the end of a confrontation, Ruiz de Velasco regains his composure and moves on to the next business in hand, in a professional and rational manner.

7. The lawyers from Urdangarín Mendoza argue that the contracts are worthless because they have been signed through coercion and blackmail. Gonzalo responds that this may be true, but if TechSpania decided to pursue legal action against JBlock, the negative publicity of their security weaknesses would cause even greater damage.

8. Lola doesn't go for a drink with the rest of the team because she says that she has some loose ends to tie up. She needs to return Park to the house of Eugenio and Concha, and she wants to find out if they have resolved their misunderstanding.

9. Eugenio explains to Lola his secret life as a freelance spy, working on behalf of international intelligence agencies extracting persons of interest from rogue nations.

10. At the end of the story, Park reminds Lola of the promise that she made to him earlier that day. He tells her that he wants her to extract Kim Dae-won from North Korea. Will Lola be able to fulfil this promise? Find out in the next book!

ANSWERS TO BUSINESS ENGLISH QUIZ

1. With this first big sale to a national supermarket, we have finally got a FOOTHOLD in the fruit and vegetable market.

2. We consider there to be tremendous SYNERGIES from this merger, which will allow us to produce higher quality goods at a much lower cost.

3. He always goes into a negotiation with an ACE UP HIS SLEEVE, a proposal that nobody expects, helping him get the best deal possible for the company.

4. One of our junior salespeople has just caught a WHALE. They have signed up the biggest purchaser of metallic paint in the market.

5. Before we invest a lot of money in this new technology, we would like you to offer a basic version for our London office to test, over the next quarter, as a PROOF OF CONCEPT.

6. We may not be the largest supplier of language classes in the market, but we do offer BEST IN CLASS business communication coaching.

7. I think we can demand another 2% discount because our supplier is very dependent on our business, and we therefore HOLD THE UPPER HAND in this negotiation.

8. In the battle between Coke and Pepsi for the domination of the Cola market, it was Coke that BLINKED FIRST in the 1980s and introduced a new recipe, called "New Coke", that nobody liked.

9. The regulators are watching us very carefully after the recent financial scandals in the banking sector, so I would like everyone to do everything BY THE BOOK.

10. The new head of sales is a real STRAIGHT SHOOTER. She's honest, open, and direct and even though you might not like what she says all the time, she does at least tell you the truth.

11. Before we WRAP UP this meeting and head off for lunch, I would just like to thank you all for making a really big effort to be here today.

12. Let's RUN THROUGH the speech one last time before you go up on stage.

13. This contract is not WORTH THE PAPER IT'S WRITTEN ON because it was signed by the wrong person.

14. I'm a bit stressed, at the moment, because I have a lot of LOOSE ENDS TO TIE UP in the office, before I leave for my summer holiday.

15. Just remember, as recent graduates of this university, you have opportunities waiting to be grasped, the WORLD IS YOUR OYSTER.

NEXT STEPS

If you are you are looking for ways to keep bringing Business English in your life in an entertaining way, here are some suggestions:

You can listen to the podcast of The Adventures of Lola Badiola on all major streaming platforms, as well as the LinkedIn Learning platform.

You can join both Sam and Marina at Club Gratton for live and interactive Business English classes on a weekly basis. Just search "Club Gratton" on Google and you will find us.

And, of course, watch out for the sequel to this novel. There are more adventures to come!

ACKNOWLEDGEMENTS

This book would not have been possible without the help and advice of my business partner and "partner partner", Marina Solana Gabeiras. Muchas gracias, Sweetie!

I'd also like to thank all the wonderful people at Club Gratton for their support and feedback.

Cover Art by: Zana at 99designs

BIBLIOGRAPHY

The definitions and explanations used in the footnotes of this book have been written in our own words, but they have been cross-referenced with a wide variety of sources, including:

dictionary.com
merriam-webster.com.
dictionary.cambridge.org
collinsdictionary.com
oed.com
macmillandictionary.com
britannica.com/dictionary
thefreedictionary.com
vocabulary.com/dictionary
wikipedia.org
investopedia.com
Transparency International
Economics Intelligence Unit

INDEX

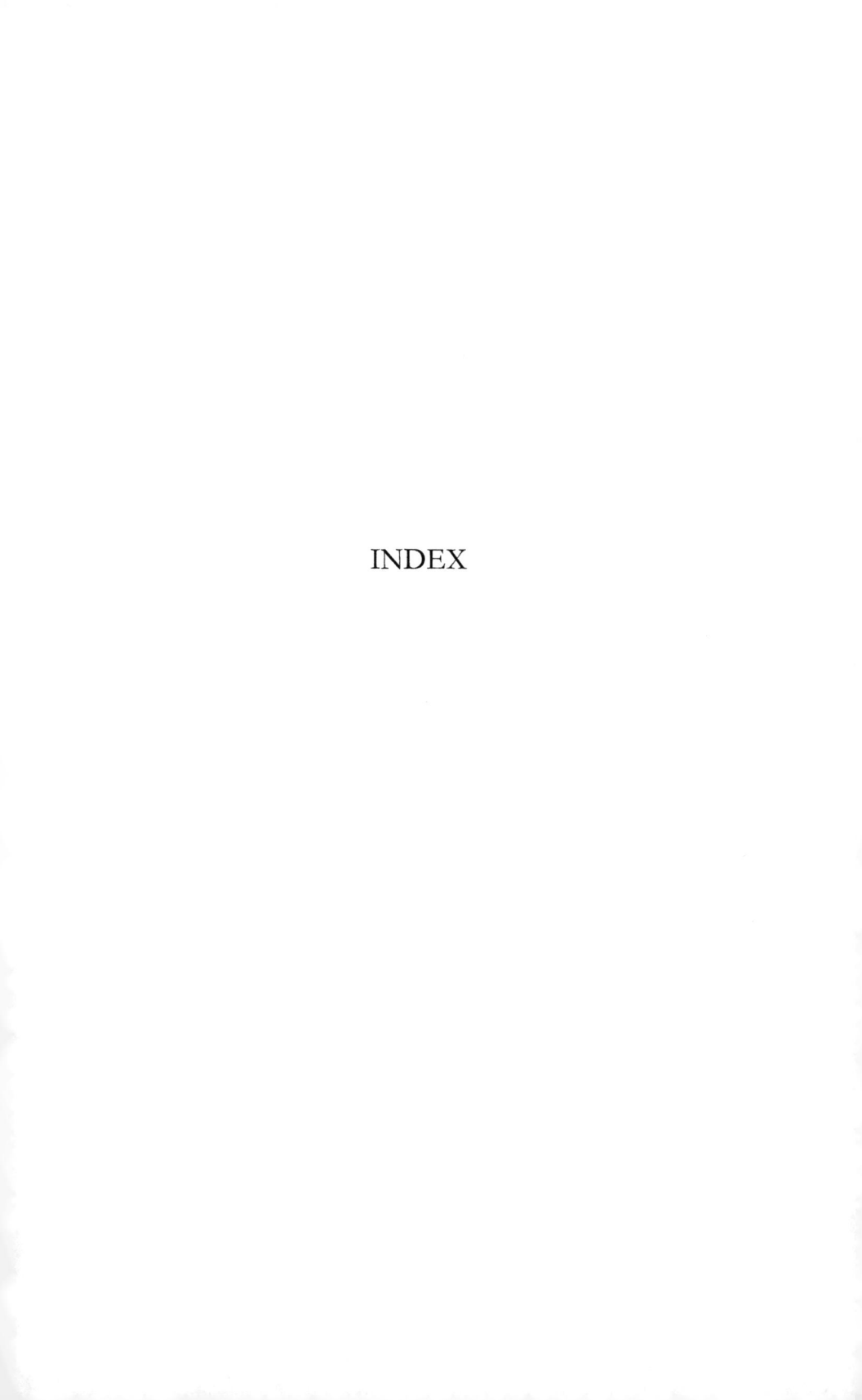

A

abbreViations, 97
above the law, 125
abuela, 105
ace up your sleeve, 347
acre, 121
annual general meeting, 93
army marches on its, 291
assets, 225
average Joe, 14

B

Bachelor's degree, 216
bad apple, 280
bad mood, 38
bankrupt, 167
baptism of fire, 103
be fired, 17
beat your budget, 4
bend down, 253
best in class, 352
bewildered, 136
big fish, 104
bigger fish to fry, 224
binding contract, 324
bite to eat, 313
bitterly, 245
bittersweet, 151
black market, 125
Black Sky Event, 194
blackmail, 288
blind date, 70
blink first, 354
blood runs cold, 220
blow your mind, 292
Board of Directors, 183
boarding school, 248
boil over, 79
boutique, 152
brainstorm, 38
brainteasers, 48
brand image, 35
breach, 69, 155
bread and butter, 287
break, 103
break down, 79
breathe down someone's neck, 198
breeze through, 293
bribe, 125, 287
bring down, 45
brood, 167
bucks, 35
bug, 132
bully, 248
bump into, 42
bungalow, 95
bureaucratic, 296
burn down, 212
burn your boats, 6
burst into, 211
burst into tears, 285
butterflies in the stomach, 107
buzz, 101

C

call in favours, 277
Campeones!, 359
capitalism, 99
carry out, 212, 222
cash burn, 229, 283
catch the eye of someone, 161
catch up, 103, 153
Chairman, 183
challenge the status quo, 13
chaperone, 101
chew, 249
childhood sweethearts, 149
chorizo in the paella, 106
chuckle, 157
civil case, 224
civil servant, 41
clam up, 78
clauses, 332
cliché, 17
close a deal, 124
close in on, 36
cold calls, 281
come together, 39, 190
come up with, 30
comfortable, 254
commit suicide, 134
communism, 99
compound number adjective, 95

core values, 14
corporate bonds, 183
Corruption, 219
coup de grace, 279
cousin, 47
cover, 363
cover for, 253
cover story, 293
cover up, 289
crush, 108
culture shock, 291
cunning, 135
CV, 216

D

daily commute, 197
damages, 225
David vs. Goliath, 63
dawn on, 34, 215
dead-end road, 9
deadline, 39
deadpan, 259
deadweight, 262
deafening silence, 31
deal with, 39
Death-Eater, 331
debrief, 294
debt, 93
deer in the headlights, 73
degree, 29
Democracy, 219
derail, 332
desk jockey, 296
dessert, 71
diligent, 245
disdain, 345
Disney, 94
disruption, 159
distraught, 150
do everything by the book, 357
do the dirty work, 296
do the trick, 211
dodgy, 191
dog-eat-dog world, 2
double check, 155
down to earth, 316
drag on, 166

dread (something), 40
drum your fingers, 351
duck down, 222
dumbfounded, 298

E

easier said than done, 185
economical with the truth, 186
Economist Intelligence Unit, 219
elephant in the room, 66, 184
employee share ownership, 15
end up, 34
entrepreneur, 63
equity stake, 47, 283
Ethereum blockchain, 9
existential threat, 79, 187
expedite, 193
exponential growth, 3
eye of the storm, 328

F

façade, 195, 278
face-off, 331
facetious, 95
figure out, 198
financial black hole, 3
financial multiples, 226
FinTech, 65
fire up, 244
fish out of water, 46
five stages of grief, 150
five-star (hotel), 6
flatten out, 251
flick through, 228
flight-or-fight, 196
flinch, 349
flirt, 277
folk hero, 160
foothold, 347
freak, 29
freak out, 137
freelancer, 74, 163
freight, 62
from time to time, 123
fry your mind, 108
functionary, 42, 197

G

gatecrash, 323
geek, 29
gender equality, 96
gender pay gap, 191
German Shepherd, 330
get it, 32
get straight to the point, 4, 321
get the show on the road, 75
ghost, 150
gifted child, 12
go off, 12, 285
go with the flow, 242
godsend, 223
grin from ear to ear, 129
grown up, 29
grunt, 260

H

hairs on the back of your neck, 318
half-hearted, 36
hands-on experience, 160
hang out, 163
hard skills, 63
hard-working, 149
haute cuisine, 292
have a lot on your plate, 30, 75
head and shoulders above the rest, 2
head spinning, 312
headhunter, 315
headquarters, 8, 322
hear (something) through the grapevine, 32
heart skips a beat, 97, 158
hidden agenda, 46
HiPos, 2
hit the ground running, 16
hold the upper hand, 353
hostile acquisitions, 159

I

IBEX 35, 319
impeccable, 278
import, 257
in a daze, 294
in the flesh, 316
in the moment, 123
in the mood, 70
income streams, 228
incumbent, 80
index finger, 99
inside job, 67, 189
intern, 169
introverted, 42
iron out, 31
ironic comment, 47
irony, 295

J

jelly, 259
just around the corner, 284

K

keep a straight face, 97
keep an eye on someone, 183
key in, 154
kick out, 363
kindling, 283
knock back, 285
know something inside out, 32

L

last-minute change, 326
lawsuit, 275
lay off, 168
lean forward, 218
living beyond your means, 46
loan, 93
lock up, 130
logistics, 62
lookalike, 243
loose strings to tie up, 360
lost for words, 7, 127, 277
love at first sight, 14

M

Magna Cum Laude, 138
make a good first impression, 30
make ends meet, 125

make fun of, 48
malicious, 356
malware, 40
margin, 184
Marxist Revolution, 98
Master's degree, 216
meltdown, 37
middle-aged, 6
mind (to go) blank, 36
mind map, 5
mind your own business, 198
mission statement, 15
mole, 279
money laundering, 130
monopoly, 39, 159
monopoly position, 9
mortgage, 93
move on, 158
munch, 249

N

nail it, 103
necessary evil, 32
Nemesis, 138
nervous breakdown, 187
non-compete clause, 155
North Korea, 246
notice period, 168

O

office politics, 244
on a roll, 283
on a rollercoaster, 213
on the house, 244
on the line, 39
on your guard, 286
open plan office, 186
operating in a (marketing) vacuum, 16
operating profits, 226
orphanage, 248
overwhelmed, 255
overwhelming, 101

P

panic attack, 45
partner, 138
pass away, 13, 182
patch, 322
patience of a saint, 31
patronisingly, 346
payments, 297
penny drops, 323
people person, 163
perish, 261
pickpockets, 46
pieces of advice, 10
pin down, 277
pinchos, 46
pitch, 103
plug in, 154
poker face, 333
pop out, 128, 217
pop up, 151
postcard, 259
post-traumatic stress disorder, 292
Prado, 321
private equity firm, 62
profits, 16
proof of concept, 31
proofreading, 332
propaganda, 129
property ladder, 96
proprietary software, 169
public company, 92
public debt, 184
pull some strings, 11
pull the trigger, 276
purge, 126
put away, 249
put bread on the table, 213
put yourself in someone else's shoes, 44

Q

quash, 104
question tags, 321

R

R&D, 161
ragdoll, 262
rags-to-riches story, 160
rainmaker, 4
ramp up, 102
ransomware, 38
real-time data, 161
recipe, 106
reckless, 162
red tape, 219
relentless, 136
rendez-vous, 216
resolute, 5
resourcefulness, 212
revenues, 16
rhetorical devices, 66
ring road, 295
rockstar, 32
rogue nations, 362
roll out, 102
round peg in a square hole, 13
run late, 214
run out, 228
run risks, 94
run through, 12, 361
rush hour, 1
ruthless, 2, 135

S

safe and sound, 295
sallow, 330
sanctions, 125
sarcasm, 356
schedule, 199
scribble, 154
secret police, 125
sell something for a song, 285
serial entrepreneur, 13
set up, 276
settle down, 290
severance pay, 168
shadow of one's former self, 170
shadow of your former self, 65
sign-on bonus, 169
silent partner, 225
single out, 163
sink in, 349
Situation Room, 188
skillset, 163
skin someone alive, 137
slanderous, 356
slow down, 251
small talk, 8, 62
smartest guys in the room, 43
snake in the grass, 223
snatch back, 219
soft skills, 63
sort out, 311
soulmates, 149
spamming, 152
speed up, 251
sponsor, 11
spur on, 244
squirm, 351
stake, 227
stakeholder, 15
stalls, 279
standard of living, 98
Star Wars, 132
state of mind, 258
steak, 122
stigmatise, 45
straight shooter, 357
stretch targets, 5
stroke someone's ego, 319
succession, 184
sue, 225
swap over, 251
swimming with sharks, 76
synergies, 347

T

tailor-made suit, 330
take your breath away, 314
take your eye of the ball, 220
target on your back, 104
Terminator, 213
the end doesn't justify the means, 327
think on your feet, 230
thirtysomethings, 242
three-generation rule, 133

throw up, 35
time heals all wounds, 185
time to kill, 43
tip, 107
tip off, 134
tiptoe, 37
to bite the hand that feeds, 2
tongue-tied, 197
totalitarian state, 221
touch down, 290
trace, 228
track down, 213
train of thought, 16
Transparency International, 219
treasure trove, 93
trial and error, 42
trip, 313
trip an electrical circuit, 199
trolling, 152
tug, 255
turn a blind eye, 125
twenty-four seven, 223
twinkle in our eye, 352
twitch, 351
two-year rotation, 160

whale, 348
when in Rome do as the Romans, 288
white collar crime, 288
wind down, 241
Windsor-knotted tie, 330
win-win scenario, 257
word of mouth, 221
work around the clock, 189
work-life balance, 38
world is your oyster, 364
worst case scenario, 282
would you mind, 153
wrap up, 249
wrap up a meeting, 358
wrath, 150
writhe around, 263

U

unconscious bias, 191
unlawful entry, 327
utterly, 260

V

vast, 16
vigilantes, 156
virgin, 99
Virgin of Guadeloupe, 316
voting rights, 225

W

walk out, 79
WannaCry, 41
water under the bridge, 103
weak link, 80
wearing different hats, 312
weigh up the pros and cons, 127

Printed in France by Amazon
Brétigny-sur-Orge, FR

Leopold Kohr

Probleme der Stadt

Leopold Kohr

Probleme der Stadt

Gedanken zur Stadt- und Verkehrsplanung

Mit einer Einführung von Ivan Illich
und einem Vorwort von Johannes Hahn

Aus dem Englischen von Andreas Wirthensohn

Herausgegeben von Ewald Hiebl
und Günther Witzany

OTTO MÜLLER VERLAG

Mit freundlicher Unterstützung von:
Stadt und Land Salzburg
Bundesministerium für Wissenschaft und Forschung

Leopold Kohr: Werkausgabe
Wissenschaftlicher Beirat der Leopold Kohr-Akademie
(Salzburg – Neukirchen):

Univ.-Prof. Dr. Reinhold Wagnleitner (Leitung)
Christine Bauer-Jelinek
Gesandter Dr. Michael Breisky
Univ.-Prof. Dr. Christian Dirninger
Mag. Manfred K. Fischer
Mag. Erwin Giedenbacher
Dr. Ewald Hiebl
Dipl. Päd. Gerald Lehner
Univ.-Prof. Dr. Ulrich Müller
Dr. Elisabeth Schreiner
Mag. Dr. Günther Witzany
Prof. Alfred Winter

Bildnachweis:
The New Yorker Magazine, Inc. (S. 38);
El Mundo (S. 46); *El Mundo* (S. 72); *Time Magazine* (S. 83);
El Mundo (S. 101)

Leopold Kohr-Akademie:
Leitung: Susanna Vötter-Dankl und Christian Vötter
Tauriska-Kammerlanderstall
A-5741 Neukirchen a. Grv.
www.leopold-kohr-akademie.at, www.tauriska.at, office@tauriska.at
Tel. 0043-(0)6565-6145, Fax 0043-(0)6565-6145-4

www.omvs.at

ISBN 978-3-7013-1154-5
© 2008 Otto Müller Verlag Salzburg/Wien
Alle Rechte vorbehalten
Satz: Media Design: Rizner.at, Salzburg
Umschlaggestaltung: Stephanie Winter
Druck und Bindung: Druckerei Theiss GmbH., A-9431 St. Stefan

Für Manning Farrell

Inhalt

Vorwort von Bundesminister Dr. Johannes Hahn — 9
Vorwort der Herausgeber — 11

Danksagung — 13

Einführung von Ivan Illich — 14
Einleitung — 17

Teil I: Stadtplanung — 21
Ganz gewöhnliche Pflastersteine — 22
Zerstörung durch Architektur — 25
Pferd oder Kamel — 28
Planorama — 32
New Town Blues — 35
Romantiker vs. Rationalisten — 39
Das Wesen der Slums — 41
Der Ursprung der Slums — 44
Die Stadt der Plätze — 48
Die Vorstädte urbanisieren — 51
Geschwindigkeitsbedingte Bevölkerung — 54
Gemeinschaft von Gemeinden — 59
Gemeinschaft wunderschöner Gemeinden — 62

Teil II: Im Verkehr ersticken — 67
Eine Metropole für Fußgänger — 68
Planungen für den Sturm — 71
Stewardessen oben ohne — 75
Rückentwicklung der Verkehrsdichte — 78
Das Zweite Eisenbahnzeitalter — 81
Regionale Souveränität — 87
Modell vs. Stadt — 91

Teil III: Docklands — 97
Anatomie der Stadtplanung — 98

Die Schönheit der Slums	103
Die Stadt außerhalb der Mauern	106
La Puntilla in Split	110
Die Saat für einen Kern legen	114
Der Glockenturm	118
Den Verkehr absorbieren	122
Nachschrift zu La Puntilla	126
Die „Witkars" in Amsterdam	130
Teil IV: Ein erstrebenswertes Herzogtum	131
Der Herzog von Buen Consejo	132
There is No Gold in Them Thar' Hills	146
Anhang	153
Glauben in der Stadt	154
Phoenix World City	157
Nachwort	159

Vorwort
Leopold Kohr als Philosoph der Stadt

Der große „Philosoph des Kleinen" Leopold Kohr beschäftigt sich im vorliegenden Buch damit, wie eine menschengerechte Stadt errichtet werden kann. Menschengerecht bedeutet, dass als Maßstab der Stadtplanung und -entwicklung nicht Parkplätze, Autos, Wirtschaftswachstum oder Außenwirkung dienen, sondern die Rücksicht auf das menschliche Maß. Kohr setzt sich für Plätze statt Straßen ein, für ein Miteinander von Wohnen und Arbeiten und für die aktive Beteiligung der Bürgerinnen und Bürger an der Gestaltung und am Ausbau ihrer Stadt.

Bemerkenswert sind nicht nur die modernen Visionen Kohrs, sondern auch der Zeitpunkt, wann er diese Forderungen aufstellte. Es waren die 1960er und frühen 1970er Jahre, als Kohr seine Gedanken zur Stadtentwicklung in puertoricanischen Zeitungen publizierte. Damals schon warnt er vor Fehlern in der Stadtplanung, welche die Lebensqualität in der Stadt vermindern. So tritt er stets gegen die Schaffung von Wohnsiedlungen am Stadtrand ein, wenn die Stadtzentren Mittelpunkt des wirtschaftlichen und gesellschaftlichen Lebens sind. Dadurch würde ein Verkehrsaufkommen entstehen, das einen beträchtlichen Teil der zur Verfügung stehenden Fläche einer Stadt für sich beansprucht. Verkehrsprobleme durch eine Ausweitung der für den Verkehr zur Verfügung stehenden Flächen zu lösen, lehnt Kohr ab, denn das führe schließlich zu noch mehr Verkehr. Eine Lösung für das Verkehrsproblem sieht Kohr zum Teil in Eisenbahnen und öffentlichem Verkehr, vor allem aber in einer radikalen Umgestaltung der Stadtplanung.

Leben und arbeiten, wo man wohnt, so sieht Kohrs ideale Stadt aus, die nicht ein Zentrum besitzt, sondern viele kleine Zentren, die dem Menschen fast alles bieten, was er im alltäglichen Leben braucht, vom Konsum bis hin zur Kultur und vor allem die Möglichkeit sozialen Kontakts auf den Plätzen. Kohrs Stadt ist also eine Stadt autonomer überschaubarer Bezirke. Seine Forderung lautet: „Urbanisiert die Vororte!" und versieht sie mit neuen zentralörtlichen Funktionen.

Wie heruntergekommene Stadtviertel wieder „revitalisiert" werden können, führt Leopold Kohr am Beispiel von „La Puntilla" an, einem Slum der puertoricanischen Hauptstadt San Juan. Als Vorbild für den Neuaufbau von La Puntilla sieht Kohr die Genese mittelalterlicher Städte an. Was es brauche, um eine menschengerechte Stadt zu gestalten, seien äußere Grenzen, also Mauern, und ein inneres Zentrum. Die restliche Gestaltung würden die Bürgerinnen und Bürger selbst erledigen. Damit wendet er sich gegen uniforme Stadtentwicklungsprojekte, die ohne Rücksicht auf traditionelle Strukturen neue Funktionen für städtische Areale vorgaben. Da diese meist einer Funktion, Wohnen oder Arbeiten, vorbehalten sind, müssen die Menschen zur Befriedigung vieler ihrer Lebensbedürfnisse in andere Stadtviertel ausweichen, was wiederum das Verkehrsaufkommen steigert.

Sein Ziel, die Visionen der Stadtentwicklung in einem Staatsroman über den „Herzog von Buen Consejo" auszuführen, konnte Leopold Kohr leider nicht mehr verwirklichen.

Ob Leopold Kohrs Visionen in der Stadt des beginnenden 21. Jahrhunderts jemals umgesetzt werden könnten und wie eine Stadt nach Kohrs menschlichem Maß in der Realität aussehen würde, bleibt vorerst dahingestellt. Tatsache ist, dass viele seiner Ideen und vor allem viele seiner Warnungen von Stadtplanern bereits aufgegriffen wurden. Die „Grätzelisierung" der Städte und die Versuche einer Eindämmung des Individualverkehrs sind Beispiele dafür. Einmal mehr war Leopold Kohr in Zeiten, als Stadtplanung und Architekten sich nur für Teilbereiche wie Verkehr, Bevölkerungsdichte oder Baumaterialien interessierten, ein Vordenker für eine Philosophie der Stadt als organisches Ganzes.

DR. JOHANNES HAHN
Bundesminister für Wissenschaft und Forschung
Wien, August 2008

Vorwort der Herausgeber

Als „The Inner City" erschien das vorliegende Buch erstmals 1989 auf Englisch. Es beinhaltete Artikel, die Leopold Kohr für die puertoricanischen Zeitungen „El Mundo", „San Juan Star" und „The World Journal" schrieb, während er in den 1960er und frühen 1970er Jahren an der Universität von Puerto Rico in San Juan lehrte.
Deshalb spielen Beispiele aus Puerto Rico eine große Rolle. So entwickelt Kohr Vorschläge, wie der Slum *La Puntilla* in der Hauptstadt San Juan in eine lebenswerte Stadt verwandelt werden könnte (Teil III: Docklands). Doch dieses Buch ist mehr als ein Einblick in die Stadtentwicklung der 1960er und 1970er Jahre auf der Insel Puerto Rico. Kohr bietet auch Lösungen für Probleme, mit denen Städte auf der ganzen Welt konfrontiert sind, etwa im Bereich des Verkehrswesens und der Stadtentwicklung. So fordert er Plätze statt Straßen, eine fußgängertaugliche Stadt und die Urbanisierung der Vororte, die zu neuen Zentren werden und die Bedürfnisse der Menschen befriedigen sollen, auch um den Verkehr einzuschränken. Mit diesem Buch beweist Leopold Kohr, dass er nicht nur der Philosoph des richtigen Maßes ist, als der er mehr als ein halbes Jahrhundert lang für überschaubare soziale Einheiten plädiert und sich der Manie des Wachsens und des Fortschrittes um jeden Preis entgegengestellt hat. Mit „Probleme der Stadt" zeigt er, dass er auch in wichtigen Fragen der Stadtentwicklung zukunftsweisende Gedanken entwickelt hat. Manche von ihnen, wie die Einführung verkehrsberuhigter Zonen, klangen den Zeitgenossen in den 1960er Jahren illusorisch und sind nun Alltag in vielen Stadtzentren. Andere sind noch heute weit von einer Realisierung entfernt, etwa das Vertrauen in die Bürgerinnen und Bürger selbst, was die Planung ihrer Stadt betrifft. Noch immer sind es Experten aus Harvard, vom MIT oder anderen renommierten Einrichtungen, denen Kohr stets kritisch auf die Finger blickte, die Städte planen. Auch ihnen sei die Lektüre dieses Buches ans Herz gelegt, geschrieben von einem bekennenden Anarchisten.
Die Herausgeber danken vor allem dem österreichischen Bundesminister für Wissenschaft und Forschung, Herrn Dr. Johannes Hahn, der als Experte für die Philosophie der Stadt und Anhänger der

Kohrschen Ideen ein Vorwort beigesteuert hat. Schließlich gilt es – stellvertretend für alle, die an der Realisierung des Buches mitgewirkt haben – auch Dr. Andreas Wirthensohn zu danken, der den Text im Sinne Kohrs mit Esprit und Präzision übersetzt hat.

Dass das vorliegende Buch nicht *Innenstadt*, *Innere Stadt* oder *Kernstadt* heißt, liegt daran, dass die wörtliche Übersetzung dem Sinn von „inner city" nicht gerecht wird. Denn während beim Begriff „Innenstadt" im Deutschen das historische Zentrum einer Stadt gemeint ist, das in der Regel positiv konnotiert ist, bezeichnet „inner city" vor allem auch problematische Aspekte der Stadtentwicklung wie die Entstehung von Slums und die Abwertung von Stadtzentren. Deshalb wurde für die deutsche Ausgabe der Titel „Probleme der Stadt" gewählt, wobei im Begriff Probleme auch Wege zur Lösung enthalten sind, die Leopold Kohr im vorliegenden Buch skizziert.

EWALD HIEBL
GÜNTHER WITZANY
Salzburg, August 2008

Danksagung

Als meine Freunde Tom und Lucilla Marvel, beide Architekten, anläßlich meines 60. Geburtstags in ihrem bezaubernden Haus in Puerto Rico eine kleine abendliche Party gaben, erhob der Gastgeber sein Champagnerglas und bemerkte mit einiger Überraschung, daß das Geburtstagskind zur Zunft der Wirtschaftswissenschaftler zu rechnen sei, doch unter den geladenen Freunden befinde sich nur ein einziger Ökonom, nämlich Alfred Thorne, mein verehrter Kollege an der Universität. Alle anderen waren Architekten und Planer: Vivi Thorne, Henry und Elas Klumb, Mabbie und Simon Schmiderer, Rafael Corrada, Albert Mangones aus Haiti, Charles Frankenhoff, Nestor Acevedo und natürlich Tom und Lucilla selbst, deren einzigartiges selbst entworfenes Wohnhaus auf einem kleinen Flecken städtischen Terrains den Zauber des Universums zu atmen scheint.

Dort wurden auf Cocktail- und Dinnerpartys in unzähligen geistvollen Gesprächen mit anderen Freunden – Jaime Benitez, Serero Colberg, Donna Pace, Ivan Illich, Sir Herbert Read, Anatol Murad, Angel Ruiz, Alex Maldonado – die Ideen auf den Prüfstand und in Frage gestellt, für gut befunden oder verworfen, ehe sie Eingang in meine Kolumnen im *San Juan Star* und in *El Mundo* fanden und, auf diesen Seiten gesammelt, in die Entwicklungsstrategie von *Der Herzog von Buen Consejo* mündeten. Ihnen allen bin ich zu größtem Dank verpflichtet.

Gloucester, Februar 1989

Einführung

Begegnet bin ich Leopold Kohr ein Jahrzehnt, bevor ich ihn verstanden habe, damals, als wir beide gerade an der Universität von Puerto Rico gelandet waren. Über Jahre lasen wir in der Faculty Lounge und im Planning Board Office seine Aufsätze sowie seine wöchentliche Kolumne und betrachteten seine wunderliche Weisheit als vergnügliche Denkanstöße eines nützlichen Störenfrieds. Keiner von uns erkannte damals, daß Kohr eine dimensionale Analyse der gesellschaftlichen Realität betrieb und uns ständig dazu aufforderte, ein Gefühl für Proportion und Größe zu entwickeln, das seiner Ansicht nach ein viel besserer Leitfaden bei der Entwicklung physischer Pläne war als die quantitativen Meßgrößen, an denen sich der Fortschritt orientierte.

Aus der Ferne stimmt es heute traurig, auf diese zwanzig Jahre puertoricanischer Geschichte zurückzublicken und sich an die Zeit zu erinnern, da Kohrs realistische Vorschläge die Probleme der drohenden industriellen Bösartigkeiten noch hätten minimieren können, indem sie Schönheit und persönlicher Effektivität den Vorrang vor statistischer Effizienz gaben; als die Entscheidung für ein hoch verdichtetes Leben inmitten geringer Verkehrsdichte noch nicht zugunsten der Betonschicht entschieden war, die heute den besten Boden dieser tropischen Insel überzieht. Heute hallen Kohrs Vorschläge in einer Umgebung wider, die zum weltweit beachteten Schauplatz bürokratisch geplanten industriellen Fortschritts und fortschreitender persönlicher Zerstörung geworden ist. Heute läßt sich der damalige Slum La Perla, der sich in den Schoß des alten San Juan schmiegt, nicht mehr erlösen: Seine Bewohner sind heimatlos geworden in ihren Häusern, die vollgestopft sind mit neuen Gerätschaften, und wurden auf dem weltweit fortschrittlichsten Niveau spezialisierter Inkompetenz ausgebildet. Kohrs Vorschläge sind heute ein Aufruf, den Modernisierungsprozeß, dem die puertoricanische Armut unterworfen wurde, rückgängig zu machen. Sie drängen heute darauf, daß Befreiung auf Desillusionierung, auf Abgrenzung und Investitionsverweigerung beruhen muß.

Als ich jüngst diese Artikel wieder las, die ein österreichischer Professor, der heute an einer walisischen Universität lehrt, für zwei Lokalzeitungen einer Hauptstadt in der Karibik verfaßt hat, und zwar in einer weit zurückliegenden Zeit, in der ich ihn oft auf seiner Terrasse unter Bananenstauden sitzen sah, mußte ich mir unwillkürlich wieder einmal meine mexikanische Bibliothek vornehmen, wo ich all die Berichte über Puerto Rico deponiert habe, die in der Zwischenzeit von Bürokraten, Sozialwissenschaftlern und auch einigen Dichtern verfaßt wurden. Ich verbrachte einen ganzen Abend damit und versuchte herauszufinden, was dieses barocke Sammelsurium an Büchern irgendwelchen Menschen fernab über die einzigartige Erfahrung berichten könnte, die die Bevölkerung Puerto Ricos in den letzten beiden Jahrzehnten gemacht hat. Ich blätterte durch die neunmalklugen Forschungsarbeiten amerikanischer Wissenschaftler, von denen damals ohne irgendwelche Feldforschungen über die Versuchskaninchen in dieser einsamen US-Kolonie kaum jemand in Yale oder an der Cornell University Karriere gemacht hätte. Ich staunte erneut über die buchlangen Werbeanzeigen für die „Operation Bootstrap" („Unternehmen Selbsthilfe"), mit der so mancher heute berühmte Professor sein Geld verdient und Meriten auf der Madison Avenue der akademischen Welt erworben hat; ich verlor mich in den schmalen Bändchen elegischer Verse, gestammelt in den Überresten einer Muttersprache, die von all dem Spinglisch oder Spanglisch, wie es in der Schule oder im Fernsehen gesprochen wird, verdrängt wird. Ich merkte, daß die soziologischen Fakten der fünfziger Jahre verblaßt sind, daß die Begeisterung für statistischen Fortschritt erlahmt ist und daß die Sprache der Dichter, die die Unabhängigkeit eines Volkes besingen, von dem die Hälfte in den Slums von New York aufgewachsen ist, für jeden Außenstehenden unbegreiflich bleiben wird.

Ich wandte mich wieder Kohrs Ausführungen zu und war doppelt dankbar, daß er seine professoralen Pamphlete, die sich mit einer ganz spezifischen Situation befaßten, nun in einer Form veröffentlicht, die auch dem gemeinen Leser Zugang verschafft. Diese Abhandlung über alternative Stadtplanung vermittelt dem Leser einen Einblick in den „Unterleib" des puertoricanischen Fortschritts aus der Sicht eines Philosophen-Ökonomen. Zudem erlaubt sie es dem

Verfasser, dezent daran zu erinnern, daß er ein guter Lehrer war. Bei der Lektüre dieser Texte mußte ich beschämt erkennen, daß die Werte der Kleinheit, der Viel-Zelligkeit, der gelungenen Dezentralisierung, der Entprofessionalisierung, der Entschleunigung und der eigenständigen Strukturen, die unsere Generation „entdeckt" hat, ebenso klar und viel humorvoller schon von Leopold Kohr formuliert worden waren, noch bevor wir überhaupt verstanden, was er uns da lehrte.

IVAN ILLICH
Centro Intercultural de Documentación, Cuernavaca, 1976

Einleitung

Seit ich das erste Stück dieser Sammlung (*Ganz gewöhnliche Pflastersteine*) auf dem Internationalen Seminar zur Ausbildung von Stadt- und Landschaftsplanern, das im März 1956 unter der Schirmherrschaft der Panamerikanischen Union und der Vereinten Nationen in Puerto Rico veranstaltet wurde, als außerplanmäßigen Kommentar zu den Ausführungen von Sir William Holford (*The Training of Planners*) präsentiert habe, wurde ich von Freunden immer wieder dazu gedrängt, meine Ideen weiterzuverfolgen und auszuarbeiten. Das habe ich in meiner allwöchentlichen Kolumne getan, die über Jahre in den puertoricanischen Tageszeitungen *The World Journal*, *The San Juan Star* und *El Mundo* erschien.

Andere haben mich gedrängt, den Geltungsbereich meiner Vorstellungen zu erweitern und sie vor dem allgemeinen Hintergrund des amerikanischen Festlands und der europäischen Bühne auszuarbeiten, statt mich auf die lokalen Bedingungen der kleinen, zum US-Commonwealth gehörenden Insel Puerto Rico zu beschränken.

Das habe ich nicht getan. Das wäre geradezu so gewesen, als hätte man Darwin gebeten, als Hintergrund seiner Evolutionstheorie die Tierwelt der Isle of Wight statt der fernen Galapagosinseln zu nehmen; oder Jesus dazu gedrängt, seine Gleichnisse aus Rom, Capua oder Syrakus zu beziehen statt aus Kafarnaum, Bethanien oder Nazareth. Letzteres war selbst Natanael, der aus dem ebenso unbekannten Nachbarort Kana stammte, dermaßen unbekannt, daß er ungläubig fragte: „Aus Nazareth? Kann von dort etwas Gutes kommen?"

Nun, dem war tatsächlich so. Und ähnlich kamen auch ein paar gute Dinge von der kleinen Karibikinsel Puerto Rico: ein paar Miss World; *Don Q.* (für Don Quichotte), angeblich – um Stephen Potters „Wort des Jahrzehnts" zu benutzen – der weltbeste Rum; das Cello von Pablo Casals, das in den letzten Jahren des großen Meisters nur in San Juan zu hören war; der soziologische Bestseller von Oscar Lewis über den Slum von San Juan (deutsch 1971 unter dem Titel *La Vida. Eine puertoricanische Familie in der Kultur der Armut*); die letzte Vorlesung von Sir Herbert Read, *The Limits of*

Permissiveness in Art, die er selbst für seine beste hielt und die speziell für die Universität von Puerto Rico verfaßt wurde, wo er sie 1968, ein paar Monate vor seinem Tod, *urbi et orbi* verkündete; viele von Ivan Illichs Ideen und Schriften, die er im Zuge seiner Arbeit beim Planning Board des Landes und als Präsident der katholischen Universität in Ponce entwickelte und formulierte; die beispiellose mystische Herrlichkeit des Ionosphärenteleskops, des schärfsten Auges auf Erden, das von einem schüsselförmigen Berggipfel in der Nähe von Arecibo aus still die Himmelsräume durchleuchtet; eine Reihe von Seminaren von E. F. Schumacher, der ein paar Monate vor Veröffentlichung seinem Buch *Small Is Beautiful* (1973) den letzten Schliff gab, als er in Carolina mein Gast war; das Musical *West Side Story*; und „last", aber sicher nicht „least" eine dieser unscheinbaren Tabletten, die jahrelang an den Frauen Puerto Ricos getestet wurde, ehe sie als letzte Hoffnung – neben der nüchternen malthusianischen Dreifaltigkeit aus Krieg, Hunger und Seuchen – die Menschheit davor bewahren sollte, sich bis in die frostige Leere des Universums hinein zu vermehren: die „Pille".

Doch der Hauptgrund, warum ich den Schauplatz für die Diskussion meiner stadtplanerischen Konzepte nicht an bekanntere und vielschichtigere Orte wie Boston, London oder Los Angeles verlegt habe, ist der, daß die weltweit renommiertesten Wissenschaftler und Stadtplaner aus Harvard, York, London oder vom MIT in den entscheidenden Phasen nicht London, Los Angeles oder Boston als erstes Testgelände für ihre sozialen und architektonischen Planungsideen genutzt haben, sondern Puerto Rico. Das hatte drei Vorteile: Die Insel war Teil der Vereinigten Staaten, und das ist immer gut, wenn man Geld braucht; sie war noch immer unterentwickelt, so daß man mit allem ganz von vorne beginnen konnte; und sie war klein, so daß die konkreten Auswirkungen ihrer Pläne fast über Nacht sichtbar wurden.

Während also die Projekte, die ich im Folgenden kritisch unter die Lupe nehme, alle in Puerto Rico zu finden sind, kommen ihre Propheten und Urheber aus praktisch allen großen Planungsinstitutionen dieser Welt. Es ist in der Tat so, wie Ivan Illich schreibt, daß „ohne irgendwelche Feldforschungen über die Versuchskaninchen in dieser einsamen US-Kolonie kaum jemand in Yale oder an der Cornell University Karriere gemacht hätte. Ich staunte erneut über die buchlangen Werbeanzeigen für die ›Operation Boostrap‹, mit der so mancher heute berühmte Professor sein Geld verdient und Meriten auf der Madison Avenue der akademischen Welt erworben hat."

Ich habe deshalb meine Zweifel, ob irgendein Leser überhaupt einen Wechsel des Namens, der Szenerie oder des Bezugsrahmens benötigt, um zu erkennen, daß die Probleme und Lösungen, die am Beispiel von Buen Cosejo, La Puntilla oder San Juan präsentiert werden, die gleichen sind wie in Boston, Kalkutta, Pimlico oder in den Docklands von Gloucester und London.

Zudem hätte ich meine Artikel natürlich auch aktualisieren können. Tatsächlich habe ich eine Menge Zeit damit verbracht, sie zurückzudatieren in die Zeit vor zwanzig oder dreißig Jahren, als ich sie geschrieben habe und deswegen oftmals, wie Fritz (E. F.) Schumacher, als ›crank‹ [Spinner, wörtlich aber Kurbel oder Schwengel, A.d.Ü.] galt, was mir aber genauso egal war wie meinem Freund Fritz, der sagte: „Was ist denn schon ein ›crank‹ [hier im Sinne von Kurbel, Schwengel, A.d.Ü.]? Es ist ein Werkzeug, das billig, klein, wirkungsvoll und ökonomisch ist und", so fügte er mit Nachdruck hinzu, „das für Umdrehungen [*revolutions*, also auch Revolutionen, A.d.Ü.] sorgt."

Meine Beobachtungen aus den 1940er, 1950er und 1960er Jahren werden heute oft als Vorklang zu denjenigen aus den 1970er und 1980er Jahren bezeichnet. Das ist durchaus möglich in einer Welt der politischen Akustik, in der Marx als Vorklang zu Arthur Scargill gelten könnte. Mit etwas mehr Gnade werden sie mitunter auch als prophetisch bezeichnet, was sie aber ebensowenig sind, wie auch George Orwells *1984*, geschrieben 1948, keine Prophezeiung künftiger Dinge war. Im Jahr 1937, während des Bürgerkriegs, habe ich diese Fragen mit ihm in spanischen Cafés diskutiert, und zwar nicht als Prophezeiungen künftiger Entwicklungen, sondern als Schlußfolgerungen aus den deutlich sichtbaren Verhältnissen, die wir damals, aber auch schon immer um uns herum vorfanden. So sagte Hesiod vor mehr als 27 Jahrhunderten im ersten Buch, das jemals in der westlichen Welt verfaßt wurde: „Der Mensch wird auch weiterhin die Städte anderer Menschen zerstören." Denn wie Goethe über Rom sagte: „Was die Barbaren stehenließen, haben die Baumeister des neuen Roms zerstört." Mitunter jedoch, so könnte man hinzufügen, wurden die Städte aber auch durch die Fürsten gerettet, wie etwa von Augustus, der stolz verkünden konnte: „Ich fand Rom in Ziegelsteinen vor und habe es in Marmor hinterlassen."

Gloucester, Februar 1989

TEIL I
Stadtplanung

Ganz gewöhnliche Pflastersteine

St. Petersburg in Leningrad. Veränderter Zweck von Stadtplanung. Ursache für den städtischen Glanz der Vergangenheit. Das gute Leben des Aristoteles. Platz, Kirche, Kneipe, Rathaus als Kern. Das Scheitern moderner Städte. Ganz gewöhnliche Pflastersteine. Der launische öffentliche Geschmack.

Als André Gide von einer seiner Reisen in die Sowjetunion zurückkehrte, beleidigte er seine russischen Gastgeber zutiefst, als er sagte: „Was ich an Leningrad bewunderte, war St. Petersburg."

Daran wurde ich erinnert, als sich ein Freund aus dem Planning Board Puerto Ricos darüber beschwerte, wie schwierig es sei, die Industrie gleichmäßiger über das Land zu verteilen. Da ich die wundervolle Hauptstadt San Juan kenne, verstehe ich gut, warum das so ist. André Gide gab dem St. Petersburg dort, wo heute Leningrad ist, aus dem gleichen Grund den Vorzug, aus dem Industrielle es vorziehen, nahe der Altstadt von San Juan zu leben und nicht an Orten, wo sie so viel Platz haben können, wie sie nur wollen: Weder das alte St. Petersburg noch das alte San Juan wurden von modernen Planern erbaut.

Alte Städte haben offenbar einen grundlegenden Zweck urbanen Lebens erfüllt, der den Stadtplanern unserer Zeit entgangen ist. Sir William Holford hat einmal den Vorzug früherer Epochen benannt. Sie hätten, so meinte er, über ein genau definiertes moralisches Ziel verfügt, das all ihren Planungen die Richtung vorgegeben habe: Die Antike strebte nach Harmonie; das Mittelalter nach mystischer Erfüllung; die Renaissance nach der Eleganz der Proportionen; neuere Zeiten nach der Aufklärung des Humanismus. Sie alle wußten genau, was sie wollten.

Im Gegensatz dazu orientieren sich moderne Planer einzig und allein am Dienst an der Gesellschaft – und dieses Ziel verändert sich von Tag zu Tag und läßt sich deshalb nur mühsam definieren. Und genau darin, so läßt uns Sir William wissen, liege die Schwierigkeit moderner Planung. Frühere Planer wußten, was sie bauten, weil sie einzig und allein das ausführten, was sie sich ausgedacht hatten. Moderne Planer hingegen irren im Dunkeln umher. Bestrebt, den öffentlichen Geschmack zu bedienen, haben sie größte Mühe, überhaupt herauszufinden, wie dieser Geschmack aussieht.

Da der Herrgott es versäumt hat, diesen launischen Gebieter mit einer Stimme auszustatten, muß der Planer ganze Forschungsteams engagieren, um herauszufinden, in welche Richtung der Wind weht. Und was muß er erleben, wenn er endlich seinen Entwurf entsprechend den Winden, Strömungen und Stimmungen der Zeit umgesetzt hat? Daß diejenigen, für die er gebaut hat, nach einem ersten Blick darauf wieder in den alten Kern der Stadt zurückdrängen, der vor vierhundert Jahren erbaut wurde, ohne daß man sich um die angeblichen Erfordernisse kommunaler Zwecke kümmerte und auf Schulen für Planung zurückgreifen konnte.

Entgegen Sir William Holfords Kategorisierung des veränderten Zwecks von Stadtplanung scheint es so etwas wie einen *veränderten* Zweck überhaupt nicht zu geben. Daß alte Städte so bezaubernd sind und neue nicht, liegt darin begründet, daß die Stadtplaner früherer Zeiten – im antiken Griechenland, in mittelalterlichen Stadtstaaten oder im modernen Paris – nicht verschiedenen Zwecken dienten, sondern einzig und allein dem unveränderlichen Zweck, aufgrund dessen die Menschen seit jeher in derartigen Gemeinwesen leben wollen.

Dieser Zweck wurde von Aristoteles philosophisch zum Ausdruck gebracht, als er sagte, die Menschen würden nicht um des Friedens, der Gerechtigkeit, der Verteidigung, des Verkehrs oder des Handels willen Gemeinwesen gründen, sondern um ein gutes Leben führen zu können. Und das gute Leben in Gemeinschaft bedeutete zu allen Zeiten die Befriedigung der drei sozialen Grundbedürfnisse des Menschen, denen frühere Planer in ihren Strukturen durchweg Gestalt verliehen. Diese Bedürfnisse sind Geselligkeit, Religiosität und Politik. Daher bestand der Kern ihrer Städte trotz aller stilistischen Varianten stets aus den gleichen Grundstrukturen. Wirtshäuser und Theater für die Geselligkeit; Kirchen für die Religiosität; und Rathäuser für das politische Naturell.

Die Gründe, warum es Menschen in die Regionen um alte Städte wie San Juan herum zurückzieht, sind somit nicht der Hafen, die Arbeitsmöglichkeiten, die Verkehrseinrichtungen oder die Stadt-autobahnen. Was sie aus ihren Siedlungen ohne Kern zurückbringt, sind die alten, ganz gewöhnlichen Pflastersteine, die den Verkehr nicht beschleunigen, sondern verlangsamen, die engen Gassen, die Wirtshäuser, die Theater – kurz: die Intensität und das Aufregende einer Stadt, deren alte Planer nicht in Kategorien von gesellschaftlicher Dienstleistung, Mystik, Symmetrie oder Harmonie dachten, sondern in den Kategorien von Geselligkeit, Religiosität und Politik.

Um Industrie erfolgreich zu dezentralisieren, braucht man deshalb nicht kostenlose Gebäude oder Steuererleichterungen, sondern die Errichtung urbaner Kerne an primitiven Kreuzungen – ein Straßencafé, ein kleines Theater, ein Restaurant, das ausgezeichnetes Essen serviert, eine bezaubernde Kirche von Henry Klumb, einen hübschen Versammlungssaal. Dann werden Unternehmer sogar dann bleiben, wenn sie ihre Fabriken selbst bauen und obendrauf auch noch Steuern zahlen müssen.

Der Grund für den Erfolg alter und das Scheitern moderner Stadtplaner läßt sich in Kurzform so zusammenfassen: Alte Planer wußten um den unveränderlichen aristotelischen Zweck, warum Menschen in Gemeinschaften leben, und verwendeten all ihr Talent auf den Bau des gemeinschaftlichen Kerns – der Gasthäuser, der Kirchen, der Rathäuser. Der Rest der Stadt – Wohnhäuser, Schulen, Fabriken, Geschäfte – folgte dann von selbst. Moderne Planer hingegen bauen unablässig am Rest der Stadt. Doch ohne Kern läßt sich nichts zusammenhalten. Und den Kern können sie nicht bauen, weil sie davon überzeugt sind, daß jedes Zeitalter einem anderen Zweck folgt. Der aber ist ihnen, kaum haben sie ihn ausgemacht, schon wieder unter den Füßen weggeschmolzen.

Dieser Text erschien erstmals in der United Nations Series No. 11 über Housing, Building and Planning (New York 1957, S. 73f.).

Zerstörung durch Architektur

Die Kirche von Hormigueros. Goethe über Rom. Main Street, Oklahoma. Organische Anpassung. Stadtplanung als Kunst. Die Bedeutung von Instinkt, Leben und Liebe. Moderne Errungenschaften in alter Umgebung. Staatlicher Denkmalschutz reicht nicht. Gefahr der Musealisierung. Bühne und Drama. Nackte Fassaden.

Auf Puerto Rico gibt es eine Kirche, die erhaben, schön und einsam wie eine edle Dame auf einem windumtosten Hügel oberhalb des Dorfes Hormigueros in einem entlegenen Teil der Insel thront. Steigt man zu ihr hinauf, fühlt man sich an Schillers Verse in seiner Ballade *Der Kampf mit dem Drachen* erinnert:
„Auf dreimal dreißig Stufen steigt
Der Pilgrim nach der steilen Höhe,
Doch hat er schwindelnd sie erreicht,
Erquickt ihn seines Heilands Nähe."
Steigt man jedoch die dreimal dreißig Stufen ins Dorf hinunter, fühlt man sich eher an Goethes Bemerkung über Rom erinnert: „Was die Barbaren stehen ließen, haben die Baumeister des neuen Roms zerstört."

Hormigueros ist noch nicht völlig ruiniert. Doch wie so viele andere himmlische Überbleibsel früherer Zeiten ist es akut bedroht, von Architekten zerstört zu werden. Inmitten seiner anmutigen alten Häuser dürfen sich neue Gebäude erheben, die vielleicht ins Zentrum von Oklahoma City passen, aber der lateinamerikanischen Eleganz und dem tropischen Charme, wie sie für die alten Städte der Insel typisch sind, völlig zuwider laufen.

Und sie sind allesamt umso erbärmlicher, weil es eigentlich überhaupt keinen Grund gibt, architektonische Muster aus Bestellkatalogen zu kopieren, wenn doch die Häuser nebenan Stile zu bieten haben, die sich organisch und sensibel nicht nur den klimatischen Bedingungen und der Umgebung anpassen, sondern sich auch bestens in Geschichte und Tradition des Landes einfügen.

Der Fehler scheint in unserer Zeit zu liegen, deren stadtplanerische Aktivitäten ihren eigenen Vollkommenheitsprinzipien folgen und sich ausschließlich an wissenschaftlichen Leitlinien orientieren. Doch Stadtplanung ist wie Dichtung, Bildhauerei oder Malerei weniger Wissenschaft als vielmehr Kunst.

Das heißt nicht, daß Häuser, Straßen oder Parks nicht funktional angelegt sein sollen, damit sie Luft zum Atmen sowie Vorrichtungen für moderne Erfordernisse bieten. Doch das sind Nebenprodukte guter Planung, die deshalb nicht im Mittelpunkt des sozialen Designs stehen sollten, wie das heute der Fall ist, so wie einer effektiven Technik des Betonmischens, so wichtig sie auch ist, nicht die primäre Aufmerksamkeit guter Architektur gelten sollte.

Um zu verhindern, daß es durch den Bau moderner Betonkästen inmitten der historischen Architektur eines Landes zu einer weiteren Verschandelung der Stadt- und Dorflandschaft kommt, muß es vor allem darum gehen, daß eine staatliche Instanz damit betraut wird, die Bauaktivitäten in alten kommunalen Zentren unter streng organischen und ästhetischen Gesichtspunkten zu überwachen. Anders ausgedrückt: Ihr sollten nicht nur Ingenieure, Planer, Ökonomen oder Soziologen angehören, sondern in erster Linie Architekten, Biologen, Dichter, Historiker und Maler. Denn Schönheit ist nur selten das Ergebnis von Wissenschaft. Sie ergibt sich vielmehr aus Instinkt, Geschmack, Liebe und Leben.

Das bedeutet wiederum nicht, daß alte Städte nicht auch die modernsten Errungenschaften in sich aufnehmen sollten – sie sollten das durchaus tun. Doch sollten diese unter der kundigen Anleitung von Meistern ihres Faches integriert werden, wie etwa des Archäologen Ricardo Alegria oder des Architekten Henry Klumb; denn deren Entwürfe, die ihre Inspiration aus dem jeweiligen fachlichen Hintergrund beziehen und auf kühlende „Brisen" statt auf Klimaanlagen setzen, haben auf brillante Weise gezeigt, daß sich das Neue harmonisch mit dem Alten verbinden läßt, das Amerikanische mit Latinoelementen, das Funktionale mit den klimatischen Bedingungen, das Kleid mit dem Antlitz, ohne daß das eine dem anderen Gewalt antut.

Die Politik, alte Gebäude wie in England unter Denkmalschutz zu stellen, ist ein Anfang, reicht aber nicht aus. Denn um deren Schönheit erstrahlen zu lassen, ist es ebenso wichtig, daß sie in einem entsprechenden Umfeld stehen, daß sie von anderen Gebäuden in ebenbürtigem Stil flankiert und umgeben sind und daß die Straßen, deren Teil sie sind, entsprechend angepaßt werden. Denn ein konserviertes Haus ist für sich allein ein Museumsstück, das künstlich erhalten und pflichtschuldig besucht wird. Eine erhaltene Stadt oder ein erhaltenes Dorf hingegen ist ein lebendiger Organismus, zu dem die Menschen strömen, um nicht nur die Bühne zu besichtigen, sondern auch das Drama zu erleben.

Hormigueros hat noch immer seine bezaubernde Kirche, die unzugänglich für die Planer hoch oben auf ihrem Hügel thront – erhaben, schön und einsam. Doch um diese Vision von Schönheit zu bewahren, sollten die Straßen darunter von dem nackten Utilitarismus neuer Rohbauten befreit werden, die vom MIT oder von Corbusier entworfen wurden und den Vorhof der Kirche verschandeln. Andernfalls wird Hormigueros, wie so viele andere Städte und Dörfer überall auf der Welt, Schwierigkeiten haben, der Zerstörung, die Rom erlebte, zu entgehen – eine Zerstörung, die nicht Generäle zu verantworten hatten, sondern Architekten.

World Journal, San Juan, 3. Januar 1957

Pferd oder Kamel

Kosten und Nutzlosigkeit kollektiver Planung. Bedarf an Experten, nicht an Untersuchungen. Zeitbedingte Erosion der Daten. Rasches Handeln in Sachen Stadterneuerung. Die Umgestaltung von Naranjito. In einer Nacht geplant, von den Bewohnern gebaut, von der Regierung ignoriert, von Künstlern bemalt, vom Bischof eingeweiht, mit Schweiß finanziert, binnen eines Monats fertiggestellt: Kosten für den Staat – null.

Die amerikanische Regierung hat für die Evaluierung von Modellstadtprojekten Zuschüsse in Millionenhöhe bereitgestellt. Für diese erstaunliche Summe an Geld, mit der man sich die Dienste ganzer Bataillone hochbezahlter Experten erkauft, wird man allerdings mit einiger Wahrscheinlichkeit nicht das Porträt einer Stadt erhalten, sondern das eines Kamels, das als von einem Ausschuß entworfenes Pferd definiert wurde.

Wenn es überhaupt solcher fachlicher Analysen bedarf – wobei man annehmen muß, daß die Behörden, die mit der Lösung urbaner Probleme betraut sind, offenbar auch nach Jahrzehnten kostspieliger wissenschaftlicher Vorarbeiten und dem noch kostspieligeren Prozeß, aus den Mißerfolgen der eigenen praktischen Erfahrung zu lernen, noch immer nicht wissen, woran sie sind –, dann sollte man nicht eine einzige kollektiv koordinierte Studie in Auftrag geben, sondern eine Vielzahl individueller, konkurrierender Untersuchungen, Modelle und Pläne.

Bei zwanzig verschieden konzipierten Projekten besteht statistisch gesehen die Wahrscheinlichkeit, daß dreizehn unbrauchbare und sieben gute dabei sind; zudem weist vermutlich jeder der dreizehn Mißerfolge einzelne Merkmale auf, die sich ausgezeichnet dafür eignen, von den siegreichen Modellen übernommen zu werden. Wird hingegen eine kollektive Untersuchung in Auftrag gegeben oder entscheidet man sich kollektiv für ein einziges Leitprinzip, so ist die statistische Wahrscheinlichkeit groß, daß diese Untersuchung einem Kamel ähnelt, das zwar in der Wüste von Wert ist, wo es weder Städte noch Slums gibt, nicht aber am Lagunenstrand von Orten wie Santurce im ärmlichen Puerto Rico, dessen Probleme zu untersuchen sich Washington angeblich mehr als 250.000 US-Dollar kosten läßt.

Die wirkliche Frage ist, ob man überhaupt teure Studien zur Stadtverbesserung braucht. Wenn jemand krank ist, wird er nicht einen Freund beauftragen, Medizin zu studieren. Bis letzterer seinen Abschluß macht, wird er längst tot sein. Er wird vielmehr einen Arzt aufsuchen, der sein Studium schon lange beendet hat und in der Lage ist, mit einem Blick die Krankheit zu diagnostizieren und eine geeignete Medizin zu verschreiben. Der Patient muß nur das Honorar für die Behandlung zahlen und nicht die Kosten einer ganzen medizinischen Ausbildung tragen.

Bei Kosten in Höhe von einer Viertelmillion Dollar gehen die Behörden, die eine solche Untersuchung in Auftrag geben, ganz offensichtlich davon aus, daß ihre Planer erst eine Ausbildung erhalten müssen. Wenn das aber der Fall ist, sollten Menschen, die derart viel Geld kosten, nicht gleich zu Anfang in Erscheinung treten. Stattdessen sollten diejenigen mit der Entwicklung von Modellen betraut werden, deren Kenntnis urbaner Probleme sie in die Lage versetzt, diese schon morgen zu präsentieren, nicht erst nach jahrelangem Sammeln von Daten, die allein dadurch schon wieder obsolet sind.

Noch viel angebrachter wäre ein solches Vorgehen in einem mittellosen, unterentwickelten, kleinen Inselstaat wie Puerto Rico, wo eine Reihe ideenreicher junger Architekten und Planer unter der Anleitung von Nestor Acevedo und Gabriel Ferrer ein höchst erfolgreiches Beispiel für einen kostengünstigen, schnell umsetzbaren Ansatz geliefert haben: die grundlegende Neugestaltung der Berggemeinde Naranjito. Statt auf Forschungszuschüsse oder regierungsamtliche Unterstützung zu warten, entwarfen sie eines Nachts zwischen 21 und 4 Uhr einen Plan. Die Kosten: ein oder zwei Flaschen Rum und ein paar Tassen Kaffee für weniger als fünf Dollar. Statt ihr Büro in die Slums von Naranjito zu verlegen und gemeinsam mit Soziologen, Bildungsexperten, Inzestforschern und Beratern aus dem Gesundheitsministerium danach zu fragen, was die Slumbewohner *wollen*, machten sie sich dorthin auf und erklärten den dort Lebenden, was sie *brauchten*. Hätten sie die Slumbewohner nach ihren Wünschen gefragt, hätten sie zu hören bekommen: Kühlschränke, Fernseher, Autos, Kaffeepausen, Bierpausen, Rumpausen, Abwanderung in die strahlende Hauptstadt und Geld. Doch statt die Slumbewohner danach zu fragen, gaben sie ihnen – Schweiß und Arbeit.

Die dabei mobilisierte Arbeitskraft, die nicht gegenseitige Ausbildung, sondern nur Überredung kostete, verwandelte das Gemeinwesen von einem Slum in eine ansehnliche urbane Wohngegend – und das nicht binnen Jahren, sondern binnen weniger Monate. Und als diese Leistung mit der Weihe der Gemeinde durch den Bischof aus dem nahegelegenen Caguas ihren Höhepunkt erreichte, bemalte ein Großteil der Bevölkerung jedes Haus in der wieder aufgebauten Gegend – einige der Häuser schmücken nun Wandgemälde der berühmtesten Künstler des Landes wie etwa Lorenzo Homar oder Rafael Tufiño – binnen 24 Stunden, und das Ganze kostete den Staat (auf nationaler wie kommunaler Ebene) genau 0,00 (in Worten: null) US-Dollar. Zudem ließ die umfassende Neugestaltung den unschätzbar wertvollen Beitrag der Slumbewohner zur Stadtplanung unberührt: die unerreichte Schönheit ihrer Siedlungen und die auf instinktive Weise organische Anordnung von Strukturen, die wie etwa Geschäfte, Wirtshäuser, Wohnhäuser und Kirchen dem gesellschaftlichen Leben seine wahre Fülle verleihen.

Als die ersten Schritte des Experiments von Naranjito abgeschlossen waren, trat die empörte Regierung auf den Plan und versprach reichlich Gelder, um zu beweisen, daß das, was Architekten billig vollbringen können, Bürokraten auch für viel Geld schaffen. Doch bestätigt wurde damit nur Oscar Wildes schöner Spruch, wonach gute Vorsätze wie ein Scheck sind, der auf eine Bank ausgestellt ist, bei der man kein Konto hat. Von dem Geld jedenfalls kam nie auch nur irgendetwas an.

Da sich Projekte umso mehr verzögern, je länger die Untersuchungen dauern, und Untersuchungen umso länger dauern, je mehr Mittel dafür bereitstehen, sollte eine lokale Regierung die üppigen Forschungsgelder, die Washington in seiner skurrilen Großzügigkeit zu vergeben hat, am besten entweder geradewegs ablehnen und die Stadtentwicklungsprojekte denen übertragen, die ohne umfassende Voruntersuchung damit beginnen können; oder das Geld in eine Vielzahl kleinerer Zuschüsse aufteilen, was die Chance eröffnet, deutlich mehr Modellentwürfe zu erhalten, und das auch noch in einem Zwanzigstel der Zeit, die man für einen einzigen kollektiven Modellentwurf benötigt.

San Juan Star, 18. Dezember 1969

Planorama

Autonomie oder berufliche Leutseligkeit. Planung als Kunst. Adam Smiths Liaison mit Aphrodite. Die Einsicht von Außenseitern. Die Bedeutung der Zeitungskolumne. Inspiration aus dem geselligen Diskussionszentrum. Das achteckige Café. Wiener oder Pariser Touch.

Einer der Gründe für die Erbärmlichkeit moderner Planung liegt darin, daß es an einer angemessenen Planungskritik fehlt. Nur wenige Zeitungen widmen ihr ähnlich regelmäßig eine Kolumne wie etwa der Theater- oder der Musikkritik. Und auch die Ausbildungsstätten für Planung bieten keine entsprechenden Lehrveranstaltungen an.

Natürlich gibt es jede Menge Kritik, die von den *Opfern* der Planung kommt. Und auch der Beruf des Planens bringt ein gewisses Maß an Kritik mit sich. Doch Kritik an Planern, von Planern und für Planer führt stets zu einer Einigung entweder durch Mehrheitsentscheidung oder durch einen braven Kompromiß, die vielleicht die Methode verändert, selten aber die Grundausrichtung. Wenn man dialektische Straßenblockaden beiseite räumt, sorgt das einzig und allein dafür, daß man schneller in Richtung Abgrund gelangt.

Um ihre Funktion zu erfüllen, muß konstruktive Kritik von außerhalb der Berufs*praxis* kommen. Ein Theaterkritiker muß die Prinzipien dramatischer Kunst verstehen, nicht aber selbst Dramatiker sein. Gleiches gilt für die anderen Künste. Maler, die über andere Maler urteilen, sind Sieger, die über die Besiegten zu Gericht sitzen, oder umgekehrt. Alles, was sie in dieser Eigenschaft tun können, ist, ihrer Mißgunst freien Lauf zu lassen und ihre Beschränktheiten zu verstärken – und das alles unter dem Deckmantel, einen klaren Blick und Objektivität zu liefern, indem sie ihre Schlußfolgerungen in die dritte Person kleiden.

Das heißt nicht, daß der gute Kunstkritiker zwangsläufig von außerhalb des Berufsstands kommen muß. Er muß aber von außerhalb des praktizierenden Teils kommen. Als Vertreter des kritischen Segments ist er nicht nur ein integraler Bestandteil des Berufsstands, sondern die unverzichtbare ausgleichende Säule, auf der dieser Berufsstand ruht. Ja, er ist von so vitaler Bedeutung für die Künste, daß die Praktiker dort, wo er fehlt, möglicherweise die Bodenhaftung verlieren; doch sie werden kaum in der Lage sein, sich in der Luft zu halten.

Das alles stellt niemand ernsthaft in Frage. Die eigentliche Frage ist, ob die Planung ähnlich wie die Musik oder das Theater ebenfalls eine Kunstform ist. Entgegen dem Konsens, der unter den heutigen technikorientierten Praktikern besteht, lautet die Antwort eindeutig ja. Selbst *ökonomische* Planung ist eine Kunst, was nicht weiter überrascht, wenn man daran denkt, daß die moderne Ökonomie der Liaison von Adam Smith mit keiner geringeren Dame als der Ästhetik persönlich entsprungen ist. Und was für die ökonomische Planung gilt, gilt in umso stärkerem Maße auch für die Stadtplanung, die ähnlich wie Verse in der Dichtung oder die Melodie in der Musik eine Übung nicht nur in Anordnung, sondern in Komposition ist.

Akzeptiert man also, daß Planung eine Kunst und Kritik von essentieller Bedeutung für jegliche Planung ist, wie läßt sich dann der gegenwärtige defizitäre Zustand beheben?

Zunächst einmal müssen in diesem Zeitalter massiver Urbanisierung die Zeitungen in jeder Stadt der Planungskritik eigene Kolumnen widmen – und diese dürfen nicht allgemeiner Natur sein, sondern sie müssen lokal verortet sein und zudem mit der gleichen Regelmäßigkeit erscheinen wie Theater- und Musikkritiken. Denn Kunstkritik welcher Art auch immer läßt sich einzig und allein über die Presse kommunizieren.

Zweitens muß die Kommune dem Planungskritiker eine Operationsbasis bieten. Der Bühnenkritiker hat das Theater; der Musikkritiker hat den Konzertsaal; der Kunstkritiker hat die Ausstellungen. Für den Planungskritiker gibt es jedoch keine derartige Einrichtung.

Es gilt deshalb ein Institut ähnlich dem Theater zu schaffen, wo Planer, Kritiker und Öffentlichkeit das Produkt der Planer zu einem Zeitpunkt begutachten, diskutieren und analysieren können, an dem es wie bei einem Theaterstück noch möglich ist, Korrekturen vorzunehmen und etwa die Umrisse zu verändern, statt das ganze Gebäude abzureißen. In früheren Zeiten, als man ein Gebäude nach dem anderen baute und auftretende Mängel in den jeweils folgenden Bauten behoben werden konnten, war ein formelles Zentrum für die Planungskritik von geringerer Bedeutung. Doch in einer Zeit, da über Nacht ganze Städte aus dem Boden gestampft werden und man für Generationen darin leben muß, ist das Fehlen eines solchen Zentrums fatal.

Wie sollte sein solches Institut, dem man den Namen „Planorama" geben könnte, physisch aussehen? Man könnte es sich als hübschen Pavillon vorstellen, vielleicht rund oder achteckig, und es sollte so gestaltet sein, daß sich eine Reihe von Ausstellungsräumen um einen großzügig angelegten zentralen Innenhof oder ein Foyer gruppiert, wie man das heute häufig in Gewerkschaftszentralen findet. Das würde eine Anziehungskraft entfalten, die die leidende Öffentlichkeit anlockt; und es würde genügend Raum bieten, um sowohl konkurrierende Modelle aktueller Bauprojekte präsentieren und betrachten zu können als auch Seminare abzuhalten, bei denen die Planer in regelmäßig stattfindenden Anhörungen mit ihren Kritikern zusammentreffen.

Am wichtigsten aber ist: Das Planorama müßte Platz haben für ein Café nach Pariser oder Wiener Art, in dem man in entspannter Umgebung diskutieren kann. Nirgends nämlich können sich die Musen der Planung angenehmer mit den anderen Musen vermischen als in der lockeren Atmosphäre eines geselligen Treffpunkts. Denn wenn sie sich nicht mit den anderen Musen vermischen könnten, wäre es unmöglich, die erste Voraussetzung für eine effektive Planungskritik zu erfüllen: die Komposition einer geistreichen Zeitungskolumne, die die nötige Schärfe, Wucht und literarische Eleganz vereint, um die regierende Zunft der Stadtplaner aus der Ruhe zu bringen.

San Juan Star, 2. Januar 1967

New Town Blues

Der Schock des Planers. Spinnerte Soziologen. Sanierung vs. Zerstörung. Das Glanz-Muster der Slums. Die großen Örtlichkeitsexperten: Adlige, Gastwirte, Slumbewohner. Die Sterilität von Satellitenstädten. Das Gesetz der molekularen städtischen Anziehung. Implodierende Grüngürtel. Einkünfte aus Romantik.

Laut Zeitungsberichten war ein hochrangiger Regierungsvertreter aus Washington schockiert über die „gewalttätige Art", in der seine Ansichten zur neuen Stadt von den jungen Mitgliedern eines lokalen *Environmental Betterment Teams* kritisiert wurden; sie seien „mit Grafiken und Karten bewaffnet in dem offensichtlichen Bestreben aufgetaucht", sein Treffen zu „sprengen". Keine Rede war hingegen vom Schock über die gewalttätige Art, mit der er bei seiner Ankunft zwei Tage vor dem Treffen aus der Hüfte schoß, als er laut den gleichen Berichten seine Kritiker als „spinnerte Soziologen" beschimpfte, die eine „nostalgisch-irrationale Sicht der Slums" pflegten, welche er ablehne, denn sie repräsentierten „keine Gemeinschaft, außer vielleicht eine Abhängigkeitsgemeinschaft". Daher dann auch sein Vorschlag, das Problem der Slums durch Zerstörung statt durch Sanierung zu lösen.

Es stimmt natürlich in gewisser Weise, daß Slums „Abhängigkeitsgemeinschaften" sind. Aber das gilt für jede urbane Siedlung. Wie N.N. Baransky, kein spinnerter Soziologe, sondern ein hellsichtiger sowjetischer Rationalist, behauptet, sind alle Städte imperialistische Einrichtungen, die das umliegende Land, von dem sie abhängig sind, melken. Der einzige Unterschied, den ich bei den Slums erkennen kann, ist der, daß sie nicht gelernt haben, wie man das Land in der rechtlich akzeptablen Form von Baranskys metropolitanem Imperialismus melkt, und deshalb den Rest der Stadt mitunter auf weniger legale Weise melken müssen. Das bedeutet aber nicht, daß sie, einmal saniert, nicht in der Lage sein sollten, der übrigen Stadt als vollwertiger Partner bei der Ausbeutung der ländlichen Kolonien, von denen sie beide abhängen, behilflich zu sein.

Ein weiteres Argument für die Sanierung ist die tatsächliche Erfahrung, die man damit gemacht hat. Alle alten Städte, die bis heute florieren, sind im Kern sanierte Slums, die ursprünglich von Armen geschaffen und aufgrund des selbst erarbeiteten steigenden Wohlstands allmählich ausgebaut wurden. Und da Slumbewohner, anders als rationalistische Stadtplaner, mit Adligen, Gasthausbesitzern, dem Militär und der Kirche über einen sehr ausgeprägten Sinn für Örtlichkeiten verfügen, erwiesen sich die „Standorte", die sie ausgewählt hatten, bei der nachfolgenden städtischen Entwicklung stets als die wertvollsten. Man denke nur an die Lagunen von Venedig, an die strahlende Erhabenheit italienischer und spanischer Hügelstädte, an die von Schlössern und Burgen bestimmten Flußstädte in Österreich, Frankreich oder England oder an die Hafenstädte am Mittelmeer, wo trotz aller marmornen Eleganz in den Porto Finos, Salzburgs und Sienas von heute noch immer die humanistische Struktur von Slums wie etwa Buen Consejo, La Perla, Las Croabas oder El Fanguito in Puerto Rico sichtbar ist, aus der sie vor Jahrhunderten entstanden sind. Und wie sieht es aus mit den üppigen kommerziellen Gewinnen aus der Erneuerung einstmals „verslumter" Stadtzentren, wie man sie in Philadelphia oder im alten San Juan findet?

Im Gegensatz zu sanierten Slums erwiesen sich neue Städte – die man auch gerne passenderweise als Satellitenstädte bezeichnet – als so mangelhaft im Hinblick auf urbane Kultur und die natürlichen Reize des Lebens, daß eine bislang unbekannte krankhafte Form von Außenbestimmtheit aufgetreten ist, die man im Englischen als „new-town blues" bezeichnet. Diese sterilisierten Künstlichkeiten sind unfähig, so etwas wie eine Identität, eine geistige Existenz oder lokalen Stolz auf sich selbst zu entwickeln, und wuchern sogleich wieder zurück in Richtung des urbanen Kerns, von dem sie abgeschnitten wurden, und zwar mit einer Intensität, die gemäß Henry Charles Careys „Gesetz der molekularen städtischen Anziehung" umgekehrt proportional zur Entfernung ist. Doch Carey konnte Anfang des 19. Jahrhunderts noch nicht vorhersehen, daß diese Anziehungskraft auch direkt proportional zur motorisierten Leistungsfähigkeit ist. Die daraus resultierende Bevölkerungsimplosion von jenseits des Grüngürtels wird somit das Problem der Überfüllung und Verslumung (welches die neuen Städte eigentlich aus der Welt schaffen sollten) wieder verschärfen, indem sie den Zwischenraum füllt, der ursprünglich dazu gedacht war, zwischen den Städten einen dünn besiedelten Raum zum Atmen zu schaffen.

Ich stimme jedoch mit dem Rationalismus des 20. Jahrhunderts darin überein, daß es eines beträchtlichen Maßes an irrationaler Romantik bedarf, in den Anordnungen der Slums, die immer wieder von Künstlern bemalt werden, Kraft, Sinnlichkeit und Schönheit zu entdecken, während ich noch nicht erlebt habe, daß jemand völlig begeistert eine „sanierte" Vorstadt betrachtet. Es bedarf romantischer Irrationalität, in sumpfigen Lagunen zu bauen, für die offenbar kein moderner Rationalist Möglichkeiten städtischer Nutzung findet, die sich rechnen. Man muß denn auch ungefähr ein halbes Jahrtausend zurückgehen, um Planer zu finden, die „spinnert" genug sind, um das Problem wie etwa in Venedig und Amsterdam dadurch zu lösen, daß sie auf den Pfeilern bauen, die diese Gemeinwesen, glaubt man dem computerisierten Hausverstand, vor zweihundert Jahren in den Schlamm hätten ziehen sollen. Laut jüngsten Berichten stehen sie aber noch immer und bescheren den Nachfahren verrückter mittelalterlicher Bauherren dank der Horden rationalistischer Touristen jährlich ein Sümmchen, das um ein Vielfaches höher liegt als das, was ihre nüchternen, modernen, auf Industrie spezialisierten Nachfolger erwirtschaften.

San Juan Star, 26. Februar 1965

„Wie schön, nach Hause zu kommen!"
Zeichnung von Alan Dunn

Romantiker vs. Rationalisten

G.K. Chestertons Brief an den *San Juan Star*. Das Beste für Buen Consejo. Mehr nötig als nur Mißbilligung. Transzendentale Liebe. Schmückung von Dingen, die bereits wunderschön sind. Buen Consejo schöner als Florenz binnen eines Jahres. Wie Städte bedeutend wurden. Was machte Rom so schön? Die Lehre aus Pimlico. Stimme aus dem Jenseits.

An den Herausgeber des San Juan Star

Gestatten Sie mir, der gegenwärtigen Diskussion zwischen Romantikern und Rationalisten in Sachen Stadtplanung Folgendes hinzuzufügen:

„Nehmen wir einmal an, wir haben es mit einer hoffnungslosen Sache zu tun – sagen wir, dem Slum von Buen Consejo. Wenn wir überlegen, was für Buen Consejo wirklich am besten wäre, werden wir merken, daß der gedankliche Faden zum Thron oder ins Mystische und Willkürliche führt. Es reicht nicht, daß man Buen Consejo mißbilligt; dann kann man sich gleich die Kehle durchschneiden oder nach Condado ziehen. Es reicht aber ebensowenig, Buen Consejo zu akzeptieren: denn dann wird es Buen Consejo bleiben, und das wäre schlimm.

Der einzige Ausweg scheint darin zu bestehen, daß man Buen Consejo liebt; daß man es mit einem Hang zum Transzendentalen und ohne irdische Vernunft liebt. Gäbe es jemanden, der Buen Consejo liebt, würden in Buen Consejo Elfenbeintürme und goldene Zinnen in den Himmel wachsen: Buen Consejo würde sich herausputzen, wie eine Frau, die geliebt wird. Denn der Schmuck soll nicht schreckliche Dinge verbergen, sondern Dinge schmücken, die schon bewundernswert sind. Eine Mutter bindet ihrem Kind keine blaue Schleife ins Haar, weil es ohne diese so häßlich wäre. Ein Liebhaber schenkt seinem Mädchen keine Halskette, um ihren Hals zu verbergen. Würden die Leute Buen Consejo lieben, wie Mütter Kinder lieben, ganz gleich ob es die ihren sind, könnte Buen Consejo binnen ein oder zwei Jahren hübscher als Florenz sein. Einige Leser werden nun sagen, das sei bloße Phantasie. Denen entgegne ich, daß das die wirkliche Menschheitsgeschichte ist. Genau so erlangten Städte ihre Größe. Man gehe zurück zu den finstersten Wurzeln der Zivilisation, und man wird sie um einen heiligen Stein geschlungen oder sich um einen heiligen Quell rankend finden. Die Menschen erwiesen zunächst einem Punkt die Ehre und ernteten später dafür Ruhm. Die Menschen liebten Rom nicht, weil es großartig war. Rom war großartig, weil die Menschen es liebten."

Da ich seit vielen Jahren tot bin, nehme ich mir die Freiheit, dem *Star* meine Gedanken über meinen treuen Schüler Professor Leopold Kohr von der Universität Puerto Rico zu übermitteln; ihm habe ich auch die Erlaubnis erteilt, Buen Consejo für Pimlico einzusetzen und Condado in Santurce für Chelsea. Mehr dazu kann man in meiner *Orthodoxie* (*Eine Handreichung für die Ungläubigen*, orig. 1908, jüngste dt. Ausgabe Frankfurt/M.: Eichborn 2000) nachlesen.

G.K. Chesterton
„Die Wolke" über Buen Consejo
San Juan, P.R.

27. Februar 1965

Das Wesen der Slums

Die Vorzüge von Slums. Keine Einsamkeit, keine Kriminalität. Das Gespür der Slumbewohner für gute Lagen. Die zerstörerische Vision von Planern. Was einen Slum ausmacht. Wo jeder jemand ist, ist niemand irgendwer. Der Wohlstand auf der Couch des Psychoanalytikers. Gesellschaftliche Pyramide. Unterste Einkommensebene wie der letzte Waggon eines Zuges: Läßt sich nicht abhängen.

Eines der vielgepriesenen Prinzipien, an denen sich Modellstadtprojekte orientieren, besteht darin, herauszufinden, was die Bewohner von Slums, die saniert werden sollen, selbst wollen. Was sie wollen, sind Slums! Darum leben sie ja dort. Und sie leben gern dort, weil Slums trotz aller Defizite Vorzüge aufweisen, die keine der Neubausiedlungen, welche die Behörden an deren Stelle gesetzt haben, zu bieten hat.

Die wichtigsten Vorzüge von Slums sind 1. ihre Lage und 2. ihre dichte und organische Anordnung von Straßen, Plätzen, Läden und Behausungen. Letzteres verhindert Einsamkeit im Alter und sorgt für wenig interne Kriminalität, wenngleich es nicht unbedingt auch von Verbrechen gegen Außenstehende abhält, so wie ja auch der innere Frieden einer Nation diese nicht von munteren Aggressionen jenseits der eigenen Grenzen abhält. Und was Punkt 1) betrifft, so haben Slumbewohner schon immer ein einzigartiges Gespür für gute Lagen gezeigt; in dieser Hinsicht können es allenfalls Gastwirte, Adlige, das Militär und die Kirche mit ihnen aufnehmen.

Nun sind es genau diese Vorzüge, die Stadtplaner und Sanierer – deren Instinkte aufgrund wissenschaftlicher Voreingenommenheit abgestumpft sind – abzuschaffen versuchen. Und sie erliegen dieser Versuchung mit umso größerer Wahrscheinlichkeit, je gewissenhafter sie die Vorgaben ihrer Modellstadtkontrakte erfüllen, in denen sie dazu angehalten werden, die Prioritätenliste der Slumbewohner zu eruieren, indem sie inmitten der Slums Wohnhäuser und Geschäfte errichten.

Denn die Slumbewohner werden ihnen sagen, was sie wollten, seien nicht die Vorzüge, über die sie verfügen (ideale Lagen und organische Lebensformen), sondern das, was sie nicht haben (Spielplätze, Parkplätze, Fernsehen und sanitäre Einrichtungen). Die Sanierer werden deshalb vorschlagen, was sie schon immer vorgeschlagen haben, nämlich Örtlichkeiten, die in ihrer Schönheit mit Amalfi, Venedig oder Assisi mithalten können, abzureißen und an ihrer Stelle neue Viertel mit sanitären Einrichtungen, Fernsehen, Park- und Spielplätzen zu errichten. Dabei vergessen sie völlig, daß die schönsten Spielplätze schon immer die zufälligen Lücken, Nischen, Seitenwege, stillen Plätzchen, Winkel und unerwarteten Zugänge zum Wasser waren, die überall dort zu finden sind, wo der offizielle Planungsprozeß seinen Entwurf nicht umsetzen konnte.

Wenn man deshalb nach den angeblichen Wünschen der Slumbewohner fragt, wird man kaum brauchbare Ergebnisse bekommen. Viel ergiebiger ist die Frage nach den Bedingungen, die dafür verantwortlich sind, daß aus Siedlungen überhaupt Slums werden. Eine Kommune wird zu einem Slum, wenn sie durchgängig von den untersten Einkommensschichten bevölkert ist. Dabei spielt es keine Rolle, auf welchem Niveau diese unterste Einklassengesellschaft lebt, denn man kann selbst auf hohem Niveau unter vielen der unterste sein. Wenn alle anderen Einserschüler sind, dann wird der Schüler mit der Note zwei diese als Versagen betrachten. „Wo jeder jemand ist, ist niemand irgendwer."

Ein Slum ist deshalb nicht durch das Fehlen sanitärer Einrichtungen bestimmt, sondern durch die fehlende Differenzierung. Unsere Stadtumgestalter sollten deshalb nicht herauszufinden versuchen, was die Slumbewohner wollen, sondern was wohlhabende Menschen, wie beispielsweise den Leiter der städtischen Baubehörde, dazu veranlassen könnte, sich in einem Slum niederzulassen. Denn nur dann bekommt man die Einkommensunterschiede und die Säulen sozialer Führerschaft, um die herum sich der Rest des Gemeinwesens weitgehend aus eigener Kraft nach oben arbeiten kann, indem er in Eigeninitiative einem Beispiel folgt und nicht auf militärische Art einem Plan.

Kurz gesagt: Modellstädte zu bauen sollte nicht heißen, daß man die Armen auf ein höheres Armutsniveau hievt (das wäre nur Wohlstand, den man auf die Couch des Psychoanalytikers legt), sondern daß man aus der planen Fläche sozialer Uniformität eine ökonomisch differenzierte Pyramide entstehen läßt. Es sollte nicht heißen:

Bauen der Bedürftigen durch die Bedürftigen und für die Bedürftigen, sondern *weg* von den Bedürftigen in Richtung des gelobten Wohlstandslandes, das die Reformer ihnen seit jeher vor Augen halten.

Ebensowenig sollte sich eine Modellstadt über Gebühr der Abschaffung des untersten Einkommensniveaus widmen. Es gibt notwendigerweise immer ein unterstes Niveau, so wie es in einem Zug immer einen ungemütlich ruckelnden letzten Waggon gibt, den man nicht aus der Welt schafft, indem man ihn abhängt. Das führt einzig und allein dazu, daß nun ein anderer Wagen der letzte ist. Eine Modellstadt muß vielmehr aus dem Material, das am Boden herumliegt, eine Pyramide immer höherer Ebenen errichten, die sich unablässig von der Armut darunter ernähren, sie aber allmählich aufsaugen, ohne die unterste, grundlegende Schicht auszuhöhlen, auf der eine gesunde Stadt ebenso gründen muß wie eine kranke.

Die einzige andere Alternative ist die Lösung, die ich in meiner nächsten Kolumne vorschlagen werde und die sich anders als die oben präsentierte nicht am Wesen der Slums orientiert – nämlich ihrem Mangel an sozialen Differenzierung –, sondern an der Ursache und dem Ursprung von Slums – der übermäßig effizienten Mechanisierung der Landwirtschaft. Diese zweite Alternative versucht deshalb einen der zentralen städtischen Mißstände dadurch zu lösen, daß sie nicht die Stadt, sondern das Land umgestaltet.

San Juan Star, 12. Dezember 1967

Der Ursprung der Slums

Landflucht aufgrund der Mechanisierung. Flucht in die Städte. Die aufregenden Erlebnisse der Arbeitslosigkeit, der Aktivismus der Untätigkeit. Die Freuden des Slumlebens. Langsame Abhilfe durch technologische Effizienz. Zurück auf die Farm. Kanonenfutter für Napoleon.

Die Slums in den Städten sind ländlichen und nicht urbanen Ursprungs. Darin liegt auch der Grund, warum selbst noch so viel traditionelle Stadtplanung ihnen bislang nicht beikam.

Slumbewohner sind geflohene Landarbeiter, die sich am noch verbliebenen Platz in oder in der Nähe von Städten versammeln und in hastig zusammengezimmerten Hütten oder Zelten ohne wirkliche Straßen, ohne Licht, ohne sanitäre Einrichtungen leben.

Das Anwachsen der Slums in den Städten läßt sich deshalb nur eindämmen, wenn man den Zustrom der Flüchtlinge vom Land eindämmt. Und die Flüchtlinge lassen sich nur aufhalten, wenn man den Feind besiegt, der sie entwurzelt und vertreibt.

Wer aber ist der Feind, der die Landbewohner in solchen Massen vertreibt, daß die Städte trotz ihres explosionsartigen Wachstums nicht schell genug wachsen können, um sie alle in ihr System aufzunehmen?

Der Feind ist der Fortschritt oder genauer: das übermäßige Tempo des Fortschritts. Es ist die zu rasante Mechanisierung des Bauernhofs oder der Farm, die dazu führt, daß die landwirtschaftliche Effizienz derart große Sprünge vorwärts macht, daß keine lokale Industrie in der Lage ist, all die Arbeitskräfte aufzunehmen, die durch die Einführung der allerneuesten landwirtschaftlichen Methoden frei werden. Erschwerend kommt hinzu, daß die Industrie selbst im Übermaß Arbeitsplätze einspart; das hat dazu geführt, daß die Fabrik heute noch einstellungsresistenter ist als die Farm.

Angesichts dessen führt das galoppierende Tempo moderner Landwirtschaftstechnik zunächst dazu, daß sich die arbeitslosen Landarbeiter in nahegelegenen ländlichen Slums sammeln. Da es die relativ geringe Größe der Slums auf dem Land erlauben würde, die Behausungen mit Hilfe der beschäftigungslosen Landarbeiter binnen relativ kurzer Zeit zu sanieren, ließe sich dieses Problem lösen, wenn man diese Arbeitskräfte dazu bringen könnte dazubleiben.

Doch arbeitslose Landarbeiter werden nicht bleiben. Statt im ländlichen Slum ihren künftigen Heimatort zu sehen, betrachten sie ihn nur als eine Art Zwischenstation auf dem Weg zu ihrer eigentlichen Zuflucht – der großen Stadt. Denn anders als frühere Phasen technischen Fortschritts bietet ihnen die jüngste Phase der Automatisierung keinerlei Hoffnung darauf, in der Nähe ihrer Heimat wieder eine neue Beschäftigung zu finden. Was Arbeit auf dem Land angeht, sind sie zu dauerhafter Untätigkeit verdammt. Und anhaltende Untätigkeit sucht naturgemäß nicht in der frustrierenden Suche nach nicht vorhandener Arbeit Befriedigung, sondern in aufregenden Erlebnissen, wie sie sich in der Beschaulichkeit und sozialen Überschaubarkeit kleiner ländlicher Gemeinden nicht finden lassen.

Das erklärt, mit welcher Kraft das heimatlose ländliche Proletariat unwiderstehlich aus dem provinziellen Stilleben ins magnetisch wirkende Neonlicht der Städte gezogen wird. Denn im pulsierenden Leben der Städte werden Untätigkeit und fehlende *Arbeit* erträglich, weil es eine solche Fülle von Möglichkeiten für *Aktivität* und *Aktivismus* gibt, daß das Leben im Slum von den Neuankömmlingen nicht mehr als soziales Problem betrachtet wird, sondern als aufregender Ausgangspunkt für bislang unbekannte Abenteuer. Ein soziales Problem sind die Slums nur in den Augen von Reformern, Regierenden und Bürgertum, da sie deren Vorliebe für behagliche Wohlanständigkeit zuwiderlaufen. In den Augen ihrer Bewohner hingegen stellen sie oftmals eine willkommene Lebensform dar, wie sich jüngst im puertoricanischen Slum La Perla gezeigt hat (dem Schauplatz von Oscar Lewis' internationalem Bestseller *La Vida*): Die dortige Bevölkerung nämlich demonstrierte dafür, die aufregende Schönheit ihres Gemeinwesens vor den unsensiblen Plänen ästhetisch gleichgültiger Regierungsbehörden zu schützen, die beauftragt waren, diese zu zerstören.

Angesichts dessen lassen sich die *städtischen* Slums nur auf eine Weise abschaffen: indem man zuvor die Quelle, die sie immer wieder neu füllt, zum Versiegen bringt – den Slum *auf dem Land*.

La Perla

Die *Evolution* wird dies letztlich schaffen, indem sie die landwirtschaftliche Mechanisierung so weit treibt, daß die daraus resultierende Entvölkerung der ländlichen Regionen jede weitere Entlassung von Farmarbeitern ökonomisch unmöglich machen wird. Wenn praktisch die gesamte Bevölkerung in Städten lebt, werden die Slums auf dem Land endlich die Chance haben zu versiegen. Gleiches wird mit ihrem städtischen Sproß geschehen, der mangels Nahrung aus dieser Quelle zu schwinden beginnen wird. Das ist dann vermutlich im Jahr 2084 der Fall – dauert also noch eine gehörige Zeit.

Das gleiche Ergebnis läßt sich freilich auch mittels einer *Revolution* erreichen, was naturgemäß sehr viel schneller geht. Statt hilflos den Flüchtlingstransfer von öden ländlichen in aufregende städtische Behausungen zu organisieren, muß man dafür nur den Prozeß der landwirtschaftlichen Mechanisierung rückgängig machen, denn er vor allem war es, der den Menschen die Beschäftigung genommen hat. Mit anderen Worten: Man muß sie wieder in ihre ursprünglichen Berufe zurückbringen, und zwar ganz einfach dadurch, daß man die Effizienz landwirtschaftlicher Maschinen so weit *reduziert* (statt sie stetig zu erhöhen), bis man beim Produktionsprozeß wieder jede Hand braucht. Das ist die Bedeutung der sogenannten mittleren Technik. Wenn Reformern das als reaktionär erscheint, muß man sie nur daran erinnern, daß das die gleiche Methode ist, mit der sich „fortschrittliche" Gewerkschaften gegen den „reaktionären" Entlassungsaspekt supereffizienter moderner Ausrüstung im Kohlebergbau, bei der Eisenbahn oder in Druckereien wehren.

Doch in einer Zeit, die noch immer fälschlicherweise technischen mit sozialem Fortschritt gleichsetzt, ist der Gedanke, die Lage der Menschen durch eine Effizienz*reduktion* des Maschinenparks zu verbessern, nur schwer zu vermitteln. Doch selbst Planer könnten ihn aufgreifen, sobald sie merken, daß der Zweck der Landwirtschaft schließlich darin besteht, die Gesellschaft mit Nahrungsmitteln und Rohstoffen zu versorgen, nicht mit Menschen, die man braucht, um städtische Slums zu bevölkern, oder, wie bei Napoleon, mit Kanonenfutter.

San Juan Star, 18. Januar 1968

Die Stadt der Plätze

Psychologie der Eigenständigkeit. Die Anziehungskraft des Supermarkts. Altmodische Marktplätze als Magnet. Das Getränkekistenmuster der urbanen Struktur. Industrieghettos. Prunkvolle Fabriken. Tod durch urbane Strangulierung. Gesellige Dezentralisierung. Eine Föderation von Plätzen.

Ein Hauptziel unserer Modellstadtplaner ist es, die Gegenden, die saniert werden sollen, mit einem gewissen Maß an Eigenständigkeit auszustatten. Als leidenschaftlicher Befürworter der Eigenständigkeit kleiner Gemeinwesen könnte ich mir kein besseres Ziel vorstellen. Betrachtet man jedoch das in der Vergangenheit Erreichte, besteht wenig Grund zu der Annahme, daß die dabei anvisierte Form von Eigenständigkeit auch nur irgendein Problem löst.

Ein Gemeinwesen ist nicht nur dann eigenständig, wenn niemand sich in andere Gegenden begeben *muß*, um seinen täglichen Aktivitäten nachzugehen, sondern auch wenn niemand sich dorthin begeben *will*. Das ist zur Hälfte keine Frage der Ökonomie, sondern der Psychologie. Deshalb wird eine Fülle an kleinen Läden um die Ecke die Anziehungskraft des weiter entfernten Supermarkts *nicht* verringern, solange letzterer etwas zu bieten hat, was eine Ansammlung keiner Läden nicht bieten kann: die Möglichkeit, wie in einer Buchhandlung in einer reichhaltigen Auswahl zu stöbern, was einem das befriedigende Gefühl von Überfluß verschafft, selbst wenn man nichts kauft.

Genau das hatte der alte *Marktplatz* zu bieten, der nicht das gleiche ist wie eine Plaza (die Nestor Avecedo als das Wohnzimmer eines Gemeinwesens definiert). Eine der Antworten auf das Problem lokaler Eigenständigkeit ist deshalb die Schaffung von Marktplätzen, die, wollen sie der Anziehungskraft von Supermärkten entgegenwirken, so zahlreich sein müssen, daß die große Mehrheit der Bevölkerung alles bekommt, was sie haben will, ohne sich zu weit von ihrem Zuhause entfernen zu müssen. Denn sobald die Menschen mehr als eine minimale Entfernung zurücklegen müssen, werden sie das Auto benutzen, und sobald sie das Auto benutzen, werden sie das Gefühl haben, daß es umso ökonomischer ist, je länger und nicht je kürzer sie damit unterwegs sind. Also können sie genausogut in den Supermarkt gehen. (Das soll nicht heißen, daß nicht der gelegentliche Besuch im Supermarkt durchaus von Wert ist, sowenig der Charme lokaler Musikgruppen über die Vorzüge eines großstädtischen Symphonieorchesters hinwegtäuscht oder die kleine Pfarrkirche über den Glanz der Kathedrale.)

Die Eigenständigkeit kleiner Lokalitäten innerhalb des Kontexts einer Metropole hängt deshalb in erster Linie davon ab, daß es wie bei einer Getränkekiste viele identische Marktplätze gibt, die einen ansonsten lawinenartigen Verkehrsstrom verteilen, und nicht ein Kanalsystem von Straßen, die an einem einzigen geselligen oder zum Einkaufen gedachten Platz konvergieren. Das hat Salzburg, Lucca, Cambridge oder das alte San Juan zu so lebendigen, liebens- und lebenswerten Städten gemacht: daß sie als „Föderation" von Plätzen und Märkten gewachsen sind, die durch Straßen miteinander verbunden sind, und nicht als Verbund von Straßen, die in Plätzen nichts anderes sehen als entweder Parkplätze oder Verkehrshindernisse (und dabei nicht erkennen, daß das Verkehrhindernis die Grundlage des Handels darstellt).

Wichtigste Voraussetzung für Eigenständigkeit ist jedoch nicht nur, daß man alles vor Ort kaufen kann oder daß Schulen, Kirchen, Kinos und Gasthäuser in der Nähe sind, sondern auch daß der überwiegende Teil des Einkommens in der unmittelbaren Nachbarschaft verdient wird. Für Ladenbesitzer ist das kein Problem, denn sie können dort wohnen, wo sie arbeiten. Schon eher ein Problem ist das für Arbeiter, ob nun Handwerker oder Facharbeiter. Und da die Bevölkerung einer Stadt in der Mehrzahl nun einmal nicht aus Ladenbesitzern besteht, sondern aus Arbeitern, machen es die Regeln für die Eigenständigkeit kleiner Areale erforderlich, daß die Industrien, die diese Menschen beschäftigen, nicht, wie das heute der Fall ist, in dicht bebauten, unbewohnten Fabrikghettos abgesondert sein dürfen, die auf unökonomische Weise tagsüber übermäßig genutzt werden und nachts völlig verlassen sind; sie müssen vielmehr wieder inmitten ihrer jeweiligen Belegschaft zu finden sein.

Das sollte nicht allzu schwer sein, wenn man bedenkt, daß die moderne Architektur genauso gut in der Lage ist, Fabriken in elegante Stadtstrukturen einzufügen, wie sie diese in Reihen von prunkvollen Gebäuden entlang von Schnellstraßen unterbringt, die die Transportkosten mit arithmetisch zunehmender Entfernung von der Stadt geometrisch anwachsen lassen. Sobald die industrielle Umgebung in der Stadt so attraktiv geworden ist wie das geschäftliche und gesellige Umfeld von Plätzen und Märkten, werden nicht nur die Arbeiter lieber vor Ort bleiben und ihren Vergnügungen in unmittelbarer Umgebung nachgehen, sondern auch Bankiers, Lehrer, Ärzte, Schauspieler und all die anderen Beförderer des guten Lebens.

Nur dann wird es für kleine Kommunen angesichts der amorphen Ausdehnung einer modernen Metropole möglich sein, die einzige Art von Eigenständigkeit zu entwickeln, die den Tod durch Ersticken im städtischen Verkehr verhindern kann. Das ist die *gesellige* Eigenständigkeit ihrer Viertel und Bezirke; sie erreicht man, indem man dafür sorgt, daß die Bewohner ihre Arbeit und ihr Vergnügen nicht nur nicht anderswo suchen *müssen*, sondern das auch gar nicht *wollen*.

San Juan Star, 22. Dezember 1967

Die Vorstädte urbanisieren

Das Ende des Parkens. Pferde schneller als Autos. Chicago 1900. Los Angeles 1984. Die verlangsamende Wirkung besserer Verkehrswege. Numerischer vs. geschwindigkeitsbedingter Druck. Malthusianische Verkehrslehre. Polynukleare Lösung. Michelangelo über Architektur und menschliche Struktur. Anmut und Vollständigkeit ins Viertel zurückbringen.

Vor einigen Jahren gab es innerhalb der Stadtgrenzen noch ein paar Ecken, in denen ziemlich wenig Verkehr herrschte. Sie sind heute verschwunden. Noch vor einem Jahr fand ich an der Universität einen Parkplatz. Heute bin ich länger auf der Suche nach einem Parkplatz, als ich für die zehn Meilen zur Uni brauche. Infolgedessen komme ich in meine Seminare oft eine Viertelstunde zu spät, obwohl ich mehr als rechtzeitig von zu Hause aufgebrochen bin.

Kein Wunder also, wenn die Menschen wehmütig an den romantischen Beginn des Jahrhunderts zurückdenken, als von Pferden gezogene Straßenbahnen wie etwa in Chicago 11 Meilen pro Stunde schafften, während im Zeitalter des Düsenflugzeugs ein nagelneues Auto innerstädtisch gerade einmal 10,3 Meilen in der Stunde zurücklegt.

In einer modernen, weitgehend staatlich gelenkten Ökonomie sind solche Ergebnisse nur möglich, wenn sie tatsächlich geplant sind. Das läßt nur zwei mögliche Schlußfolgerungen zu. Entweder wollten die Planer den Verkehr absichtlich verlangsamen oder ihre Mathematiker haben sich verrechnet.

Nimmt man letzteres an, welche Theorie könnte dann für die fortschreitende Lähmung der städtischen Bewegung verantwortlich sein? Ursprünglich muß die Idee gewesen sein, den Verkehrsdruck zu verringern, indem man die Verkehrswege ausbaut. Daher der unablässige Bau von breiteren Straßen, Einbahnstraßen, Parkgaragen und schnelleren Autos.

Obwohl sich in der Folge die Lage stets verschlechterte, fiel den Planern nichts anderes ein, als ihre Straßenbauanstrengungen zu verdoppeln. In Los Angeles haben sie sage und schreibe drei Viertel der riesigen Fläche der Stadt dem Verkehr geopfert – noch immer ohne Erfolg.

Sie müssen erst noch erkennen, daß zusätzlicher *Raum* möglicherweise gerade die Ursache für zusätzlichen *Druck* ist und daß die Verringerung des Verkehrsdrucks vielleicht auf die genau entgegengesetzte Weise gelingt – nicht durch einen weiteren *Ausbau* der Verkehrswege, sondern durch eine *Reduzierung* des Verkehrs.

Aber warum sollte zusätzliche Infrastruktur den Verkehrsdruck erhöhen, statt ihn zu verringern? Sie *hätte* reduzierende Wirkung, wenn andere Größen unverändert bleiben würden wie etwa die Zahl und Masse der Autos, die Größe der Städte, der Lebensstandard, die Bevölkerung. Doch wir leben in einem Zeitalter des Wachstums: dem Zuwachs von Produktivität, von Ausstoß, von Autopopulation, von Lebensstandard, von allem.

Und da sich der steigende Lebensstandard in erster Linie in der Suburbanisierung der Städte manifestiert mitsamt all dem, was dies an geometrisch zunehmenden Pendlerströmen mit sich bringt, müssen neue Straßen, die sich bestenfalls in arithmetischem Maße ausbauen lassen, allein schon aus diesem Grund immer inadäquater werden.

Denn jeder Reduktionseffekt, den zusätzliche Straßen im Hinblick auf den arithmetisch gestiegenen *physischen* Verkehrsdruck aufgrund der größeren Zahl an Vorstadtautos möglicherweise haben, wird mehr als „kompensiert" durch eine geometrische Zunahme des *Geschwindigkeits*drucks, welche die verbesserte Verkehrsinfrastruktur mit sich bringt. Denn der Verkehrsdruck steigt nicht nur mit der Zahl, sondern auch mit der Geschwindigkeit der Autos, die durch zusätzliche neue Straßen stets zunimmt.

Das erklärt, warum ähnlich wie beim malthusianischen Verhältnis zwischen Bevölkerungsdruck und Nahrungsmittelversorgung der Verkehrsdruck mathematisch zwangsläufig den verfügbaren Raum für Straßen übertrifft, selbst in den reichsten Gesellschaften, die diesen Raum in ihrem vergeblichen Bemühen, den Druck zu verringern, stetig vergrößern. Daher auch das scheinbare Paradoxon: je reicher eine Gesellschaft, desto großzügiger ihre Straßen; und je großzügiger die Straßen, desto größer das Verkehrschaos.

Und genau aus diesem Grund muß das Problem des Staus vom anderen Ende der Gleichung her angegangen werden: Die Verkehrswege dürfen nicht ausgebaut werden, sondern der Verkehr muß reduziert werden. Aber wie läßt sich das bewerkstelligen? Ganz offensichtlich, indem man die Voraussetzung, die zu seiner Zunahme geführt hat, umkehrt. Wenn der Verkehrsdruck infolge der Suburbanisierung der Städte zugenommen hat, folgt daraus, daß er durch die Urbanisierung der Vorstädte geringer wird.

Eine solche Urbanisierung läßt sich einzig und allein dadurch erreichen, daß man die Vorstädte wenn schon nicht physisch, dann zumindest administrativ von den Städten trennt und sie in ein polynukleares System in sich geschlossener, autonomer Zentren verwandelt, die ihre Bewohner in ihren eigenen Magnetfeldern halten, indem sie ihnen nicht nur Arbeit, sondern auch so viele Attraktionen des eleganten Stadtlebens bieten, daß keiner von ihnen den Wunsch hegt, den eigenen Sprengel zu verlassen, außer vielleicht für gelegentliche Besichtigungstouren, wie man sie von San Juan auf die Jungferninseln oder von London nach Paris unternimmt. Doch da jede Frage der Anziehung stets ästhetischer Natur ist, folgt daraus auch, daß mit dieser Umwandlung der urbanen Struktur nicht die Planungstechniker betraut werden dürfen, sondern die Planungsgourmets – eine Spezies, die unsere spezialisierten Einrichtungen höherer Bildung nicht mehr hervorbringen.

Sobald Planer mit Michelangelo wieder erkennen, daß die Struktur eines Gebäudes wie auch einer Stadt der Struktur des menschlichen Körpers entspricht und nicht nur soziologisch oder technisch, sondern auch ästhetisch betrachtet werden muß, werden sie merken, daß sich das Problem des Verkehrsdrucks auf ein schlichtes Problem von Proportionen und Form reduziert. Dann besteht auch keinerlei Bedarf mehr an all den staatlich finanzierten Untersuchungen, die nur deswegen Jahrzehnte brauchen, damit sie die üppigen Summen, die ihnen zugedacht sind, auch verdienen.

San Juan Star, 9. Februar 1967

Geschwindigkeitsbedingte Bevölkerung

Vaterschaft auf dem Motorrad. Der massenvergrößernde Effekt der Geschwindigkeit. Die Panikgröße von Theaterpublikum. Überbevölkerung: Folge technologischer Geschwindigkeit, nicht der Zeugungsfreude. Lösung ist Motivations- und nicht Fortbewegungsproblem. Was läßt Sammy rasen? Fehlende Schönheit in der Nähe. Nationale und urbane Dezentralisierung. Wirtschaftliche Eigenständigkeit der Regionen. Der ästhetische Charme von Stadtvierteln.

Broadus Mitchell, der eine Biographie über Alexander Hamilton verfaßt hat und zu den bedeutendsten Wirtschaftshistorikern Amerikas gehört, erzählt die amüsante Geschichte von einem etwas irritierten Arzt, der in einem großen Gebiet im Süden der Vereinigten Staaten bei der Geburt ungewöhnlich vieler unehelicher Kinder dabei war.

Was den Arzt irritierte, war in erster Linie die Tatsache, daß alle Mädchen als den Vater ihres Babys die gleiche Person angaben. Völlig von den Socken war er dann allerdings, als er dem Vater der Kinder zum ersten Mal begegnete und dieser sich als Mann von über achtzig Jahren erwies. „Wie um alles in der Welt haben Sie es angestellt, all diese Kinder zu zeugen?" fragte der Arzt. „Nun", antwortete der erstaunliche Achtziger mit altersgemäß krächzender Stimme, „ich gebe zu, ich hätte es nicht geschafft, wenn ich nicht ein Motorrad gehabt hätte."

Mit anderen Worten: Die Geschwindigkeit der modernen Verkehrsmittel erlaubte es dem alten Kerl, in einem beachtlichen Gebiet zu leisten, was nur im Umkreis einer Quadratmeile möglich gewesen wäre, wenn er zu Fuß unterwegs gewesen wäre. Und innerhalb einer Quadratmeile hätte es natürlich nicht so viele Mädchen für eine solche Zufallsmutterschaft gegeben.

Doch die Geschwindigkeit, mit der man heute unterwegs ist, hat noch einen viel wichtigeren Effekt, als nur die Bevölkerung quantitativ zu vergrößern, indem man ihre Zahl vergrößert. Die eigentliche Sensation ist, daß die Geschwindigkeit die Bevölkerung auch qualitativ wachsen läßt, indem sie deren Masse vergrößert, so wie eine höhere Geschwindigkeit die Zahl der Atomteilchen erhöht oder eine schnellere Zirkulation die „Geldmenge" vergrößert, wie jedem Wirtschaftsstudenten beigebracht wird.

Das erklärt, warum Theater zusätzlich zu den normalen Ausgängen auch über Notausgänge verfügen müssen – für den Fall, daß das Publikum in Panik gerät und schneller als normal hinaus möchte. Denn wie jeder Theaterbesitzer weiß, hat eine schnellere Menge den gleichen materiellen Effekt wie eine größere Menge. Die Zahl der verfügbaren Ausgänge muß deshalb nicht der numerischen, sondern der effektiven (oder Geschwindigkeits-) Größe des Publikums entsprechen; sie ergibt sich, wenn man die numerische Größe mit der Geschwindigkeit multipliziert.

Was für Menschen gilt, die sich im Gebäude eines Theaters bewegen, gilt natürlich auch für Bevölkerungen, die sich im geschlossenen Raum von Städten oder Nationen bewegen. Je schneller sie sich aufgrund der modernen Verkehrsmittel, vom Motorrad bis zum Düsenflugzeug, bewegen, desto stärker nimmt ihre effektive Größe zu. Abgesehen von ein paar wenigen Ausnahmen wie Indien ist das Problem der weltweiten Überbevölkerung weniger wegen der übermäßigen Zahl an Menschen so beunruhigend, sondern wegen der übermäßigen Geschwindigkeit, mit der sie sich bewegen.

Angesichts dessen besteht eine Möglichkeit, des Problems Herr zu werden, darin, ähnlich wie im Theater eine Art „Notraum" schaffen, um die Phasen zu überstehen, in denen sich die Menschen schneller als gewöhnlich bewegen, wie dies in jeder Stadt zu den Stoßzeiten der Fall ist. Das tun Planer ohnehin, indem sie ständig neue Straßen bauen und die alten verbreitern.

Das Problem dabei ist nur: Anders als im feststehenden Raum des Theaters lindert die Einrichtung zusätzlichen „Notraums" innerhalb der dehnbaren Grenzen einer Stadt nichts an der Überfüllung; in Wirklichkeit verstärkt sie diese sogar noch, denn sie ermutigt die Bevölkerung, sich über die „Stadtmauern" hinaus in immer größere Gebiete auszubreiten. Doch je weiter sich eine zusammengehörende Bevölkerung ausbreitet, desto größer wird die Entfernung, die sie zurücklegen muß, um ihren täglichen Verrichtungen nachzukommen. Und je schneller sie sich bewegt, desto stärker nimmt ihre effektive (oder Geschwindigkeits-) Größe zu.

Im Falle einer Stadt von der Größe San Franciscos, Bristols oder San Juans in Puerto Rico bedeutet das, daß eine numerische Bevölkerung von – sagen wir – 600.000 Menschen zu einer effektiven Bevölkerung von vielleicht 2.000.000 Menschen aufgebläht wird, während ihr Netzwerk an Notstraßen bestenfalls für 1.000.000 Menschen ausgelegt ist. Und diese Kluft läßt sich niemals schließen. Denn jedes Mal, wenn in einem *arithmetischen* Verhältnis neue Straßen hinzukommen, steigt die effektive oder geschwindigkeitsbedingte Bevölkerung einer Stadt genau deshalb in *geometrischem* Verhältnis an. Aus diesem Grund erreichte der 1948 eröffnete New Jersey Turnpike die für das Jahr 1975 prognostizierte Verkehrsdichte bereits eine Woche nach seiner Eröffnung; und deshalb hat, zur Überraschung von Inspektor Martin West vom Straßenverkehrsdezernat der Polizei von Surrey (*The Times*, 18. August 1988), der durch seinen Distrikt führende Abschnitt der Autobahn (M 25) schon in den 1980er Jahren „eine Verkehrslast zu bewältigen, wie sie erst für die 1990er Jahre prognostiziert worden war". „Das Verkehrsaufkommen verursacht Chaos" nicht trotz, sondern wegen der neuen Autobahnen.

Damit bleibt als die einzig praktikable Lösung nur die zweite Methode, mit der die Theater der massenvergrößernden Wirkung der Geschwindigkeit zu begegnen versuchen, wenn sie ihr Publikum dazu ermahnen: „Im Falle eines Brandes **gehen, nicht rennen**." Denn ebenso wie erhöhte Geschwindigkeit den Druck und die Masse einer Menschenmenge erhöht, verringert eine reduzierte Geschwindigkeit Druck und Masse. Doch wie jeder Theaterbesitzer ebenfalls weiß, läßt sich die effektive oder geschwindigkeitsbedingte Größe eines Publikums nicht reduzieren, indem man es vor den verheerenden *Folgen* des Rennens warnt, sondern einzig und allein, indem man ihm den *Anlaß* nimmt, überhaupt zu rennen – das heißt, indem man sicherstellt, daß es zu keinem Brand kommt. Die wahre Antwort auf das Problem, das durch die vergrößernde Wirkung beschleunigten Schrittes entsteht, besteht somit weniger in Notausgängen denn in einer feuersicheren Struktur.

Gleiches gilt für die Antwort auf unsere urbanen und nationalen Probleme – zumindest solange der übermäßige Druck auf den Raum, den wir mit dem Begriff der Überbevölkerung verbinden, noch hauptsächlich durch eine Zunahme der motorisierten Geschwindigkeit und weniger der Zahl der Menschen verursacht ist. Deshalb müssen unsere Planer für eine Situation sorgen, die den Menschen nicht die *Mittel* für eine Fortbewegung mit hoher Geschwindigkeit nimmt, sondern das *Motiv*, das sie dazu zwingt, sich überhaupt immer schneller zu bewegen. Oder anders ausgedrückt: Womit sie sich befassen müssen, ist nicht die *Fortbewegung*, sondern die *Motivation*; sind nicht Fahrzeug- und Straßentypen, die Sammy rasen lassen, sondern der Grund, warum Sammy rast – und dann müssen sie ihm diesen Grund nehmen.

Auf nationaler Ebene läßt sich das erreichen, indem man zu einem hohen Maß an Langstreckenverkehr und -geschwindigkeit zurückkehrt, was die regionale Eigenständigkeit fördert, *wie dies die Anhänger der Regionalisierung anstreben*; und auf kommunaler Ebene durch ein hohes Maß an städtischer Dezentralisierung oder, wie man es besser nennen sollte, an *multizentrischer Umgestaltung*. Das bedeutet: Statt die zentralen Behörden einer Stadtregion über die verschiedenen Bezirke zu verstreuen, gilt es, die Stadtteile wieder zu autonomen, eigenständigen Gemeinwesen zu machen, in denen der Bürger alles, was er fürs tägliche Leben braucht, an Örtlichkeiten findet, die zentral, aber klein und in der Nähe sind. Die Antwort ist deshalb keine Dezentralisierung im eigentlichen Sinne, sondern *eine Zentralisierung im kleinen Maßstab*.

Das ist die einzige Möglichkeit, wie sich der steigende Verkehrsdruck unserer motorisierten geschwindigkeitsbedingten Überbevölkerung reduzieren lässt, ohne daß man zu handfesteren Methoden Zuflucht nehmen muß: nicht indem man zentrale Einrichtungen regionalisiert (Autozulassung in Swansea, eine Londoner Kunstgalerie mit einer Dependance im Hafenviertel von Manchester), sondern indem man die Regionen zentralisiert und ihnen zu diesem Zweck ein hohes Maß an Autonomie gewährt; und in den Städten, nicht indem man die Slums suburbanisiert, sondern indem man die Vorstädte urbanisiert; nicht indem man die Viertel der Armen, für die Armen, durch die Armen in Viertel der Yuppies, für die Yuppies, durch die Yuppies verwandelt, die beide 15 Meilen von ihren von nur einer Schicht bewohnten Orten entfernt arbeiten, sondern indem man jede Gegend in eine kleine, alle Schichten umfassende

Stadt verwandelt, die über eine so spezifische Identität, eine so gesellige Eigenständigkeit und einen so großen ästhetischen Charme verfügt, daß kaum jemand sie verlassen muß oder will.

Vor dem Ende des 20. Jahrhunderts, wenn das schreckliche Gespenst der numerischen Überbevölkerung umgehen wird, ist das alles, was man im Augenblick braucht, um die nicht zu bewältigende geschwindigkeitsbedingte Überbevölkerung von Städten wie Cardiff, San Francisco oder Bristol von bis zu zwei Millionen auf eine zu bewältigende Größenordnung von 600.000 zurückzufahren. Und warum nicht, wie im Falle Londons, den überwiegenden Teil am Ende des Jahrhunderts in eine Föderation von Dörfern verwandeln, wie es der fröhliche Anarchist William Morris für die britische Hauptstadt vorgeschlagen hat. Oder die Stadt abschreiben.

El Mundo, 8. Juni 1973

Gemeinschaft von Gemeinden

Die Nutzlosigkeit schneller Nahverkehrssysteme. Von schlimm nach schlimmer. Effektive vs. numerische Bevölkerungsgröße. Der ignorierte Geschwindigkeitsfaktor. Lösung des Stauproblems durch urbane Kontraktion. Zurück ins Viertel.

Eines scheint gewiß: Schnelle Nahverkehrssysteme werden kein bißchen zur Lösung des Verkehrsproblems beitragen. Sie werden nur eine bereits schlimme Situation noch weiter verschlimmern. Das ist bisher in jeder Kommune so gewesen, die ein solches System eingeführt hat. Kennt irgendjemand eine Stadt, in der die Verkehrssituation heute besser ist als letztes Jahr? Oder als vor fünf Jahren? Oder als vor fünfzig Jahren? Eine solche Stadt gibt es nicht.

Der Grund dafür liegt darin, das mehr Verkehrsadern unweigerlich nicht zu weniger, sondern zu mehr Verkehrsaufkommen führen. Und da das Verkehrsaufkommen mit jedem arithmetischen Zuwachs bei den Verkehrswegen geometrisch ansteigt, folgt daraus (wie ich in den beiden vorangegangenen Kolumnen gezeigt habe): Statt das erstickende Problem des Staus zu lindern, verschärft jede Ausweitung des Verkehrssystems dieses Problem nicht nur, sondern tut das auch noch in überproportionalem Maße.

Ich habe das Prinzip, das dieses Verhältnis zum Ausdruck bringt, die *Geschwindigkeitstheorie der Bevölkerung* genannt. Analog zur Geldmengentheorie geht sie davon aus, daß die Masse der Bevölkerung nicht nur mit jedem zahlenmäßigen Zuwachs zunimmt; ungeachtet numerischer Veränderungen wächst sie auch mit jeder Erhöhung der Geschwindigkeit, mit der eine Bevölkerung zirkuliert. Wie ich schon oft betont habe, ist das wahre Problem unseres Zeitalters denn auch nicht eines der numerischen, sondern der geschwindigkeitsbedingten Überbevölkerung.

Planer, die es gewohnt sind, ihre Entwürfe dem *numerischen* Bevölkerungszuwachs in einer Kommune anzupassen, greifen deshalb in ihren Projektionen zwangsläufig zu kurz, weil sie die unendlich viel wichtigeren Zuwächse der *effektiven oder geschwindigkeitsbedingten Bevölkerung* außer acht lassen, also die numerische Bevölkerung multipliziert mit der Geschwindigkeit ihrer Bewegung. Denn ein Zuwachs der effektiven Bevölkerung bedeutet einen Anstieg des Verkehrsdrucks. Zunehmender Verkehrsdruck steigert den Bedarf an zusätzlichen Verkehrswegen. Neue Verkehrswege führen zu einem weiteren Zuwachs der effektiven oder geschwindigkeitsbedingten Größe der Bevölkerung – mit dem Ergebnis, daß, hat dieser spiralförmige Prozeß einmal begonnen, neue Einrichtungen nie mehr mit dem wachsenden Mehrbedarf mithalten können, den sie selbst erzeugen. Darin liegt der Grund, warum nach einer Ausweitung der Stadt ein schnelles Nahverkehrssystem genau die Verkehrsverhältnisse, die es zu lindern sucht, nicht verbessert, sondern verschärft.

Welche Implikationen die Geschwindigkeitstheorie der Bevölkerung hat, habe ich bereits in drei Büchern ausführlich dargelegt – *Die überentwickelten Nationen*, *Entwicklung ohne Hilfe* und *The City of Man* –, so daß man es mir hoffentlich verzeiht, wenn ich angesichts des begrenzten Raums dieser Kolumne auf mathematische Einzelheiten verzichte. Schließlich kommt es für praktische Zwecke nicht auf die Theorie an, sondern auf die Lösung, die sie anzubieten hat. Worin aber besteht die Lösung?

Gehen wir von der Annahme aus, daß die verstopften Städte unserer Zeit nicht unter zu wenig, sondern unter zu viel Verkehr leiden, so ist offensichtlich, daß die eigentliche Frage nicht ist, wie man die verfügbaren Schnellverkehrseinrichtungen *ausbaut*, sondern wie man zuallererst den Bedarf nach ihnen *reduziert*. Und die einzige Möglichkeit, das zu schaffen, ist die urbane Kontraktion mittels einer geographischen Neugestaltung unseres persönlichen und beruflichen Lebens. Man sorge dafür, daß jeder in der Nähe seines Arbeitsplatzes lebt und Arbeit dort sucht, wo er lebt, und bringe dann all die übrigen Einrichtungen, die er für ein vollständiges Leben benötigt – Geschäfte, Schulen, Kirchen, Theater, Erholungseinrichtungen – in seine unmittelbare Umgebung.

Mit anderen Worten: Man verwandle eine integrierte Metropole von einem zentralisierten Kraken, wie sie heute einer ist, in eine locker föderierte Gemeinschaft von Gemeinden, deren lokal verankerte Bewohner wenig Anlaß dazu sehen werden, jeden Tag mit hoher Geschwindigkeit innerstädtische Entfernungen zwischen 20 und 50 Meilen zurückzulegen in der Hetze eines Daseins, das so viel reicher und zivilisierter sein könnte, wenn die täglichen Strecken auf locker machbare zwei oder drei Meilen reduziert werden und die Menschen ihre gesellschaftlich notwendigen Aktivitäten auf ihre zu Fuß erreichbare unmittelbare Umgebung beschränken könnten.

Dahin zu kommen erfordert allerdings nicht nur, daß man die wirtschaftlichen, geselligen und beruflichen Aktivitäten der Bürger neu um eine Reihe konkurrierender städtischer Kerne herum anordnet, die mit einem hohen Maß an Eigenständigkeit versehen und über die gesamte Metropolregion verstreut sind. Die Gemeinschaft von Gemeinden muß auch eine Gemeinschaft wundervoller Gemeinden sein. Denn nur eine wunderbare Kommune wird, ähnlich wie eine wunderschöne Frau, verhindern, daß ihre Bewohner ständig anderswo herumsausen auf der Jagd nach Lebensunterhalt und Vergnügen.

El Mundo, 8. Juni 1973

Gemeinschaft wunderschöner Gemeinden

Wohnen, wo man arbeitet. Die Verlockung der Innenstadt. Rückkehr durch ministeriale Überzeugungsarbeit. Rang. Örtlichkeit und Chic. Wohnprestige. Ökonomie des Fußgängertums. Die Urbanisierung der Vorstädte. Die zentrale Rolle der Ästhetik. Architektonische vs. urbane Schönheit.

Schnelle Nahverkehrssysteme sind, wie ich in der vorangegangenen Kolumne gezeigt habe, keine Antwort auf die epischen Verkehrsprobleme der Metropolen unserer Zeit. Sie können die Probleme allenfalls noch verschlimmern. Die wirkliche Antwort liegt in einer urbanen Neuordnung, in der man ein solches System gar nicht mehr braucht, weil die enormen Entfernungen wegfallen, die die meisten von uns zurücklegen müssen, um unsere weit verstreuten Wohnungen wieder mit den Orten im Stadtzentrum zu verbinden, wo wir arbeiten, einkaufen, beten, entspannen oder uns vergnügen.

Im Falle meines Lieblingsbeispiels, nämlich San Juan, ließe sich das recht einfach bewerkstelligen, wenn man, wie das auch schon Ursula von Eckardt kurz vor ihrem viel zu frühen Tod forderte, die Menschen, die in der Altstadt arbeiten, dazu bringen könnte, auch dort zu wohnen. Dann bräuchte man kein schnelles Nahverkehrssystem, um das Beamtenheer jeden Morgen hereinzukarren und abends wieder hinauszubefördern. Obwohl Dr. von Eckardt diese Idee für ausgezeichnet hielt, fügte sie mit Bedauern hinzu, daß das nicht ausreiche, damit sie auch offizielle Politik wird.

Tatsächlich wäre es recht einfach, die Idee in die Praxis umzusetzen. Die einzige Frage ist: Wie könnte man unsere modernen Vorstadtbewohner dazu bringen, wieder als dauerhafte Bewohner ins Stadtzentrum zurückzukehren und nicht nur als kilometerfressende, die Straßen verstopfende Pendler?

Obwohl viele dieser armen Seelen Staatsangestellte sind, wäre es für die Regierung unmöglich, sie per Dekret zurückzubeordern. Es wäre jedoch möglich, sie qua gutem Beispiel zurückzulocken, indem man ihnen vor Augen führt, daß die Altstadt von San Juan eine bessere Wohnadresse ist als selbst die schickste der modernen Vorstädte. Dazu müßte man lediglich zu Anfang wichtige Kabinettsmitglieder überreden, das zu tun, was hochrangige Menschen zu allen Zeiten getan haben: so wie der glückliche Gouverneur an ihrem Arbeitsplatz zu wohnen – der Justizminister im Justizministerium; der Außenminister im Außenministerium; der Finanzminister im alten Finanzministerium.

Diese Gebäude, die jetzt tagsüber überfüllt und nachts kaum genutzt sind, gehören heute schon zu den schönsten im Land. Es gibt deshalb keinen Grund, warum ein Kabinettsmitglied, das dazu gedrängt wird, dort zu wohnen, dies als Einschränkung seiner Entscheidungsfreiheit oder als Degradierung empfinden sollte. Viel eher würde er es als Statussymbol betrachten, das es ihm ermöglicht, endlich so zu wohnen, wie es nicht nur der Macht seines Amtes, sondern auch der Würde der Menschen, denen er dient, entspricht.

Wohnen erst einmal die Kabinettsmitglieder wieder in der Stadt, dürfte es nicht allzu schwierig sein, auch die leitenden Beamten der verschiedenen Ministerien anzulocken, indem man ihnen als Teil ihrer Entlohnung weniger eine Wohnung als vielmehr eine ihrem Rang angemessene Wohn*lage* anbietet – das heißt, nicht in ihren Bürogebäuden, aber in unmittelbarer Nähe. Gleiches läßt sich mit den meisten rangniedrigeren Beamten anstellen, indem man in der übrigen Altstadt angemessene Unterkünfte für sie bereitstellt. Und dieser Prozeß wäre damit natürlich noch nicht beendet. Denn eine elegante Hauptstadt, in der ein Großteil der Staatsdiener wohnt, würde schon bald viele andere „stadtwichtige" Menschen – Bankiers, Unternehmensführer, Restaurantbesitzer, Schauspieler, Lehrer, Kellner – dazu animieren, deren Beispiel zu folgen, sobald die Verwaltungselite deutlich gemacht hat, daß eine Wohnung in der Nähe des Arbeitsplatzes keine Degradierung, sondern Zeichen eines schicken Lebensstils ist. Zudem hätte eine Rückkehr ins Zentrum natürlich auch die enormen energie- und kostensparenden Vorteile des Fußgängertums, die für sich genommen einem dreißigprozentigen Einkommensanstieg entsprechen dürften, ohne daß der Staat auch nur einen Cent für höhere Löhne zahlen müßte.

Doch die Pendler wieder im alten San Juan anzusiedeln ist nur die eine Hälfte der Sache. Um den Druck auf die Straßen zu verringern, muß dieser Prozeß auch in den anderen Gegenden der Metropolregion erfolgen. Dort aber muß das Problem vom anderen

Ende her angegangen werden. Was man in der Altstadt von San Juan braucht, um aus Pendlern Bewohner zu machen, sind Wohnungen. Was man in den anderen Stadtbezirken braucht – Santurce, Ocean Park, Puerto Nuevo, Isla Verde, Country Club, Villa Fontana –, ist die Kultiviertheit des Stadtlebens. Das bedeutet, daß man dichte Stadtkerne aufbaut, die aus Theatern, Cafés, Plätzen, Kirchen, Gasthäusern, Rathäusern inmitten der bereits in Hülle und Fülle vorhandenen Wohngebiete bestehen, und diese insofern funktional mit den Arbeitsplätzen verknüpft, als diese zu Fuß erreichbar sein sollen und man kein Auto braucht. Andernfalls werden die dortigen Bewohner weiter ihre Pendlerexistenz führen, um ihr Dasein mit der Vielfalt zu bereichern, die wir uns alle wünschen.

Und hier wird, wie ich in der vorangegangenen Kolumne gezeigt habe, die administrative Aufgabe einer Neugestaltung der Stadt zu einem ästhetischen Problem. Denn es reicht eben nicht, die städtischen Kernstrukturen funktional im engen Fußgängermaßstab zu gestalten; die Struktur muß auch die Sinne ansprechen.

In der Altstadt von San Juan ist das kein Problem, denn sie wurde mit dem unfehlbaren Geschmack früherer Jahrhunderte erbaut und mit dem unfehlbaren Geschmack von Ricardo Alegria, dessen Leistung beispiellos ist, restauriert. In allen anderen Bezirken der Metropolregion liegt darin jedoch das Hauptproblem. Vielerorts haben wir eine Fülle schöner Wohngebäude und Fabrikstrukturen von herausragender architektonischer Schönheit. Ihre urbane Anordnung ist jedoch alles andere als schön, und es gibt keinen nahegelegenen Allzweckkern, der die Bürger davon abhalten würde, auf der Suche nach aufregenden Erlebnissen, die umgekehrt proportional zur Entfernung sind, die man dafür zurücklegen muß, in ihre Autos zu springen.

Das wäre also die zivilisierte Alternative zur zunehmenden städtischen Geschwindigkeit, wie sie das Nahverkehrssystem bietet: nicht mehr, sondern weniger Verkehrswege. Doch weniger Verkehrswege sind nur dann angemessen, wenn sich die Größe der Bevölkerung verringern läßt. Und das läßt sich gemäß der Geschwindigkeitstheorie der Bevölkerung nicht nur durch eine zahlenmäßige Dezimierung erreichen, sondern viel humaner auch durch eine Verringerung ihrer Geschwindigkeit. Denn eine Bevölkerung, die sich langsamer bewegt, hat die gleiche Wirkung wie eine numerisch kleinere Bevölkerung, wie ja auch umgekehrt eine schnellere Bevölkerung numerisch größer ist.

Es sei jedoch noch einmal betont: Eine Verringerung der Geschwindigkeit und damit der effektiven (im Gegensatz zur numerischen) Größe einer Stadt erfordert nicht nur die funktionale und administrative Umgestaltung eines weit ausgreifenden, aber zentralisierten Stadtgebiets zu einem föderierten System kleiner Städte; eine solche Neustrukturierung wird das angestrebte Ziel nur dann erreichen, wenn sie von einem Geist des ästhetischen Bewußtseins beseelt ist. Oder anders ausgedrückt: Wenn Ursula von Eckardts lobenswerter Traum Wirklichkeit werden soll, darf San Juan – wie jede zu groß gewordene Stadt auf dieser Welt – nicht nur einfach zu einer Gemeinschaft von Gemeinden werden. Es muß vielmehr zu einer Gemeinschaft wunderschöner Gemeinden werden.

El Mundo, 10. Juni 1973

TEIL II
Im Verkehr ersticken

Eine Metropole für Fußgänger

Der Glanz der Ausstellung. Die Bedeutung individueller Entwürfe. Die Armseligkeit einer kollektiven Vision. Den Verkehr unter den Teppich kehren. Verschlimmernde Wirkung des Zentrumskonzepts. Der Bedarf an eigenständigen, konkurrierenden Zentren. Rückkehr zum Muster der Vergangenheit. Urbane Konföderation.

Jeder wird die Ausstellung in der Chase Manhattan Bank begrüßen, in der das Modell und die Entwürfe von sechs unserer herausragendsten Architekten und Stadtplaner für die künftige Gestalt von Hato Rey präsentiert werden – dem im Entstehen begriffenen Zentrum der Metropolregion San Juan, Puerto Ricos viel beachtetem internationalen Paradebeispiel für eine explodierende Hauptstadt.

Das Ergebnis ist ein solcher Augenschmaus, daß, aus der eigenen Perspektive betrachtet, dem Kritiker kaum etwas bleibt, an dem er sich festbeißen könnte. Allein als Ausstellung ist sie fast perfekt. Nicht nur sind die Modelle und Illustrationen wunderbar gestaltet und umfassend erläutert, sogar die Sockel, auf denen die verschiedenen Plätze errichtet sind, sind so elegant, daß sie allein einer Ausstellung kubistischer Kunst zur Ehre gereichen würden. Und fast perfekt ist auch die Art und Weise, wie der geplante Typus des künftigen Stadtzentrums präsentiert wird – er fügt sich zu einem organischen Ganzen: Büros, Banken, Wohnhäuser, politische, kulturelle und freizeitspezifische Strukturen; und von den weit ausgreifenden, entspannten Fußgängerplattformen ist aller Autoverkehr in Verkehrsadern verbannt, die unsichtbar darunter verlaufen.

Es gibt jedoch durchaus Anlaß für ein paar grundlegende kritische Anmerkungen. Zum ersten ist der Plan ein kollektives Produkt. Doch Planung ist, anders als das Ingenieur- oder Maurerwesen, keine Technik, sondern eine Kunst. Und wie jede Kunstform leidet sie, wenn sie zu einem Gemeinschaftsunternehmen wird, besonders dann, wenn, wie im vorliegenden Fall, die Mitwirkenden allesamt zur Spitzenklasse gehören und deshalb vermutlich im Wettbewerb und nicht in Kooperation jeweils die beste Arbeit leisten. Man fragt sich deshalb, ob es nicht besser gewesen wäre, wenn jeder der sechs für sich genommen brillanten Architekten und Planer seine eigene Vision der künftigen Stadt vorgelegt hätte statt zu einem Gemeinschaftswerk beizutragen, das nicht Eskridge, Molther, Marcel, Toro, Reid und Padilla zeigt, sondern weder das Gepräge von Eskridge noch von Molther, Marvel, Toro, Reid oder Padilla aufweist. Angesichts dessen müssen deshalb dringend eine Reihe konkurrierender Pläne vorgelegt werden, damit der Bürger die Möglichkeit hat, sich zwischen verschiedenen Alternativen zu entscheiden, wobei am Ende dann durchaus die gegenwärtige Ausstellung das Rennen machen kann.

Der viel wichtigere Kritikpunkt betrifft jedoch weniger die kollektive Form des Plans als vielmehr die ihm zugrundeliegende Vorstellung von Stadt. Nach außen hin soll das Hato Rey der Zukunft den Fußgängern gehören. Aber wird das zunehmende Problem der Verstopfung durch den Verkehr wirklich gelöst? Oder kehrt man dieses Problem nicht einfach unter den Teppich der hübsch gestalteten Fußgängerplattformen?

Hato Rey wird in jeder Hinsicht keine eigenständige Kleinstadt sein, sondern das Zentrum einer sehr viel größeren Metropolregion. Das aber bedeutet, daß der Verkehr eines viel größeren Gebiets weiterhin in einem viel kleineren konvergiert, mit der Folge, daß das Zentrum allein aufgrund der räumlichen Dynamik im Verkehr ersticken wird, so wie heute überirdisch dann eben unter der Erde.

Die einzige Möglichkeit, ein Gemeinwesen mit wirklich fußgängerspezifischen Proportionen zu schaffen, besteht darin, den Großteil der Bewegungen zu Berufs-, Bildungs-, Wirtschafts-, Freizeit- und Privatzwecken auf den wirklich fußgängerspezifischen Rahmen einer Reihe lebendiger kleiner, *konkurrierender* Zentren zu beschränken, die jeweils über ein eigenes Magnetfeld verfügen. Dazu bedarf es nicht der Übernahme, sondern der Abschaffung der zentralistischen Vorstellung vom metropolitanen Zentrum, wie sie heute besteht.

Mit anderen Worten: Soll Hato Rey den Fußgängern gehören, muß man es sich grundlegend anders vorstellen, nämlich als weitgehend eigenständige Stadt mit vielleicht 50.000 Einwohnern, nicht als Verkehr erzeugendes Zentrum einer Megacity, dem allein schon deshalb die völlige Strangulierung droht. Denn die Situation wird umso schlimmer werden, je attraktiver das entstehende Zentrum ist, was die paradoxe Folge hat, daß gerade die Schönheit des in der Ausstellung präsentierten Plans das Verkehrsschicksal des künftigen San Juan besiegelt.

Die einzige Lösung für das Problem des geschwürartigen Wucherns in unserer massebestimmten Zeit scheint deshalb, wie in so vielen anderen Bereichen auch, nicht in einem Voranschreiten zu bestehen, sondern in einer Rückkehr zu den Mustern der Vergangenheit. Anders ausgedrückt: Man muß dem altehrwürdigen Beispiel vergangener Zentren des guten urbanen Lebens wie London, Paris, Rom oder Wien folgen. Das heißt, wir müssen unsere größeren städtischen Ballungsräume wieder in Föderationen hochgradig autonomer Kleinstädte umwandeln, die in der Lage sind, die nach außen gerichteten Bewegungen ihrer Bewohner überflüssig zu machen, und zwar durch feine Unterschiede in ihrem Charme, den jede von ihnen für sich ausstrahlt, während gleichzeitig die symphonische Einheit des Ganzen gewahrt bleibt.

San Juan Star, 24. Mai 1967

Planungen für den Sturm

Anpassung an das Massenzeitalter. Städte mit 60 Millionen Einwohnern auf dem Zeichentisch des MIT. Präventive vs. adaptive Planung. Die Gebärfreude am Leben in der Masse. Der Geruch Venedigs. Die Faszination Londons. Der Mensch, nicht die Menschheit ist das Maß aller Dinge.

Wenn ein normaler Mensch erfährt, daß ein Sturm im Anmarsch ist, wird er Vorbereitungen treffen, um ihn aus seinem Haus fernzuhalten. Er wird Fenster und Fensterläden schließen, die Türen verrammeln, das Dach ausbessern und sich dann in seinem Haus verkriechen, das zur Burg geworden ist. Wenn ein Planer von einem Sturm erfährt, wird er heutzutage wahrscheinlich genau gegenteilig reagieren. Er wird Türen und Fenster entfernen, Schindel vom Dach nehmen und Vorkehrungen treffen, die seiner Ansicht nach notwendig sind, damit der Sturm ungehindert über und durch sein Haus fegen kann. In beiden Fällen steht dahinter die Vorstellung, die drohende Zerstörung abzuwenden. Doch in dem einem Fall erreicht man das, indem man dem Hausbesitzer Rechnung trägt, im anderen Fall, indem man dem Sturm Rechnung trägt.

Der Sturm, dessen Bedürfnis nach ungehindertem Durchzug moderne Planer all ihre Entwürfe anzupassen scheinen, ist der reißende Strom der Menschheit, der die letzen Überreste des Individuums zu vernichten droht. Daß heute allerorten vom ökologischen Gleichgewicht die Rede ist, lenkt die Aufmerksamkeit auf diese Tatsache, doch trotz großartiger Manifeste wie dem *Blueprint for Survival* von Edward Goldsmith (dt. 1972 unter dem Titel *Planspiel zum Überleben*) scheint die Zeit abgelaufen zu sein. Man baut Autobahn auf Autobahn, was immer größere Automassen anzieht und die Verkehrsverhältnisse, die man damit eigentlich verbessern wollte, noch verschlimmert. Flughäfen werden vergrößert in der Annahme, daß mehr Menschen reisen wollen, während das Problem genau umgekehrt darin besteht, daß mehr Menschen reisen wollen, weil die Luftfahrtinfrastruktur ausgebaut wird. Gibbon sagte, die Prophezeiung führe häufig zu ihrer eigenen Erfüllung; in unserem Fall könnte man davon sprechen, daß die *Antizipation* des Bedarfs fast unweigerlich zu tatsächlichem Bedarf führt, der dann, ist er erst einmal vorhanden, im allgemeinen weit über all das hinausgeht, was antizipiert wurde oder angeboten werden kann.

Sobald deshalb die Statistiker vorhersagten, auf dem Gebiet einer kleineren amerikanischen Stadt wie San Juan, Puerto Rico, würden am Ende des Jahrhunderts 1,5 Millionen Menschen leben, taten die Planer sogleich alles, um die Stadt diesem Ansturm anzupassen. Und sobald dies geschehen war, beschleunigte sich der Ansturm plötzlich. Ähnlich war es im Falle Kalkuttas: Als die Propheten eine Bevölkerung von 60 Millionen für die Stadt vorhersagten, entwarf das Massachusetts Institute of Technology (MIT) sogleich Modelle urbaner Konzentration, die dieser Entwicklung Rechnung tragen sollten. Doch sobald ein Plan einmal auf den Zeichentischen im MIT liegt, kann keine Macht auf Erden verhindern, daß er am Ende dann auch realisiert wird.

Eigentlich aber sollten Planer auf derartige Prognosen und Projektionen damit reagieren, daß sie all ihre Kräfte mobilisieren, um

Rio Mar en Lunguillo – ein Beispiel für Planung zum Schutz des Einzelnen

zu *verhindern*, daß sie Wirklichkeit werden. Sie sollten in dieser Hinsicht dem Beispiel der Politiker folgen, die bei düsteren Wahlprognosen nicht panikartig die politikwissenschaftlichen Fakultäten in Oxford und Harvard bitten, sich mit den Englischlehrstühlen in Cambridge und Yale zusammenzutun und eine lautstarke Kapitulationserklärung zu entwerfen, um damit die Siegeserwartungen ihrer politischen Gegner zu erfüllen. Sie nutzen die Prognosen vielmehr, um zu verhindern, daß sie eintreffen.

In dieser Spätphase kommunaler Vernichtung bedarf es deshalb nicht anpassender oder antizipierender, sondern präventiver Planung. Doch das ist, wie alle gesellschaftlichen Dinge, auch eine Frage der Philosophie. Vielleicht ist die Entwicklung in Richtung urbaner Konzentration, stetig zunehmender Bevölkerung, Kollektivierung, Sozialisierung, Integration, Automation, Vereinheitlichung genau das, was die Natur für die Menschheit vorgesehen hat. Was ist schon an den Bienen schlecht? Vielleicht verfügten sie vor dem Menschen über Intelligenz, bis ihre Technik es ihnen ermöglichte, die angesammelte Masse zu verringern, indem sie ihre individuellen Körper auf so ökonomische Dimensionen reduzierten, daß sie nur noch zwei Dinge brauchten: Honig als Nahrung und Wachs für die Behausung. Und ich bin sicher, sie haben sich schon lange mit der an Kalkutta erinnernden Beengtheit ihrer gegenwärtigen miniaturisierten Situation abgefunden und genießen sie sehr. Warum sollte also nicht auch die Menschheit Freude daran haben?

Es besteht denn auch keinerlei Zweifel, daß die Menschheit es natürlich genießen würde, wenn sie sich an ihre neue komprimierte Bienenstocksituation akklimatisiert hat, so wie die Venezianer den Gestank ihrer verschmutzten Lagunen lieben, der für sie mehr als alles andere die Wasserromantik und den Wesenskern dessen, was Venedig ausmacht, widerspiegelt. Aber das ist genau die Gefahr: nicht, daß wir das Leben in den Monsterballungsräumen der Zukunft verabscheuen, sondern daß wir liebend gerne dort leben, sobald es sie gibt. Ich selbst bin immer wieder überrascht, welch fürchterliche Faszination London auf mich ausübt. Sollte man also die Zeit und den Computer einfach weitermarschieren lassen?

Doch hier stellt sich die eigentliche Frage: Ist *die Menschheit* das Maß aller Dinge? Oder ist *der Mensch* das Maß? Bisher war es der

Mensch, an dem alles ausgerichtet war: seine Behausungen – von der Tonne des Diogenes bis zum Prunk von Versailles –; seine Werkzeuge; und besonders seine Städte, die nach *seinen* Vorgaben und nicht nach denen der *Gesellschaft* gebaut wurden. Vielleicht ist der Mensch ein Auslaufmodell. Doch wenn er in irgendeiner anderen Verfassung denn als Ameise oder Biene überleben soll, muß die gegenwärtige Entwicklung in Sachen Planung völlig umgedreht werden: Statt dem Sturm nachzugeben gilt es wieder das kleine Individuum auf seinem Weg zu beschützen.

El Mundo, 8. November 1972

Stewardessen oben ohne

Verkehrsstau durch Gebärfreude. Explodierende Städte. Der Fußgängerhafen des Luxushotels. Autos, die durch die Kleinheit des Ganzen nutzlos werden. Zwischenzeitliche Maßnahmen: Parken entsprechend der Autogröße. Die Elite wieder ins Zentrum locken. Steigerung der Freuden des Bus- statt des Autofahrens mit Hilfe von Zeitungen, Kaffee, barbusigen Stewardessen.

Der Juli ist die Zeit im Jahr, in der Verkehrsplaner aktiv werden sollten, um das plötzlich anwachsende Verkehrsaufkommen abzuwenden, das alljährlich mit dem Ende der Sommerferien zu erleben ist. *Warum* das mit solcher Regelmäßigkeit der Fall sein sollte, ist umstritten; die Geburtenexplosion wird nur vereinzelt als Ursache genannt. Es *ist* jedenfalls jedes Jahr so gewesen, seit ich 1955 nach Puerto Rico kam, als man in den Stoßzeiten mit dem Auto noch schneller unterwegs war als zu Fuß.

Tatsächlich wird vermutlich keine der langfristigen Maßnahmen, die man in Erwägung zieht, zu einer Verbesserung führen, solange man am gegenwärtigen Stadtentwicklungskonzept festhält, das die zunehmende Benutzung des Autos verlangt, damit man die geometrisch wachsenden Entfernungen bewältigen kann, die sich aus dem nach außen gerichteten, explosionsartigen Wachstum unserer Städte ergeben.

Nur wenn die Städte ähnlich wie die eigenständigen Anlagen moderner Luxushotels wieder zum Hort des Fußgängerdaseins werden, in dem man sich nicht den Autos anpaßt, sondern diese weitgehend überflüssig macht, lassen sich die langfristigen Probleme nicht nur des Verkehrsstaus, sondern auch der Luftverschmutzung lösen. Doch die Situation muß sich offenbar erst noch deutlich verschlimmern, ehe die Planer von ihrer Gewohnheit lassen, den Trends hinterherzulaufen statt sie zu setzen.

Es gibt jedoch ein paar kurzfristige Maßnahmen, die zumindest vorübergehende Erleichterung bringen könnten, ohne daß man dafür erst kostspielige Studien in Auftrag geben muß. Eine davon wäre, getrennte Parkbereiche für große und kleine Autos auszuweisen. Das gegenwärtige Parksystem erlaubt es, daß einzeln markierte Parkplätze unterschiedslos von beiden Autotypen genutzt werden, was bedeutet, daß jeder Parkplatz an den Dimensionen der größeren Fahrzeuge ausgerichtet werden muß, die bis zu 30 Prozent mehr Platz brauchen als kleinere Autos. Der geringere Platzbedarf kleinerer Autos wird somit den gesamten verfügbaren Parkraum um durchschnittlich mindestens 20 Prozent vergrößern, sobald Kleinwagen nur für sie reservierte Bereiche zugewiesen bekommen. Wenn sie zudem bevorzugte Standorte in der Nähe der Hauptzufahrtsstraßen bekommen, wird sich aus der Bevorzugung von Kleinwagenbesitzern aller Wahrscheinlichkeit nach der willkommene Sekundäreffekt ergeben, daß sich die Zahl der klobigen, spritfressenden Autos allmählich verringert. Damit vergrößert sich dann der verfügbare Parkraum noch weiter, ohne daß man auch nur einen Quadratmeter knappen städtischen Bodens dafür opfern müßte.

Eine weitere Methode, um das Verkehrsproblem zu lindern, wäre, hohe Regierungsbeamte dazu zu bringen, dem Beispiel ihrer Vorgesetzten zu folgen und, wie ich das in einer meiner früheren Kolumnen vorgeschlagen habe, an ihrem Arbeitsplatz auch ihr Wohndomizil aufzuschlagen: der Außenminister im Außenministerium, der Finanzminister im Finanzministerium, der Justizminister im Justizministerium. Im Falle San Juans sind diese Gebäude von solch florentinischer Anmut, Geschichte und Lage, daß nur ein Barbar statt der zivilisierten Freude eines pendlerlosen Lebens in der von Balkonen bestimmten Süße der Altstadt lieber weiter ein autogeplagtes Dasein in der halbländlichen Idiotie der Vorstädte führen wollte, wie Marx das genannt hätte. Und sobald es für Kabinettsmitglieder schick ist, in der Nähe ihrer Büros zu wohnen, würde ein Statusmultiplikator dafür sorgen, daß schon bald ein ganzer Schwung niederer Beamter folgt, was das Problem verstopfter Straßen zusätzlich signifikant verringern würde.

Die effektivste kurzfristige Maßnahme aber wäre, die Mehrzahl der Autofahrer, die weiterhin in den Vororten wohnen und zur Arbeit in die Stadt pendeln, ganz von den Straßen zu bekommen und zu diesem Zweck die Freude am Busfahren zu vergrößern, bis das geplante alternative U-Bahn-System fertig ist. Wie ich vor gut zwei Jahren im *San Juan Star* vorgeschlagen habe, läßt sich das erreichen, indem man einen abgestuften Busservice einrichtet: Busse wie die heutigen für den autolosen Normalpendler; Erster-Klasse-Busse für die Besitzer von Mittelklassewagen und Luxusservice für den Rest. Die Busse der beiden letztgenannten Kategorien würden höhere Fahrpreise verlangen. Doch im Gegenzug würden sie alle Annehmlichkeiten bieten wie bequeme Sitze, Kaffee, Zeitungen, Börsentipps und Horoskope, die von Stewardessen in kurzen Röcken vorgelesen werden – eine Kombination, die den Druck auf die Straßen mit Sicherheit deutlich verringern würde.

San Juan Star, 30. Mai 1967

P.S. Tatsächlich ist seit damals Washington, D.C., San Juan bei der Verwirklichung des Ideals zuvorgekommen, wie sich einem Bericht in *Newsweek* (11. Februar 1974) entnehmen läßt. Dort heißt es: „Die Regierung berichtet von einem erfolgreichen Experiment, bei dem die Verkehrsstaus während der Hauptstoßzeiten verringert werden sollten, indem man die Menschen aus ihren Autos lockte und mit einem ›Premium‹-Busservice verwöhnte… Das vierzehnmonatige Projekt verlockte sogar Pendler mit kostenlosen Parkplätzen dazu, ihr Auto zu Hause stehen zu lassen und den Bus zu nehmen." Leider erwähnt der Bericht nicht, wie der „Premiumservice" genau aussah, der als so erfolgreiches Lockmittel fungierte. Waren es vielleicht Stewardessen oben ohne, die einem auch noch aus der Hand lesen?

Rückentwicklung der Verkehrsdichte

Grenzen des Wachstums. Rettung durch Haiabwehr. Entworfen von der Anti-Destination-League. Die zerstörerische Kraft der Anziehung. Der Bedarf an mehr Hauptstädten. Verkehrsverringerung durch politische Teilung. Zentralisierung kleingeschrieben.

Ähnlich wie die eine Viertelmillion Dollar teure *Modellstadtuntersuchung* leidet auch die *Verkehrsstudie*, für die Washington der Stadtregierung des verkehrsgeplagten San Juan sogar eine volle Million Dollar zur Verfügung gestellt hat, unter vielen der grundsätzlichen Mängel, die auch die meisten anderen gegenwärtigen Bemühungen zur Stadterneuerung in der übrigen Welt aufweisen. Dazu gehört ihre Anpassung an die Aussicht auf eine Stadt, deren Einwohnerzahl sich bis 1999 von jetzt 700.000 auf dann 1,5 Millionen mehr als verdoppeln wird.

Wie ich in einer früheren Kolumne bemerkt habe, gehörte es angesichts dieser Bedrohung ja offensichtlich zu den ersten Aufgaben der Stadtplaner, zu verhindern, daß diese Prognose Wirklichkeit wird, statt ihre Realisierung vorzubereiten. Etwas anderes zu tun wäre gerade so, als würde der Planungsausschuß, wenn er hört, daß Puerto Rico 1999 im Meer versinkt, dafür sorgen, daß jeder Bewohner die nötige Ausrüstung für die Haiabwehr bekommt. Wie alle anderen Hauptstädte dieser Welt ist San Juan schon schlimm genug, so wie es ist. Zuzulassen, daß sich seine Größe verdoppelt, würde nichts anderes bedeuten, als daß sich seine Verkehrprobleme vervierfachen, was wiederum zur Folge hat, daß man sich Lösungen, selbst wenn sie möglich wären, nicht mehr leisten kann.

Die Frage lautet deshalb nicht, wie man neue Schnellstraßen oder ein U-Bahn-System mit zwei Linien, die sich an einem einzigen Punkt schneiden, baut – eine Idee, die offenbar Stephen Potters „Anti-Destination-League" ausgeheckt hat –, sondern wie man den weiteren Zustrom in die Metropolregion verhindert.

Das läßt sich einzig und allein dadurch erreichen, daß man in einem anderen Teil des Landes eine Stadt entwickelt, die an Glanz, Entwicklungsstand, Unterhaltung, Meinungsvielfalt und öffentlichen

Dienstleistungen genau das aufweist, was bislang allein San Juan vorbehalten war.

Da es San Juans Eigenschaft als „Hauptstadt" ist, die ähnlich wie in Paris, London oder Mexiko-Stadt eine so zerstörerische Anziehungskraft ausübt, folgt daraus, daß Puerto Rico eine zweite Hauptstadt bekommen sollte. Da nur ein Staat eine Hauptstadt haben kann, heißt das, daß Puerto Rico einen zweiten Staat haben sollte, einen Staat, der als Commonwealth unabhängig mit den USA assoziiert ist; ein 51. oder 52. Bundesstaat, der sowohl von den USA als auch von Puerto Rico unabhängig ist, was den Unabhängigkeitsbefürwortern gefallen dürfte, denn je mehr Unabhängigkeit, desto besser; oder als Teil einer puertoricanischen Föderation von 2, 5 oder bis zu 20 gleichberechtigten Staaten, wie dies Gwynfor Evans und J.P. Mackintosh für Großbritannien vorgeschlagen haben. Nur ein konkurrierender Staat braucht eine Hauptstadt, und nur eine neue Hauptstadt kann den wachsenden Druck vom Magneten der bestehenden nehmen. Das hat nichts mit verträumter Theorie zu tun, sondern mit Verwaltungsarithmetik. Denn Verkehrsprobleme sind wie die meisten anderen Kompliziertheiten des Lebens in zu groß gewordenen Städten und Nationen letztlich nicht technischer, sondern politischer Natur; und um sie zu lösen, braucht man keine millionenteuren Verkehrsexperten, sondern einen Funken philosophischer Erkenntnis, der vielleicht, wie im Falle Newtons, kommt, während man unter einem Baum liegt.

Ein weiterer Mangel, den unsere Studie mit ähnlichen Untersuchungen zur Stadterneuerung gemeinsam hat, betrifft die Vorstellung von einer „polyzentrischen" Stadt, also einer Reihe spezialisierter, wenn auch wechselseitig sich ergänzender Regionen auf dem Gebiet der puertoricanischen Metropole. Einige Ministerien sollen in Bayamon angesiedelt sein, einige in Santurce, einige in Rio Piedras, einige in San Juan. Zudem sollen die Banken in Hato Rey konzentriert sein, der Handel in Santurce, die Bildung in Rio Piedras und die Unterhaltung in Condado.

Doch gerade weil diese Einrichtungen sich gegenseitig ergänzen, muß der Durchschnittsbürger die meisten von ihnen jeden Tag aufsuchen, was zur Folge hat, daß der durch die spezialisierte Vielköpfigkeit ausgelöste Kreuz-und-quer-Verkehr viel größer ist als in einer Stadt mit einem einzigen Zentrum. Man braucht deshalb nicht nur viele Köpfe, sondern auch ebenso viele Körper, die diese ernähren. Das aber ist genau das Gegenteil der Vorstellung von einem vielköpfigen Monstrum auf dem einen Körper einer Metropole. Mit anderen Worten: Abgesehen von den relativ wenigen und eher selten besuchten zentralen Behörden, die für alle Regionen zuständig sind und folglich in einem einzigen Gebiet wie der historischen Altstadt von San Juan konzentriert und nicht auf eine Vielzahl verschiedener Orte verstreut sein sollten, müssen all die Einrichtungen, die der Bürger tagtäglich braucht – Supermarkt, Kirche, Theater, Schule, Nachtclub, Schwimmbad –, in fast völliger Eigenständigkeit in unmittelbarer Umgebung jedes Einzelnen angesiedelt und zu Fuß erreichbar sein. Nur dann läßt sich der Verkehrdruck, der aus dem integrierten, spezialisierten und daher interdependenten Langstreckenpendeln resultiert, signifikant verringern.

Berichten zufolge scheint unter den Stadterneuerern tatsächlich eine wachsende Bereitschaft zu bestehen, nicht nur eine vielköpfige Spezialisierung in Betracht zu ziehen, sondern auch ein gewisses, zögernd zugestandenes Maß an lokaler Eigenständigkeit. Das Problem dabei ist, daß sich beides nur schlecht vermischen läßt. Eigenständigkeit muß „on the rocks" serviert werden – oder zumindest fast. Mischt man sie in einem wie auch immer gearteten größeren Maß mit dem konzentrierten Rauschmittel der Spezialisierung, kann sie ebensowenig einen klaren Kopf garantieren wie Soda gemischt mit Rum.

San Juan Star, 13. Juni 1967

Das zweite Eisenbahnzeitalter

Letzter Zug. Zähfließender Verkehr auf den Schnellstraßen. Zurück zur Schiene. Die Freuden der Reisebegleitung. Japan als Vorreiter. Mythos von der Unrentabilität der Eisenbahn. Fremd für Land und Zeit. Die Profitabilität von Milchbars und Espressocafés. Die Romantik der Eisenbahn. Lage und Glanz der Bahnhöfe. Die Schönheit der Waggons. Das Erfolgsgeheimnis.

Als ich 1955 nach Puerto Rico kam, wurde die letzte verbliebene Eisenbahnstrecke der Insel gerade stillgelegt. Ich erinnere mich noch, wie ich mit meinen drei Kollegen Severo Colberg, Alfred Thorne und Anatol Murad faul in einem Café an einer Landspitze hoch über dem wunderbaren Küstenstreifen in der Nähe von Aguadilla saß, als aus der finsteren Tiefe eines Tunnels plötzlich ein Zug auftauchte, der traurig pfeifend in sanfter Resignation auf einer seiner letzten Reisen in die Vergessenheit unterwegs war.

Und ich erinnere mich noch an die Diskussion, die wir über die paradoxe Situation führten, daß nämlich die Eisenbahn als alternatives Beförderungsmittel genau zu dem Zeitpunkt aus dem Verkehr gezogen wurde, da die Aufnahmekapazität der Schnellstraßen so gut wie erschöpft war und alle verkehrsökologischen Zeichen darauf hindeuteten, daß die Welt an der Schwelle zum Zweiten Eisenbahnzeitalter stand.

Angesichts dessen ist es schwer zu verstehen, warum das Thema Eisenbahn von den Planern immer so außerordentlich ängstlich behandelt wird. Der einzige, der sich in den letzten Jahren unzweideutig für die Wiederherstellung unseres Eisenbahnsystems aussprach, war denn auch ausgerechnet Tony Beacon, der bekannte und gefürchtete Klatschkolumnist.

Alle anderen nähern sich dem Thema, als würde es vor Obszönität geradezu strotzen. Man spricht mit Inbrunst von einem „integrierten Schnellverkehrssystem auf der gesamten Insel", schwadroniert von Einschienenbahnen, Kanälen und U-Bahnen für San Juan und landet am Ende immer wieder bei der wunderbaren Lösung für alle Probleme: dem „integrierten Schnellverkehrssystem". Das Wort Eisenbahn aber ist nirgendwo zu hören.

Gibt es außer Tony Beacon niemanden, der es wagt, in Begeisterung auszubrechen bei dem Gedanken an diese eleganten Waggons, die auf glänzenden Schienen sanft zwischen Dörfern und Städten dahingleiten, völlig unbehindert von den zähen Staus auf den Schnellstraßen? Oder bei der Aussicht, daß der müde Passagier nicht nur das beruhigende Panorama der vorbeifliegenden Landschaft geboten bekommt, sondern auch die anregende Gesellschaft von Mitreisenden (in der fast vergessenen ursprünglichen Bedeutung von Reisegefährten), die sich wieder einmal frei von den ideologischen Zwängen und anderen Unpäßlichkeiten, die sie beim Autofahren quälen, unterhalten können?

Nur Japan hat bislang Weitblick bewiesen und sich auf das Zweite Eisenbahnzeitalter vorbereitet, was zur Folge hat, daß Puerto Rico seine Zuggarnituren demnächst möglicherweise aus Yokohama und nicht aus Ponce oder Pittsburgh beziehen muß.

Haupteinwand gegen eine Wiederbelebung der Eisenbahn ist die Annahme, sie sei nicht profitabel. Das Gleiche behauptete man von der „Operation Bootstrap" oder von der Idee, in einem Puerto Rico, das so arm war, daß niemand besonders scharf auf einen Abstecher dorthin zu sein schien, Luxushotels zu errichten. In England brachte man Ähnliches gegen italienische Espressobars vor, in Frankreich gegen Milchbars amerikanischer Provenienz. Doch entgegen den Prophezeiungen der Experten erwies sich jedes dieser Unternehmen als so phänomenal profitabel, daß sie heute angeblich die Traditionen und sogar die Identität der Länder gefährden, in denen sie angeblich keinerlei Chance hatten.

Zugegeben, die Eisenbahn ist nicht mehr so profitabel, wie sie es einmal war. Aber nicht deswegen, weil die Idee obsolet wäre, sondern weil man zuließ, daß sie im Laufe ihres Einsatzes und der Zeit immer schlechter wurde.

Züge haben die Phantasie der Menschen schon immer zutiefst fasziniert. Selbst heute gibt es nur wenige Kinder, die nicht lieber Lokomotivführer oder Schaffner werden möchten als General, Politiker oder Testpilot. Und es gibt nur wenige Väter, die ihren Söhnen eine Spielzeugeisenbahn kaufen und sich nicht darauf freuen, selbst ihren Spaß damit zu haben.

Time behauptet: „Amerika kehrt wieder auf die Schiene zurück. Wegen der Landschaft, der Geselligkeit und der Beschaulichkeit fahren die Reisenden wieder mit der Eisenbahn."

Um eine auch ökonomisch funktionierende Nachfrage nach Eisenbahnfahrten aus ihrem gegenwärtigen Dornröschenschlaf zu wecken, muß man offenbar nur das verblaßte Image wiederbeleben und das Bahnfahren wieder mit den Attributen Effizienz, Zuverlässigkeit, Sicherheit, Luxus, Eleganz, Komfort und Romantik in Verbindung bringen, mit denen es lange Zeit assoziiert wurde, im Gegensatz zur Vulgärheit der nervenaufreibenden und lebensgefährlichen Hetze auf den verstopften und abgasverpesteten Schnellstraßen.

In Österreich, der Schweiz oder Italien ist die Eisenbahn deshalb besonders attraktiv, weil die Ausgangspunkte der Bahnfahrt, nämlich die Bahnhöfe, nicht nur architektonisch herausragen, sondern auch mitten in der Stadt liegen, an Plätzen, die gesäumt sind von Brunnen und umgeben von Luxushotels. Die Bahnhofsrestaurants gehören durchweg zu den besten und beliebtesten Gaststätten. Die Bahnhofshallen erfreuen den Reisenden mit dem Schauspiel von Einheimischen, die gut gelaunt herumlaufen, und den Einheimischen mit dem Schauspiel exotischer Reisender aus fernen Ländern, die ihre steifen Glieder auf dem Bahnsteig recken und sich in fremden Sprachen unterhalten. Und in kleinen Ortschaften ist der Bahnhof oft der wichtigste Treffpunkt der Gemeinde; er lockt Menschen an, die einen Blick auf einen Schnellzug werfen wollen, wenn der nachmittags um fünf mit gedrosselter Geschwindigkeit durchfährt und dabei einen Hauch von großer weiter Welt hinterläßt.

Soll die Eisenbahn für Reisende wieder attraktiv werden, muß neben dem Bahnhofstreiben und den Reisemöglichkeiten jedoch vor allem eines erneuert werden: die Züge selbst. Sie müssen ins Auge stechen. Die Gänge, die Abteile, die Speise- und Schlafwagen müssen einen Hauch von Luxus und nicht nur Funktionalität verströmen. Das Personal muß wieder *alt*modische Höflichkeit lernen, denn eine *neu*modische Entsprechung dazu gibt es nicht. Kurz: All die Merkmale müssen erneuert werden, welche die Ökonomisierer so weit verkommen ließen, daß niemand mehr Zug fahren will: nicht weil die *Vorstellung* obsolet ist, sondern weil die *Ausstattung* verwahrlost.

Unsere Verkehrstechniker müssen deshalb wieder lernen, daß der wirtschaftliche Erfolg der Eisenbahn wie bei jedem anderen Unternehmen nicht darin besteht, Kosten zu sparen, bis nichts mehr übrig ist, was der Kunde kaufen möchte, sondern dem Kunden wieder eine Dienstleistung anzubieten, die so angenehm ist, daß er gerne den Mehrpreis bezahlt, den das Unternehmen erheben muß, um seine Ausgaben zu decken.

Geographisch und demographisch könnte Puerto Rico mindestens zwei Strecken einrichten, die sich rechnen, wenn diese Voraussetzungen erfüllt sind. Die eine wäre eine Küsteneisenbahn, die um die Insel herumfährt und gleichzeitig in beiden Richtungen unterwegs ist; die andere wäre eine Strecke quer über die Insel von San Juan nach Ponce. Das würde automatisch das gegenwärtige Verkehrsaufkommen auf den Schnellstraßen auf ein erträgliches Maß reduzieren, denn der Straßenverkehr würde fortan in erster Linie nur noch gebraucht, um kurze Strecken zurückzulegen (zwischen den Orten im Innern der Insel und zwischen dem Innern und dem nächstgelegenen Bahnhof an der Küste).

Ein erneuertes Eisenbahnsystem würde aber nicht nur das erstickende und die Luft verpestende Problem verstopfter Straßen lösen, sondern wäre auch als touristische Einnahmequelle von unschätzbarem Wert. Denn Inselumrundungen im luxuriösen Komfort der Züge wären unverzichtbarer Teil jedes Besuchsprogramms. Allein damit käme man auf eine Million Zugfahrten jährlich – und diese Zahl ließe sich verdoppeln, wenn man zusätzlich noch ein paar Schmalspurbahnen ins Innere der Insel anlegt, die in Ländern wie der Schweiz oder Wales auf Kinder ebenso wie auf ihre erwachsenen Begleiter eine unwiderstehliche Faszination ausüben. In Puerto Rico könnte man mit solchen Strecken den Regenwald erkunden oder Ausflüge zum Ionosphärenteleskop in der Nähe von Arecibo unternehmen, um nur zwei Beispiele zu nennen; darüber hinaus gibt es bereits die alte Zuckerlinie in Fajardo, deren Beliebtheit offenbar von Monat zu Monat wächst.

Doch der Wiederaufbau eines Eisenbahnnetzes, das ohne die verseuchenden Nebeneffekte des Straßenverkehrs auskommt, löst das wachsende Verkehrsproblem unserer Zeit nur zur Hälfte. Die andere Hälfte hängt davon ab, ob unsere Planer in der Lage sind, die ökonomische Notwendigkeit zu reduzieren, der zufolge eine zunehmende Zahl von Menschen aufgrund der sinnlosen Zusammenschlußpolitik, die alle modernen nationalen Gesellschaften verfolgen, immer weitere Wege an immer weiter entfernte Orte zurücklegt.

Dazu muß freilich nicht nur unser gegenwärtiges, straßenorientiertes Monoverkehrssystem verändert werden, sondern auch die zentralisierte Struktur unseres Lebens auf nationaler wie kommunaler Ebene. Wie meine nächste Kolumne zu zeigen versucht, wird ein Schnellverkehrssystem welcher Art auch immer, ob mit oder ohne Eisenbahn, die Situation, die es eigentlich lindern sollte, nicht lösen, sondern noch verschärfen, wenn nicht beide Aspekte gleichzeitig in Angriff genommen werden.

El Mundo, 29. Juni 1970

Regionale Souveränität

Zunahme der Verkehrsvielfalt. Verringerung der Verkehrsabhängigkeit durch föderale Rückentwicklung. Das Hindernis des Vorurteils. Hoher Lebensstandard durch geringe Transportkosten. Careys Prinzip von Webstuhl und Amboß. Munoz, Kilbrandon und Maud. Zentralisierung verkleidet als Dezentralisierung. Urbane Verschönerung durch nationale Kantonalisierung. Vergnügen statt Schrecken auf den Straßen.

In der vorangegangenen Kolumne habe ich behauptet, ein Eisenbahnsystem, das gegenüber dem Straßenverkehr konkurrenzfähig ist, sei die einzige Möglichkeit, um das Verkehrsaufkommen auf den Straßen auf nationaler Ebene zu reduzieren, aber nur, wenn sich gleichzeitig unser zentralisiertes Muster kommunalen Daseins ändert. Denn selbst wenn zusätzliche Verkehrseinrichtungen die Schnellstraßen entlasten, bewirken sie mit ziemlicher Sicherheit das genaue Gegenteil, falls ihre Einführung einhergeht mit der Notwendigkeit zunehmenden Verkehrs zwischen den Kommunen, wie sie sich immer dann ergibt, wenn ein Land seine politische und wirtschaftliche Integration verstärkt.

Wenn nun die Interdependenz, die sich aus der Integration ergibt, den Verkehr anwachsen läßt, folgt daraus, daß die Wiederherstellung eines hohen Maßes an kommunaler Eigenständigkeit diesen zwangsläufig wieder verringert, denn die verminderte Notwendigkeit, zwischen Ponce und San Juan hin und herzusausen, mindert auch den Wunsch, zwischen den beiden Städten hin und herzureisen.

Die vollständige Antwort auf die Frage, wie sich das Verkehrsaufkommen reduzieren läßt, lautet deshalb:

1. Man erhöhe die Vielfalt der Verkehrswege durch die Einführung von Eisenbahnen und anderen alternativen Beförderungssystemen.

2. Gleichzeitig verringere man die Notwendigkeit, dieses Mehr ans Verkehrswegen in Anspruch zu nehmen, indem man den regionalen Einheiten mittels politischer Dezentralisierung ein hohes Maß

an Eigenständigkeit zugesteht. Das ist das, was ich mit einem veränderten Muster kommunalen Daseins meine.

Im konkreten Fall Puerto Ricos bedeutet das, wie ich bei anderer Gelegenheit ausgeführt habe, einen Wechsel vom gegenwärtigen Einheitsstaat, in dem die Belange jeder Region eng mit den Belangen aller anderen Regionen verknüpft sind, zu einer Föderation von zwei bis vielleicht zwanzig hochgradig autonomen Kantonen, die über ein solches Maß an wirtschaftlicher, sozialer und politischer Eigenständigkeit verfügen, daß sie ihre Probleme allein mit Hilfe lokaler Ressourcen lösen können.

Gegen einen derartigen Vorschlag gibt es noch immer große Vorbehalte, weil man völlig unbegründet der Ansicht ist, kommunale Eigenständigkeit verringere zwar die Verkehrsabhängigkeit, impliziere aber gleichzeitig einen enormen Verlust an Spezialisierung, was zwangsläufig zu einem Rückgang der Produktivität wie zu einem sinkenden Lebensstandard führe.

Doch ein hoher Lebensstandard hängt nicht nur von hoher Produktivität ab, sondern auch von niedrigen Transportkosten, die mit jedem arithmetischen Mehr an regionaler Spezialisierung geometrisch zunehmen und letztlich unweigerlich größer sind als der Nutzen, den Größen- und Integrationsvorteile mit sich bringen. Aus diesem Grund hat sich der große amerikanische Ökonom H.C. Carey Anfang des 19. Jahrhunderts gegen einen weit ausgreifenden Handel ausgesprochen und statt dessen vorgeschlagen, jede Industrie solle in dem ländlichen Umfeld angesiedelt sein, das unmittelbar von ihr abhängt. „Webstuhl und Amboß müssen ihren natürlichen Platz an der Seite von Pflug und Egge einnehmen", schrieb Carey, um den Verkehr, der notwendig ist, um sie miteinander in Verbindung zu bringen, so gering wie möglich zu halten. Denn „die erste und schwerste Steuer, die das Land und die Arbeit zu zahlen haben, sind die Transportkosten".

Tatsächlich ist die Vorstellung, zu einem verkehrssparenden Maß an wirtschaftlicher, sozialer und politischer Eigenständigkeit zurückzukehren, längst nicht mehr so schockierend wie noch vor ein paar Jahren, als die Integrationsmanie auf ihrem Höhepunkt war. Da ist zum einen die aufstrebende *Fourth World* Bewegung, die versucht, den Menschen aus seiner Verkehrsverseuchung zu befreien, und ihn dazu ermuntert, seine täglichen Verrichtungen auf die eine Gemeinschaft zu beschränken, in deren Rahmen die meisten seiner Probleme zu lösen sind: seine unmittelbare Umgebung. Und anderswo gibt es immer mehr Pläne, die Industrie zu „dezentralisieren" und die lokale Regierung zu stärken, wie dies etwa Luis Munoz Marin in seinem Programm *Purpose of Puerto Rico* für das puertoricanische Commonwealth oder der Maud- (bzw. der Kilbrandon-) Bericht 1969 (bzw. 1974) für Großbritannien vorgeschlagen hat.

Problematisch an diesen Regionalisierungs- und Kommunalisierungsplänen ist nur: Solange die „barrios", Bezirke, Städte und Stadtregionen nur administrative Untereinheiten eines einheitlich verwalteten Landes sind, dient eine „Dezentralisierung" nur dem Ganzen, nicht aber den Teilen, nur den zentralen, nicht aber den regionalen Autoritäten. Statt die Bindungen an den gemeinsamen Regierungssitz zu lockern, verstärkt sie diese Bande noch. Statt neue Posten zu schaffen, um lokale Talente auch lokal zu „absorbieren", schafft sie ein bequemes Sprungbrett, von dem aus lokale Talente in Positionen an der Spitze der bürokratischen Pyramide gelangen können; diese Spitze aber befindet sich weiterhin in der aufregenderen Hauptstadt, auf die auch weiterhin alle Augen gerichtet sind.

Die einzige Möglichkeit, damit Dezentralisierung und Kommunalisierung wirklich funktionieren, besteht darin, den Kommunen die einzige Eigenschaft zu übertragen, die ihnen ein eigenes und weitgehend eigenständiges, nach innen gerichtetes Gravitationsfeld verschafft. Wie die Kantone der Schweiz oder die prunkvollen Stadtstaaten der Renaissance gezeigt haben, ist dieses Attribut ein hohes Maß nicht an delegierter Autorität, die unweigerlich zum Zentrum zurückführt, sondern an lokaler politischer Souveränität, die in den Regionen selbst verankert ist.

Nur dann werden die „pocenos" weitgehend in Ponce unterwegs sein, die Bewohner Cabo Rojas in Cabo Roja und die Barranquitener in einem Staat Barranquitas, und erst dann wird es schließlich zu einer dauerhaften Verringerung des Verkehrsdrucks kommen. Und nicht nur das. Von Careys „schwerster Steuer" – den übermäßigen Transportkosten – befreit, können die Bürger die daraus resultierenden Ersparnisse in die Verschönerung ihrer neuen Hauptstädte stecken, und zwar so üppig, daß nicht nur die Notwendigkeit, sondern auch der Wunsch, zwischen den Städten hin und herzufahren, so weit nachläßt, daß auf den Straßen statt Schrecken die reinste Freude herrscht.

El Mundo, 13. Juli 1970

Modell vs. Stadt

Wenn eine Frau ein Kleid kauft. Die Stadt als Happening. Nicht genügend Stühle. Erregung der Menschenmengen. Anordnung durch Kompression. Funktion der Stadtmauer. Die Notwendigkeit von Eigenständigkeit. Selbstgenerierende Stadtjobs. Verkehr innerhalb der Mauer. Vertrautheit, Schönheit, Liebe und Heimat. Chesterton über Rom. Identitätsstrukturen. Romantischer Schrott.

Die Frage, die sich eine Frau stellen muß, wenn sie ein neues Kleid kauft, ist nicht, was ihre Maße *sein sollten*, sondern was ihre Maße *sind*. Sonst bekommt sie ein Kleidungsstück, das zwar toll aussieht, aber nichts taugt oder nicht paßt.

Aus dem gleichen Grund lautet die Frage für Stadtplaner nicht, was eine Stadt *sein sollte*, sondern was sie *ist*, und entsprechend gilt es einen Entwurf zu präsentieren, der zur *Stadt* paßt und nicht zu dem *Modell*, das sie sich im Kopf zurechtgelegt haben.

Es müssen vor allem vier Voraussetzungen erfüllt sein, damit ein Gemeinwesen kein Modell, sondern eine Stadt ist.

1. In erster Linie muß sie dicht bevölkert sein. Im Gegensatz zum friedlichen Landleben ist eine Stadt ein Ort der Erregung und der Aktivität. Eine Stadt ist ein „Happening", das durch Zusammenstoß entsteht und nicht, indem man jede Berührung vermeidet. Das erreicht man dadurch, daß man sie auf weniger Raum zusammendrängt, als für den Luxus des Sich-Ausbreitens nötig wäre. Ähnlich dem, was Churchill über das britische Unterhaus sagte, ist die Stadt ein Drama, dessen Wirkung zerstört würde, wenn die Planer jedem einen bequemen Stuhl zur Verfügung stellen würden, der sich bei den Anlässen, zu denen die Menschen massenhaft strömen, hinsetzen *möchte*. Denn wenn sich jeder hinsetzen kann – wenn es also letztlich für jeden einen Sitzplatz gibt –, ist die Art von städtischem Schauspiel nicht mehr möglich, dessen Faszination ja zum Teil gerade auf dem Spektakel beruht, das die nach Sitzplätzen Suchenden bieten.

In der Geschichte haben Städte für diese Belebtheit am einfachsten dadurch gesorgt, daß sie einen Raum mit Mauern umgaben und ihn dann vollstopften. Als die „urbane Mischung" da drinnen dann aktiv zu werden und zu brodeln begann, ergab sich nicht nur spontan die Anordnung von Gebäuden, Plätzen und Straßen, wie sie für die „natürliche" Stadt charakteristisch ist, auch der Bedarf an weiterer bewußter Planung innerhalb der Mauern reduzierte sich auf ein Minimum.

Heute sind die physischen Mauern möglicherweise durch rechtliche ersetzt. Doch ob rechtlich oder physisch, ohne Mauern gibt es nur wild wuchernde Stadtgebiete, aber keine Städte. Denn Mauern sind für die Vorstellung von Stadt von so entscheidender Bedeutung, daß sie einem Gemeinwesen, wie klein auch immer, nicht selten den herausgehobenen Status einer Stadt verliehen. Als Romulus die größte aller Städte gründete, tat er nichts anderes, als einen bestimmten Bereich mit Mauern zu umgeben. Rom entstand dann von selbst, ähnlich wie sich ein See bildet, wenn ein Damm dem sprudelnden Fluß eines Baches Einhalt gebietet.

2. Die zweite Voraussetzung für eine gute Stadt ist ein hohes Maß an Eigenständigkeit. Wie Edward Wakefield, ein Ökonom des 19. Jahrhunderts, in einem nach ihm benannten Prinzip zeigte, leben annährend neunzig Prozent der städtischen Bevölkerung davon, daß sie sich gegenseitig Arbeit verschaffen. Wenn einzig Rohstoffe und Nahrungsmittel von außerhalb herbeigeschafft werden müssen, läßt sich allein aufgrund der gesparten *externen* Transportkosten erklären, warum Stadtbewohner seit jeher über einen höheren Lebensstandard verfügen als die Menschen auf dem von großen Entfernungen geplagten Land. Und die Kluft zwischen diesen beiden Lebensstandards vergrößert sich sogar, wenn eine Stadt von Einsparungen bei den *internen* Transportkosten profitieren kann, was überall dort möglich ist, wo das Prinzip der Eigenständigkeit auch für die Beziehungen zwischen den einzelnen Bezirken innerhalb der Stadtmauern gilt; denn die zurückgelegten Wege innerhalb einer bevölkerungsreichen Stadt sind naturgemäß unendlich viel zahlreicher als die Bewegungen außerhalb der Stadtmauern, über welche die Stadt mit dem Land verbunden ist.

Die einzige Frage dabei ist: Wie lassen sich die einzelnen Bezirke im Verhältnis zueinander eigenständiger machen? Ich habe diese

Frage in *The City of Man** funktional zu beantworten versucht. An dieser Stelle will ich sie historisch angehen und einen Blick auf die großen Städte der Vergangenheit werfen. In deren Fall *mußten* die einzelnen Stadtviertel aus dem ganz einfachen Grund über ein hohes Maß an Eigenständigkeit verfügen, weil die damals verfügbaren Transportmittel so langsam waren, daß man, wenn es nur irgendwie ging, auf alle zeitraubenden innerstädtischen Fahrten verzichtete. Statt also das gesamte Spektrum an komplementären bürgerlichen Aktivitäten und Berufen in einem zentralen Kern zu konzentrieren, gruppierte man sie um eine Vielzahl konkurrierender kleinerer Kerne herum. Abschließend machte man sich, wie etwa in Paris im Falle der Arrondissements, daran, jeden dieser zahlreichen kleineren Kerne mit einer solchen Fülle an geselligen, ästhetischen und architektonischen Annehmlichkeiten zu versehen, daß nur wenige lokale Bewohner ihr Vergnügen anderswo suchen mußten. Und schließlich reduzierte man aus dem gleichen Grund, wo immer es ging, die Entfernung zwischen Zuhause und Arbeitsplatz, bis aus Fahrzeug- Fußgängerdimensionen geworden waren, indem man die Wohnungen in die Nähe der Einkommensquellen rückte.

3. Die dritte Voraussetzung einer guten Stadt ergibt sich aus den ästhetischen Aspekten der zweiten und betrifft die Verfügbarkeit Dutzender attraktiver alternativer Straßen, die der Bürger nutzen kann, um zwei gleiche Punkte seines täglichen Unterwegsseins wie etwa Wohnung und Arbeitsplatz miteinander zu verbinden. Fehlen solche Alternativrouten, beschränkt sich seine Vertrautheit auf einen einzigen engen Streifen, während der Rest der Stadt eine schwammige graue Masse links und rechts davon bleibt. Ich selbst wohne in einem wunderbar gebauten Haus in der Via 18 in Villa Fontana, Carolina. Doch der Rest des Stadtteils weist zwar wundervolle Wohnarchitektur auf, könnte aber ebenso das Bettlaken eines Geistes sein. Ich war noch nie in Via 17 oder 19. Vielleicht gibt es sie auch gar nicht. Die Straße in und aus meinem Büro ist ein dünner Laserstrahl, der mein Ziel an der zehn Meilen entfernten Universität von Puerto Rico mit der Präzision eines Scharfschützen trifft

---

* Vgl. dazu S. 150.

und entlang der gleichen dünnen Linie zwischen den beiden Zielen wieder zurückwandert. Doch er verhindert jede Vertrautheit mit den Stadtvierteln, die er durchschneidet.

Da aber Vertrautheit den Wesenskern von Heimat wie auch die Basis der Liebe bildet, heißt das: Wenn man nicht mit seiner Stadt vertraut wird, kann sie nie wirklich Zuhause und Heimat werden. Und aus dem gleichen Grund kann man sie niemals lieben. Und wenn man sie nicht liebt, wird man sich nicht um sie kümmern oder sie verschönern. Und wenn sie nicht verschönert wird, wird sie nicht in der Lage sein, einen zu halten, außer vielleicht in dem Sinne, wie einen die Cocktaillounge am Flughafen hält, bevor man in grünere Gefilde abhebt. Wie Chesterton schon sagte: Die Römer „liebten Rom nicht, weil es großartig war. Rom war großartig, weil die Römer es liebten." Und sie liebten es wegen des Gewirrs aus faszinierend unterschiedlichen Alternativwegen, die ihnen zur Verfügung standen und die sie mal hierhin, mal dorthin zogen, bis sie mit jedem Winkel und jeder Ecke innerhalb der Stadtmauern vertraut waren.

4. Und schließlich muß eine Stadt wie jedes Gemeinwesen Strukturen haben, die ihrer Identität physischen Ausdruck verleihen und gleichzeitig ihren Bürgern eine allen gemeinsame emotionale „Erhebung" verschaffen. Solche „Identitätsstrukturen" müssen naturgemäß für alle von nah und fern sichtbar sein. Die symbolischste dieser Strukturen muß sich deshalb weit über die Dächer und die Betriebsamkeit des Tages erheben. Zudem dürfen sie nicht zweckorientiert sein wie etwa Fabrikschornsteine oder Wassertürme, deren erdgebundene Funktion den Geist nach unten zieht, nicht nach oben. Wie auf Anhöhen thronende Burgen, Kirchturmspitzen oder Domtürme müssen sie gen Himmel weisen und den müden Geist der Menschen erfrischen, indem sie seinen Blick über die engen physischen Grenzen hinaus und aus dem langen Schatten der engen irdischen Höhle herausführen, ihn hinlenken zum himmlischen Sitz der platonischen Idee von seiner Stadt, wo die mystischen Bande gewoben werden, die die Menschen unten auf dem Boden in ihren Gemeinwesen zusammenhalten.

Das einzige Problem mit diesen vier entscheidenden Voraussetzungen der guten Stadt ist, daß für das gegenwärtige Völkchen harter Mit-beiden-Beinen-auf-dem-Boden-Planer, wie Anatol Murad sie nennen würde, der Gedanke, Mauern zu errichten statt sie einzureißen, um den Geist des Universums zu fassen zu bekommen; die Vorstellung mystischer Bande, die irgendwo darüber gewoben sind, statt irdischer Rationalität, die unten zerbröckelt; und der Gedanke, daß Türme leer in den Himmel weisen statt die Armen mit dringend benötigtem Wohnraum zu versorgen – daß all das für sie nichts als romantischer Schrott ist.

El Mundo, 19. Januar 1970

TEIL III
Docklands

Anatomie der Stadtplanung

Preisgekröntes Modell. Architektur vs. Stadtplanung. Michelangelos Nackte. Entwurf und Arrangement. Stadt als Podest. Goethe über die Zerstörung Roms durch Krieg und Architekten. Der Petersdom im Dschungel. Die Stadt als Kasernensiedlung. Militarisierung durch Architektur. Der Charme der Hafenviertel. Ein hanseatisches Faubourg. Die Zeitlosigkeit der Vergangenheit.

Anfang Januar 1968 verlieh eine fünfköpfige Jury unter Vorsitz des Dekans für Architektur am renommierten MIT den Hauptpreis des 15. „Annual National Design Competition of the United States" an ein Wohnungsbauprojekt, das in Puerto Ricos Hafengegend La Puntilla verwirklicht werden sollte, um dorthin dann die Menschen aus La Perla, einem der größten Slums des Landes, umzusiedeln.

Es überraschte weder, daß der Preisträger ein MIT-Absolvent war, noch, daß der renommierte Vorsitzende des Preiskomitees diese Art ganz allgemein und den siegreichen Entwurf des ehemaligen Studenten seiner Universität im Besonderen in höchsten Tönen pries, weil er zeige, „in welche Richtung die Architektur sich bewegt".

Dem Foto dieses preisgekrönten Modells nach zu urteilen, scheint die moderne Architektur sich von „schlimm" nach „noch schlimmer" zu bewegen. Denn zum einen zeigt sich, wie sehr technische Prinzipien in der Architektur Fuß gefaßt haben, zum anderen, in welchem Maße die Architekten selbst sich als Stadtplaner gerieren, und zwar ungeachtet der Tatsache, daß das eine mit dem anderen so wenig gemein hat wie die plastische Chirurgie mit der organischen Chirurgie.

Hauptaufgabe des Architekten ist es, individuelle Gebäude zu entwerfen, während der Stadtplaner diese dann in ein kollektives Ensemble einfügen muß. Diese beiden Aufgaben sind so unterschiedlich wie das Malen von Bildern durch einen Künstler und das Aufhängen dieser Bilder durch den Leiter einer Galerie. Wenn daher Michelangelo von Architekten verlangte, zu ihrer Ausbildung müsse auch das Aktzeichnen gehören, denn „die Struktur eines Gebäudes und die des menschlichen Körpers ist dieselbe", so könnte man mit gleichem Recht von Stadtplanern verlangen, daß zu ihrer Berufs-

vorbereitung das Studium der Anatomie gehört. Denn die Anordnung der Organe innerhalb des menschlichen Körpers und von individuellen Gebäuden innerhalb einer Stadt ist die gleiche.
Vermengt man die beiden Disziplinen und überträgt die im wesentlichen technische und kollektive Aufgabe des Stadtplaners der im wesentlichen individuellen und künstlerischen Hand des Architekten, ergeben sich daraus zwei mögliche Folgen: Entweder wird die Stadt dann so gestaltet, daß sie nur noch als Podest für die vorteilhafteste Zurschaustellung ihrer großen architektonischem Monumente dient; oder sie nimmt die Form nicht eines symphonischen Arrangements von Gebäuden an, sondern eines unorchestrierten Wohnkomplexes, der nur einem einzigen Zweck dient. Das ist, als würde man den Körper nur um ein einziges menschliches Organ herum entwerfen.
Die erste der genannten Folgen zeigt sich am Schicksal Roms, von dem Goethe meinte: „Was die Barbaren stehen ließen, haben die Baumeister des neuen Roms zerstört." Wenn sich der Pilger dem Petersdom näherte, war es bis vor ein paar Jahrzehnten noch so, daß er zunächst nur eine geheimnisvolle Ahnung der großen Kathedrale verspürte, bevor sie dann plötzlich mit ihren überwältigenden Proportionen über ihn hereinbrach wie eine unbekannte Lichtung, die sich inmitten eines Dschungels aus eng gedrängten Häusern und engen Gassen öffnete. Heute, da dieses aufregende städtische Konglomerat um den Petersdom herum durchschnitten ist von der breiten Narbe einer Prachtstraße, die gesäumt ist von der unterkühlten Langeweile moderner Regierungsgebäude, ist der Dom schon von so weit her zu erkennen, daß die eindrucksvollste Erfahrung des Pilgers das schimmernde Strahlen des Pflasters ist, nicht aber die Proportionen einer Kirche, die jetzt geradezu klein wirkt aufgrund der großen Entfernungen, wie man sie vom Land, nicht aber aus den Städten kennt.
Das zweite Ergebnis, das zu verzeichnen ist, wenn Architekten Stadtplaner spielen und ein urbanes Umfeld bauen, als hätten sie es mit einem einzigen Wohnkomplex zu tun, läßt sich an dem preisgekrönten Modell für La Puntilla beobachten. Es heißt, die offenen Räume sollten an die Plätze und das Straßensystem des alten San Juan erinnern. In Wirklichkeit erinnern sie nicht an die Plätze und

die Straßen einer Stadt, sondern an den Innenhof und die Verbindungskorridore einer kommunalen Einrichtung wie etwa eines Gefängnisses oder einer Kaserne, wo Ordnung nicht aus einer Vielzahl zufälliger frontaler Kollisionen entsteht, wie dies für eine Stadt charakteristisch ist, sondern durch die ökonomische Künstlichkeit von Disziplin und Drill.

Die eigentliche Kritik an dem preisgekrönten La-Puntilla-Modell richtet sich jedoch nicht gegen seinen funktionalen Kasernencharakter. Denn ob wir das nun mögen oder nicht: In einer Zeit, die durch den wachsenden Druck unserer zunehmenden Menschenmengen immer weiter in Richtung Uniformität des Militarismus

Das preisgekrönte maßstabsgetreue Modell für La Puntilla des Bostoner Architekten Jan Wambler

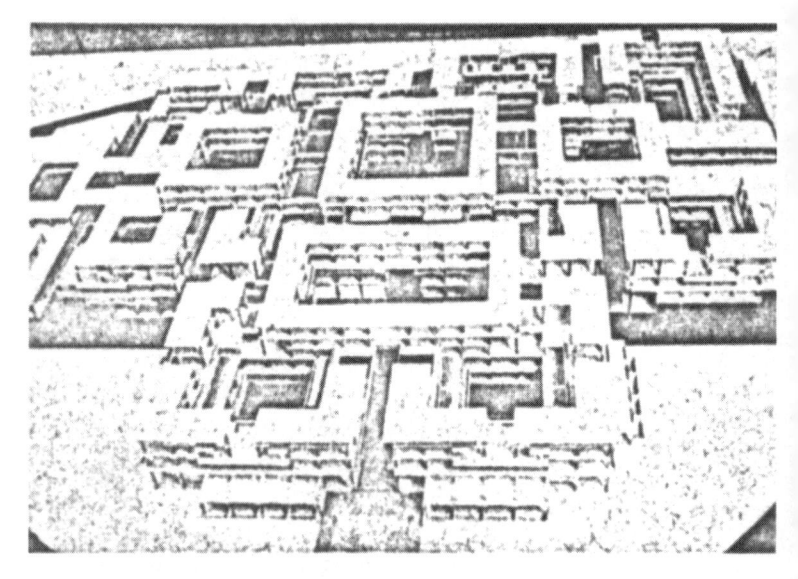

Dieser architektonische Entwurf für ein staatliches Bauprojekt in La Puntilla, einem Stadtteil in der Altstadt von San Juan, gewann den Ersten Preis beim 15. jährlichen Design Awards Competition, der von der Zeitschrift *Progressive Architecture of the United States* gesponsert wird.

getrieben wird, steht dieses Modell in der Tat für die Richtung, in die Architektur und Stadtplanung sich bewegen (müssen). Das Tadelnswerte an diesem Modell ist, daß es in La Puntilla gebaut werden soll.

Denn La Puntilla mit seinen Hafenanlagen und der Landzunge, die in die Bucht von San Juan hinausragt, ist nicht nur der letzte noch weitgehend unzerstörte Ausläufer der Altstadt, der sich nach Art alter Vorstädte über die Grenzen seiner formidablen Mauern hinaus ausbreitete; mit seinen angenehm unspektakulären Gebäuden und Straßen und seinen ganz eigenen dreieckigen Plätzen, die an vielen Kreuzungen entstanden sind, bildet es auch eines der schönsten städtischen Ensembles in ganz Puerto Rico.

Und nicht nur das Ensemble ist schön. Anders als die „untraditionellen" Strukturen, die um das Castillo del Morro herum „plattgemacht" werden sollen, sind die meisten Gebäude in La Puntilla

La Puntilla

zwar relativ jung, gehören aber potentiell zu den herausragendsten Beispielen des spanischen und puertoricanischen Stils. Dieser Stil ahmt nicht nur die von Veranden bestimmte Eleganz der Altstadthäuser nach, die einem anderen Zweck dienten; er steht auch für die großzügigen Kais und die gediegene Funktionalität, wie sie zu einem hanseatischen *faubourg* passen, wo Seehandel, Großhandelsgeschäfte, Verschiffung, Zollwesen und all die anderen Aktivitäten betrieben werden, die an den Toren einer Stadt am Meer gedeihen.

Es wäre tragisch, würde man zulassen, daß diese Perle zugunsten einer monströsen kasernenartigen Siedlung zerstört wird, auch wenn letztere die alles nivellierende Welle der Zukunft darstellt. Um sicherzustellen, daß sie bewahrt wird, wäre es jedoch nötig, daß man dieses Gebiet einer Stadterneuerungsbehörde wegnimmt, die sich naturgemäß dem inhärenten Militarismus dieses grundstürzenden Massenzeitalters unterwirft, und es den bewährten Händen von Ricardo Alegria übergibt, dessen Institut für puertoricanische Kultur sich bei allem, was man über einige seiner Rationalisierungen sagen kann, vor allem durch eines auszeichnet: Sein untrüglicher künstlerischer Geschmack und sein anerkennendes Gespür für die Errungenschaften einer zu Recht gepriesenen Vergangenheit haben dazu geführt, daß das Flair vergangener Zeiten auf eine Weise bewahrt, wiederbelebt und restauriert wird, die nirgendwo sonst auf der Welt ihresgleichen findet – weder in England noch in Frankreich, weder in Italien noch in Spanien.

San Juan Star, 26. April 1968.

Die Schönheit der Slums

Grausamer Entwurf. Die Bienenstockgesellschaft. Urbane Schönheit. Härtezulage für Brasilia. Gutes Leben in St. Ives. Die organische Schönheit von Slums. Vom Dreck zum Marmor. Im Schoß der Slums schlummernde Reichtümer. Mensch aus einem anderen Jahrhundert. Das Opfer heutiger Planung.

Ein paar Punkte in der vorangegangenen Kolumne, die für den Erhalt der Hafenanlagen von La Puntilla plädiert, bedürfen offenbar genauerer Erläuterung. Darauf läßt zumindest ein kritischer Brief schließen, den mir der Urheber des preisgekrönten Modells geschickt hat, das dort umgesetzt werden soll.

Ich habe seinen Entwurf als monströs bezeichnet. Ein befreundeter Architekt nannte ihn „grausam", was mir der bessere Ausdruck zu sein scheint. Ich habe jedoch weder den Entwurf verurteilt noch bestreite ich dessen Verdienste im Kontext unseres Massenzeitalters, das uns mit seinem Bevölkerungsdruck unausweichlich zu einer hochgradig regulierten Bienenstockgesellschaft machen wird. Und da sich der entsprechende Bienenstockstil am besten in der Wabenstruktur von Kasernengebäuden widerspiegelt, kann sich die moderne Massenarchitektur nur in eine Richtung entwickeln, nämlich hin zu einer Art von Siedlung, wie sie das siegreiche Modell für La Puntilla vorsieht.

Gemeint habe ich, daß der Entwurf *im Kontext von La Puntilla* monströs ist, in einem Umfeld, das den Stil einer anderen Zeit widerspiegelt und das in seinen gegenwärtig bestehenden Strukturen erhalten bleiben sollte, nicht weil es Geschichte hat, sondern weil es schön ist und deshalb selbst den Menschen des 20. Jahrhunderts eine angenehme Lebensweise bieten kann.

Vor allem verfügt La Puntilla über *urbane* Schönheit, was etwas anderes ist als *architektonische* Schönheit. Es mag Städte geben, die Unmengen an wunderbarer Architektur aufweisen, denen aber urbane Schönheit völlig abgeht. Ein Beispiel ist etwa Brasilia, das sich wie die Niagarafälle zu einer Sehenswürdigkeit entwickelt hat – zu einem Ort, den man *gesehen* haben muß. Doch als Ort zum *Bleiben* hat es sich für seine an Rio de Janeiro orientierte Bevölkerung als so hoffnungsloser Fall erwiesen, daß man den Politikern Erschwerniszuschläge zahlen muß, damit sie in ihrer eigenen Hauptstadt ihren Geschäften nachgehen.

Auf der anderen Seite gibt es Städte, die über kein einziges architektonisches Prunkstück verfügen, aber durch so große urbane Schönheit bezaubern, daß sie fortwährend in Gefahr sind, von den Flüchtlingsschwärmen aus modernen Stadtagglomerationen überschwemmt zu werden, die auf der Suche nach Orten sind, welche zwar nicht unbedingt so toll aussehen, aber mit Sicherheit die Essenz eines guten Lebens bieten können.

Ein Beispiel für eine solche Stadt ist St. Ives in Cornwall, dessen Mangel an *architektonischer* Schönheit mehr als wettgemacht wird durch den Überfluß an *urbaner* Schönheit. Im Gegensatz zu ersterer ist urbane Schönheit Ausdruck organischer und weniger visueller Stimmigkeit. Sie ist Ergebnis nicht eines intellektuellen Entwurfs, sondern widerstreitender Kräfte, die aufgrund der verschiedenen Schichten einer Stadtbevölkerung entstehen, wenn diese sich auf gleichem Raum drängen, bis sie in einem Gleichgewicht zur Ruhe kommen, das automatisch eine gesunde Stadtstruktur zur Folge hat. Im Gegensatz zur architektonischen Schönheit, die Ausfluß individuellen menschlichen Geistes ist, resultiert urbane Schönheit aus dem Wirken des sozialen Wesens des Menschen, und ihr ist deshalb am besten gedient, wenn man sie in Ruhe läßt.

Darin liegt denn auch der Grund, warum fast alle Slums von einzigartiger urbaner Schönheit sind. Sie haben einen Wesenskern entwickelt, der den meisten Stadtplanern fehlt. Um La Perla zu einem Positano zu machen, Buen Consejo zu einem Assisi oder El Fanguito zu einem Venedig, muß man deshalb einzig und allein Holz in Stein und Stein in Marmor verwandeln; muß man der natürlichen Arbeit der Menschen die künstlerische des Architekten hinzufügen und darf sie nicht durch das künstliche Schaffen des modernen, ökonomisch denkenden Stadtplaners ersetzen. Und alles, was man an einem Ort wie La Puntilla braucht, der bereits urbane Schönheit mit einem beträchtlichen Maß an architektonischer Schönheit verbindet – sogar ohne die Balkone, die in Boston vielleicht „unecht" aussehen, nicht aber in den Tropen –, ist, die potenziellen Reichtümer zu nutzen, die in seinem Schoß schlummern.

Aufgrund dieser Vorstellung behauptet mein Kritiker, ich sei „offensichtlich nicht in diesem Jahrhundert zu Hause". In meiner vorangegangenen Kolumne über La Puntilla sind mir ein paar Fehler unterlaufen, etwa daß ich ihm einen MIT- statt einem Harvard-Abschluß angedichtet habe, aber das dürfte angesichts der engen Zusammenarbeit zwischen den beiden Architekturfakultäten und des gleichermaßen hohen Renommees, an einer der beiden Universitäten sein Studium absolviert zu haben, keinen großen Unterschied machen. Falsch war auch meine Behauptung, er sei Architekt und nicht Stadtplaner, aber das hätte an meiner Einschätzung nichts geändert, sondern allenfalls dazu geführt, daß ich diese Kolumne hier vor der anderen geschrieben hätte, wenn ich um dieses nebensächliche Detail gewußt hätte.

Ich glaube jedoch kaum, daß mein Anliegen, nämlich La Puntilla dagegen zu verteidigen, daß es zum Schauplatz für die Umsetzung des preisgekrönten Projekts wird (während es Dutzende andere gibt, die nicht die Zerstörung einer bezaubernden, bestehenden Kommune erfordern), mich zwangsläufig zu einem Menschen aus einem anderen Jahrhundert macht. Der ganze Grund für meine Kritik an der gegenwärtigen Stadtplanung ist ja gerade, daß ich ein Opfer der Planung des 20. Jahrhunderts und eben nicht des 17. oder 19. Jahrhunderts bin. Denn sie hat das Schlamassel angerichtet, in dem wir leben, weil sie eines nicht erkannt hat: Worauf es wirklich ankommt, ist nicht, wie eine Stadt aussehen sollte, sondern was eine Stadt ist. Das Aussehen folgt dann automatisch.

Wie ich schon des öfteren festgestellt habe, wußten frühere Zeiten all das. Nicht aber unsere. Ansonsten müßte man nicht für den Erhalt von La Puntilla plädieren, denn niemand würde je auch nur auf den Gedanken kommen, es abzureißen.

San Juan Star, 7. Juni 1968

Die Stadt außerhalb der Mauern

Schönheit in der Geschichte. Realität einer Idee. Unsichtbare Türme. *Genius loci*. Die Schrecken der urbanen Diaspora. Verringerung der Entfernungen für die Pendler. Die Bauphilosophie von Sir Herbert Read. Bruchbuden und Klospülungen.

In meinen ersten beiden La-Puntilla-Kolumnen habe ich mich vehement gegen den preisgekrönten Entwurf und seine „Sanierung" ausgesprochen, und zwar weniger wegen seiner „Grausamkeit", denn die ist unvermeidlicher Auswuchs unseres monströsen Massenzeitalters, und dafür kann der Urheber dieses Entwurfs nun wahrlich nicht verantwortlich gemacht werden. Wogegen ich mich wehrte, war die Tatsache, daß dieses Projekt ausgerechnet in der Gegend von La Puntilla umgesetzt werden sollte, die gar nicht dafür geeignet ist, wo es doch im Rest des Landes noch genügend Raum gibt, um den Wohnungshunger einer explodierenden Bevölkerung zu stillen, ohne daß man dafür die historische Gegend rings um die Altstadt von San Juan zerstören muß.

Mein Vorschlag für La Puntilla lautete Erhalt. Man hat behauptet, der Ort enthalte keine historisch wertvollen, erhaltenswerten Gebäude. Die höchst eindrucksvolle Appartmentsiedlung in El Monte oder Henry Klumbs großartige Parke-Davis-Fabrik an der Straße nach Carolina haben auch keinen historischen Wert. Sollte man sie deshalb ebenfalls abreißen?

Was erhalten zu werden verdient, ist nicht Geschichte, sondern Schönheit. Und die Schönheit La Puntillas ist überwältigend. Das mag für einige einzelne Gebäude nicht gelten. Doch sie ist kollektiv vorhanden in dem von Plätzen bestimmten Gepräge, das seine gemächlichen, einfachen Strukturen zu einem organischen Ganzen vereint, welches heute zwar von Verfall bedroht ist, sich aber mit der gleichen natürlichen Leichtigkeit und Anmut in die „außerhalb der Mauern" gelegene Hafenumgebung schmiegt, wie eine Katze dies überall dort tut, wo sie schläft.

Das allein sollte Grund genug sein, eine der potenziell schönsten Stadtlandschaften der Karibik zu erhalten. Doch tatsächlich kann

La Puntilla nicht nur mit Schönheit aufwarten. Es *hat* Geschichte, auch wenn die vielleicht nicht in den dortigen Gebäuden steckt, von denen ihre unphilosophischen Kritiker unter Eid behaupten, keines sei älter als fünfzig Jahre. Wie im Falle der unvollendeten und daher noch immer unsichtbaren zweiten Türme gotischer Kathedralen liegen die Geschichte und die Realität La Puntillas in seiner *Idee*, die so alt ist wie der Plan, der die Stadtmauern von San Juan entwarf, und nicht von Wohnungsbauexperten stammte, sondern der kreativen Kraft seiner natürlichen Umgebung entsprang, dem *genius loci*. Und der *genius loci* bestimmte von Anfang an, daß La Puntilla der angrenzenden Stadt nicht als Auffangbecken für die aus dem Slum von La Perla Umgesiedelten dienen sollte, sondern als freundlicher Vorort, der aufgrund seiner Lage zwischen Stadtmauer und Hafen dazu bestimmt war, einerseits seinem Nachbarn als zusätzliches, auf dem Wasser schwimmendes Hafenviertel zu dienen, sich gleichzeitig aber um einen ganz eigenen Kern herum zu entwickeln.

Das heißt jetzt nicht, daß La Puntilla zwangsläufig wieder zum historischen Zentrum wasserorientierter Aktivitäten werden sollte, so wie ja auch Salzburgs Salzbergbauvergangenheit nicht bedeutet, daß sich die glamouröse Mozart-Stadt jetzt von den Festspielen ab- und wieder dem Abbau des Kristalls, das ihm einst den Namen gab, zuwenden sollte. La Puntilla eignet sich gleichermaßen dafür, als Ort des Handwerks zu dienen oder als innerstädtisches Universitätszentrum, wie es schon längst eines geben sollte am Urquell der spanisch-amerikanischen Geschichte des Landes.

Das heißt also: Welches spezielle Flair man ihm auch immer gibt – La Puntilla, das schon auf natürliche Weise durch die formidable Umschließung alter Mauern vom Rest der Stadt getrennt ist, sollte wieder eine abgeschlossene, kleine, eigenständige Allzweckstadt werden. Es sollte sein, was Murano für Venedig ist, San Angel für Mexiko-Stadt, Montmartre für Paris, Clifton für Bristol oder Grinzing für Wien: *ein Teil* von San Juan und doch davon *getrennt*; eine Kommune in der Umlaufbahn, aber mit eigenem Gravitationsfeld, das verhindert, daß eine Unmenge an Pendlern sie wie Sternschnuppen ihrer Substanz beraubt und in alle Richtungen auseinanderstiebt. Wenn La Puntilla über eine Universität verfügt, dann sollte es kein Universitäts*campus* sein, sondern eine Universitäts*stadt*, die wie Princeton, Cambridge oder Heidelberg denjenigen, die dort leben (statt denjenigen, die nur zu Besuch kommen), die ganze Palette an städtischen Einrichtungen bietet: Wohnungen, Kirchen, Uferpromenaden, Straßencafés, Antiquariate, Arztpraxen, Geschäfte, kurz: alles, was sich für eine voll strukturierte, vertikal integrierte Kommune gehört.

Was es unter keinen Umständen werden sollte, ist eine dieser tödlichen horizontalen Kommunen, die nur einem Zweck dienen und ein so großes Problem unserer Zeit sind. Dabei ist es völlig egal, ob sie in Gestalt von billigen Wohnungsbauprojekten, Wohngegenden für die Mittelschicht, Hotelarealen oder Industrieparks daherkommen. Solche Kommunen hängen völlig von außen ab – von Arbeitsplätzen, wenn es sich um Wohngegenden handelt, von Arbeitskräften, wenn es sich um Industrieansiedlungen handelt, von Kunden, wenn es reine Geschäftsgegenden sind, und von Touristen, wenn sie auf Erholung ausgerichtet sind – und sind deshalb nicht nur auf untragbare Weise unwirtschaftlich, da sie die halbe Zeit zu wenig genutzt sind und während der anderen Hälfte zu stark in Anspruch genommen werden; sie tragen auch entscheidend zur erstickenden Verkehrsflut bei, die daraus entsteht, daß die „amputierten" Menschen täglich damit beschäftigt sind, all die Funktionen wieder miteinander zu verbinden, welche die Ein-Zweck-Planer so effektiv überall verstreut haben.

Als eigenständiger kleiner Vorort außerhalb der Tore würde La Puntilla nicht zusätzlich zum städtischen Verkehrsstau beitragen, im Gegenteil: es würde ihn enorm verringern, wenn man bedenkt, daß die meisten Distanzen dort zu Fuß zurückzulegen wären. Als Viertel, das sich auf Wohneinrichtungen spezialisiert, wird es hingegen pro Tag 10.000 bis 16.000 Verkehrsmeilen je 1.000 Einwohner generieren, wenn diese in günstigen Wohnblocks leben, und zwischen 5.000 und 9.000 Meilen, wenn sie zur Mittelschicht gehören; denn letztere finden wahrscheinlich eher Arbeit in der Nähe, in der Altstadt von San Juan oder in Hato Rey, während die Haupteinkommensquelle für erstere die Fabriken in der entfernten Peripherie wären.

Allein das sollte die Planer von dem verrückten Vorhaben abbringen, in La Puntilla nur Wohnungen, *welcher Art auch immer*, zu bauen, die nur für eine Bevölkerungsschicht gedacht sind. Doch wichtiger noch als das, was sie *bleiben lassen* sollten, ist, was sie *tun* sollten: nämlich wie die Planer vergangener Zeiten wieder auf den *genius loci* zu hören und auf diesen unbezahlbaren Flecken mit Hafenanlagen und urbanem Land eine kleine, vertikal integrierte Stadt zu setzen, in der die historische Idee seiner natürlichen, vom Wasser geprägten und von Mauern umschlossenen Umgebung zumindest zu spüren ist. Denn was Sir Herbert Read über Gebäude sagte, gilt auch für Kommunen: „Sie müssen vor Ort beginnen, nicht in einem Büro", und sie müssen „im Einklang mit der Natur gebaut werden", nicht mittels preisgekrönter Entwürfe oder sozialer Prinzipien, die seit jeher dafür gesorgt haben, daß die Menschen in Bruchbuden leben – auch wenn die heute vielleicht mit Klospülung und Fernsehantennen ausgestattet und in hurrikanerprobter Betonbauweise errichtet sind.

El Mundo, 14. November 1969

La Puntilla in Split

Die Stadt innerhalb eines Palasts. Enge durch Geschwindigkeit. Der Triumph des Autos über den Menschen. Die Verwandlung der Stadt in einen Parkplatz. Die menschliche Lösung. Freiheit von der Entfernung. Hohe Dichte. Langsame Fortbewegung. Das Universum in einem kleinen Raum. Zu klein, um lebensfähig zu sein. Das Wakefield-Prinzip der städtischen Ökonomie. Die geringen Kosten der Dichte. Die Geißel des Automobilismus.

Glücklicherweise wurde die Umgestaltung von La Puntilla um weitere zwei Jahre verschoben. Das bietet der Regierung die Gelegenheit, dieses heute schmucklose, früher aber einmal ziemlich hübsche Großhandels- und Lagerhausviertel, das unvergleichlich schön gelegen ist, wieder aufzubauen, wenn man sich an anderen Prinzipien als denen der modernen Planungsschulen orientiert, die sich überall auf der Welt als so katastrophal erwiesen haben.

La Puntilla, das sich außer- und unterhalb der beeindruckenden alten Mauern der Hauptstadt in die Bucht von San Juan hinaus erstreckt, umfaßt eine Fläche, die grob gerechnet derjenigen der dalmatinischen Hauptstadt Split (ital. Spalato) am Mittelmeer entspricht; diese ist, wie man vielleicht weiß, innerhalb des Terrains des Palastes errichtet worden, in den sich der römische Kaiser Diokletian nach seiner Abdankung an der Wende zum dritten nachchristlichen Jahrhundert zurückzog. Vor einiger Zeit begann Split über seine ursprünglichen Grenzen hinauszuwachsen und hat heute eine Bevölkerung von über 50 000 Menschen. Doch mehr als zwei Drittel davon leben noch immer auf dem engen Raum des ursprünglichen Kaiserpalasts.

Nimmt man Split als zufälliges Beispiel für kompakte städtische Lebensverhältnisse, die so großen Reiz ausstrahlen, daß die Stadt heute zu einer der beliebtesten Ausflugs- und Erholungsgegenden in Jugoslawien geworden ist, stellen sich zwei Fragen: Könnte man La Puntilla in ähnlicher Weise sanieren? Und würde dies die allgemeinen Probleme der wuchernden Ballungsräume lösen?

Wie ich in früheren Kolumnen ausgeführt habe, hat das urbane Hauptproblem unserer Zeit nichts damit zu tun, daß zu viele

Menschen in einer bestimmten Stadt leben. Es rührt vielmehr aus der übermäßigen Geschwindigkeit, mit der sich die Menschen bewegen müssen, um die verschiedenen Punkte ihrer täglichen Aktivitäten wieder miteinander zu verbinden, die infolge der autobedingten, zerstreuten Lebensgewohnheiten voneinander getrennt wurden.

Eine Möglichkeit, diese Situation zu bewältigen, ist, die Städte den gewachsenen Geschwindigkeitsbedürfnissen des zerstreuten Lebens anzupassen und immer mehr städtische Fläche für Verkehrsadern, Tankstellen und Parkplätze zu nutzen. Am Ende wird das, wie Russel Baker in einer seiner Kolumnen anschaulich gezeigt hat, darin gipfeln, daß man ganze Städte unter dem Asphalt begraben muß und damit den endgültigen Triumph des Autos über den Menschen besiegelt. Natürlich hat Baker spaßeshalber übertrieben. Doch gerade als ich mich an diese Kolumne setzte, fiel mein Blick auf die Schlagzeilen in *El Mundo* und im *San Juan Star*, die genau diese Art von Nachricht vermittelten: daß nämlich „nach langem Streit La Puntilla asphaltiert und als Parkplatz für 800 Autos genutzt werden wird". Zugegeben, das ist nur als vorübergehende Maßnahme gedacht. Doch wie vorübergehend ist ein asphaltierter Parkplatz, der sofort wieder eine auf ewig irreversible Verkehrsflut anzieht?

Das Problem läßt sich jedoch auch noch anders lösen, nämlich nicht mit Blick auf die Kraftfahrzeuge, sondern auf die Menschen. Passen wir La Puntilla nicht den Erfordernissen der Autos an, die durch unsere modernen, zerstreuten Lebensgewohnheiten unentbehrlich geworden sind; passen wir La Puntilla lieber den Bedürfnissen der Menschen an, die dort leben könnten, wenn nicht die Gefräßigkeit der Autos allen urbanen Raum, denn es noch gibt, verschlingen würde.

Mit anderen Worten: Verändern wir unsere Lebensgewohnheiten so, daß sie nicht vom Auto abhängig sind. Das ist dann der Fall, wenn jeder Ort, den der Bürger im Laufe eines normalen Tages aufsuchen muß – Schule, Kirche, Krankenhaus, Geschäfte, Cafés, Arztpraxen, Häuser von Freunden, kommunale Behörden –, wieder in unsere unmittelbare, zu Fuß erreichbare Umgebung zurückgebracht wird. Und keine Gegend bietet eine bessere Gelegenheit dafür als eine von Natur aus kleine Halbinsel wie La Puntilla.

Das heißt: La Puntilla muß zunächst und vor allem als Kommune mit hoher Dichte wiederaufgebaut werden. Doch wenn Autos weitgehend entbehrlich sein sollen, muß es auch zu einer Kommune mit großer Vielfalt werden. Oder wie Christopher Marlowe sagen würde: „In einem kleinen Raum unendlichen Reichtum" umfassen. Es kann keine *Ein-Klassen*-Gesellschaft sein, die von entfernten Einkommensquellen abhängig ist, wie das der Fall wäre, folgte man den Vorstellungen derjenigen, die La Puntilla zu einer Wohngegend entweder für umgesiedelte Slumbewohner, für Arme, für die Mittelschicht, für die Oberschicht oder für Regierungsbeamte machen wollen, die über den gesamten Großraum San Juan verstreut arbeiten. Es muß eine *All-Klassen*-Gesellschaft sein, in der die meisten von denen, die in La Puntilla wohnen, auch in La Puntilla arbeiten.

Es muß, kurz gesagt, zur einer wirtschaftlich weitgehend autonomen, kleinen und eigenständigen Fußgängerstadt umgestaltet werden, wo nicht nur Parkplatzwächter oder Pendler mit weit entfernten Arbeitsplätzen wohnen, sondern die ganze Palette städtischer Berufe zu finden ist, vom Hausmeister bis zum Arzt, vom Kellner bis zum Gastwirt, vom Schneider bis zum Priester, vom Studenten bis zum Lehrer, vom Handwerker bis zum Musiker, vom Bäcker bis zum Briefträger, vom Straßenkehrer bis zum Richter. Dann – und nur dann – werden Autos weitgehend überflüssig sein.

Aber ist die Gegend von La Puntilla groß genug, um eine ausreichend große Bevölkerung zu beherbergen, damit die ganze Bandbreite städtischer Aktivitäten zur Verfügung steht? Das ist der Grund, warum ich Split erwähnt habe. Wenn der Diokletianpalast groß genug ist, um in Renaissanceprunk und ohne Hochhäuser mehr als 35.000 Einwohner unterzubringen, warum sollte das in La Puntilla nicht möglich sein?

Bedeutsamer ist die Frage, ob eine solche Bevölkerung, wie bunt sie sich auch immer zusammensetzt, nicht doch zu klein wäre, um eine wirtschaftlich lebensfähige Einheit zu bilden? Aber auch das ist nicht wirklich kompliziert. Denn wie Edward Wakefield, ein Ökonom des 19. Jahrhunderts, in einem nach ihm benannten Prinzip zeigte, werden 85 bis 90 Prozent des Einkommens in einer Stadt, ganz gleich wie groß sie ist, nicht durch Austausch mit der Außenwelt erwirtschaftet, sondern durch Geschäfte, welche die Einwohner untereinander tätigen.

Ein weitgehend eigenständiges und autoloses La Puntilla wäre also keineswegs zu Stagnation verdammt. Im Gegenteil: Befreit von der Last eines kostspieligen Verkehrs- und Pendlersystems, könnte es die städtischen Verschönerungsaktivitäten bescheidener mittelalterlicher Städte nachahmen: Diese konnten nicht deshalb Kathedralen, Universitäten, Rathäuser bauen und ihre mit Marmor gepflasterten Plätze mit Brunnen schmücken, weil sie Zentren des internationalen Handels waren; das waren nur ganz wenige Städte. Sie konnten sich diese öffentlichen Ausgaben vielmehr leisten wegen des günstigen Lebens in dicht bevölkerten Stadtvierteln und wegen der Ersparnisse, über die eine Gesellschaft vor der Heraufkunft dessen verfügte, was Professor Anatol Murad bereits zu einer Zeit „die Geißel des Automobilismus" nannte, als die übrigen Propheten diese Geißel noch für ein Symbol des Fortschritts hielten.

El Mundo, 28. Juli 1973

Die Saat für einen Kern legen

Die Bedeutung von Schönheit. Der Sexappeal einer Stadt. Anatomie der Planung. Funktionale Atonalität. Das magnetische Zentrum einer Kommune. Notwendige Grenzen. Romulus und seine Mauer. Entwicklung durch Implosion. Verfall durch Explosion. Kernstrukturen: Kneipe, Kirche, Rathaus.

In der vorangegangenen Kolumne habe ich behauptet: Wenn man La Puntilla zu einer eigenständigen Stadt umgestaltet statt zu einem Wohnungsbauprojekt oder einem riesigen Parkplatz, könnte es eine Bevölkerung beherbergen, die nicht nur groß und vielfältig genug ist, um eine hochgradig eigenständige Wirtschaftseinheit zu bilden; die fehlende Belastung durch Pendlerkosten würde sie auch so wohlhabend machen, daß sie sich den Luxus städtischer Verschönerung in Renaissancemanier leisten könnte. Und genau dieser scheinbare Nebeneffekt enthält die Antwort auf die zweite Frage, die ich gestellt habe: Könnte der Umbau La Puntillas zu einer weitgehend autonomen Kommune nicht nur die Probleme der dortigen Bevölkerung lösen, sondern auch zur Lösung der allgemeineren Probleme des angrenzenden Ballungsraums beitragen?

Daran kann überhaupt kein Zweifel bestehen. Eine Metropole darf nicht nur eine Stadt sein, wie ich schon des öfteren betont habe. Sie muß vielmehr eine Föderation von Städten sein; keine Kommune, sondern eine Gemeinschaft von Gemeinden. Wenn jedoch eine föderale Struktur den Stau wirkungsvoll bekämpfen und den Verkehr verteilen soll, dann muß sie mehr sein als das. Sie darf nicht nur eine Gemeinschaft von Gemeinden sein, sondern eine Gemeinschaft wunderschöner Gemeinden; nicht nur eine Föderation von Städten, sondern eine Föderation von schönen Städten. Denn nur wenn die Schönheit in der Nähe der dort lebenden Menschen ist, wird sie verhindern, daß die Bürger ständig überall in der Gegend herumschwirren auf der Suche nach den verstreuten Teilen.

Deshalb ist die Fähigkeit La Puntillas, sich dank der geringen Kosten einer dichten und weitgehend eigenständigen Lebensweise mit eigenen Mitteln zu verschönern, nicht nebensächlich, sondern ganz zentral für die Probleme, die seine Umgestaltung lösen soll. Sie ist nicht nur die Voraussetzung für die eigenen Fußgängerdimensionen; sie wird auch im übrigen Ballungsraum einen Großteil des Pendlerverkehrs von den Straßen und Autobahnen fernhalten.

Wie aber schafft man Schönheit? Um diese Frage zu beantworten, will ich wiederholen, was ich in einer früheren Kolumne gesagt habe, nämlich daß wir uns zunächst bewußt machen müssen, daß es zwei Arten von Schönheit gibt, die in einer Stadt eine Rolle spielen: architektonische Schönheit und urbane Schönheit. Erstere findet ihren Ausdruck im Stil einzelner Gebäude; letztere in der organischen Anordnung, in der diese wie die Organe des menschlichen Körpers in Relation zueinander gesetzt sind. Urbane Schönheit ist oft auch dort vorhanden, wo architektonische Schönheit fehlt, so wie die Schönheit einer Frau mitunter auch dann strahlt, wenn ihre individuellen Merkmale nicht schön sind. Wir sprechen dann von ihrem Sexappeal.

Genauso verhält es sich mit der *urbanen* Schönheit. Sie ist sozusagen der Sexappeal der Kommune. Sie sorgt für das Aufregende des Stadtlebens ebenso wie für das Magnetfeld, das die Stadtbewohner davon abhält, sich in der galaktischen Weite des außerhalb der Stadtmauern gelegenen Raums zu verlieren. Im brodelnden Mischmasch der Slums ist sie stets vorhanden, während sie in den gepflegten Wohnanlagen moderner Ballungsräume fast immer fehlt.

Für die ästhetische Entwicklung La Puntillas braucht man deshalb sowohl Architekten als auch Stadtplaner. Letztere müssen seine anatomische Struktur entwerfen, erstere seine individuellen Merkmale. Und da die Funktionen der beiden so unterschiedlich sind wie die von plastischem Chirurgen und Internisten, können sie nur in den allerseltensten Fällen von ein und derselben Person ausgeübt werden. Denn wenn der Architekt in ihm vorherrscht, wird er seine Gebäude wie in Brasilia wie Monumente behandeln, die inmitten geräumiger Umgebungen gut sichtbar und mit großzügigen Zufahrten auf Podeste gestellt werden – das ist das Markenzeichen von Ausstellungsgeländen, negiert jedoch die überraschungsgeladene, anarchische Beengtheit, die das Wesen der Stadt ausmacht. Und wenn der Planer in ihm vorherrscht, wird er die funktionale Atonalität und innere Nacktheit der Struktur so sehr betonen, daß dabei weder eine Stadt noch ein Ausstellungsgelände herauskommt, sondern ein lebloser, benzingetriebener Automat, der alles hat außer Gefühl und Pissoirs.

Wenn also La Puntilla als weitgehend selbständige, den Verkehr absorbierende und nicht Verkehr produzierende Kommune von architektonischer wie urbaner Schönheit erstehen soll, mögen die Architekten sich auf das beschränken, was sie können – das Entwerfen von Gebäuden; und die Planer mögen sich auf die Anatomie konzentrieren – den Entwurf einer gesunden Stadtstruktur. Letztere müssen sich keineswegs mit *umfassender* Planung verlustieren, die üblicherweise so viele Details ausarbeitet, daß sie meist nicht in der Lage ist, diese dann auch in die passende organische Form einzufügen. Alles, was man braucht, ist *Kernplanung*, die nur zwei grundlegende Aufgaben hat: 1. Sie muß das Magnetzentrum einer Kommune festlegen, das ihre Kernstrukturen enthält und den Großteil der ökonomischen, politischen und geselligen Bewegungen nach innen lenkt; 2. sie muß diese energiegeladenen, nach innen gerichteten Bewegungen verstärken, indem sie die äußeren Grenzen festlegt, über die die Stadt nicht hinauswuchern kann, und damit das gefürchtete Geschwür peripheren Verfalls verhindert.

Als Romulus die berühmteste aller Städte gründete, tat er nichts weiter, als einen noch leeren Raum mit Mauern zu umgeben. Den Rest überließ er den Kräften, die durch *Im*plosion freigesetzt werden; diese konzentriert soziale Energie wie in einem Schnellkochtopf und schafft organische Formen in Reaktion nicht auf Vorgaben, sondern auf die zufälligen Interaktionen der Bewohner, die ihren Geschäften, Vergnügungen und allem übrigen nachgehen. Die Menschen, die nach innen Richtung Zentrum drängten und vom äußeren Ring unveränderlicher, in Fels und Stein gehauener Grenzen zurückprallten, schufen selbst das Gassengewirr und die Plätze, die Durchgänge und Abkürzungen, die man brauchte, um Läden, Büros, Tempel und Gasthäuser miteinander zu verbinden, bis alles an den Ort gequetscht war, an den es organisch gehörte. Das steht in deutlichem Gegensatz zur modernen Form des Wachstums durch *Ex*plosion; statt die urbane Form zu schaffen und zu bewahren, zerstört sie sie, indem sie die Kernaufgabe einer Stadt über die riesige Weite des extramuralen Raums verstreut, bis ihre Bruchstücke entlang stetig weiter zurückweichender Peripherien herumliegen, wohin sie organisch *gar nicht* gehören.

La Puntilla hat heute den großen Vorteil, daß die Grenzen seines extramuralen Wachstums durch Explosion nicht erst gesetzt werden müssen. Sie stehen schon lange fest. An drei Seiten sind sie durch das sanft gewellte Wasser der Bucht von San Juan vorgegeben; und an der vierten Seite existieren sie in Gestalt der imposanten historischen Mauern, von denen die alte Hauptstadt würdevoll und aufmerksam wie von einem blumengeschmückten Balkon hinabblickt. Um La Puntilla mit urbaner Schönheit zu versehen – dem anziehenden Sexappeal, der verhindert, daß die Bewohner die Straßen der übrigen Stadt verstopfen –, muß ein Planer angesichts dessen einzig und allein festlegen, wo der zentrale Platz liegen soll, um den herum sich die Kernstrukturen der Kommune gruppieren: Kirche, Gasthaus, Rathaus. Alles andere kann man getrost den eingeschlossenen Kräften überlassen, die Form schaffen, indem sie gegeneinander und gegen die Mauern des kommunalen Schnellkochtopfs prallen.

El Mundo, 4. August 1973

Der Glockenturm

Die Stadt als Föderation von Plätzen. Die Lage des Kernplatzes. Der Beginn des Jobs für den Architekten. Industrialisierung vs. Denkmalschutz. Elektrischer Strom, Telephon, Kanalisation. Stil der Dauerhaftigkeit. Von schattenspendenden Bäumen geprägte Realität. Das Markenzeichen einer Kommune. Keine Zweckbauten. Über den Dächern. Campanile, Eiffelturm, Akropolis. Der Glöckner von Nôtre-Dame. Romantiker? Aber ja.

Wie gesagt: Alles, was der Stadtplaner in La Puntilla tun muß, wenn die Gegend als kleine, eigenständige Stadt wiederaufgebaut werden soll, ist, ihre beiden grundlegenden Merkmale festzulegen: ihre physischen Grenzen und den Ort des zentralen Platzes, um den herum sich ihre Kernstrukturen gruppieren sollen – Kirche, Gasthaus, Rathaus. Alles andere kann man den natürlichen Kräften überlassen, die durch die zufälligen Interaktionen der Bewohner selbst freigesetzt werden.

Da die Grenzen La Puntillas bereits feststehen, ist die Aufgabe des Planers darauf beschränkt, den Kernplatz festzulegen. Natürlich muß es viele Plätze geben. Denn so wie eine gesunde Metropole eine Föderation von Städten sein sollte, sollte eine gesunde Stadt eine Föderation von Plätzen sein, deren verdoppelnde und nicht komplementäre Funktionen das sicherste Mittel sind, um Verkehrsstaus zu vermeiden und den Verkehr gleichmäßig über das gesamte Gebiet zu verteilen. Doch da diese sekundären Plätze gewöhnlich spontan in Reaktion auf die normalen Ströme der urbanen Aktivitäten entstehen, muß sich der Planer um sie nicht weiter kümmern. Worüber er entscheiden muß, ist: Wo soll sich der Kernplatz befinden?

Normalerweise sollte er in der Nähe des Zentrums einer Kommune liegen. Doch in einer vom Wasser umgebenen Stadt liegt sein natürlicher Ort wie in Venedig an der Peripherie, am Wasser, was sicherstellt, daß er von allen Seiten leicht zugänglich ist. Im Falle von La Puntilla empfiehlt sich das ganz besonders, denn dessen Territorium ist so klein, daß sogar Orte entlang der Peripherie am Wasser praktisch gleich weit von allen anderen Lokalitäten entfernt sind.

Doch um La Puntillas eigenständige Identität zu stärken, sollte sein Kernplatz nicht nur am Wasser liegen; er sollte sich auch an dem Punkt befinden, der am weitesten von seiner Grenze zur Altstadt von San Juan entfernt ist, also ganz an der Spitze, die über die Bucht Richtung Catano ragt. Da der Kernplatz der Ort ist, auf den hin die meisten Bewegungen in einer Kommune ausgerichtet sind, würde dies auf doppelte Weise sicherstellen, daß der lokal erzeugte Verkehr auch durch La Puntillas eigene Adern zirkuliert und nicht vom viel stärkeren Gravitationsfeld des verstopften Rests der Metropole absorbiert wird.

Damit endet die Aufgabe des Planers, und die Arbeit des Architekten beginnt. Ähnlich wie der Stadtplaner steht auch der Stadtarchitekt nur vor zwei Hauptproblemen: Er muss den *allgemeinen* architektonischen Stil der Kommune festlegen und über den *besonderen* Stil der Kernstrukturen entscheiden, deren Funktion darin besteht, die Identität einer Stadt zum Ausdruck zu bringen und bei ihren Bewohnern das heitere Gefühl einer gemeinsamen Erfahrung zu erzeugen.

Was La Puntillas allgemeinen Stil angeht, so scheint es naheliegend, daß sich darin das mediterrane spanische Erbe des Landes spiegeln sollte. Es macht gleichermaßen wenig Sinn, sein Aussehen dem modernen Industrialismus anzupassen oder es im gotischen Stil des deutschen Mittelalters mit seinen spitzen Dächern wiederaufzubauen. Genauso wenig sinnvoll ist es, es in eine impressionistische Abstraktion des alten San Juan zu verwandeln, wie dies der Bostoner Stadtplaner Jan Wampler vorgeschlagen hat, dessen preisgekrönter Entwurf für San Juan das war, was Picassos „Guernica" für das wirkliche Guernica war – ein Ausstellungsstück für eine Galerie, aber kein Lebensraum für Menschen.

Das heißt jedoch nicht, daß La Puntilla nicht über die neuesten Errungenschaften der Moderne verfügen sollte wie Bäder, Telephone, elektrischen Strom, Aufzüge, Fernsehen oder Kanalisation, so wie ja auch die altmodische urbane Gestaltung des brandneuen La Tropez in Frankreich keineswegs die fortschrittlichsten Gerätschaften, welche die moderne Technik zu bieten hat, ausschloß. Es bedeutet vielmehr, daß sein architektonischer Stil weder das Alte noch das Neue widerspiegeln sollte, sondern das Dauerhafte. Er sollte nicht das hechelnde Tempo des industriellen Wandels zum Ausdruck bringen, sondern das langsame Momentum von Geschichte, Tradition und Kontinuität. La Puntilla darf kein Wohnungsbauprojekt sein, sondern muß eine kleine Stadt sein, die kein impressionistisches *Bild* von San Juan bietet, sondern die typisch puertoricanische, von Balkonen und schattenspendenden Bäumen geprägte *Realität*. Seine Häuser dürfen nicht in die Höhe schießen, sondern sollen von mittlerer Höhe sein, voller Innenhöfe, und an lauschige kleine Plätze grenzen, die wie Perlen an einer Schnur von einem Netzwerk lauschiger, enger, nur für Fußgänger geeigneter Straßen zusammengehalten werden, welche zum Wasser und entlang des Wassers fließen, bis sie aus allen Richtungen am glänzenden Zentralplatz zusammenkommen.

Das bedeutet jedoch wiederum nicht, daß La Puntilla wie San Juan oder irgendeine andere puertoricanische Stadt aussehen sollte. Es sollte im *allgemeinen* Stil des Landes wiederaufgebaut werden. Aber es sollte keine Kopie anderer Städte sein, so wie ja auch ein Mädchen kein Duplikat eines anderes Mädchens ist, nur weil beide einen Minirock tragen. Es ist vielmehr sogar von entscheidender Bedeutung, daß es über die allgemeine nationale Ähnlichkeit hinaus einen markanten Unterschied schafft, so daß seine Bewohner die gemeinsame emotionale Bindung entwickeln können, die ihre Bewegungen nach innen richtet und aufs Zufußgehen beschränkt.

Und genau das ist die zweite Aufgabe des Stadtarchitekten. Während der Planer die *Lage* der Kernstrukturen festlegen muß, muß der Architekt ihnen die *Form* geben, die fortan als Signatur der Kommune dient und die Identität zum Ausdruck bringt, durch welche sie ein eigenes Leben führen kann.

Um ihren Zweck zu erfüllen, müssen die Kernstrukturen zwei Eigenschaften aufweisen. Sie müssen sich über die Dächer und das Straßengewirr erheben und dem zurückkehrenden Bewohner deutlich signalisieren, daß er sich in der Nähe des kommunalen Hafens befindet, der sein individuelles Zuhause schützt. Und sie dürfen keine Zweckbauten sein. Es dürfen keine Fabrikschlote, Wassertürme oder Wolkenkratzer sein, die zwar hoch in den Himmel ragen, aber deren erdgebundene materielle Funktion sie nach unten zeigen läßt. Wie der Eiffelturm in Paris, die St. Paul's Cathedral in London, der

Stephansdom in Wien, der Campanile oder die Säulen von San Marco in Venedig, die Festung in Segovia oder die Ruinen der Akropolis in Athen müssen sie nach oben weisen und so die Seele des Bürgers zum mystischen Sitz des Gemeinschaftsgeistes über den Wolken emporheben, wo die Bande gewoben werden, welche die Menschen unten am Boden zusammenhalten. Ganz gleich also, welche Gestalt die Identitätsstrukturen von La Puntilla annehmen: der Teil, der sich über die Skyline erhebt, darf keinem materiellen Zweck dienen, außer vielleicht dem, Fledermäuse und Glocken und den Glöckner von Nôtre-Dame zu beherbergen.*

Ist das Romantik? Natürlich. Das Leben ist romantisch. Sich aus dem Staub zu erheben und zu Staub zurückzukehren ergibt für den Rationalisten keinen Sinn. Der einzige, für den das Leben einen Sinn hat und für den Glockentürme, Ornamente, Verse, Lieder und schöne Städte bedeutungsvoll sind, ist der Romantiker. Und ich will mich nicht dafür entschuldigen, daß ich einer bin.

El Mundo, 11. August 1973

---

* Bei der Zusammenstellung dieses Buches merke ich, daß ich in meiner Kolumne *Modell vs. Stadt* drei Jahre zuvor (19. Januar 1970) praktisch das Gleiche über die Identität einer Stadt gesagt habe. Ich habe aber nicht dort abgeschrieben. Der Absatz entstand vielmehr praktisch mit den gleichen Worten. Statt sie zu streichen, lasse ich sie stehen, so wie Homer das des öfteren getan hat oder wie es Musiker mit dem Leitmotiv tun, als Refrain zum Zwecke der zusätzlichen Betonung.

Den Verkehr absorbieren

Die magnetische Anziehungskraft von Schönheit. Spezifischer Stil. Bögen und Arkaden. Administrative Autonomie. Konföderierte Urbanität. Vom Auto zu den Füßen. Fußgängertum vs. Nahverkehr. Allroundstadt und Universitätsstadt für spezielle Zwecke. Heimat aller Schichten. Cafés, Uferpromenade, Fischläden, Glockenturm. Bierbrauende Förderer. Die Bulldozer der Regierung.

Ich habe stets betont: Wenn La Puntilla die Probleme des Großraums San Juan reduzieren und nicht vergrößern soll, muß es zu einer kleinen, eigenständigen Stadt umgebaut werden und nicht zu einer komplementären Unterabteilung einer riesigen urbanen Masse.

Und ich habe auch betont: Wenn es eine Stadt sein soll, muß die Bevölkerung so vielfältig sein, daß sie weitgehend eigenständig ist, und müssen ihre Strukturen so schön sein, daß die Bewohner davon abgehalten werden, ständig in ihr Auto zu springen und anderswo nach ästhetischer Befriedigung zu suchen. Zu diesem Zweck muß sie sowohl mit urbaner wie mit architektonischer Schönheit ausgestattet sein – mit urbaner Schönheit, die in ihrer gesunden organischen Struktur zum Ausdruck kommt; und mit architektonischer Schönheit, die sich äußert (a) im *allgemeinen* Stil, der dafür sorgt, daß sie der hispanischen Eleganz des Landes entspricht, und (b) im *spezifischen* Stil ihrer „Kernstrukturen", die ihr wie der Eiffelturm in Paris, der Koloß im antiken Rhodos oder der Gateway Arch in St. Louis ihre Identität verleihen.

Doch auch das reicht noch nicht, um La Puntilla das unabhängige Leben zu verschaffen, das es benötigt, wenn es den Stau im Großraum San Juan verringern und nicht noch vergrößern will. Zu diesem Zweck muß es letztlich nicht nur über eine architektonische, sondern auch über eine politische Identität verfügen. Es muß sein eigenes Oberhaupt haben. Seine Autonomie muß nicht nur ökonomischer, sondern auch administrativer Art sein. Denn wenn die grundlegenden Entscheidungen kommunalen Daseins nicht von den eigenen Bürgern getroffen werden können, werden sie kein Interesse daran haben, die Seele oder das Aussehen ihres Gemeinwesens zu gestalten. Sie werden nur abstrakte Posten in den Büchern eines fernen Herrn sein, der sie von außen regiert. Deshalb muß La Puntilla ähnlich wie die verschiedenen Arrondissements in Paris seinen eigenen Stadtrat, seinen eigenen Bürgermeister, seine eigene Pfarrei, seine eigenen Schulen, seine eigenen Gerichte haben.

Aber damit mich unser tatkräftiges Stadtoberhaupt nicht der Anstiftung zum Landesverrat verdächtigt, sei gesagt: Damit ist keine Abspaltung von San Juan gemeint. Gemeint ist damit nur ein Wandel von einem zentralisierten Verhältnis, das in La Puntillas beispielloser Lage lediglich einen Parkplatz sieht, hin zu einer föderalen Beziehung, die ein beträchtliches Maß an Verwaltungsaufgaben von der Metropolregierung, für die sie zu groß sind, auf die eigenen Behörden überträgt, die sie aufgrund von La Puntillas geringer Größe leicht bewältigen können. Mit anderen Worten: Politische Autonomisierung und Föderalisierung werden den Bürgermeister von San Juan nicht vertreiben. Sie werden ihm vielmehr eine Menge Arbeit abnehmen, seine übrige Arbeit effizienter machen und ihn in den ehrwürdigeren Stand eines Oberbürgermeisters erheben.

Doch der Prozeß der Kommunalisierung sollte natürlich nicht auf La Puntilla beschränkt bleiben, das den Vorteil hat, von Grund auf neu erbaut zu werden. Er muß auf all die anderen, hier nicht näher genannten identitätslosen Gegenden des Großraums San Juan ausgedehnt werden. Dazu muß man nur in jeder die Saat für Kernplätze und Identitätsstrukturen legen, die den Löwenanteil der täglichen urbanen Bewegungen anziehen und damit die einzige Möglichkeit darstellen, den Verkehrsdruck zu verringern, indem sie den Durchschnittsbürger vom Auto quasi wieder auf die eigenen Füße stellen. Ein schnelles Nahverkehrssystem wird ihn zwar auch vom Auto wegbringen, aber in die andere Richtung: zu Fahrzeugen, die noch schneller unterwegs sind und damit den Fußgängersinn urbanen Daseins noch weiter zerstören.

Ein letzter Punkt noch: Die Tatsache, daß La Puntilla als kleine Stadt innerhalb einer Föderation von Städten, versehen mit einem hohem Maß an Eigenständigkeit, wiederaufgebaut werden sollte, bedeutet nicht, daß sie nicht zugleich einem speziellen Zweck dienen kann, der über ihre Grenzen hinausgeht. Sie könnte zum Beispiel Sitz der Graduiertenkollegs der Universität sein, deren Studentenschaft naturgemäß nur von begrenzter Größe ist, oder die Juristische Fakultät oder Ricardo Alegrias schon erwähntes Graduierteninstitut für puertoricanische Studien beherbergen, an dem auf dem amerikanischen Festland so viel Interesse besteht. Oder sie könnte ein Verlagszentrum sein. Das Entscheidende dabei ist, daß La Puntilla einem speziellen Zweck dienen kann, aber keine *Stadt* für einen speziellen Zweck sein darf, denn das würde genau die Verkehrsströme erzeugen und vergrößern, die durch die Autonomie eigentlich ausgetrocknet werden sollen.

Mit anderen Worten: Ganz gleich, ob es dort nun Graduiertenkollegs gibt oder nicht, es darf keine Kollegstadt sein, die nur von Lehrern und Studenten bewohnt ist. Es muß eine Stadt sein, in der Architekten, Bäcker, Mechaniker, Ärzte, Krankenschwestern, Hausmeister, Müllmänner, Kellner, Metzger, Anwälte und natürlich die Lehrer und Studenten der jeweiligen Kollegs leben. Und diese müßten dort wohnen, sie dürften keine Pendler sein.

Ich war versucht, einen Führer von La Puntilla zu verfassen, in dem seine Straßen und Plätze und Ecken beschrieben sind, seine Cafés am Wasser, seine Fischläden, seine schattigen Bänke, seine Bibliothek, seine wunderschönen Gebäude, sein prächtiges Rathaus und seine Hauptkirche am Kernplatz, mit ihrem Glockenturm und dem Geläut, das bei Einbruch der Nacht sanfte Melodien über die Bucht wehen läßt, und seine vielen anderen begeisternden Merkmale – als würde die kleine Stadt schon existieren.

Ich habe jedoch eine bessere Idee. Möge ein bierbrauender oder rumbrennender Förderer der Künste oder vielleicht Ricardo Alegria oder Luis Ferré die begabten Maler Puerto Ricos oder alle Maler einer urbanen Vision, die im Mittelalter so zahlreich waren, einladen, ihre Vorstellung von einem *La Puntilla Reborn* auf die Leinwand zu bringen, und an die Besten von ihnen hübsche Preise verleihen. Keiner von ihnen muß sich um die Umsetzung kümmern. Die wirkliche Aufgabe bleibt dann doch Architekten und Stadtplanern überlassen. Aber das Interesse, das durch einen solchen Wettbewerb geweckt wird, hilft möglicherweise nicht nur den Marken der Sponsoren, sondern könnte auch eine Wiederholung dessen verhindern, was Goethe über Rom sagte: „Was die Barbaren stehen ließen, haben die Baumeister zerstört." Es wäre ein Jammer, wenn unsere Kinder über La Puntilla sagen würden: „Was die Bulldozer stehen ließen, hat unsere Regierung zerstört."

El Mundo, 18. August 1973

Nachschrift zu La Puntilla

Das Paradoxon eines Einheimischen. Die Un-Urbanität breiter Straßen. Enge Straßen und weniger Autos. Vertikales Parken. Autos gemeinsam besitzen. Verringerter Bedarf an Autos. Ästhetische Heilung des Autowahnsinns. Das Luxushotel als Stadtstaat. La Tropez. Portmeirion. Churchills Architektur der Demokratie. Freihafen für Schnaps. Ein schottisches Hochzeitsgeschenk für Norma Acevedo.

Die Kolumnenreihe, die ich über La Puntilla geschrieben habe, bedarf einer Nachschrift. Ein sehr guter Freund aus dem Planungsausschuß Puerto Ricos machte mir das sehr schöne Kompliment, er habe sie interessant gefunden. „Ich weiß sehr wohl", sagte er, „welche Freude es ist, in einer dicht bebauten Stadt wie der Altstadt von San Juan zu leben, denn ich wohne selbst dort. Und wenn Freunde zu Besuch kommen, schwärmen sie immer von der Schönheit und Geräumigkeit meines Hauses. Das Problem ist nur, daß man in einem motorisierten Zeitalter wie dem unseren einen Ort wie das alte San Juan nicht mehr bauen kann. Heute *müssen* die Straßen breit sein..."

„Aber", unterbrach ich ihn, „wenn man breite Straßen baut, dann baut man sie für Autos, und wenn man sie für Autos baut, sind sie gleich wieder zu eng, ganz gleich, wie breit man sie anlegt. Man muß sich am Fußgänger, am Bürger, am Menschen orientieren, nicht am Auto."

Das erinnerte mich daran, daß ich in keiner meiner La-Puntilla-Kolumnen irgendetwas über Autos gesagt habe. Doch so sehr wir Fußgängerdimensionen genießen, so sehr schätzen wir es auch, ein Auto zu haben, selbst wenn es ein Nahverkehrssystem gibt, das einen Großteil der Autos überflüssig macht. Doch genau deshalb würden wir sie umso mehr genießen als Luxusgüter für gelegentliche Ausflüge aufs Land, für Besuche bei Freunden, die uns noch nicht nach La Puntilla gefolgt sind, oder ganz einfach für ein gemächliches, „zweckfreies" Dahinzuckeln durch Straßen und an den Lagunen entlang.

Doch um diese Freuden des Fahrens zu genießen, braucht nicht jeder ein *eigenes* Auto. Das ist der Grund, warum so viel Wert auf die ästhetischen Aspekte des Städtebaus gelegt werden muß: um den Wunsch, über den zu Fuß erreichbaren Radius hinauszufahren, so klein wie möglich zu halten. Und mit dem Wunsch herumzufahren wird sich entsprechend auch die Notwendigkeit, Tausende von Autos zu besitzen, verringern, im Falle von La Puntilla auf, sagen wir, rund 200 bis 300 Autos.

Wenn also nie ein größerer gleichzeitiger Bedarf besteht, wäre es am besten, diese 200 oder 300 Autos gemeinschaftlich zu besitzen und zu unterhalten, wobei jeder berechtigt wäre, sie zu benutzen, wann immer er will. Wenn man gerne einen Volkswagen haben will, dann soll man einen Volkswagen bekommen. Wenn man lieber einen Mercedes oder einen Cadillac will, kann man einen solchen nehmen, wobei die gemeinsame Eigentümerschaft effizienter funktionieren würde, wenn es nur *eine* Art von Auto gibt, und hier vorzugsweise natürlich Kleinwagen. Und da man in La Puntilla selbst kein Auto braucht, ließe sich der ganze Fuhrpark am besten unterbringen, indem man den imposanten Fels hinter dem Gefängnis La Princesa in eine Art mit Arkaden versehenen Kaninchenbau für PKW verwandeln würde, was sich architektonisch ebenso spektakulär wie anmutig bewerkstelligen ließe.

Auf jeden Fall ist das eine Gegend, in der gemeinschaftlicher Besitz dessen, was dann ein Luxusgut wäre, sinnvoll wäre. Und das wiederum würde es erlauben, den Gassen den engen städtischen Charakter zu geben, den breite Straßen einfach nicht haben. Doch es heißt, die Menschen unserer Zeit wollten nicht mehr auf ein eigenes Auto verzichten. Das stimmt, aber nur deshalb, weil es keine Städte mehr gibt, die so wunderbar sind, daß sie die Menschen von den geliebten Straßen fernhalten.

Doch überall dort, wo die Voraussetzung kommunaler Schönheit erfüllt ist, kehren die scheinbar autovernarrten Bürger sofort zum Fußgängertum zurück. Deshalb war das Problem mit den amerikanischen Touristen in Puerto Rico in der Vergangenheit nicht, sie mit genügend Autos zu versorgen, mit denen sie übers Land brausen können. Das Problem war vielmehr, sie aus den Enklaven ihrer Luxushotels wieder auf die Straßen zu bringen. Warum? Weil die Luxushotels von heute zu den modernen Pendants des eigenständigen, auf Fußgänger ausgerichteten Stadtstaats des Mittelalters geworden sind; sie haben vom Gasthaus bis zur Kirche, von Geschäften bis zur Unterhaltung alles in so hübscher und konzentrierter Form zu bieten, daß man nie auch nur einen Fuß nach draußen setzen muß. Alles, was man in Rockefellers Dorado Beach Hotel vielleicht haben will, ist ein hauseigener kleiner Golfkart, mit dem man die Hotelanlagen erkundet. Wie der französische Ausdruck *Hotel de Ville* noch immer signalisiert, wird die Kernstruktur einer Stadt nicht nur als Hotel *bezeichnet*. Die Stadt *ist* seit jeher ein Hotel.

Es sollte deshalb keinen Hinderungsgrund geben, La Puntilla nach dem engen urbanen Muster wiederaufzubauen, das den Charme von Viejo San Juan ausmacht. La Tropez in Frankreich wurde vor gerade einmal zehn Jahren nach diesen Prinzipien von Grund auf errichtet – und was für ein sagenhafter Erfolg ist es geworden. Gleiches gilt für Portmeirion in Wales, dessen neunzig Jahre alter Architekt, Sir Clough Williams Ellis, mir sagte, die Fachleute hätten prophezeit, seine große Vision, ein Hotel in Form eines dicht gebauten italienischen Dorfes zu errichten, werde niemals funktionieren. Sie bezeichneten es als Millionärsspielzeug. „Ich hätte es mir nie leisten können", sagte er. „Es war sein Erfolg, der *mich zum Millionär gemacht hat.*"

Als das britische Unterhaus nach dem Krieg wieder aufgebaut wurde, bestand Churchill darauf, daß es seine „antiquierte" länglich enge Form behalten müsse, wenn man den Debattiergeist der Demokratie bewahren wolle. „Wir formen unsere Gebäude", sagte er in einer seiner eingängigsten Wendungen, „aber später dann formen unsere Gebäude *uns*." Gleiches gilt für den öffentlichen Geschmack. Eingezwängt zwischen Schnellstraßen und eingehüllt in giftige Benzinschwaden, wird er zulassen, daß La Puntilla als Freihafen dient, an dem billiger Fusel verkauft wird, aber, so heißt es, er wird nie erlauben, daß es im erhabenen Stil des alten San Juan wiederaufgebaut wird.

Aber braucht der Planungsausschuß die Erlaubnis des öffentlichen Geschmacks? Er muß einzig und allein La Puntilla im Stil seiner jahrhundertealten Umgebung wieder aufbauen, dann wird er merken, daß der öffentliche Geschmack darin schon bald ebensoviel Ruhm und Ehre erkennt wie die Engländer heute in Churchills beengtem Unterhaus oder die Polen im alten Aussehen ihres nagelneuen Warschau. Den Geist städtischen Lebens so einzufangen, daß er nur deshalb alt wirkt, weil er überzeitlich ist, ist nicht zwangsläufig das gleiche wie ein Disneyland zu bauen.

P.S. Eigentlich wollte ich diese Kolumne einer Sammlung von geflügelten Wendungen widmen wie etwa Sokrates' „Erkenne dich selbst", Goethes „Sei du selbst" und meinem auf eigener Erfahrung beruhenden „Inszeniere dich selbst" und sie wie ein sparsamer Schotte als Hochzeitsgeschenk Norma Avecedo überreichen, einer ehemaligen Studentin von mir, die ebenso brillant wie entzückend ist und heute Vormittag in Mayagües heiratet.

Doch gerade als ich mit meiner Kollektion beginnen wollte, bekam ich einen Brief von Norma von der York University in England, wohin sie mit ihrem Magisterabschluß und dem jungen Mann aus Chile, der, da sie dies liest, ihr Gatte sein wird, zurückkehrte. In diesem Brief schrieb sie: „Ich habe einen Ihrer Artikel über La Puntilla gelesen. Das ist die Art von Artikel, die ich bei Ihnen liebe. Er unterscheidet sich von denen über Marx und... Nun, ich will nicht schon wieder anfangen, Sie zu kritisieren."

Also habe ich mein Vorhaben geändert und überreiche ihr, um auf der sicheren Seite zu sein, mit Dank für die erfrischende Kritik, mit der sie stets meine Seminare belebt hat, eine andere schottische Form von Hochzeitsgeschenk: die letzte meiner La-Puntilla-Kolumnen.

El Mundo, 15. September 1973

Die „Witkars" in Amsterdam

Für das Magazin *Time* (Juni 1979) sehen sie aus wie „eine Kreuzung zwischen einem Golfkart und einem Mondfahrzeug". *Newsweek* (8. April 1974) erinnern sie an eine „trächtige Schildkröte". Den Menschen in Amsterdam erscheint der „Witkar" – ein kleines weißes Elektrofahrzeug, das über zwei Sitze verfügt, batteriebetrieben ist, selbst gesteuert wird und mit bis zu zwanzig Meilen pro Stunde die 2,4 Meilen zwischen strategisch gelegenen Aufladestationen (das Aufladen dauert fünf Minuten) zurücklegt – wie ein „Zylinderhut auf Rädern".

Doch bei all den amüsanten Assoziationen, die der Witkar weckt, könnte er sich, wie es in *Time* heißt, durchaus „als der größte Fortschritt im innerstädtischen Verkehr erweisen, seit Straßenbahnen an die Stelle von Dreirädern traten".

Anders als von mir in meiner La-Puntilla-Kolumne vom 15. September 1973 vorgeschlagen, ist der Witkar mit seiner begrenzten Reichweite für die Fortbewegung im Zentrum gedacht und nicht Gemeinbesitz. Aber er wird einer Kooperative gehören, was meinem Vorschlag durchaus nahe kommt. Er ist nicht käuflich zu erwerben. So berichtet *Newsweek*: Die Flotte, die insgesamt 1.500 Wagen umfassen wird, „kann von Leuten genutzt werden, die der Witkar-Kooperative beitreten und eine Jahresgebühr von 20 US-Dollar zahlen. Steckt man an der Witkar-Station einen speziellen Mitgliederschlüssel in eine Kontrollvorrichtung, wird die Mitgliedschaft von einem Computer überprüft und man bekommt ein Auto. Ist die Spritztour beendet, vermerkt der Computer dies und belastet das Konto des Fahrers mit 3 Cent je Minute.

TEIL IV
Ein erstrebenswertes Herzogtum

Der Herzog von Buen Consejo

Politische Fiktion. Die erstaunliche Lage von Slums. Der Herzog von „Guter Rat". Verschlafene Zuflucht für die Individualität. Die Privatisierung von Entwicklung. Reichtum, Titel und Geschmack als Stimulus. Palast in den Slums. Demonstrative Enthaltsamkeit. Kreatives Schwelgen. Die Klagen der Herzogin. Gesellschaftlicher Nutzen aus privatem Gewinn. Der Stil der Medici. Die Einsparungen durch geringe Größe. Kettenreaktion der Nachahmung. Kein Bedarf an öffentlichen Geldern. Vielfalt an Klassen und Stilen. Der Kopf des Herzogs. Die Geschichte der Kernsaat. Utopische Fiktion? Von Peisistratos bis Venedig. Der Wert der Monarchie.

Ich hege immer wieder einmal den Gedanken, das zu schreiben, was die Deutschen als „Staatsroman" bezeichnen – eine Übung in literarischer Fiktion zu dem Zweck, die Implikationen einer Gesellschaftstheorie zu veranschaulichen. Schauplatz meines geplanten Staatsromans wäre aller Wahrscheinlichkeit nach der völlig überfüllte Slum Buen Consejo, ein Hügel am Rande des Stadtgebiets von San Juan in Puerto Rico. Dieser Ort wurde nicht von Fachleuten vom MIT ausgewählt, sondern von den Slumbewohnern, und deshalb ist er, wenig überraschend, von so überwältigender Schönheit, daß er selbst die höchsten Ansprüche an einen Wohnort und ein geschäftliches Umfeld erfüllen würde. Mit Sicherheit aber hat er mich aus der Planungsmüdigkeit meiner Träume gerissen. Zudem hat er einen unglaublich bezaubernden Namen – Buen Consejo, Guter Rat. Ich habe noch nicht entschieden, welche Art machiavellischer Liebeshandlung ich in die Geschichte einbauen sollte. Von allem übrigen aber habe ich ziemlich klare Vorstellungen. Und vor allem habe ich schon einen Titel: *Der Herzog von Buen Consejo*.

Selbst in seinem gegenwärtigen Zustand besitzt Buen Consejo alles, was eine prächtige Kleinstadt ausmacht, und oft weise ich Besucher darauf hin, die zunächst befremdet, dann belustigt und schließlich hingerissen sind, sobald es ihnen gelingt, unter der scheinbar unappetitlichen Oberfläche die exquisite Schönheit zu erkennen. Die geschäftig summenden Straßen fallen kaskadenartig die Hänge eines steilen Hügels hinab und münden freudig in die Strudel

Dutzender gemütlicher Plätze, die wie blumengeschmückte Balkone über Gullies, Häusern und Tälern hängen. Die Fußpfade, die durch die Bewegung des Lebens entstanden sind, winden sich ganz natürlich nach oben und nach unten, und sie enden oftmals abrupt an kühnen Treppenfluchten, die himmelwärts führen zu eindrucksvoll gelegenen Häusern, die wie exotische Vögel auf schlanken Beinen hoch über den Niederungen von Verkehr und Streit thronen. Die Blicke schweifen über die unterhalb liegenden Nachbargemeinden, über die von Bäumen umgebenen, spiegelglatten Augen rätselhafter Lagunen in der Ferne bis zu der schäumenden, weißen Pferden gleichenden Brandung, bis sie sich in der schimmernden Weite des blauen Ozeans am Horizont verlieren. Die ganze Siedlung ähnelt dem Kegel des Mont St. Michel, San Marino, Fiesole oder, in geringerem Maße, Segovia oder Toledo – wenn man einmal davon absieht, daß es sich um einen elenden Slum handelt. Aber das waren auch die anderen einmal. Und wie die anderen in ihren noch immer dicht bevölkerten Vierteln ist es erfüllt vom Summen warmherziger Menschen, die, von der Sonne gebräunt, vom Winde gekühlt, glücklich in der kooperativen Enge ihrer Gemeinschaft leben und in der Souveränität ihrer Hütten eine verschlafene Zuflucht für ihre Individualität finden.

Doch statt Buen Consejo von der Erdoberfläche zu kratzen und es in einen weiteren bewaldeten Park zu verwandeln, in den außer Vergewaltigern niemand auch nur einen Fuß setzen wird; oder statt jahrzehntelang zu warten, bis eine sozial gesinnte, ängstliche Regierung, die sich schließlich um das ganze Land kümmern muß, den Slum endlich auf der trägen Prioritätenliste eines umfassenden nationalen Plans nach oben hievt und die nötigen Finanzmittel zur Verfügung stellt, träumt mein Staatsroman von einer Regierung, welche die Sanierung dieser spezifischen Kommune – zusammen mit der lokalen und nicht nationalen Entwicklung einer Reihe ähnlicher Kommunen – einem privaten Unternehmer anvertraut.

Grund dafür ist die unausweichliche Tatsache, daß die staatlichen Finanzmittel nicht ausreichen, um gleichzeitig eine so große Zahl von gleichermaßen dringlichen Entwicklungsprogrammen durchzuführen (denn sonst würde natürlich die Regierung selbst diese Aufgabe übernehmen), und daraus folgt, daß der Privatunternehmer, der für Buen Consejo verantwortlich ist, die erwarteten Verbesserungen aus eigener Tasche bezahlen können muß. Oder anders ausgedrückt: Er muß ein bemittelter Mensch, Kapitalist von Format, vielfacher Millionär sein.

Doch trotz des pathetischen Bestrebens, dem Gemeinwohl zu dienen statt auf privaten Gewinn aus zu sein, das unser Massenzeitalter dem verängstigten Völkchen der modernen Wohlfahrtskapitalisten quasi aufgezwungen hat, ist zweifelhaft, ob sich ein Rockefeller oder ein Luis Ferré dazu animieren ließen, eine Aufgabe dieser Größenordnung zu übernehmen. Zwar könnte sie zu seinem Ruf als Wohltäter der Menschheit beitragen, doch er weiß, daß seine Bemühungen noch immer mißbraucht und seine Motive in Zweifel gezogen würden von den Marxisten, den Zynikern, den Politikern, den Wissenschaftlern, den Psychologen, den Nutznießern, den Journalisten, den Konkurrenten, von Chruschtschow, der das Evangelium zitieren würde, und von Adam Smith, dessen Stimme von fern aus seinem Grab aus dem *Wohlstand der Nationen* vorlesen würde. Er bräuchte deshalb einen konkreteren Anreiz als nur die Ehre oder vorgetäuschten Beifall, einen Anreiz, der nicht an sein soziales Verantwortungsgefühl appelliert, sondern sich an die stets verläßlichen, altmodischen menschlichen Triebkräfte des Stolzes, der Eitelkeit und des Eigeninteresses richtet.

Geld würde freilich in diesem Fall aus einer Vielzahl von Gründen nicht funktionieren. Der Staat hat keines zu bieten, der Millionär hat genug davon und würde sich, wenn er sich von der Aussicht auf zusätzliche Reichtümer verlocken lassen *sollte*, vermutlich für profitablere Investitionsobjekte entscheiden als den Bau moderner Unterkünfte für verarmte Slumbewohner. Doch es gibt andere, zwingendere Anreize für das private Interesse. Was ein millionenschwerer Unternehmer vielleicht um einer zusätzlichen Million willen nicht in Angriff nehmen würde, würde er vielleicht, wie England so ertragreich vorgeführt hat, für einen der Eitelkeit schmeichelnden, imposant klingenden Adelstitel tun. Es gibt viele reiche Menschen auf dieser Welt, aber nur wenige von ihnen sind Herzöge. Um also die nötige Begeisterung zu wecken, beschließt die Regierung in meiner Geschichte, nicht nur einen reichen Millionär damit zu beauftragen, das zentrale lokale Entwicklungsprojekt des Romans durchzu-

wenn die Sanierung in deren Fall nicht mehr aus der Privatschatulle des Herzogs finanziert wird. Das wird jedoch ihre rasche Verschönerung nicht behindern. Denn wie die Geschichte schon so oft gezeigt hat, stellen viele Dinge, die außerhalb der finanziellen Möglichkeiten wohlhabender, vereinter, kostspieliger Supermächte liegen, arme Gemeinwesen vor keinerlei Finanzierungsprobleme, solange sie klein sind. Die berühmten Einsparungen durch Größenvorteile – in diesem Fall der geringen Größe – sind alle auf ihrer Seite, denn es besteht von Seiten des Staates kein Bedarf, die Bürger mit durchschnittlich 13,4 Meilen vierspuriger Autobahn pro Kopf auszustatten und sie auch noch finanziell dafür in die Verantwortung zu nehmen.

Doch selbst ein marmorgepflasterter Platz wird nicht reichen, um die ästhetischen Ansprüche der Herzogin zu befriedigen. Seine Durchlaucht wird deshalb als nächsten Schritt die Wellblechhüttennachbarn animieren, ihre Behausungen mit Hilfe entsprechender Subventionen umzubauen, so daß sie von ihrem Material und Stil her zum neuen Umfeld passen. Doch viele werden, angeregt durch sein Vorbild, bereits damit begonnen haben, in Eigeninitiative genau das zu tun, und somit werden die erforderlichen Subventionen dermaßen unbedeutend sein, daß sie kaum ein Loch in die herzogliche Schatzkammer reißen. Benötigt wird weniger finanzielle Unterstützung als vielmehr ästhetische und technische Hilfestellung. Bedenkt man zudem, daß von der neuen Verschönerungswelle von nun an nicht mehr nur der Herzog deutlich spürbar profitiert, sondern jeder, dessen Grundstück an den frisch mit Marmor versehenen Platz grenzt, werden die Anwohner schon aus diesem Grund gerne bereit sein, den Großteil der Sanierungskosten selbst zu tragen. Die einzige Frage dabei ist: Sind sie dazu auch in der Lage? Schließlich sind sie als Slumbewohner noch immer zutiefst arm. Doch sie sind arm, weil sie jahrhundertelang die kostspieligste Entwicklungsressource in Händen hatten, nämlich ihre Arbeitskraft, ohne sie entsprechend nutzen zu können. Wenn sie den Großteil der Kosten tragen, bedeutet das also nur, daß sie endlich die einzige Ware, über die sie bereits im Überfluß verfügen, angemessen zum Einsatz bringen können.

Infolgedessen umfaßt die zweite Phase städtischer Erneuerung zwar nunmehr auch ein hohes Maß an *öffentlicher* Sanierung, doch durchgeführt wird sie wiederum mittels strikt privater Ressourcen, die zudem nicht mehr allein vom Herzog mobilisiert werden, sondern gemeinsam mit seinen aufgerüttelten und gleichermaßen profitierenden Nachbarn. Mit anderen Worten: Aus ökonomischer Sicht ist die zweite Phase sogar weniger problematisch als die erste. Das einzige, was vom Herzog an diesem Punkt verlangt wird, ist, einen relativ geringen Betrag seiner Verschönerungsgelder in den Platz außerhalb seiner Residenz zu investieren. Da sich hier seine eigenen privaten Interessen und die Interessen seiner Nachbarn sowie ihrer beider Interessen und das öffentliche Interesse überschneiden, wird eine Finanzspritze an diesem strategisch wichtigen Ort genügen, um eine Kettenreaktion ergänzender privater Aktivitäten auszulösen, so daß sich der marmorgepflasterte Platz schon bald zu einem echten Stadtkern entwickelt – ohne daß man dafür auch nur einen Cent öffentlicher Gelder anzapfen muß. Und dieser Prozeß wird damit natürlich noch nicht zu Ende sein. Denn sobald der von außen kommende Stimulus, so klein er zu Anfang auch gewesen sein mag, die ungeheuren schlummernden Selbsthilfekräfte freigesetzt hat, wird er sich von Platz zu Platz, von Straße zu Straße ausbreiten, bis vom Slum nichts mehr übrig ist außer seiner exquisiten geographischen Lage. Zudem wird die gesamte umwälzende Entwicklung, beseelt vom Geist der Nachahmung und der Konkurrenz, nicht das ermüdende Ergebnis eines langfristigen, aus penibel aufeinanderfolgenden Phasen bestehenden Plans sein, der feierlich in majestätischer Lethargie vollzogen wird, sondern Resultat einer Reihe kurzer Energieeruptionen, die mit vulkanhaftem Furor an allen Ecken und Ende gleichzeitig ausbrechen.

Die nun einsetzende dritte Entwicklungsphase hat ein anspruchsvolleres Ziel. Sie ergibt sich auf natürliche Weise aus der zweiten Phase und ist in erster Linie damit befaßt, Vielfalt in das tödliche Einheitsschema zu bringen, das nicht nur unausweichliche Folge jeder zentralen Planung ist, sondern auch Hauptmerkmal aller Slums, der Wohlstandsslums genauso wie der Armutsslums. Doch auch hier wird sich wieder zeigen, daß sich das Programm, das Supermächte vielleicht gar nicht bewältigen könnten, im Herzogtum Buen Consejo praktisch von selbst entfaltet und finanziert. Auf die herzoglichen Mittel kann man vielleicht sogar ganz verzichten. Denn der Ausbruch an Aktivitäten, der die zweite Phase belebt hat, hat auch das Einkommensniveau im Herzogtum so weit ansteigen lassen, daß man über die Entwicklungsfinanzen für die dritte Phase verfügt. Und die gleichen Aktivitäten, die für die nötigen Finanzmittel gesorgt haben, haben auch den Boden bereitet, auf dem sich die Vielfalt ausbreiten kann. Denn die Tatsache, daß die Mehrzahl dieser Aktivitäten grundsätzlich unkoordinierten Selbsthilfe- und Laissez-faire-Charakter hat, hat dazu geführt, daß sich allmählich eine Vielzahl verschiedener Geschmäcker, Temperamente und Fertigkeiten herausbildete, und zwar nicht nur in architektonischer, sondern auch in gesellschaftlicher, beruflicher und wirtschaftlicher Hinsicht.

Unter der ästhetischen Führung des Herzog oder wohl eher der Herzogin, aber sonst ausschließlich die eigenen, vielfältigen Interessen verfolgend, haben einige Bürger größer gebaut, manche kleiner. Einige bleiben Arbeiter, andere werden Handwerker. Einige verzeichnen wachsenden Wohlstand, andere hinken hinterher. Im Zuge der zunehmenden geschäftlichen Transaktionen in einer nun nicht mehr lethargischen Kommune werden einige zu Anwälten, andere zu Bankern. Angesichts der Zunahme an persönlichen Beziehungen beschließen einige, Psychoanalytiker zu werden, andere werden Priester. Da zudem die aufstrebende Mittelschicht dem Beispiel der Herzogs folgt, flieht sie nicht wieder in die kostspielige, unstädtische Langeweile der Vororte, sondern betrachtet es als chic, in den Geschäftsräumen zu wohnen. Das fügt dem Bild eine zusätzliche Dimension architektonischer Unterschiede hinzu, insofern nämlich eine Reihe von Häusern so stattlich werden, daß einige von ihnen sogar der herzoglichen Residenz Konkurrenz machen. Der gleiche Prozeß wird auch kirchliche Gebäude erfassen, und die Kirche wird begeistert wieder ihre traditionelle Rolle als Schrittmacherin prächtiger Architektur und als kundiger Förderer der Künste einnehmen. Das wiederum schafft Möglichkeiten für die anarchistische Vielfalt der Künstler. Und Künstler müssen natürlich in Cafés sitzen, die sich der neuen gesellschaftlichen Szenerie anpassen, in vielfältigen Stilformen und in unterschiedlichem Luxus aus dem Boden schießen und damit die letzte der geselligen Annehmlichkeiten hinzufügen, indem sie sich auf die Gehsteige an verkehrsberuhigten Straßen ausbreiten; denn der Autoverkehr ist angesichts der dichten, fußgängerfreundlichen Lebensbedingungen, die als eine der wichtigsten gesellschaftlichen Errungenschaften des ursprünglichen Slums überlebt haben, weitgehend entbehrlich geworden.

All das steht in deutlichem Gegensatz zu den Idealen moderner Planung, die alles daran setzt, Unterschiede nicht zu betonen, sondern einzuebnen. Doch glücklicherweise gehört unser Herzog nicht zu ihren Verfechtern. Er glaubt, eine gute Stadt zeichne sich nicht durch Einheitlichkeit, sondern durch Vielfalt auch; nicht durch Reichtum, sondern durch Fülle; nicht durch ein diffuses Flachland ganz gleich auf welcher Höhe, sondern durch eine Pyramide, die sich von einer genau definierten Basis aus über eine Reihe schmaler werdender Ebenen gen Himmel streckt. Er weiß mit Aristoteles, daß „ein Staat nicht nur aus vielen Menschen besteht, sondern aus ganz verschiedenen Menschen; denn Gleiche bilden keinen Staat. Er ist kein Militärbündnis." Und er stimmt mit Gilbert und Sullivan überein, wenn sie über ein Fest sagen, zu dem nur *Grandes* Zutritt haben: „Wo jeder jemand ist, ist niemand irgendwer."

Nun, da sich die ästhetischen, ökonomischen und materiellen Bedingungen verbessert haben, haben wir die letzte Entwicklungsphase erreicht. In ihr geht es um mehr als nur urbane Erneuerung. Sie ist auf das höchste Ziel ausgerichtet: die Steigerung des Bildungsniveaus im Herzogtum. Das steht erneut im Widerspruch zu gängigen Entwicklungsmustern, die zumeist versuchen, zuerst zu bilden und später dann die materiellen Bedingungen zu verbessern. Doch unser Herzog hat schon längst erkannt, daß eine verfrühte Bildung eine rasche Entwicklung ebenso behindert wie gar keine Bildung. Denn der gebildete Mensch hat höhere Lohnforderungen und andere Bedürfnisse, als sie sich ein zu wenig produktives, unterentwickeltes Gemeinwesen leisten kann. Da eine verfrühte Bildung Forderungen nach einem kommunalen Produkt weckt, das es noch gar nicht gibt, führt sie zwangsläufig zu Frust statt zu Befriedigung; zu einem schmerzlichen Ungleichgewicht statt zu einem neuen Gleichgewicht auf höherem Niveau; zu einem Anstieg der Kosten, während der Fortschritt gerade verlangt, den Gürtel enger zu schnallen und deshalb die Kosten niedrig zu halten; zu Streiks, wo man doch jede Hand brauchen kann.

Doch nun ist die Zeit reif, die kulturelle Krönung der herzoglichen Herrschaft zu schaffen. Wie wir gesehen haben, verlangt eine der wenigen Beschränkungen, die dem Herzog auferlegt sind, daß er und seine Familie ihren Wohnsitz innerhalb der Grenzen des Herzogtums haben. Das macht es Seiner Durchlaucht unmöglich, seine Kinder aus Buen Consejo wegzuschicken, sobald sie im schulpflichtigen Alter sind. Da er gleichwohl sehr darauf bedacht ist, ihnen die bestmögliche Schulbildung zukommen zu lassen, hat er keine andere Wahl, als auf eigene Kosten die besten Lehrer ins Herzogtum zu bringen. Und da er ebenso darauf bedacht ist, seine Kinder so normal wie möglich aufwachsen zu lassen, wird er sich nicht damit zufrieden geben, die besten Lehrer zu importieren. Er wird sie auch in angemessen eingerichteten und ausgestatteten Schulen unterbringen, zu denen auch die Kinder der Ärmsten kostenlosen Zugang haben. Das wird den Wohlhabenden ein gewisses Maß an demokratischer Härte vermitteln und den Armen ein wenig vom feinen Geschmack des Adels, bis alle sozialen Schichten in Buen Consejo kulturell so anspruchsvoll und wirtschaftlich so stark geworden sind, daß sie nicht nur selbst die besten Lehrer hervorbringen, sondern auch die abschließende und höchste Schicht der Kulturproduzenten: Philosophen, Dichter, Komponisten, aber auch das kleine Konzerthaus und das intime Theater, in dem sie auftreten können.

Und selbst hier, auf der höchsten Ebene, werden die Kosten all dessen ein zu vernachlässigendes Problem darstellen. Ein erster Anstoß kommt aus der Privatschatulle des Herzogs, der dieses Geld aus Gründen rein persönlicher Verbesserung aufbringt, doch in den nachfolgenden und anspruchsvolleren Phasen kann die Kommune selbst leicht die Kosten tragen, nicht weil sie dann schon so viel produziert, sondern weil – wie das bei allen kleinen Unternehmen der Fall ist – die laufenden Kosten dafür so gering sind. Mit anderen Worten: Buen Consejo wird seine Kultur schlicht und einfach deshalb finanzieren können, weil es zweierlei *nicht* finanzieren muß: (a) die Art von bürokratielastiger Regierungsmaschinerie, die man braucht, um eine große Gesellschaft mit all ihren Extremformen zusammenzuhalten; und (b) das prohibitiv teure Straßennetz, das man braucht, um zu verhindern, daß sich die Gesellschaft selbst aus dem Auge verliert, ganz zu schweigen von all den arm machenden und privat getragenen Zusatzkosten, die ein solches Straßennetz mit sich bringt: die endlos hin und her rasenden Autos, die vergeblich versuchen, mit den immer weiter zunehmenden technologischen Entfernungen Schritt zu halten; die Reparaturen, die nötig sind, um die Autos in Schuß zu halten; und das Benzin, das ihren unstillbaren Durst stillt.

Reine Utopie? Keineswegs! Denn eine Utopie verspricht die Beseitigung allen Elends. Buen Consejo hingegen hat die absolut realistischen Vorteile geringer Größe zu bieten. Da es so viel kleiner ist als die meisten modernen politischen Gemeinwesen, wird es ganz natürlich die Probleme des Zusammenlebens auf ein *Minimum reduzieren*. Und es wird sie im geometrischen Maßstab minimieren, so daß sie eher der kleinen Statur des Menschen entsprechen. Aber es wird keines dieser Probleme lösen, das heißt, keines außer dem Hauptproblem unserer Zeit, nämlich das Problem übermäßiger Größe. Auf völlig unutopische Weise akzeptiert es die Unvollkommenheiten von Mensch und Gesellschaft, so wie sie sind.

Es wird somit weiterhin ein gewisse Maß an Krankheit, Leidenschaft, Frust, Intrige, Gewalt, Idiotie und Betrügerei geben. Und soweit ich das bisher überblicke, endet meine Geschichte möglicherweise mit einer saturierten Bürgerschaft, die zu den soliden alten Formen einer wahrhaft republikanischen Regierung zurückkehrt und den Herzog unehrenhaft entläßt, sobald er seine wichtige Entwicklungsfunktion erfüllt hat, ihn vielleicht sogar enthauptet und in einer würdevollen Zeremonie seiner ertragreichen Herrschaft gedenkt, indem sie eine nette Kneipe oder einen Nachtclub nach ihm benennt (und damit dem Vorbild der zurückhaltenden Engländer folgt, die, wie Voltaire einmal bemerkte, sich ihren Vergnügungen traurig widmen, während sie nicht selten gewillt scheinen, ihre Hinrichtungen mit Freude aufzunehmen).

Doch in dieser Hinsicht bin ich, ganz unpuritanisch, noch nicht festgelegt. Vielleicht behalte ich den Herzog auch. Schließlich ist gerade in den turbulenten Zeiten wirtschaftlicher Entwicklung und sozialen Wandels eine der stärksten Bindungskräfte ein persönliches, herzogliches, monarchisches Zentrum, eine paternalistische Vaterfigur, die Vertrauen ebenso ausstrahlt wie die nötige Autorität und die regiert, indem sie ein Beispiel gibt und nicht durch Dekrete das Verhalten vorschreibt. Das macht viele Dinge deutlich einfacher und billiger. Wie wir gesehen haben, muß unser Herzog nur eines tun, wenn er ein anschließend selbsttragendes Bedürfnis nach allgemeiner Bildung wecken will: Er muß dafür sorgen, daß sein Volk Zeuge seiner Bildungsbemühungen in der eigenen Familie wird. Um den Menschen ein Gefühl für Eleganz und Stil zu vermitteln, sind die beispielgebenden Gewohnheiten der Herzogin mindestens so effektiv wie kostspielige Kurse in Sachen Geschmack. Um bei den Menschen Begeisterung für das Theater und die Künste zu wecken, muß der Herzog nur selbst demonstrativ sein Interesse daran zeigen, wie dies der Herzog von Weimar zu Goethes Zeiten tat; das hatte zur Folge, daß jeder Kutscher und jedes Dienstmädchen mit den jüngsten literarischen Errungenschaften so vertraut war, wie sie das heute mit dem „Pop" wären. Und um die wirtschaftliche Entwicklung voranzutreiben, muß er nur demonstrativ und ausgiebig konsumieren, was gesellschaftlich alles andere als anstößig ist und die gleiche Funktion erfüllt wie eine nationale Messe, eine Modenschau oder ein Versandkatalog. Die Menschen erfahren aus dem strategisch günstigsten Zentrum, was los ist und was produziert wird. Monarchische Symbole sind denn auch als Instrumente effizienter Geschäftstätigkeit so wertvoll, daß der *Economist* vor kurzem im Zuge eines Überblicks über amerikanische Werbung zu dem Schluß kam, kein Land sei der Krone so sehr ergeben wie die USA.

Also behalte ich den Herzog vielleicht lieber bis zum Happy End, statt Buen Consejo wieder in den Schoß der Republik mit ihren höchst ehrenwerten Regeln zurückkehren zu lassen. Aber diese Regeln neigen dazu, jeden offiziellen Vertreter des Staates, der dabei beobachtet wird, wie er aus seinem Dienstwagen steigt und einen Nachtclub betritt, so lange zu jagen, bis er entweder zurücktritt oder in das schattenhafte Dasein demonstrativer Abstinenz abtaucht. Was ihn möglicherweise fürs Kloster qualifiziert. Doch in Zeiten der Entwicklung ist das wirtschaftlich ungefähr so nützlich wie eine genügsame Regierung, die sich auf die Sterilität des Sparens statt aufs Ausgeben verlegt.

Alles Fiktion? Ich habe es als Staatsroman bezeichnet. Was Buen Consejo angeht, handelt es sich in der Tat um einen Roman mitsamt seinen Helden und Heldentaten, die leider kaum Ähnlichkeiten mit lebenden Personen oder Ereignissen aufweisen. Doch darüber hinaus hat es damit nichts zu tun. Es illustriert nicht Theorie, sondern Geschichte, wie sie sich in einer Vielzahl von Dörfern, Städten und Stadtstaaten überall in Europa während des Mittelalters abgespielt hat oder in den unzähligen Stadtgründungen der griechischen und phönizischen Antike. Sie alle entwickelten sich aus der Saat eines Kerns und weniger durch umfassende Planung. Und sie haben sich auch lange Zeit auf stagnierendem Niveau jenseits ihrer eigentlichen Möglichkeiten bewegt und darauf gehofft, es möge ihnen jemand zu Hilfe kommen, bis sie schließlich einem Tyrannen, einem Herrn, einem adligen Kaufmann, einem Herzog, einem Fürsten, einem König in die Hände fielen, der entschied, daß man keine ausgeklügelte ökonomische Wachstumsmaschinerie brauchte, sondern ein wenig ästhetischen Ehrgeiz; daß man am schnellsten vorankam, wenn man nicht auf Hilfe von außen wartete, sondern die Dinge selbst anpackte; daß es nicht so ist, daß Kommunen nicht bauen können, weil sie arm sind, sondern daß sie arm sind, weil die Kerle nicht bauen wollen; daß man nicht zunächst für Einheit sorgen muß, bevor man sich Luxusgüter leisten kann, sondern daß man ein gewisses Niveau an Luxus erreicht haben muß, bevor man sich das teure Parasitentum einer Union leisten kann.

So einfach ist die Ökonomie der Entwicklung im lokalen statt im nationalen oder internationalen Maßstab und so groß ist der Skalenvorteil einer geringen Größe, daß in der Vergangenheit in einer Reihe erbittert konkurrierender Städte oftmals eine ganze Reihe von „Saatlegern" zur gleichen Zeit auftauchte und mehrmals in einer Kettenreaktion sich vervielfältigender Anstrengungen schaffte, was keine Großmacht mit vereinten Kräften je hätte bewerkstelligen können: Ihr Territorium, oftmals in der kurzen kreativen Zeitspanne einer einzigen Generation, von einem Slum zu einer marmornen Stadt zu machen. Als Peisistratos die Bühne betrat, bestand Athen großteils aus Bruchbuden. Als er sie verließ, stand dort eine Phalanx an Gebäuden, über deren unsterbliche Schönheit der Dichter Pausanias noch mehrere Jahrhunderte später schreiben konnte, sie hätten schon altehrwürdig ausgesehen, als sie noch ganz neu waren. Nun, da sie alt seien, sähen sie noch immer neu aus. Auch Venedig begann seine funkelnde Karriere als völlig heruntergekommener Slum. Wäre es dem modernen Rat gefolgt und hätte mit seiner Entwicklung gewartet, bis Italien geeint, die Vereinten Nationen begründet und der Gemeinsame Markt etabliert waren, wäre es noch heute ein Slum. Gleiches gälte für Urbino, Perugia, Assisi, Parma, Padua und für den Großteil des prachtvollen Rests. Indem Venedig nach Art des Herzogs von Buen Consejo eigenständig voranging, verstieß es gegen alle Prinzipien vernünftiger Politik, Ökonomie, Planung, Standorttheorie, ja sogar des gesunden Menschenverstands. Denn wer außer einem Narren oder einem exzentrischen Slumbewohner würde inmitten einer Lagune bauen? Aber dem haben wir Venedig zu verdanken.

The San Juan Review, August 1964

There is No Gold in Them Thar' Hills

Die Kritik von Lewis. Würde ich Hitler wegen seiner Städte vergeben? Der Sonderfall Kuba. Mörder, die regieren. Der Anarchismus des Verfassers. Seine Romantik. Die mittelalterlichen Wohnungsstandards in den Cotswolds. Adlige, Kirche, Gastwirte und Slumbewohner als Fachleute für gute Lagen. Was ist ein Sklave? Lohnsklaverei in der Goldmine. Griechische Städte als Produkt der Sklaverei. Diogenes: der Sklave als Herr. Twiggy vs. Mae West. *The City of Man*. Das Ferment der Kleinheit. Stratford, Oxford, Oberndorf. Die Freude des Verfassers an der Bissigkeit des Kritikers.

Das Problem an Gordon Lewis' Besprechung von *The City of Man* (University of Puerto Rico Press, San Juan 1976) ist, daß ich wie so oft nicht weiß, wen er damit attackiert – das Objekt seiner Kritik oder sich selbst. Er wirft mir vor, ich würde mich nur selektiv auf die Vergangenheit berufen und mir nur die Fakten herauspicken, die *meine* These stützen, und prompt zitiert er im nächsten Augenblick die Vergangenheit selektiv und pickt sich die Fakten heraus, die zu *seiner* These passen. Ich erwähne den Glanz alter Städte, er spricht von dem Preis, den sie an Plackerei, Blut, Schweiß und Tränen forderten. Ich spreche von Schönheit, er von deren Ausbeutung, als wären männliche Chauvinistenschweinereien auf den Kapitalismus beschränkt. Er wägt seine „Worte sorgfältig" und sagt, „wenn Stalin oder Hitler eine sorgfältig geplante Stadt hinterlassen hätten, wäre Kohr möglicherweise bereit, ihnen ihre schweren Verbrechen zu vergeben", und einige Absätze später entschuldigt er sowohl die massiven Verbrechen in Stalins Sowjetunion, denn sie habe dafür gesorgt, daß „die Schätze St. Petersburgs intakt blieben", als auch die Hinrichtungen von Regimegegnern und Andersdenken nach dem Sieg der kubanischen Revolution, denn „das sozialistische Kuba hat zum ersten Mal ein wirkliches Gleichgewicht zwischen Stadt und Land geschaffen". Hätte er meine Worte so sorgfältig gewogen wie die seinen, dann wüßte er, daß ich in jeder Kneipe und in jedem Fakultätsclub zwischen Aberystwyth und Rio Pedras verkündete, daß es für mich keinen Unterschied gibt zwischen Regierungen, die morden, und Mördern, die regieren. Ganz gleich, ob sie Hitler oder

Battista, Stalin oder Castro heißen. Als anarchistischer Nonkonformist hätte ich unter keinem von ihnen große Chancen.

Darüber hinaus geißelt Lewis mich dafür, ich würde so tun, als hätte ich recht und alle anderen unrecht, gerade so als hielte er es für die Tugend eines Autors, zu glauben, man selbst liege falsch und alle anderen richtig. Wenn Lewis sich gezwungen fühlte, seine glänzenden Werke über die Karibik zu schreiben, würde ich zu behaupten wagen, daß auch er seine Interpretation nicht für falsch, sondern für richtig hielt, wenngleich einige seiner Kritiker vom Gegenteil überzeugt waren. Wer zudem so reichlich aus den Werken anderer zitiert, wie er und ich das gewöhnlich tun, kann das nur tun, weil er glaubt, viele andere hätten ebenfalls recht.

Gordon Lewis glaubt zudem, ich sei ein Romantiker. Selbstverständlich bin ich das. Von Staub sind wir genommen, zu Staub kehren wir zurück; aus dem Nichts kommen wir und kehren nach einer Menge Aufwand ins Nichts zurück – für einen Rationalisten ergibt das Leben überhaupt keinen Sinn. Für einen Ökonomen ist es ein irrationales Verlustgeschäft. Nur für einen Romantiker hat es Sinn. Doch ein Romantiker zu sein bedeutet nicht, daß ich mich nach dem „Unzivilisierten" sehne. Gordon Lewis selbst äußerte sich nach einem Besuch in meiner mittelalterlichen Schäferhütte in den Cotswolds recht begeistert, und zwar nicht nur, weil er selbst ein Romantiker ist, wie jeder erkennen kann, der seine begeisterte Hymne auf die Schönheit karibischer Frauen am Ende seines faszinierenden Buches über Puerto Rico liest; er war auch deshalb begeistert, weil er ganz offensichtlich erkannte, daß ein robustes mittelalterliches Steinhaus alles andere als „unzivilisiert" ist, denn es muß einem englischen Schäfer einen Wohnstandard geboten haben, der vielleicht nicht so hoch ist wie der eines Landarbeiters im sozialistischen Kuba, aber genügend Annehmlichkeiten bietet, um selbst einen modernen Reformer, der entschlossen ist, die Klasse der Schäfer abzuschaffen, mit nostalgischer Sehnsucht nach einigen Vorzügen zu erfüllen, die dieser Berufsstand im Mittelalter genoß.

Des weiteren macht mir Lewis zum Vorwurf, meine Helden des Städtebaus seien die Kirche des Mittelalters und der Landadel, ich hätte jedoch versäumt, darauf hinzuweisen, von welch immensem Reichtum deren Aktivitäten getragen worden sein, was für jeden außer offenbar Leopold Kohr ein Skandal ist. Er erwähnt nicht, daß zu meinen Helden, die städtische Lagen auswählen und als Ästheten fungieren, auch drei andere Klassen gehören: das Militär, die Wirtshausbesitzer und die Slumbewohner. Insbesondere die Slumbewohner habe ich wegen ihres beispiellosen Gespürs für urbane Schönheit und Lage hervorgehoben, wie er aus dem Untertitel zu *The City of Man* hätte erschließen können: *Der Herzog von Buen Consejo*. Wie der verstorbene Gilberto Concepcion de Gracia oder meine vielen Architekten- und Planerfreunde in Puerto Rico hätte Gordon Lewis ohne zusätzliche Erklärungen erkennen müssen, daß mein wahrer Held natürlich nicht der Herzog ist. Er hätte auch Kommissar sein können. Der Held meiner Geschichte ist Buen Consejo. Und was den skandalösen Reichtum der mittelalterlichen Kirche angeht, so hatte seine Anhäufung nichts damit zu tun, daß die Kirche die Kirche war, sondern damit, daß sie wie der Gutsherr in vielen Fällen der Staat war (oder zumindest wie der Staat), und der in seinen Händen akkumulierte Reichtum ist – für die, die sich dadurch gestört fühlen – immer suspekt, ob es sich nun um einen katholischen, calvinistischen, arabischen, kremlsowjetischen, kapitalistischen oder castroistischen Staat handelt.

Aus diesem Grund habe ich die Kategorie der gesellschaftlichen Klasse – eine englische Obsession – auch nicht als Instrument der Stadtanalyse verwendet. Mein Büchlein handelt von der „Stadt des Menschen" und nicht von der „Stadt des Proletariers". Aus dem gleichen Grund habe ich mich auch nicht weiter mit der Behauptung befaßt, die Schönheit der griechischen Städte beruhe auf einer Sklavengesellschaft. Natürlich tut sie das. Aber sollte ich deshalb Schönheit verachten? Alle Gesellschaften außer den ganz kleinen sind Sklavengesellschaften. Als Marx von „Lohnsklaven" sprach, meinte er damit nicht die Bewohner Griechenlands, sondern die Menschen in den Fabriken, deren Versklavung durch Fließband und Maschinen in sozialistischen Gesellschaften genauso schlimm ist wie in kapitalistischen. Das haben mir zumindest meine „Feldforschung" in sowjetischen Fabriken und meine Erfahrung in kanadischen Goldminen vor Augen geführt, als ich für einen Stundenlohn von 24 Cents schuftete, und zwar nicht als „Pop-Soziologe", wie Lewis vermutet, sondern als Lohnsklave des 20. Jahrhunderts, der in unterirdischen Stollen voller Kondenswasser beschissene Bohrer in beschissene Felsen trieb, bis er taub war. Ich bezweifle, daß das Leben in den Silberminen Athens so viel schlimmer war. Aber darum geht es auch nicht.

Entscheidend ist, daß die Sklaverei, ungeachtet ihrer rechtlichen Form und Etikette, Teil nicht der kapitalistischen oder sozialistischen Ordnung ist, sondern der natürlichen Ordnung. Das behauptete zumindest Aristoteles, der sich, anders als Lewis glaubt, nicht als „Verteidiger der Sklaverei" erwies. Er stellte ganz einfach fest, daß es „natürliche" Sklaven und „natürliche" Herren gibt. Er behauptete aber auch, daß sich natürliche Herren oftmals in der Kategorie der rechtlichen Sklaven wiederfinden, während man die natürlichen Sklaven oft unter denen findet, die rechtlich als Freie gelten. Wichtig war, *wer* man war, und nicht, *was* man war. Ich bezweifle, daß es mir wirklich etwas ausgemacht hätte, wenn ich in der Antike Sklave gewesen wäre. So sagte Horaz über die römische „Herrenrasse": „Das gefangene Griechenland nahm seinen grausamen Eroberer gefangen." (*Graecia capta ferum victorem cepit.*) Und als der Philosoph Diogenes sich als Gefangener auf dem Sklavenmarkt von Kreta wiederfand, wußte er, wovon er sprach, als er einen Mann aus Korinth vorbeikommen sah und zu seinem Besitzer sagte: „He, verkauf mich an den Mann da drüben! Er sieht aus, als könnte er einen Herrn brauchen."

Zugegeben, nichts davon habe ich erwähnt. Ich hätte über die Sklaverei schreiben können, über den Reichtum der Reichen, die Armut der Armen, die Sündhaftigkeit der Kirche, die „politisch-administrative Erscheinungsform mächtiger Wirtschaftsgruppen", wie Lewis das weihevoll formuliert, über multinationale Unternehmen, das Elend der Philosophie (der populären wie der anderen) und viele andere Dinge, die ich weggelassen habe, was meinen alten Freund dazu veranlaßt, mich als verantwortungslosen Amateur aus seiner Lehrervereinigung hinauszuschmeißen. Das Problem mit meinem „schlanken" Bändchen, das sich zu Gordons Büchern verhält wie Twiggy im Vergleich zu Mae West, ist, daß ich darin keines dieser Themen behandeln *wollte*. Ich wollte *mein* Buch schreiben, nicht *seines*. Ich erforschte die Stadt nicht als Übung in Sachen Soziologie, Ökonomie oder Politik, sondern als allgemeine Lebens-erfahrung. Ich schrieb über die Stadt des Menschen, nicht über den Gottesstaat, den Sonnenstaat oder die sozialistische Stadt. Worauf es mir ankam, war der Wesenskern des guten Lebens als dem eigentlichen Ziel menschlichen Strebens, nicht die Langeweile der Klassenlosigkeit; die Rolle urbaner Schönheit, nicht von Status. Und Schönheit erlaubt leider nicht die Art von Feldforschung, die Gordon Lewis von mir verlangt. Sie muß wahrgenommen werden. Sie muß nicht befühlt werden – was nicht heißt, daß sie zwangsläufig so oberflächlich ist wie die „Popsoziologie".

Und wenn Lewis schließlich sich selbst als „Historiker und Politikwissenschaftler" bezeichnet, während er meine Betrachtungsweise der Geschichte als „unverantwortlich amateurhaft" abtut, behauptet er, er habe „noch nie davon gehört, daß das englische Dorf oder die amerikanische Kleinstadt für ihr geistiges Ferment bekannt" seien. Ich kann mich nicht erinnern, in *The City of Man* irgend etwas über Dörfer geschrieben zu haben, auch wenn ich das in einen anderen Buch mit dem Titel *Entwicklung ohne Hilfe* sehr wohl getan habe. Doch wenn es Dörfern und Kleinstädten wirklich so sehr an Ferment fehlt, wie erklärt er sich dann die Tatsache, daß nur ein britischer Premierminister aus London kam; daß Shakespeare aus dem ländlichen Charme Stratford-on-Avons stammte, oder daß die beiden bedeutendsten Institutionen der Gelehrsamkeit auf den Britischen Inseln nicht in der Hauptstadt zu finden sind, sondern in kleinen Provinzstädten – nämlich in Oxford (Lewis' eigener Universität) und in Cambridge? Mein kleiner Heimatort in Österreich hat „Stille Nacht" hervorgebracht (was möglicherweise auf den dortigen Mangel an geistigem Ferment hinweist). Jesus wurde in Bethlehem geboren, nicht im funkelnden Jerusalem. Und Gordon Lewis selbst stammt aus einem kleinen Bergbaudorf in den Bergen von Südwales, das der Welt Gordon Lewis geschenkt hat. Ist dies wirklich ein Beleg dafür, daß es in diesen Hügeln dort kein Gold gibt?

Aber verstehen Sie mich nicht falsch. Wie über alles, was der sonoren keltischen Feder von Freund Lewis entspringt, habe ich mich auch über seine Besprechung von *The City of Man* aufrichtig gefreut, nicht wegen dem, was er über mich und obendrein auch noch über Ivan Illich sagt, sondern wegen der ausladend bissigen Art, in der er es sagt. Ich hoffe, er wird nicht zu milde, wenn es an der Zeit ist, den Nachruf auf mich zu schreiben. Das würde ich ihm nie verzeihen. Denn auch wenn wir „uns grundlegend unterscheiden, so haben wir doch, denke ich, eine Form der intellektuellen Zivilisiertheit gemeinsam, die es uns ermöglicht, gleichzeitig ideologische Feinde und persönliche Freunde zu sein". Und um seinem Gedächtnis auf die Sprünge zu helfen: Das Zitat stammt trotz einer gewissen Ähnlichkeit nicht von David Ricardo, gerichtet an Thomas Malthus, sondern aus einem Brief, den Gordon Lewis mir geschrieben hat.

San Juan Star, 19. Januar 1976

Anhang

Glauben in der Stadt

Kirchliche Illusionen. Keine Notwendigkeit sozialer Unterstützung. Flucht der Reichen in die ländliche Idiotie. Rückkehr der Beamtenschaft ins Stadtzentrum. Der Bedarf an der feudalen Westminster-Umgebung. Die Rolle von Bischöfen und Königen. Die Bedeutung des Geschmacks. Die Auswirkungen der geschmackvollen Gestaltung. Perikles und Augustus als Beispiele. Die Rolle der Königsfamilie als Herzöge der Slums.

Frank Field hat völlig recht, wenn er sagt (*The Times*, 13. Dezember), die Enzyklika der Church of England mit dem Titel *Faith in the City* sei „nicht marxistisch". Das ist sie in der Tat nicht. Sie ist vielmehr Unsinn – zumindest mit der Idee, die Stadtsanierung zu finanzieren, indem man Geld von den Wohlhabenden zu den Habenichtsen umverteilt. Denn diejenigen, die nichts haben, haben deshalb nichts, weil sie, wie ich, üblicherweise nicht wissen, was sie mit Geld anfangen sollen.[1]

---

1 Die Church of England selbst hatte das Gefühl, ihre unter dem Titel *Faith in the City* veröffentlichten Vorschläge seien möglicherweise „nicht in allen Punkten richtig gewesen" (*The Times*, 21. April 1988). Das gilt allerdings auch für die deutlich verbesserte Fassung, wie sie unter dem Titel *Church Urban Fund* am 20. April 1988 vorgelegt wurde; sie zielt darauf ab, bereits bestehende innerstädtische Aktivitäten mit bescheideneren Summen als den ursprünglich geplanten massiven Transferzahlungen zu fördern. Das entspricht zwar eher der Regierungsphilosophie von Unternehmertum und Eigeninitiative, doch es wird nicht viel besser ausfallen als die regierungsamtlichen Vorstellungen. Wie ich zu zeigen versucht habe, muss man einen edlen großzügigen Spender in einer herausgehobenen gesellschaftlichen Stellung etablieren, der wie die Renaissancebischöfe oder -fürsten eine Kettenreaktion der Eigeninitiative auslöst, und man braucht Nachahmer, die aus eigenem Antrieb die Initiative ergreifen, auch wenn sie nur wenig Startkapital haben. Der Fürst kann natürlich auch ein Emporkömmling sein, ein Kommissar, ein Tyrann nach Art des Peisistratos oder ein Glaubensguru, dessen Worten und Beispiel die Menschen folgen, um entweder ihren Status, ihren Kopf oder ihre Seele zu retten.

Doch man muß nicht Reichtum oder Gelder in die Innenstädte transferieren, sondern die Menschen, die Reichtum und Finanzmittel schöpfen und die von ihrem Wesen her niemals soziale Unterstützung brauchten, um ihre Standards gemeinsam mit denen des ärmeren Umfelds um sie herum zu erhöhen. Das befreit die Reichen allerdings nicht von ihrer Pflicht, denn sie sind für den Verfall der einstmals prächtigen Innenstädte verantwortlich, weil sie schändlicherweise die aufregende Geselligkeit ihrer Stadtwohnungen zugunsten dessen verließen, was Marx die „ländliche Idiotie" der Vorstädte genannt hätte, und die Stadtzentren den Armen überließen, die weder über das notwendige Wissen noch um den notwendigen Geschmackssinn verfügten, um deren Schönheit und Kultiviertheit zu erhalten, selbst wenn sie bei Pferdewetten das dafür nötige Geld gewonnen hätten.

Das also ist der Hauptgrund für den Verfall der Städte, und Herr Field hat deshalb auch recht, wenn er als eine erste Gegenmaßnahme vorschlägt, die Kirche solle „ihren Verwaltungsapparat aus dem feudalen Westminster in die Innenstadt verlegen", um etwas für deren Sanierung zu tun, die ihr Bericht, nicht anders als der Prinz von Wales, so leidenschaftlich beschwört. Allerdings weist er nicht darauf hin, daß es nicht nur um eine Verlegung von Beamten geht. Was zusammen mit ihnen verlegt werden muß, ist der feudale Charakter der Westminster-Umgebung.

Armut läßt sich nur auf diese Weise bekämpfen: nicht indem man sich mitleidsvoll mit den Armen identifiziert, sondern indem man ihnen einen Sinn für Schönheit und luxuriösen Geschmack vermittelt, wie ihn die Könige, Bischöfe, Adligen, Kaufleute und Architekten besaßen, die für die gebaut haben. Sie bauten großartige Städte, indem sie selbst zusammen mit den Armen dort lebten, und sie taten das nicht als Investoren, Steuererhebungsexperten, Sozialarbeiter oder Prediger wider die Sünde, sondern als Könige, die Paläste brauchten, als Bischöfe, die Kathedralen, Komponisten, Chöre und Ministranten benötigten; als Adlige, die Handwerker, Bewunderer, Nachahmer, Köche, Bedienstete, Weber, Drucker, Schauspieler, Theater und Dichter brauchten, die sie kritisierten oder ein Loblied auf sie sangen; als Händler, die Lagerhäuser, Banken, Zeitungen, Buchhalter, Läden benötigten; und als Arbeiter, die

Schulen, Kneipen, Wettbüros und dazwischen immer mal wieder ein Bordell brauchten.

Dieser Prozeß ist es, der zu allen Zeiten aus Slums Städte, aus Verfall Überfluß und aus pflichtvergessener Untätigkeit hart verdiente Zufriedenheit machte, und zwar ohne daß man dafür Wohltätigkeit, Gewalt oder hochfliegende sozioökonomische Theorien gebraucht hätte. Den Staat kostet das nur eine „Spritze", nicht an Geld, sondern an Willen und Geschmack, wie das Augustus schaffte, der zu Recht von sich sagen konnte: „Ich fand Rom in Ziegelsteinen vor und habe es in Marmor hinterlassen." Oder Perikles, der eines Tages wegen Veruntreuung zu einer Geldstrafe verurteilt und wie Präsident Nixon aus dem Amt vertrieben wurde, doch über seine Bauten im Stadtzentrum konnte Pausanias noch Jahrhunderte später schreiben: „Als sie neu waren, sahen sie bereits altehrwürdig aus. Nun, da sie alt sind, sehen sie noch immer neu aus." Doch um das zu schaffen, mußten die Fürsten und politischen Führer zunächst selbst in Stein und Ziegel und Dreck leben – und sich nicht damit abfinden.[2]

---

[2] Damit will ich nicht behaupten, der Prinz von Wales – dessen scharfsinnige Wahrnehmung und Theorien über den Verfall der Innenstädte ich nicht berücksichtigen konnte, weil meine Kolumnen lange, bevor seine Empfindungen bekannt wurden, verfasst wurden – sollte nach Art des Herzogs von Buen Consejo selbst in ein verfallenes Innenstadtviertel ziehen. Schließlich hat er als Erbe eines größeren Throns einen deutlich darüber hinausreichenden Auftrag. Doch was ist mit den vielen anderen Mitgliedern der königlichen Familie oder mit den „Non-Royals", die über Geschmack und die nötigen Mittel verfügen? Das ist das, was ich mit „die Saat für einen Kern legen" statt rein finanzieller Investition meine. Man soll Menschen mit den nötigen Mitteln transferieren, nicht Gelder ohne Menschen!

Phoenix World City

Leser haben kritisiert, ich hätte in einer meiner Kolumnen im *San Juan Star* (vom 8. November 1963) die „modernen Medici" nicht näher spezifiziert, die in rasantem Tempo die Macht von unseren verkehrsbesessenen Stadtplanern übernehmen. Diesen Mangel habe ich in einem ergänzenden Hinweis einen Tag später behoben. „Es sind die Gastwirte", schrieb ich. Nach Jahrzehnten der Luft und Geist verpestenden Urbanisierung „sind *sie* diejenigen, die die Zutaten einer guten Stadt – *Wohnquartiere, Geschäfte, Arbeitsräume, Postamt, Theater, Turnhalle, Swimmingpool, Glaubenszentren, Clubs, Buchhandlungen, Kunstgalerien, Diskussionszirkel* – wieder auf konzentriertestem Fußgängerraum versammeln: dem Grand Hotel." Das ist das *Hotel de Ville* im wahrsten Sinne des Wortes: die Stadt als Hotel. Deshalb gilt eine Wiederbelebung der Renaissancevorstellung, wieder zur städtischen Geselligkeit des kleinen Raums zurückzukehren, die alles zu bieten hat, was sich Herz, Geist, Augen, Ohren und Zunge an luxuriösem Überfluß wünschen, als nicht mehr ganz so rückwärtsgewandt, wie die nach vorne blickenden Kommunikations-, Verkehrs-, Stadt- und Katastrophenplaner unserer Zeit gerne glauben. „Sie ist von den Gastwirten wiederbelebt worden."

Das habe ich 1963 geschrieben. 1993, dreißig Jahre später, haben sich den Gastwirten in noch viel spektakulärerem Maßstab die Schiffsbauer zugesellt, wie die ersten aufgeregten Berichte über die *Phoenix World City* nahe legen, die von der norwegischen World City Corporation A/S ersonnen und entworfen wurde und nun kurz vor der Fertigstellung steht. Gebaut wurde sie von der Howaldswerke-Deutsche Werft AG, der Bremer Vulkan AG, der Bloom & Voss AG und der Thyssen Nordseewerke GmbH, und sie wird 250.000 Bruttoregistertonnen haben, mehr als 5.600 Fahrgästen Unterkunft bieten, 400 Meter lang sein und einiges zu bieten haben: „*geräumige Kabinen mit Balkonen, Dorfplätze, die gesäumt sind von Läden und Restaurants, ein Theater, Kinos, eine Bibliothek, ein Museum, einen Universitätscampus, Fernsehen, Besprechungsräume, ein Casino*" und, zu meiner ganz besonderen Freude, ein *akademisches Wirtshaus*. Wenn sie 1993 vom Stapel läuft, wird sie das bei weitem größte Schiff sein, das je gebaut wurde.

Die einzige Frage ist: Wie kann ich dieses Schiff in meine Philosophie der Kleinheit integrieren? Wie sein Name *World City* zeigt, geht es darum, daß es nicht so sehr das größte Schiff ist, sondern der kleinste Planet; nicht die sinnlose Ausweitung der Welt, zu der auch eine Stadt gehört, sondern eine Welt für sich, „in einem kleinen Raum unendlicher Reichtum", wie Marlowe es genannt hat, oder, wie Aristoteles in seiner Bestimmung der idealen Größe eines Staates sagte: dieser müsse „leicht überschaubar" sein. Es wird keine Gefahr bestehen, von der modernen Seuche der Vernachlässigung und des Verfalls der Innenstadt befallen zu werden, denn diese Stadt wird sich nicht über ihre „Mauern" hinaus in den Ozean ausbreiten können, und die *Innenstadt* wird wieder sein, was sie schon immer war, nämlich die *ganze Stadt*. Wie Phoenix aus der Asche.

Nachwort

„Alles ist inzwischen so groß aufgeblasen, daß es dringender denn je der Verkleinerung bedarf." (David Miller, Chefredakteur Sport bei der Times, über die Olympischen Spiele von Seoul 1988)

Seltener als der Typus ist nur eines, nämlich der Archetyp: Platons Realität außerhalb der Höhle, in der wir gefangen sind, weil wir ihren Schatten fälschlicherweise für das Ding selbst halten. Einmal jedoch erblickte ich das ganz reale Ding: den Archetyp eines Engländers. Er spazierte während eines Jahrmarkts in der Nähe von Painswick in den Cotswolds übers Feld, trug bequemen, aber perfekt geschnittenen Tweed, eine rote Blume am Revers, eine bläuliche Krawatte, ein Hemd mit Knöpfen, ein Paar Handschuhe (von denen er nur einen anhatte), Gamaschen über den Schuhen, den Hund an der Leine, auf seinem Rex-Harrison-Gesicht der würdevolle Ausdruck eines imperialen Landherzogs mittleren Alters, leicht angegrautes Haar und keinen Hut – völlig entspannt, mit einem zusammengerollten Regenschirm, der in Gentlemanmanier am anmutig angewinkelten Arm baumelte.

„Schön und gut", erwiderte einer meiner amerikanischen Studenten, nachdem ich in einem Seminar dieses seltene Exemplar beschrieben hatte, „aber was ist so typisch englisch an ihm?"

„Daß es in Strömen regnete", gab ich zur Antwort.

Ähnlich werden viele, die meine Ansichten und Vorschläge zur Innenstadt lesen, sagen: „Schön und gut, aber was ist daran so Besonderes?" Sagt nicht jeder, vom Prinz von Wales, der Church of England und dem Royal Institute of British Architects bis hinunter zum jüngsten Hafeninvestor und Kneipensoziologen, so ziemlich das Gleiche? Ja, in der Tat: Heute! Entscheidend aber ist, daß ich das, wie die ursprünglichen Veröffentlichungsdaten meiner wieder abgedruckten Kolumnen zeigen, vor zwanzig, dreißig und fünfzig Jahren gesagt habe.[1] Wie David Marquand über Bertrand Russells Lehren schrieb (*The Observer*, 10. Juli 1988): „Wenn sie heute ein wenig veraltet wirken, dann hat das zum Teil damit zu tun, daß viele von ihnen Allgemeingut geworden sind." Das aber nimmt ihnen nichts von ihrer Gültigkeit.

Doch dadurch wären sie weder etwas Besonderes noch wert, ein zweites Mal veröffentlicht zu werden. Der Punkt aber ist: Zwar scheinen viele Stadtplaner ganz ähnlich zu sprechen, doch die von mir vorgeschlagenen Ideen sind eben nicht Allgemeingut geworden, so wie die originellen Innenstadtpläne von Prinz Charles oder Rod Hackney nicht allgemein geläufig sind, nur weil sie von den Redakteuren großer Zeitungen begeistert beschrieben werden. Journalisten machen Zeitungen, aber keine Städte. Ebensowenig sorgen Kunstgalerien im Hafenviertel oder der Tausch von Yuppietum gegen Hippietum in den Innenstädten schon für ein lebensfähiges Gemeinwesen. Die vorherrschenden Ideen sind die von Immobilienmaklern, Investoren und Spekulanten, die sich leiten lassen von Moden, Preis und Markterwägungen und keinerlei biophilosophisches Verständnis davon haben, was für ein lebendiger Organismus ein Stadtkern wirklich ist. Sie müssen erst noch erkennen, daß der Stadtkern kein auf das Finanzwesen, auf eine bestimmte Ethnie, auf Vergnügen, Arbeit oder Drogenhandel spezialisierter *Teil* einer Stadt ist, sondern die *ganze* Stadt. Ist der Stadtkern heruntergekommen, so bedeutet das, daß sein Strahlenkranz zu groß geworden ist, und es geht nicht darum, das Hafenviertel zu yuppifizieren, indem man muskelfördernde, geschlechtsverändernde anabole Steroide spritzt, sondern die zwanzig oder dreißig getrennten Stadtbezirke, aus denen großstädtische Ballungsräume üblicherweise bestehen, in ihrer auf ein Gravitationszentrum konzentrierten Ganzheit organisch wiederherzustellen.

Die entscheidende Krankheit unserer Zeit ist nicht Häßlichkeit, Armut, Kriminalität oder Vernachlässigung, sondern Häßlichkeit, Armut, Kriminalität und Vernachlässigung, die aus den nicht mehr zu überschauenden Dimensionen des modernen nationalen und urbanen Gigantismus resultieren, und sie läßt sich nur auf eine einzige Weise heilen: nicht durch Mitgefühl, Geld oder Genialität, sondern indem man große Dinge kleiner macht. Erst dann werden die Menschen in der Lage sein, ihre Probleme ohne Anleitung, Mitgefühl oder eine Menge Geld von außen zu lösen, indem sie die Art von Hausverstand anwenden, die wir Pferden, selten aber Männern und Frauen zuschreiben. Wir brauchen eine Rückkehr zum menschlichen Maß.

Deshalb lege ich meine Ideen zur Stadtplanung noch einmal vor. Vielleicht klingen sie wie all das übrige, was heute vorgebracht wird. Aber sie entspringen einer radikal anderen Philosophie. Deren Grundlage ist eine *allgemeine Theorie organisch optimaler Dimensionen*, der zufolge die Größe von allem und jedem bestimmt und begrenzt ist durch dessen Funktion, sei es nun eine Schale, ein Schuh, ein Zahn, ein Haus, eine Kneipe, eine Stadt oder ein Staat. Es geht nicht um die Probleme, sondern um deren Ursachen; nicht um den *Verfall* von Innenstädten, die den hilflosen Händen der verarmten untersten Bevölkerungsschicht überlassen werden, sondern um die *Bedeutung* von Stadtkernen als pyramidenförmigen Strukturen, in denen um einen Kern aus Kirche, Kneipe, Schule, Markt und Rathaus alle Gesellschaftsklassen zusammenleben – nicht getrennt in Wohn-, Verwaltungs-, Vergnügungs-, Finanz- und Arbeiterviertel, die nichts als Verkehrsstaus produzieren. Es ist völlig egal, ob eine Stadt in der Arktis oder in den Tropen liegt, ob sie in der Antike oder in der Neuzeit gegründet wurde. Die Bedeutung urbaner Existenz war stets die gleiche.

Was das vorliegende Buch am Beispiel von San Juan schildert, ist deshalb nicht typisch puertoricanisch, sondern archetypisch urban, und die Problemlösungen, die es vorschlägt, gelten für das „Herzogtum" Soho oder meinetwegen für die innerstädtische Diözese eines Londoner Bischofs, der im Exil in Westminster lebt, genauso wie in meinem tropischen Märchenland des Herzogtums von Buen Consejo, dessen Entwicklung vom Dreck zum Marmor ich vor einem Vierteljahrhundert in der August-Ausgabe 1964 des *San Juan Review* beschrieben habe.[1]

---

1 Das hat nichts mit irgendwelchen prophetischen Gaben zu tun, sondern damit, daß die Folgen der Stadtplanung damals schon ebenso mit bloßem Auge zu erkennen waren, wie die Bedingungen von *1984* für George Orwell schon 1948, als er dieses Buch schrieb, sichtbar waren oder, was das anbelangt (wie ich in meiner Einleitung bereits erwähnt habe), 1937, als wir während des Spanischen Bürgerkriegs in den Straßencafés darüber diskutierten. Das mag der Grund gewesen sein, warum die erfreulichste Besprechung meines Buches *The Breakdown of Nations* (dt. *Das Ende der Großen*) am 12. Juli 1957 in Orwells Zeitung *Tribune* erschien („Ich kann dem, was er sagt, zwar nicht zustimmen, aber ich mag ganz einfach die Art, wie er es sagt").

LEOPOLD KOHR AKADEMIE

Leopold Kohr-Forschungszentrum Universität Salzburg, Universitätsplatz 1, 5010 Salzburg HS 121

Leopold Kohrs „Rückkehr" ins alte Studiengebäude der Universität Salzburg
Zu Kohrs Schulzeit wurde die Alte Universität als Humanistisches Gymnasium genutzt, das er von 1920 bis 1928 besuchte. Sein Internat „Rupertinum" beherbergt heute die Moderne Galerie. Im Nahbereich seiner alten Klasse ist es nun über Initiative von Dr. Elisabeth Werner (GR und Universitäts-Wirtschaftsdirektorin) und Univ.-Prof. Dr. Christian Dirninger (Fachbereich Geschichte der Universität Salzburg) gelungen, ein Leopold Kohr-Forschungszentrum einzurichten, das 2008 eröffnet wurde. Rektor, Univ.-Prof. Dr. Heinrich Schmidinger engagierte sich in großartiger Weise mit allen nur denkbaren Hilfestellungen der Universität Salzburg, um dem Leopold Kohr-Nachlass eine adäquate Bleibe und Forschungsstätte zu schaffen. Das Land Salzburg mit Landeshauptmann-Stv. Dr. Wilfried Haslauer ermöglicht seit Jahren die Wissenschaftliche Ordnung des Nachlasses durch Ewald Hiebl. Um den aus den verschiedenen Wirkungsstätten Kohrs – Puerto Rico, Anquilla, USA, Kanada, Wales, England und Oberndorf – nach Salzburg evakuierten Nachlass wissenschaftlich aufzuarbeiten, entstand nun diese Forschungsstätte, die Kohrs Arbeiten auch einem internationalen Publikum zugänglich machen soll.
Bundesminister Dr. Johannes Hahn (BM für Wissenschaft und Forschung) hat sich selbst wissenschaftlich mit Leopold Kohr beschäftigt und unterstützt wie die Stadt Salzburg mit Bürgermeister Dr. Heinz Schaden, mit Mag. Claudia Schmidt (Klubvorsitzende), mit Mag. Ingrid Tröger-Gordon (Magistrat Salzburg) und Mag. Eva Weissenbacher (GR und Vorsitzende des Kulturausschusses) die Aktivitäten der Leopold Kohr-Akademie. Ein maßgeblicher Förderer des Forschungszentrums ist die Wirtschaftskammer Salzburg mit ihrem Präsidenten KommR Julius Schmalz und dem Direktor Dr. Johann Bachleitner. Zugleich soll diese neue Institution ein Mittelpunkt für wissenschaftliche Treffen, Begegnungen mit Alternativ-Nobelpreisträgern und Veranstaltungen rund um Leopold Kohr werden.

Alfred Winter - Entdecker Leopold Kohrs und Gründer der Akademie

Während der von ihm gegründeten großen Kelten-Ausstellung in Hallein, kam es 1980 zu einer historischen Begegnung. Der Zufall führte Prof. Alfred Winter mit Leopold Kohr zusammen. Dieser lebte damals in Wales, wo das keltische Erbe Europas noch viel lebendiger war als in Salzburg. Spontan bot Kohr seine Kontakte zur walisischen Kulturszene an. Es war der Anfang einer Freundschaft, die Kohr bis zu seinem Tod begleiten sollte. Prof. Alfred Winter brachte den in Österreich vergessenen Philosophen und Ökonomen wieder in das Bewusstsein von Politik und Medien. Franz Kreuzer und Günther Nenning setzten sich im Detail mit Kohrs Thesen auseinander. Wilfried Haslauer, zu jener Zeit Landeshauptmann, überreichte ihm den „Goldenen Ring des Landes Salzburg". Das Landesstudio des ORF richtete ihm zu Ehren ein international hochkarätig besetztes Symposium aus. 1986 entstand vor den Toren des Nationalparks Hohe Tauern auf Initiative Alfred Winters der Verein für Kultur und Regionalentwicklung „Tauriska". Kohr wurde Präsident und die neue Regional-Akademie in Neukirchen am Großvenediger nach ihm benannt.

Leopold Kohr-Akademie

Die Leopold Kohr-Akademie ist eine ständige Einrichtung des Vereins Tauriska ZVR-Zahl 204405414, dessen Präsidentin und gleichzeitig Geschäftsführerin der Leopold Kohr-Akademie Susanna Vötter-Dankl ist. Die wissenschaftliche Aufarbeitung des Nachlasses wird von Historiker Mag. Dr. Ewald Hiebl vorgenommen, der auch mit Mag. Dr. Günther Witzany (Philosoph, der mit Leopold Kohr befreundet war und dessen Philosophie weiterentwickelt) die Herausgabe aller Werke Leopold Kohrs betreut. Kohrs Nachlass (Bücher, Manuskripte, Schriftverkehr…) und Bibliothek sind im Besitz von Verein Tauriska/Leopold Kohr-Akademie. Unterstützt, beraten und begleitet wird die Kohr-Akademie durch den wissenschaftlichen Beirat unter der Leitung von Univ.-Prof. Dr. Reinhold Wagnleitner und seinem Stellvertreter Univ.-Prof. Dr. Christian Dirninger.

Der Philosoph und Ökonom Leopold Kohr wurde am 05. Oktober 1909 in Oberndorf bei Salzburg geboren und starb am 26. Februar 1994. Er gilt als Schöpfer des Slogan „Small is beautiful" und erhielt „für seinen frühen Anstoß zur Rückbesinnung auf das menschliche Maß" den Alternativen Nobelpreis.

Überschaubarkeit und Nachhaltigkeit waren für Kohr nicht nur wirtschaftliche und ökologische (Überlebens-) Notwendigkeit, sondern tatsächlich unverzichtbare Grundvoraussetzungen für jede Art lebendiger Demokratie und zukunftsfähige Zivilgesellschaften.

Mit Hilfe neuer Kooperationen und Medien sollen die Ideen Kohrs, die sich vereinfacht unter den Begriffen „menschliches Maß", „überschaubare Größe" und „Verhältnismäßigkeit" subsumieren lassen, einer breiten Öffentlichkeit zur Diskussion gestellt werden.

Ziele der Leopold Kohr-Akademie

Forschungszentrum in der Universität Salzburg: (Nachlass · Archiv · Veranstaltung)
- Gründung eines öffentlich zugänglichen Archivs
- Wissenschaftliche Auf- und Bearbeitung des Nachlasses
- die kommentierte Herausgabe aller vergriffenen Bücher Kohrs so wie die erstmalige Edition bisher unveröffentlicher Werke
- Vorbereitung und Durchführung eines Leopold-Kohr-Preises
- Erstellung einer Kohr-Website in englischer Sprache
- Ausrichtung von regionalen wie internationalen Symposien und Veranstaltungen mit Vernetzungen von Kunst, Kultur und Wissenschaft
- Entwicklung, Belebung und Begleitung von Regionalkultur und Projekten auf der Basis Kohrschen Gedankenguts
- interdisziplinäre Auseinandersetzung mit dem Korschen Werk in der universitären Forschung und Lehre
- die Erforschung einer „Theorie kleinräumiger Wirtschaftskreisläufe" im Werk Leopold Kohrs als spezifischer Beitrag zur Wirtschaftstheorie und als Perspektive einer möglichen Wirtschaftspolitik in Kooperation mit Vertretungsinstitutionen der Wirtschaft (Klein- und Mittelbetriebe) und anderen Institutionen (Tourismus)

Information: **www.leopold-kohr-akademie.at**